EARLY LITERACY IN PRESCHOOL AND KINDERGARTEN

JANICE J. BEATY
Professor Emerita, Elmira College

LINDA PRATT
Elmira College

Merrill
Prentice Hall

Upper Saddle River, New Jersey
Columbus, Ohio

Library of Congress Cataloging-in-Publication Data
Beaty, Janice J.
   Early literacy in preschool and kindergarten / Janice J. Beaty, Linda Pratt. p. cm.
   Includes bibliographical references and index.
   ISBN 0-13-014828-8
   1. Language arts (Kindergarten) 2. Language arts (Preschool) I. Pratt, Linda II.
   Title.
LB1140.5.L3 B43 2003
372.6—dc21
2002019576

Vice President and Publisher: Jeffery W. Johnston
Executive Editor: Kevin M. Davis
Associate Editor: Christina M. Tawney
Editorial Assistant: Autumn Crisp
Production Editor: Sheryl Glicker Langner
Design Coordinator: Diane C. Lorenzo
Cover Designer: Ali Mohrman
Cover art: Christy Terry
Production Manager: Laura Messerly
Director of Marketing: Ann Castel Davis
Marketing Manager: Amy June
Marketing Coordinator: Tyra Cooper

This book was set in Opitma Medium by Carlisle Communications, Ltd. It was printed and bound by R. R. Donnelley & Sons Company. The cover was printed by Phoenix Color Corp.

Photo Credits: All photos by Janice J. Beaty

Pearson Education Ltd.
Pearson Education Australia Pty. Limited
Pearson Education Singapore Pte. Ltd.
Pearson Education North Asia Ltd.
Pearson Education Canada, Ltd.
Pearson Educación de Mexico, S.A. de C. V.
Pearson Education—Japan
Pearson Education Malasia Pte.Ltd.
Pearson Education, *Upper Saddle River, New Jersey*

10 9 8 7 6 5 4 3 2 1
ISBN: 0-13-014828-8

To Ann Gilchrist,
director,
Mid Missouri Foster Grandparents Program—
for making a lasting contribution
to the lives of the elderly and the young
and for being such a fine friend

ABOUT THE AUTHORS

Janice J. Beaty, professor emerita, Elmira College, Elmira, New York, is a full-time writer of early childhood college textbooks and a consultant and trainer in early childhood education from her home in Taos, New Mexico. Some of her textbooks include *Skills for Preschool Teachers* (sixth edition), *Observing Development of the Young Child* (fifth edition), *Building Bridges with Multicultural Picture Books, Prosocial Guidance for the Preschool Child,* and *Picture Book Storytelling.* At present Dr. Beaty is involved in an early literacy mentoring program with Foster Grandparents in schools and Head Start in Central Missouri and with early literacy in Indian Head Start Programs in the Southwest.

Linda Pratt is the executive director of teacher education and a professor of education at Elmira College. For over 20 years she has been teaching both graduate and undergraduate courses in literacy education and has been directing the graduate program in teaching literacy, with her primary teaching interest being literacy acquisition and development. Dr. Pratt has given presentations on literacy in the United States as well as in Asia, the Bahamas and Caribbean, Canada, Europe, and South America. She and Dr. Beaty have also coauthored the textbook *Transcultural Children's Literature* (Merrill/Prentice Hall).

PREFACE

Here is the textbook early childhood educators have been waiting for. While most early literacy texts treat preschool learning in a chapter or two, this entire text focuses on early literacy in the preschool, leading up to what is expected in kindergarten. *Early Literacy in Preschool and Kindergarten* presents a unique approach to exploring literacy with preschool and kindergarten children. The current recognition that learning to read and write can emerge naturally in young children when supported by appropriate teaching methods and materials has led the authors to develop a fresh approach by using classroom learning centers, children's literature, and "cultural characters" to involve children in their own learning.

We now know that literacy begins at birth. Right from the start infants try to communicate with those around them through crying and cooing, smiling, and babbling. As toddlers, they pay close attention to their caregivers, striving to imitate the sounds they hear. By the time they are preschoolers, ages 3 through 5, young children are fully engaged in emerging into early literacy: listening, speaking, and exploring their own experimental reading and writing. By kindergarten, they are ready for more formal instruction in reading and writing while continuing their own natural emergence.

To support such development, this text presents ideas to involve teachers, student teachers, and their children in a unique "cultural character early literacy method" that uses children's picture books as lead-ins to activities for engaging children in speaking, listening, writing, and reading. These books introduce children to the multicultural world around them in a meaningful way through cultural book characters children can identify with—such as Suki, the Asian American girl who worries about whether her mother will remember to pick her up at the day care center in *Will You Come Back for Me?*; the Caribbean boy in *Hue Boy* who tries desperately to grow taller but can't seem to do it until his father returns; or the Anglo girl Anna and her Navajo friend Juanita, who build the biggest bridge in preschool when they finally put their blocks together in *Building a Bridge*.

Teachers and student teachers learn to use puppets, dolls, character cutouts, chopsticks, unit blocks, drums, painting and weaving, tape recorders, computers, role plays, flannelboards, and story reenactments to bring these book characters to life. Children take it from there, converting their adventures with these multicultural characters into accomplishments in speaking and listening, mock writing, book making, and storytelling, to name a few.

The text is divided into four parts: Part 1, "Getting Started with Early Literacy," which defines the cultural character approach and helps teachers choose picture books with exciting cultural characters that can lead children into literacy activities; part 2, "Emergent Speaking," with chapters on the foundations of early literacy, music as a natural language, and speaking and listening in preschool; part 3, "Emergent Writing," with chapters on developing eye–hand coordination, art as a natural language, and becoming a writer; and part 4, "Emergent Reading," with chapters on how reading emerges, the home book experience, and becoming a reader in kindergarten. A topical book index from Acceptance and Adoption to Worry and Writing helps readers choose from among the 200 books described in this text. Making plans for children with curriculum webs and using accomplishment cards to evaluate individual gains give teachers powerful new tools to integrate cultural education into every curriculum area.

Both teachers and student teachers can implement this approach with ease using helpful checklists such as "*Choosing Cultural Character Picture Books,*" "*Learning Center Checklist,*" "*Spoken Language Checklist,*" "*Eye–Hand Coordination Checklist,*" "*Preschool Writing Behaviors Checklist,*" "*Preschool Reading Behaviors Checklist,*" and "*Choosing Predictable Cultural Character Books.*" In total 93 engaging cultural characters from 24 different cultures shown in 200 current picture books are presented. Acquiring the books is made easy through the bookstores, publishers, and Web sites listed or inexpensively with the 60 paperback books listed from Scholastic in appendix A.

Much of the information in this text has never before appeared in print, including many of the ideas for using cultural characters to lead children into literacy activities, as well as the in-depth survey of types of reading instruction used in kindergartens across the country. The information presented has been carefully researched. The photographs of children using cultural characters in literacy activities should stimulate even more original ideas by readers. Altogether *Early Literacy in Preschool and Kindergarten* should help teachers and student teachers to solve the problems of "What kinds of reading and writing activities are really appropriate for such young children?" and "How do I go about implementing them successfully?"

ACKNOWLEDGMENTS

Our heartfelt thanks go to the teachers, parents of children, and directors from the Noah's Ark Christian Preschool in Taos, New Mexico; the Helm Nursery School in Corning, New York; and Head Start Programs in Fulton and Mexico, Missouri, for allowing photographs of their children in the classrooms; to grandmothers from the Foster Grandparents Program of Mid Missouri for allowing photographs during their literacy volunteer work with young children; to

Winona Sample and Mary Maples for sharing their knowledge during our visits to Indian Head Start Programs in New Mexico; to Elmira College research assistant Andrew Stage for his technical assistance; to husband J. Michael Pratt for his assistance and unconditional support; to Dr. Thomas K. Meier, president, and Bryan D. Reddick, vice president of Elmira College, for their continued support and recognition; to the librarians at the Gannett Tripp Library at Elmira College and the Missouri University Library at Columbia, Missouri; to editor Ann Davis for her always valuable support and ideas; to production editor Sheryl Langner for her careful and creative presentation of the book; and to the following reviewers of the manuscript: Paula D. Packer, Lock Haven University; Linda Medearis, Texas A&M International; Adrienne Herrell, California State University–Fresno; and Ithel Jones, Florida State University.

—J.J.B. and L.P.

DISCOVER THE COMPANION WEBSITE ACCOMPANYING THIS BOOK

THE PRENTICE HALL COMPANION WEBSITE: A VIRTUAL LEARNING ENVIRONMENT

Technology is a constantly growing and changing aspect of our field that is creating a need for content and resources. To address this emerging need, Prentice Hall has developed an online learning environment for students and professors alike–Companion Websites–to support our textbooks.

In creating a Companion Website, our goal is to build on and enhance what the textbook already offers. For this reason, the content for each user-friendly website is organized by topic and provides the professor and student with a variety of meaningful resources. Common features of a Companion Website include:

FOR THE PROFESSOR—

Every Companion Website integrates **Syllabus Manager**™, an online syllabus creation and management utility.

- **Syllabus Manager**™ provides you, the instructor, with an easy, step-by-step process to create and revise syllabi, with direct links into Companion Website and other online content without having to learn HTML.
- Students may logon to your syllabus during any study session. All they need to know is the web address for the Companion Website and the password you've assigned to your syllabus.
- After you have created a syllabus using **Syllabus Manager**™, students may enter the syllabus for their course section from any point in the Companion Website.
- Clicking on a date, the student is shown the list of activities for the assignment. The activities for each assignment are linked directly to actual content, saving time for students.
- Adding assignments consists of clicking on the desired due date, then filling in the details of the assignment—name of the assignment, instructions, and whether or not it is a one-time or repeating assignment.
- In addition, links to other activities can be created easily. If the activity is online, a URL can be entered in the space provided, and it will be linked automatically in the final syllabus.
- Your completed syllabus is hosted on our servers, allowing convenient updates from any computer on the Internet. Changes you make to your syllabus are immediately available to your students at their next logon.

FOR THE STUDENT—

- **Topic Overviews**—outline key concepts in topic areas
- **Web Links**—General websites related to topic areas as well as associations and professional organizations.
- **Read About It**—Timely articles that enable you to become more aware of important issues in early childhood education.
- **Learn by Doing**—Put concepts into action, participate in activities, complete lesson plans, examine strategies, and more.
- **For Teachers**—Access information that you will need to know as an in-service teacher, including information on materials, activities, lessons, curriculum, and state standards.
- **Visit a School**—Visit a school's website to see concepts, theories, and strategies in action.
- **Electronic Bluebook**—send homework or essays directly to your instructor's email with this paperless form
- **Message Board**—serves as a virtual bulletin board to post—or respond to–questions or comments to/from a national audience
- **Chat**—real-time chat with anyone who is using the text anywhere in the country—ideal for discussion and study groups, class projects, etc.

To take advantage of these and other resources, please visit the *Early Literacy in Preschool and Kindergarten* Companion Website at

www.prenhall.com/beaty

CONTENTS

PART 3: EMERGENT WRITING

CHAPTER 5
Developing Eye–Hand Coordination 137

PART 4: EMERGENT READING

INTRODUCTION

For years educators ignored literacy behaviors that preceded formal instruction in reading and writing, and assumed that the child came to the instructional context as a blank slate. Emergent literacy as a concept recognizes the child's learning about print and how it works before any kind of formal instruction in how to read and write. In essence, we appreciate what children have learned about the written language of their environment before they come to school.

Brewer (1998, p. 122)

GETTING STARTED WITH EARLY LITERACY

WHAT IS EARLY LITERACY?

HOW CAN PRESCHOOL TEACHERS PROMOTE EARLY LITERACY?

WHAT IS THE CULTURAL CHARACTER APPROACH?

HOW CAN TEACHERS CHOOSE BOOKS WITH CULTURAL CHARACTERS TO SUPPORT AN EARLY LITERACY CURRICULUM?

WHAT IS EARLY LITERACY?

Literacy begins at birth. Right from the start infants try to communicate with those around them through crying and cooing, smiling and babbling. As toddlers they pay close attention to their caregivers, striving to imitate the sounds they hear, the gestures they see—all the while attempting to make sense of the world around them. For all young children from every culture, early literacy is a process of *meaning making*.

For most of us, however, literacy means being able to read and write. Does "early literacy" actually mean that young children can learn to read and write naturally before they enter kindergarten or first grade where they receive formal instruction? The answer to this question is quite different today from what it was as recently as 20 years ago. Today research shows us how reading and writing can develop naturally in a continuum as young children make sense of their world through playful exploration and how children's brains take in this information, extracting rules from it to help children learn. Such research has changed our minds forever about the way children develop and how we can best support their growth.

We now know, for instance, that reading and writing are outgrowths of the same communication urge that drives children to express themselves orally. We also know that given the proper tools and support, children can teach themselves prereading and prewriting skills. Educators use the term *emergent literacy* to describe children's natural development of reading and writing skills. Such educators have this to say about it:

> As researchers began to observe and report the literacy activities of preschool children, they found that young children engage in a wide range of emergent literacy behaviors, such as listening to stories, discussing stories, making up stories, scribbling "letters" to family and friends, writing their names, and creating invented printlike signs. Today there is a general consensus in the research community that literacy is a process that begins at birth, when babies begin to experiment with oral language. (Gambrell & Mazzoni, 1999, p. 81)

By the time they are preschoolers, ages 3 through 5, children are fully engaged in emerging into early literacy: listening, speaking, and practicing their own experimental reading and writing, especially if the adults around them support their literacy efforts by providing materials and activities for them to progress. Adults must also commend them continually for their successes. For youngsters who receive little support in this regard, their drive to communicate and emerge into early literacy may not progress as smoothly. Becoming literate for them may take additional effort and a longer time.

Nevertheless, the preschool years are the natural time for young children to develop early literacy skills: listening, speaking, reading, and writing. As researchers learn more about the process of reading and writing, they realize that the earlier adults can support young children in their natural development of literacy skills, the more successful children of every culture will become in their ability to read and write later in the elementary school years. As noted by the International Reading Association (IRA) and the National Association for the Education of Young Children (NAEYC, 1998), "Although reading and writing abilities continue to develop throughout the life span, the early years—from birth through age eight—are the most important period for literacy development" (p. 30).

These two leading professional organizations have adopted a joint position statement on *Learning to Read and Write: Developmentally Appropriate Practices for Young Children* (NAEYC, 1998). Included in this statement is a "Continuum of Children's Development in Early Reading and Writing" to illustrate how children function at different levels of their development. Phase 1 and Phase 2 apply to early literacy:

Continuum of Children's Development in Early Reading and Writing

Phase 1: Awareness and exploration (goals for preschool)

Children explore their environment and build the foundations for learning to read and write.

Children can:

- enjoy listening to and discussing storybooks
- understand that print carries a message
- engage in reading and writing attempts
- identify labels and signs in their environment
- participate in rhyming games
- identify some letters and make some letter–sound matches
- use known letters or approximations of letters to represent written language (especially meaningful words like their name and phrases such as "I love you")

Phase 2: Experimental reading and writing (goals for kindergarten)

Children develop basic concepts of print and begin to engage in and experiment with reading and writing.

Kindergartners can:

- enjoy being read to and themselves retell simple narrative stories or informational texts
- use descriptive language to explain and explore
- recognize letter and letter–sound matches
- show familiarity with rhyming and beginning sounds
- understand left to right and top to bottom orientation and familiar concepts of print
- match spoken words with written words
- begin to write letters of the alphabet and some high-frequency words (NAEYC, 1998, p. 40)

Preschool children may function at either or both of these two phases, especially if the adults around them encourage their development and provide appropriate experiences. But it is the preschool teaching staff (including teachers, teaching assistants, student teachers, and volunteers) who can benefit most from knowledge of this continuum by learning to provide suitable literacy activities for children at their appropriate levels of development.

HOW CAN PRESCHOOL TEACHERS PROMOTE EARLY LITERACY?

Once the early childhood teaching staff understands that learning to read and write begins long before children are formally taught in elementary school, they can rearrange the preschool learning environment so that each learning center promotes literacy development, they can take time daily with individuals and small groups to engage them in literacy activities, and they can acquaint themselves with the most up-to-date information on what works best to promote early literacy among the children of many cultures present in most preschools.

This text provides such information in four parts, beginning with part 1, "Introduction," and chapter 1, "Getting Started with Early Literacy," which sets the stage; part 2, "Emergent Speaking," includes chapter 2, "Foundations of Early Literacy," which discusses the latest brain research on children's acquisition of language and how to establish an emotional, social, and physical environment with learning centers that promote early literacy development through cultural-character book activities.

Chapter 3, "Sounds of the Language: Rhyme, Rhythm, and Song," takes the reader into the music center, treating music and verse as a natural language that helps children develop phonemic awareness. Teachers learn how to use chants from picture books with cultural characters as a prelude to singing and later reading. They then progress with their children to sound making, singing, and reading song storybooks.

Chapter 4, "Sounds of the Language: Speaking and Listening," focuses on the listening center, book center, dramatic play center, and block center, using story reading and storytelling as the basis for developing these skills. In learning to recognize the preschool stages of language production, teachers provide opportunities for conversation, acceptance for the language of all children, and help for children in bonding with favorite cultural book characters. Teachers also learn how to prepare for story reading and telling, how to engage their audience, how to deliver stories, and how to follow up with exciting cultural character story extension activities in every learning center.

Part 3, "Emergent Writing," continues this presentation of classroom learning centers as the focus of literacy activities. Chapter 5, "Developing Eye–Hand Coordination," helps teachers strengthen children's small-motor coordination through three-dimensional art, cooking, and woodworking activities that are spin-offs from books containing favorite cultural characters. Cutting with scissors, stringing beads, simple sewing and weaving, and using cooking utensils and woodworking tools help prepare children for holding and controlling writing implements.

Chapter 6, "Art as a Natural Language," takes the reader into the art center, where children learn to handle drawing and painting tools as a precursor to using writing tools. Some begin by making art scribbles, then shapes and designs, and later suns, humans, and pictorials. Children learn to use their eyes to develop visual representational skills, eventually learning to communicate ideas through drawing.

Chapter 7, "Becoming a Writer," focuses on the preschool writing center, where teachers learn how to encourage children's early writing attempts such as scribble writing and mock letter writing. Teachers learn how children develop the *alphabetic principle*, and the latest alphabet books with cultural characters make their appearance. Children begin to print their names and use the computer keyboard. Books with cultural characters lead children into making lists, writing messages, and writing stories with pictures and invented spelling.

Part 4, "Emergent Reading," takes the reader through the emergent reading continuum beginning with chapter 8, "How Reading Emerges," in which developing a sense of story through dramatization is the most important concept. Children tell stories with flannel boards, cultural character dolls, and reenactment of favorite stories with themselves as characters. They also begin to read dictated stories, as well as retelling stories from books. Chapter 9, "Home Book Experience," discusses family literacy, the physical environment in the home, shared book reading with family members, and programs that support home reading.

Finally, chapter 10, "Becoming a Reader," takes both teacher and child through the transition from preschool to kindergarten. Teachers learn what is expected of the children in kindergarten and what types of reading instruction can be used, depending on how educators believe children acquire literacy. Altogether, these chapters give the teaching staff a solid foundation in theory and practice in using appropriate cultural activities to promote early literacy in preschool children.

WHAT IS THE CULTURAL CHARACTER APPROACH?

Almost all research on early literacy and reading points to one particular activity as having the most significant influence on children's success: "The single most important activity for building these understandings and skills essential for reading success appears to be *reading aloud to children*" (NAEYC, 1998, p. 33).

We already understand that young children must hear language spoken around them to learn to speak it themselves. Thus, it is not surprising to learn that

The single most important activity essential for reading success is reading aloud to children.

children's success in learning to read is also enhanced by having books read to them by adults. The extensive examination of research results by Karweit and Wasik (1996), who looked at the effects of story reading programs on literacy and language development of disadvantaged preschoolers, note, "In the current view of literacy as a process beginning long before school entry and incorporating broad definitions of reading and writing, reading stories is seen as a major vehicle through which children's vocabulary and literacy skills are developed" (p. 319).

The cultural character approach takes the position that early literacy for preschool children is best accomplished by reading aloud picture books featuring characters from diverse cultures that can then lead children into book extension activities in every learning center in the classroom. When children hear these stories read aloud, they come to identify with the characters in the stories almost as real people. They want to interact with these characters, pretend about them, build block structures for them, prepare make-believe meals for them, draw pictures about them, and make up their own stories about them with a teacher's encouragement. Most important, they come to love these books and want them read again and again.

Picture Book Characters as Cultural Models

Teachers have always tried to choose books that would interest their children. What do preschool youngsters have the most intense interest in? First, them-

One of the most effective ways for integrating cultural diversity into a curriculum is to help children identify with and bond with storybook characters like themselves from other cultures.

selves. Next on the list comes other children. Thus, we understand that if information about other cultures is to make a difference in the lives of children ages 3 to 5, it should relate directly to the children themselves and their peers. It should involve the children in learning firsthand about youngsters like themselves from different cultures. In fact, one of the most effective approaches to integrating cultural diversity into an early childhood curriculum is to help children identify with and bond with children like themselves from other cultures (Pratt & Beaty, 1999).

Where can an early childhood teacher or caregiver find these other children—and on a daily basis? They have always been available if you knew where to look. Today there are more of them around than ever before: in children's picture books. They are the real or imagined Anglo-Americans, African Americans, Asians, Europeans, Hispanics, Middle Easterners, Native Americans, and the rainbow of other children whose lives are depicted in illustrated storybooks.

Your children can come to know these cultural characters intimately by identifying and bonding with them, as you read stories about how children from diverse cultures play, work, and live; how they eat, dress, and go to preschool; how they feel, act, and even "act out." Introducing children to picture book characters in the stories and activities you provide is an especially effective way for children to get to know youngsters from other cultures. The experience can be almost as real as having a child from a different culture in the class.

Children seem to have no difficulty choosing these cultural characters as role models. Youngsters enjoy the characters in their storybooks, and if the story appeals to them, they want to hear it over and over. They come to love the characters in the stories they love. Some educators actually call children's close identification with storybook characters as "book character bonding," or "book bonding" for short (Pratt & Beaty, 1999).

To celebrate the diversity of all children everywhere, this textbook takes the distinctive approach of using such picture books as springboards into activities that not only promote early literacy but also bond children with youngsters like them from other cultures. In other words, by picking up a particular culture-based story and reading it to the children, a teacher can involve the youngsters vicariously in the lives of children from that culture. Afterward the youngsters can participate in early literacy activities in the various learning centers of the classroom that are similar to the activities experienced by the book characters. When children take on the roles of the characters in a book, they bond with the characters.

Whether or not the culture being read about is present in the classroom makes no difference. All children can celebrate any culture on a daily basis simply by looking at or listening to cultural character picture books and following up with early literacy cultural activities. Remember your own favorite childhood books? Most were undoubtedly based on characters for whom you had a strong affinity. They were children you wanted to emulate and whose adventures you wanted to experience. Today they can be children from more cultures than ever before.

Lead-ins to a Cultural Character Curriculum

Will You Come Back for Me?
(Tompert, 1988)
Hue Boy (Mitchell, 1993)
Building a Bridge (Begaye & Tracy, 1993)

But what can you do with a book besides reading it aloud to children? You and the children can make a game of it; make puppets of its characters; build a house for its characters; make costumes for its characters; make hats or masks for its characters; pretend to be a character; make a felt board of it; cook a meal from it; paint pictures about it; write letters about it; tell the story to a doll; guess what happens next; make a puzzle of it; make sound effects; write your own version of it; tape record the children's version; sing it; dance it; videotape it; anything!

Certain children's books can be the lead-ins to an entire preschool curriculum. But what books should they be? That is the important question. This text takes the position that *the best books to use in promoting early literacy for preschool children in this day and age are quality picture books featuring cultural characters that children can identify with*. Thus, the cultural character approach presented here features outstanding picture books with child characters as the basis for literacy development in the preschool.

Why picture books, you may wonder? Wouldn't any storybook that could keep a young child's attention promote literacy? Barbara Z. Kiefer (1995), author of *The Potential of Picturebooks: From Visual Literacy to Aesthetic Understanding,* believes that picture books offer a special attraction as well as important learnings for young children: "I found that picturebooks inspired imaginative experiences for children. Their language in response to picturebooks allowed them to participate in the imaginary world created by the author and artist or to create their own images. Young children often 'chose' a character that they wanted to be as they read or looked through a book" (pp. 29–30).

If the character happened to be a child from another culture, the young listeners were able to learn firsthand about a child like themselves from a different culture by actually pretending to be that character through classroom activities and dramatizations. In fact, one of the most effective approaches for integrating multicultural education into an early childhood curriculum is to help children identify with children like themselves from other cultures.

Is there any precedent for using cultural character picture books as the basis for an entire multicultural curriculum emphasizing literacy? Children's literature specialist Donna Norton recognized the role of children's books in shaping attitudes and breaking down stereotypes as early as 1985 when she stated:

> The values gained from sharing multicultural literature with children are so powerful and so persuasive that we cannot dispute them. These include:
>
> 1. Pleasure and enjoyment gained from hearing the rhythmic language of an African folktale or from vicariously seeing one's continent through the eyes of an early resident.
> 2. Information and understanding gained from reading about one's geographical and natural history, from discovering the impact of sociological change and from reading about great achievers of all backgrounds.
> 3. Pride in heritage as children identify with achievers from the past as well as the present, improve their self-concepts and develop a sense of identity.
> 4. Social development as children discover that all people are human beings who should be considered as individuals, not stereotypes.
> 5. Language development as children interact with rhymes and poetry and discuss story plots, characterizations, settings and themes.
> 6. Cognitive development nurtured through literature-related activities that emphasize observing, comparing, hypothesizing, organizing, summarizing, applying, and criticizing. (p. 103)

The United States is a multicultural nation including people from European, Asian, Hispanic, African, Middle Eastern, Pacific Island, Caribbean, and Native American backgrounds and others. However, our efforts to integrate this understanding into educational settings has not been overly successful. Too often our attempts at multicultural education have been superficial, celebrating occasional cultural holidays, heroes, and festivals, but with little integration into the overall curriculum. For multicultural education to be effective, it must be an *everyday* affair that speaks to the children. As Boutte and McCormick (1992) point out, "Multicultural ideas are 'caught' rather than 'taught'; that is, multicultural attitudes are developed through everyday experiences rather than formal lessons. Multicultural ideas and activities, therefore, should be thoroughly integrated throughout all activities every day—not only in fragmented units" (p. 140).

The cultural character approach incorporates the daily reading of appropriate picture books with cultural characters and extending book activities into

The cultural character approach incorporates the daily reading of picture books about cultural characters with whom children can identify.

every learning center of the classroom. An entire early literacy curriculum can emerge from such books. Does it work?

Teachers who have used cultural character picture books as lead-ins to literacy activities tell about children's excitement in meeting these wonderful new book friends, such as Asian American Suki who worries about whether her mother will remember to pick her up at the day care center in *Will You Come Back for Me?* Your children may also identify with such worries.

Then there is the Caribbean boy in *Hue Boy* who tries desperately to grow big and tall but can't seem to do it until his father returns. You may have boys like this as well. Or what about the Anglo-American girl Anna and the Navajo girl Juanita who worry that they won't find a friend on their first day at preschool, until they find each other in the block center in *Building a Bridge*?

Teachers, teaching assistants, student teachers, and volunteers who read cultural character books to children are then able to plan the use of puppets, dolls, and character cutouts to help bring these book characters to life. Children take it from there, converting their adventures with these cultural book characters into positive attitudes about people of all kinds, about books, and about reading and writing that can last them a lifetime. As Bieger (1996) tells us, "Through reading, we briefly share in the lives and feelings of the characters rather than dealing only with facts. Literature provides food for both the head and the heart. Books may be used as agents for change, vehicles for introducing concepts, and catalysts for activities" (p. 309).

Traditionally, teachers have used books in two ways: they read the stories to their children, and they put the books back on the shelves to be looked at or read by the children on their own. What about you? This is a serious underuse of a valuable asset in a preschool curriculum. Each picture book is an extraordinary resource for activities that can be extended throughout the curriculum as noted. Picture books can lead children into art and music activities, science projects, math and language learning, physical activities, and all sorts of dramatics, not to mention prereading and prewriting activities. In other words, picture books can and should be used as introductions or lead-ins to *all* of your curriculum activities all year long.

The books themselves should be selected by teachers for such purposes. When planning curriculum activities, teachers need to consider using a book to introduce each experience. This is an especially meaningful way to get youngsters involved in the same sorts of activities that the cultural book characters engage in. Thus, choosing the right books is an essential first step toward developing the curriculum.

HOW CAN TEACHERS CHOOSE BOOKS WITH CULTURAL CHARACTERS TO SUPPORT AN EARLY LITERACY CURRICULUM?

Choosing Appropriate Picture Books

Go into any bookstore or library featuring children's picture books and you may soon feel overwhelmed with the number and variety of picture books available. Clever cover illustrations seem to pop out at you. Catchy titles call for your attention. But which ones are appropriate? They can't all be equal in value for the children you are working with, can they? How can you choose among so many seemingly good possibilities?

For teachers who believe it is the book itself that can lead children into an entire curriculum of early literacy and cultural activities, they will want to choose carefully. They will want several picture storybooks on the broad themes or topics that are frequently pursued during the year, such as these:

Caring for ourselves

Getting along with one another

Relating to family members

Learning about our neighborhood, our world

Caring about the Earth

Some teachers organize their curriculum around the *learning centers* in the classroom, providing materials and activities in each center that will support the theme being pursued. Others organize their teaching around *units*, engaging children in preplanned activities related to the unit theme. Still others favor a *project approach* in which teachers or the children themselves decide to find out about a particular topic or theme, not knowing ahead of time in what direction their investigation will take them.

In any case, teachers will usually have some idea about a particular topic that is to be pursued. They will also know that they want a picture book that:

- features cultural characters,
- features characters who are realistic and not stereotyped,
- displays illustrations attractive to children,
- contains a minimum of text to keep the attention of preschool children,
- can serve as a lead-in to curriculum activities.

Many teachers find that checklists listing important criteria such as these can help them select the best books for their children. The checklist "Choosing Cultural Character Picture Books" as shown in Figure 1.1 has proved helpful to many teachers who plan to use these picture books as keys to unlocking a curriculum featuring early literacy.

With these ideas in mind, let's take the theme "Caring for Ourselves" to see what subtopics we might want to pursue and what books might relate to this theme. Some of the subtopics could include the following:

Who am I?

What kinds of clothes or shoes do I like?

What do I like to eat?

What is my favorite activity?

First, look at the covers of the books in the bookstore or library. If your children are from a neighborhood of Anglo-American, African American, or Hispanic people, you may be looking for books that show characters from these groups on the covers. On the other hand, if your children are mainly Anglo-American, you will still want books featuring a diversity of children because your children need to know about them. Do any of the books you see show attractive, realistic illustrations of such children? Do the books relate in any way to this topic? Here are a few of the books you may want to *consid*er for the subtopic "Who Am I?"

I Am Me (Kushkin, 2000)

Dancing in the Wings (Allen, 2000)

Cleversticks (Ashley, 1991)

Pablo's Tree (Mora, 1994)

Susan Laughs (Willis, 1999)

Now open each of the books one at a time and look at the criteria that may help you decide whether this is the book for your children. As you go

Choosing Cultural Character Picture Books

Title _____

Criteria _____ Yes   No

1. Illustrations attractive, showing cultural characters/theme   ____ ____

2. Characters children can identify with   ____ ____

3. Theme familiar to children   ____ ____

4. Words catchy; rhyme, rhythm, or repetition   ____ ____

5. Plot fast-paced, easy for preschoolers to follow   ____ ____

6. Publication date current (1990–2000+)   ____ ____

7. Characters, theme, or topic can be integrated into learning center
   activities   ____ ____

Extension Activities from This Book

Describe:

(Permission is granted by the publisher to reproduce this checklist for evaluation and record keeping.)

FIGURE 1.1

Checklist: Choosing Cultural Character Picture Books

through the checklist for the book *I Am Me* (see Figure 1.2), it becomes obvious that this story not only fulfills all the criteria but will also make an excellent beginning book for the topic "Who Am I?" The story features a little tan-skinned girl at the beach with white and tan relatives who make comments about the girl's eyes, hands, feet, and so on, mentioning in rhyme the source of each of her features (her mother's pointed chin; her dad's tan skin). At the end the little girl loudly proclaims that "I am me!"

Although the illustrations of the people are more cartoonlike than realistic, they are not stereotyped but show the characters as interesting individuals. Recent publication dates such as this book's 2000 date usually indicate that

---

Choosing Cultural Character Picture Books

Title I Am Me _____

Criteria	Yes	No
1. Illustrations attractive, showing multicultural characters/theme	✓	___
2. Characters children can identify with	✓	___
3. Theme familiar to children	✓	___
4. Words catchy; (rhyme,) rhythm, or repetition	✓	___
5. Plot fast-paced, easy for preschoolers to follow	✓	___
6. Publication date current (1990–2000+)	✓	___
7. Characters, theme, or topic can be integrated into learning center activities	✓	___

Extension Activities from this Book

Describe:
   Look-in-the-mirror game
   Art: trace around hands; do foot stampings
   Take photos of every child
   Start "Who Am I?" books for everyone

FIGURE 1.2
Checklist for I Am Me

artists and authors have not reverted to the unfortunate racial stereotypes of some older book illustrations. The simple rhyming sentences make this book a "predictable book," one in which children can predict what word comes next—very helpful for beginning readers.

The picture book **Dancing in the Wings,** on the other hand, shows a more realistic African American girl, Sassy, on the blue cover in a spectacular ballet pose (Figure 1.3). But as you go through the book, you realize that although the illustrations are expressive and wonderful, the text is too long and the plot too complicated for preschool children. In fact, now that you look closer, you realize that the girl herself is older than your children. This will be a fine book for a parent to read at home to an older child who wants to take ballet lessons.

Choosing Cultural Character Picture Books

Title Dancing in the Wings

Criteria	Yes	No
1. Illustrations attractive, showing multicultural characters/theme	✓	
2. Characters children can identify with	✓	
3. Theme familiar to children	✓	
4. Words catchy; rhyme, rhythm, or repetition		✓
5. Plot fast-paced, easy for preschoolers to follow		✓
6. Publication date current (1990–2000+)	✓	
7. Characters, theme, or topic can be integrated into learning center activities	✓	

Extension Activities from this Book

Describe:
(Story too long and complex for preschooler children. Better for grade school children.)

FIGURE 1.3
Checklist for *Dancing in the Wings*

The cover of ***Cleversticks*** shows the happily surprised face and upper torso of the Chinese boy Ling Sung, using a pair of inverted paintbrushes as chopsticks to pick up cookie pieces (Figure 1.4). As you leaf through the book, you note the large, expressive illustrations show Ling Sung in his new preschool trying but failing to tie his shoes, paint his name, and tie his paint apron like his other multicultural classmates. Then he drops and breaks his cookies but easily picks them up with inverted paintbrushes for chopsticks. Everyone claps, and his father calls him "Cleversticks" when he comes to get him after school.

The text is somewhat long for the youngest preschoolers, but large, colorful pictures on every page keep the story fast-paced and easy for most preschoolers to follow. What a grand lead-in to a whole series of eye–hand coordination, cooking, and name-printing activities this book can introduce, based on the topic "Who Am I?"

Choosing Cultural Character Picture Books

Title Cleversticks

Criteria	Yes	No
1. Illustrations attractive, showing multicultural characters/theme	✓	____
2. Characters children can identify with	✓	____
3. Theme familiar to children	✓	____
4. Words catchy; rhyme, rhythm, or repetition	____	✓
5. Plot fast-paced, easy for preschoolers to follow	✓	____
6. Publication date current (1990–2000+)	✓	____
7. Characters, theme, or topic can be integrated into learning center activities	✓	____

Extension Activities from this Book

Describe:

Snack: have cookies & chopsticks
Dramatic play: put chopsticks in center
Invite Asian parents to help children cook & eat a rice dish

FIGURE 1.4

Checklist for *Cleversticks*

The cover of **Pablo's Tree** shows a Hispanic boy with a paper lantern ready to hang on his "birthday tree" (Figure 1.5). The story describes 5-year-old Pablo and his mother's visit to his grandfather, who planted a tree when Pablo was first adopted, and has been hanging surprise decorations on the tree for each of Pablo's birthdays. Like **Cleversticks,** the story is somewhat long for the youngest preschoolers, but the colorful folk art–like illustrations nearly filling each page keep the story fast-paced. This story, too, is a fine lead-in to a unique birthday activity, which does not always have to consist of a piñata for a Hispanic child. The concepts of guessing about a surprise, as well as recalling what happened in past years, make this story personal for each child.

The cover of **Susan Laughs** shows a little red-haired Anglo-American girl on the high end of a teeter-totter (Figure 1.6). As you flip through the pages, you realize there are no children of other cultures but mainly Susan herself on

Large, colorful pictures on every page of Cleversticks *can lead to a whole series of eye–hand coordination and name-printing activities.*

each page with a simple two-word rhyming sentence describing the illustration ("Susan dances," "Susan rides," "Susan swims," and "Susan hides"). This very simple story is intriguing for the youngest listeners, not only making it an excellent book for early reading but also leading up to a most unexpected ending: Susan is sitting in a wheelchair! A dramatic lesson for everyone that although some children may look different, all children are "just like me, just like you."

Acquiring Appropriate Picture Books

Where will you find such books as those described here? Most bookstores and libraries have some or all of them or can order them for you. If you prefer to order them yourself, you may want to call or write for catalogs or go on-line to the publishers of the books or the following supply houses:

Lakeshore Learning Materials
2695 E. Dominguez Street
PO Box 6261
Carson, CA 90749
Phone: (800) 421–5354
(Multicultural books and materials)

Lectorum Publications, Inc.
205 Chubb Avenue
Lyndhurst, NJ 07071
Phone: (800) 345–5946
(Books in English and Spanish)

Choosing Cultural Character Picture Books

Title *Pablo's Tree*

Criteria	Yes	No
1. Illustrations attractive, showing multicultural characters/theme	✓	___
2. Characters children can identify with	✓	___
3. Theme familiar to children	✓	___
4. Words catchy; rhyme, rhythm, or repetition	✓	___
5. Plot fast-paced, easy for preschoolers to follow	✓	___
6. Publication date current (1990–2000+)	✓	___
7. Characters, theme, or topic can be integrated into learning center activities	✓	___

Extension Activities from this Book

Describe:

Make "Birthday Tree"; hang a paper cutout for each child's birthday. Add to "Who Am I" book about birthdays
Play music (flute, tambourine)
use new Spanish words

FIGURE 1.5

Checklist for *Pablo's Tree*

Northland/Rising Moon
PO Box 1389
Flagstaff, AZ 86002
Phone: (800) 346–3257
On-line: www.northlandpub.com
(Native American books)

Oyate
2702 Mathews Street
Berkeley, CA 94702
On-line: www.oyate.org
(Native American books)

Choosing Cultural Character Picture Books

Title *Susan Laughs* _____

Criteria	**Yes**	**No**
1. Illustrations attractive, showing multicultural characters/theme		✓
2. Characters children can identify with	✓	
3. Theme familiar to children	✓	
4. Words catchy; (rhyme,) rhythm, or repetition	✓	
5. Plot fast-paced, easy for preschoolers to follow	✓	
6. Publication date current (1990–2000+)	✓	
7. Characters, theme, or topic can be integrated into learning center activities	✓	

Extension Activities from this Book

Describe:
Children can try to imitate Susan's activities
Add new facts to "Who Am I" book
Pretend to be Susan in a "wheelchair"

FIGURE 1.6
Checklist for *Susan Laughs*

Scholastic, Inc. (see appendix A)
PO Box 7502
Jefferson City, MO 65102
Phone: (800) 724–6527
On-line: www.scholastic.com
(Multicultural books; inexpensive paperback books)

Bookstores may also be contacted on-line. The following stores have Web sites that list children's multicultural picture books:

www.amazon.com
www.barnes&noble.com
www.borders.com
www.waldenbooks.com

Affordability

For some early childhood educators, the prices of children's trade picture books may seem prohibitive at about $15 for a hardcover book, but this cost is no more than for other quality classroom equipment and materials such as unit blocks and art supplies. However, paperback copies of many of the same hardcover books may run only between $3 and $6 (see appendix A, "Cultural Character Paperback Books from Scholastic"). When we understand that young children are motivated to learn to read through listening to such books, and to a hands-on acquaintance with them, then we will budget sufficient funds annually for the purchase of the best cultural character picture books available. No longer will inexpensive little cardboard-covered books from discount stores be acceptable in the classroom book center.

Centers that still cannot afford a good collection of cultural character books such as those described in this text need to contact the parents of their children to help with fund-raising projects to purchase books for the program.

Paradigm Shift

Those of us who still look at children's picture books as merely a form of entertainment may need to make a paradigm shift when we realize that such books are actually the keys to unlocking an entire curriculum of cultural character activities—activities that can improve attitudes toward all people while at the same time helping young children emerge into early literacy. *Early Literacy in Preschool and Kindergarten* invites you to join in the excitement of this new approach.

Summary

This chapter defines early literacy and sets the stage for the chapters to come with their emphasis on the unique "cultural character approach," using picture book characters as cultural models young children can identify with, thus leading them into early reading and writing activities. Choosing appropriate picture books to support this approach is discussed along with a summary of the contents of each chapter to follow.

Learning Activities

1. Define "early literacy," telling how early it begins and what teachers can expect from children ages 3 to 5 in their classrooms.
2. How can preschool teachers promote early literacy among the children in their classes? What areas of child development does early literacy encompass?
3. What is the cultural character approach featured in this textbook, and how can it help children develop early literacy?

4. How can picture book characters become cultural models for children? Why is this important?
5. How can teachers choose books with cultural characters to support an early literacy curriculum? Give an example of one such book, and tell how it meets the criteria discussed.

REFERENCES

Bieger, E. M. (1996). Promoting multicultural education through a literature-based approach. *The Reading Teacher, 49*(4), 308–311.

Boutte, G. S., & McCormick, C. B. (1992). Authentic multicultural activities. *Childhood Education, 68*(3), 140–144.

Brewer, J. (1998). Literacy development of young children in a multilingual setting. In R. Campbell (Ed.), *Facilitating preschool literacy* (pp. 119–130). Newark, DE: International Reading Association.

Gambrell, L. B., & Mazzoni, S. A. (1999). Emergent literacy: What research reveals about learning to read. In C. Seefeldt (Ed.), *The early childhood curriculum: Current findings in theory and practice.* New York: Teachers College Press.

Karweit, N., & Wasik, B. A. (1996). The effects of story reading programs on literacy and language development of disadvantaged preschoolers. *Journal of Education for Students Placed at Risk, 1*(4), 319–348.

Kiefer, B. Z. (1995). *The potential of picturebooks: From visual literacy to aesthetic understanding.* Upper Saddle River, NJ: Merrill/Prentice Hall.

National Association for the Education of Young Children. (1998). Learning to read and write: Developmentally appropriate practices for young children. *Young Children, 53*(4), 30–46.

Norton, D. E. (1985, November/December). Language and cognitive development through multicultural literature. *Childhood Education,* 103–108.

Pratt, L., & Beaty, J. J. (1999). *Transcultural children's literature.* Upper Saddle River, NJ: Merrill/Prentice Hall.

SUGGESTED READINGS

Barclay, K., Kenilli, C., & Curtis, A. (1995). Literacy begins at birth: What caregivers can learn from parents of children who read early. *Young Children, 50*(4), 24–28.

Bobys, A. R. (2000). What does emerging literacy look like? *Young Children, 55*(4), 16–27.

Bryan, J. W. (1999). Readers' workshop in a kindergarten classroom. *Reading Teacher, 52*(5), 538–540.

Corson, P. (2000). Laying the foundation for literacy: An anti-bias approach. *Childhood Education, 76*(6), 385–389.

De Meléndez, W. R., & Ostertag, V. (1997). *Teaching young children in multicultural classrooms: Issues, concepts, and strategies.* Albany, NY: Delmar.

Gottschall, S. M. (1995). Hug-a-Book: A program to nurture a young child's love of books and reading. *Young Children, 50*(4), 29–35.

Graue, E. (2001). What's going on in the children's garden? Kindergarten today. *Young Children, 56*(4), 67–73.

Greenberg, P. (1998). Some thoughts about phonics, feelings, Don Quixote, diversity, and democracy: Teaching young children to read, Part 1. *Young Children, 53*(4), 72–82.

Greenberg, P. (1998). Warmly and calmly teaching young children to read, write, and spell: Thoughts about the first four of twelve well-known principles, Part 2. *Young Children, 53*(5), 68–82.

Hayden, R., Anderson, J., & Gunderson, L. (1997). Literacy learning from a multicultural perspective. *The Reading Teacher, 50*(6), 514–516.

Helm, J. H., & Katz, L. (2001). *Young investigators: The project approach in the early years.* New York: Teachers College Press.

Hernandez, H. (2001). *Multicultural education: A teacher's guide to linking context, process and content.* Upper Saddle River, NJ: Merrill/Prentice Hall.

Hunt, R. (2000). Making positive multicultural education happen. *Young Children, 54*(5), 39–42.

Kendall, F. E. (1996). *Diversity in the classroom: New approaches to the education of young children.* New York: Teachers College Press.

King, E. W., Chipman, M., & Cruz-Janzen, M. (1994). *Educating young children in a diverse society.* Boston: Allyn & Bacon.

Makin, L., Hayden, J., & Diaz, C. J. (2000). High-quality literacy programs in early childhood classrooms: An Australian case study. *Childhood Education, 76*(6), 365–367.

Meyer, J. (2001). The child-centered kindergarten: A position paper. *Childhood Education, 77*(3), 161–167.

Norton, D. E. (2001). *Multicultural children's literature: Through the eyes of many children.* Upper Saddle River, NJ: Merrill/Prentice Hall.

Novick, R. (1999–2000). Support early literacy development: Doing things with words in the real world. *Childhood Education, 76*(2), 70–75.

Ramsey, P. G., & Derman-Sparks, L. (1992). Multicultural education reaffirmed. *Young Children, 47*(2), 10–11.

Strasser, J. K. (2000–2001). Beautiful me! Celebrating diversity through literature and art. *Childhood Education, 77*(2), 76–80.

Wham, M. A., Barnhart, J., & Cook, G. (1996). Enhancing multicultural awareness through the storybook reading experience. *Journal of Research and Development in Education, 30*(1), 1–9.

CHILDREN'S BOOKS

Allen, D. (2000). *Dancing in the wings.* New York: Dial.

Ashley, B. (1991). *Cleversticks.* New York: Crown.

Begaye, L. S., & Tracy, L. (1993). *Building a bridge.* Flagstaff, AZ: Rising Moon.

Kuskin, K. (2000). *I am me.* New York: Simon & Schuster.

Mora, P. (1994). *Pablo's tree.* New York: Macmillan.

Mitchell, R. P. (1993). *Hue boy.* New York: Dial.

Tompert, A. (1988). *Will you come back for me?* Morton Grove, IL: Whitman.

Willis, J. (1999). *Susan laughs.* New York: Holt.

PART 2

EMERGENT SPEAKING

*Young children have enormous capacity for language
learning. They delight in the sounds and meanings
of new words, rolling the names of dinosaurs off
their tongues, for example. But oral language
development is more than facility with labels: it is
coming to understand the need for precision,
purpose, and audience in using language. One of
the best opportunities for hearing language worth
talking about—and for using language to say exactly
what one means—comes with sitting on the story
rug, and talking about children's books.*

Lapp, Flood, and Roser (2000, p. 187)

FOUNDATIONS OF EARLY LITERACY

SUPPORTING LANGUAGE DEVELOPMENT THROUGH NEW BRAIN RESEARCH

ESTABLISHING THE PRESCHOOL LANGUAGE LEARNING ENVIRONMENT

CHAPTER 2

SUPPORTING LANGUAGE DEVELOPMENT THROUGH NEW BRAIN RESEARCH

Language Acquisition in Preschool Children

Preschool children ages 3 through 5 are at the language acquisition stage of their development. Between birth and age 6, children acquire an entire native language from scratch. If they are from bilingual or multilingual families, they may acquire more than one language. This natural language acquisition in young children is so commonplace that we tend to take it for granted. We seldom stop to think what a miraculous achievement it is to go from having no spoken language at birth to speaking an entire native tongue by age 6!

The years from 2 to 5 are especially crucial in this process. During this period, a child's vocabulary expands from about 200 to 2,000 words or more. In addition, children learn by themselves the rules for putting words together to speak in sentences. Because children are often in early childhood programs during these years, the language environment you provide can have a profound effect on their language development, thus their early literacy.

New Brain Research

New brain research supports the idea that language development takes place most readily during toddlerhood and the preschool years when a "window of opportunity" for language development is also occurring in the developing brain. Kotulak (1996) describes what neurobiologists have discovered:

> The brain can reorganize itself with particular ease early in life during crucial learning periods, when connections between brain cells are being made and broken down at an enormous rate. Information flows easily into the brain through "windows" that are open for only a short duration. These windows of development occur in phases from birth to age 12 when the brain is most actively learning from its environment. It is during this period, and especially the first three years, that the foundations of thinking, language, vision, attitudes, aptitudes, and other characteristics are laid down. Then the windows close, and much of the fundamental architecture of the brain is completed. (p. 7)

Research neurobiologist Dr. Carla Shatz describes how the human brain is made up of more than one trillion nerve cells called *neurons*. As the brain develops, these neurons join together to form *synapses*, or paths that allow nerve cells to connect to one another. The synapses in turn join together to form an even more highly interconnected wiring system, the *brain circuitry* (Willis, 1997). The brain itself is organized into numerous physical "maps" that govern such things as vision and language. Such structures need to be reinforced by stimuli coming from the child's experiences in his or her environment.

Brain tissue development reaches a peak by the age of 3 years. While every child develops more synapses than he or she can possibly use, it is the environment that determines which synapses become permanent because they are used and which ones are eliminated because they are not used. In other words, the way a child is raised affects how the brain chooses to wire itself for life (Simmons & Sheehan, 1997).

But what about a child's usage of language? How does it affect the brain? Healy (1990) describes what a huge impact language has on brain development: "Language shapes culture, language shapes thinking—and language shapes brains. Language helps children learn to reason, reflect, and respond to the world. The brain is ravenous for language stimulation in early childhood."

Such research does not suggest that early childhood programs flood their classrooms with expensive learning materials or pressure the children to learn the alphabet in several languages while this window of opportunity for language learning is open. Research instead supports the theory that "learning must take place in a meaningful context and in an environment of love and support" (Newberger, 1997, p. 8). It is thus crucial that the language learning environment we establish be one of acceptance for children from a variety of cultures, support for the individual child, and abundant stimulating and fun-filled activities.

Most of all, children must hear spoken language to learn it. You and every staff member must talk with the children and with one another. You must read books to individuals and small groups on a daily basis. Young children learn the languages they hear spoken in their environment. If yours is a bilingual classroom, be sure that both languages are spoken among children and adults.

Such language experiences for young children form the basis not only for their early literacy development but also for much of their future learning through the wiring of their brains. Thus, the language environment we create must give children the freedom and encouragement to plunge into new dimensions of language learning to emerge successfully on their personal road to literacy.

ESTABLISHING THE PRESCHOOL LANGUAGE LEARNING ENVIRONMENT

Emotional Environment

Teacher–Child Acceptance

How do you feel about the children in your classroom? Do you like them? Every one of them? Or do you like many of them, tolerate some of them, and have a few special favorites? You must show your acceptance of every child in the classroom no matter what he looks like, how he dresses, how he acts or speaks; no matter what her race, religion, or ethnic background, and no matter what her family makeup. Young children are especially aware of the feelings of others toward them. If we want children to feel good about themselves

Rise and Shine, Mariko-Chan
(Tomoika, 1992)
Cleversticks (Ashley, 1991)

CHAPTER 2

The teacher must show acceptance of every child in the class no matter what she looks like or how she acts or speaks.

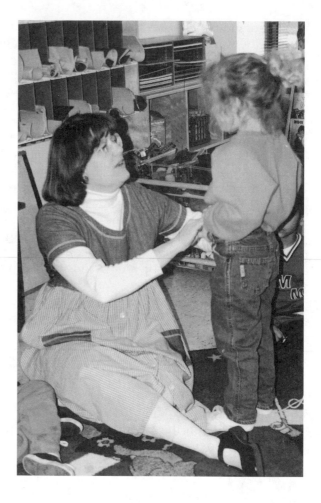

and comfortable in the classroom environment, then we must treat each of them as special, worthwhile individuals. Current research agrees: "There is consistent evidence that how teachers interact with children matters to their development. Teachers who are sensitive to children's needs and who engage, encourage, and verbally communicate with them appear to be nurturing more optimal cognitive, language, and socioemotional development" (Kontos & Wilcoz-Herzog, 1997, p. 11).

Furthermore, the emotional tone of the classroom can help set the stage for language learning if the environment is stress-free. This means the staff must be friendly and welcoming to all of the children and their families. To help children feel at ease about speaking, you need to help them feel at ease about themselves by accepting them as they are. Show them how happy you are to see them every day. Encourage but do not pressure them to participate in activities. Compliment them for their completion of a task or success at solving a problem.

Take time at the end of the day to tell them how happy you were to have them in class and how much you look forward to seeing them the next day.

If you have recent immigrants to the United States in your program, you may want to greet such newcomers in their native language to make them feel more at home. Ask their parents or sponsors what to say.

> Developing esteem can begin for child and parent when first entering a group. When a refugee Vietnamese family enrolled Thuy (Twee) in the day care center, the caregiver greeted the parents and child each day in their native language: "chao ong" to the father, "chao ba" to the mother, and "chao em" to the child. By showing affection toward the children and encouraging their mutual affection for each other, the caregiver communicates that each child is liked, and therefore, that each child should like himself. (Browne, Howard, & Pitts, 1984, p. 2)

Many cultures use greetings and farewells in a more formal manner than Americans do. Sometimes a handshake, a nod, or a bow is part of the greeting. Your children may enjoy hearing about another culture and its method of greeting through your reading of **Rise and Shine, Mariko-chan!** Little Mariko-chan, the youngest daughter in a Japanese family, enjoys greeting everyone with her cheery good mornings and good-byes as the family goes off to work and school.

The youngest children may want to try some of Mariko's greetings themselves every day when they come to school. Or they can put on a brief role play of Mariko-chan saying "good morning" and "good-bye" to members of her family with figures of block people. Be sure that your block people represent different races.

Your youngsters may also like to hear a picture book story about children like themselves who are complimented for the simple tasks they perform in preschool, such as fastening their jackets, putting on paint aprons, or making letters of their names. In **Cleversticks**, a Chinese boy named Ling Sung has trouble adjusting to his multicultural American preschool. He can't seem to do the things the others do, so nobody claps for his accomplishments until the day he drops the snack cookies by accident and picks up the pieces Chinese-style with two inverted paintbrushes used like chopsticks. Everyone is amazed and wants him to teach them how. His dad ends up calling him "Cleversticks," as mentioned in chapter 1.

Clever teachers use this book as a lead-in to using real chopsticks with small groups in the dramatic play area and cooking area. Soon everyone is looking for other hidden skills different children may possess. "Look, Silas can hop on one foot all the way across the room!" "Shamara knows how to say 'hello' in Swahili!"

Language Acceptance

In addition to showing acceptance for the children, you need to accept each child's language, no matter how poorly it is pronounced or how ungrammatical it is. Whether it is English, a dialect of English, or another language altogether, it reflects not only the child's stage of language development but also his or her family's language. Language is a very personal thing. A child's language represents the child and her family. To tell a child she is saying a word wrong is a personal put-down not only for the child but also for her family. Better to compliment her on what she is saying or doing that is right. Then she will come to feel at ease in the classroom. Your correct use of words is the language model she will eventually learn to follow.

Most preschool teachers do, in fact, accept all of the children in their class. Yet for children who do not feel good about themselves, their teacher's acceptance of them may not sink in. Greeting each child in the morning may not be enough. You and the staff may need to plan and then carry out other agreed-on procedures for helping children be aware that you notice them and appreciate their presence, for, as Kosnik (1993) points out, "For children to believe that they are valuable members of the community, they must feel individually noticed and they must feel wanted. By getting to know the children and highlighting their abilities, the teacher validates the children" (p. 36).

Use of Photos

Pascual's Magic Pictures

(Gage, 1996)

Take a photo of each child at the beginning of the year and make duplicate copies for a variety of language activities. One photo can be laminated onto an attendance card with his name typed in uppercase letters under his picture, which the teacher gives to the child when she greets him in the morning, tells him how happy she is to see him, and asks him to hang his card on the attendance board under his name.

Another photo can be pasted on the front of the child's journal, which he will be drawing or scribble-writing in every day. Don't forget to look at this booklet with the child from time to time, making positive comments on his entries and listening to stories he may want to tell about them.

An enlarged photo of the child can be pasted on cardboard and cut into a personal photo puzzle. Keep the puzzle pieces in a manila envelope with a picture of the child on the front. Each time the child completes the puzzle, it should make her feel good to see a smiling image of herself looking back at her. Be sure to encourage children to make their photo puzzles from time to time because you also like to see what they look like on their completed puzzles and hear what they have to say about themselves.

Keep a camera handy and take photos of each child during the week as he or she participates in various activities. The child can then make his own scrapbook of such photos, dictating a brief story for you to write under the photo. Be sure to let children also use a camera to take their own photos to add to their books.

To get them started you might read them **Pascual's Magic Pictures** about the Hispanic boy Pascual who lives in the jungle near the Mayan ruins of Tikal in Guatemala. When a tourist lady asks to take his picture with her little yellow disposable camera, Pascual knows he has to save his money for a camera like this to take pictures of the exciting black howler monkeys in the jungle. He finally gets his camera but then loses it in the jungle when a loud roar frightens him into dropping it and running away. It is only the howler monkeys themselves roaring at him. When he finally finds the lost camera, all the pictures are used up. He sends it in for developing anyway, and guess what the pictures show? Ask your children to guess. Did anybody say "howler monkeys"? The monkeys have stolen the camera and used it on themselves!

Your children will certainly identify with this boy from another culture and may want to reenact his story. How many children will want to be howler monkeys, do you suppose? But first you should be prepared with a little disposable camera for their use to see what pictures they will take for their personal journals. Because this is a long story for the youngest preschooler, be prepared to tell the story by "reading the pictures"—large colorful illustrations of Pascual appear on every page.

Use of Mirrors

Another way children can feel good about themselves is by looking in a mirror. A full-length mirror should be stationed in the dress-up area. You can also bring in enough hand mirrors or pocket mirrors

Kelly in the Mirror
(Vertreace, 1993)

Another way children can feel good about themselves is by looking in a full-length mirror.

to use with each child in a small story-reading group. Talk with the group about feelings, and ask them to make smiling faces in the mirrors. Tell each one by name how much you enjoy seeing them smile.

Read the book **Kelly in the Mirror** about the little African American girl who overhears her family talking about her brother and which relative he looks the most like. Kelly looks in a mirror but becomes discouraged when she does not see her own features resembling anyone in her family. Then she finds an old photo album with a picture in it of her mother as a little girl—who looks just like Kelly—and she smiles.

Do you realize how quickly young children can tell how you feel about them just by looking at you? Dorothy Briggs (1970), in her now-classic book *Your Child's Self-Esteem*, has this to say: "Mirrors create self-images. Have you ever thought of yourself as a mirror? You are one—a psychological mirror your child uses to build his identity. And his whole life is affected by the conclusions he draws" (p. 9).

What will the children in the classroom see when they look at you? Smiles? Frowns? Sparkling eyes? Nonverbal cues like this are more powerful feeling makers than words for young children—especially young children from other cultures who may not understand your words yet. Smiles speak a universal language of happiness. They help set a positive emotional tone in the classroom.

Use of Names

Little Eagle Lots of Owls
(Edmiston, 1993)
Jafta (Lewin, 1981a)

Children also feel good about themselves when they hear you using their names, but be sure to pronounce them correctly. You might consider substituting a child's name for a book character's name from time to time when you read her a story. Whenever you talk to a child, be sure to address her by name. Are you using a happy tone of voice when talking to each child? After all, you and the staff are the language models the children will imitate. Sometimes you will hear them sounding just like you when they speak. Make sure it is a happy sound!

Children like to see their names as well as hear them. Have their written names displayed on children's cubbies, their artwork, their writing, their computer printouts, name tags at the lunch table, their toothbrushes and their blankets, and even themselves when visitors are present. Children also like to hear their names being sung in greeting songs, good-bye songs, and getting-ready songs. (For example, try this verse to the tune "Lazy Mary"):

Who's getting ready to go outdoors?
Go outdoors, go outdoors;
Who's getting ready to go outdoors?
Nicolas Borda is ready! Sondra Sanchez is ready!

Children's names, however, should not be used in negative ways, such as calling out a child by name across the room when you see him doing something inappropriate. Instead, go yourself to the child and talk to him privately. Names are a personal part of every child, and their use by the teacher should boost their self-esteem and set a positive emotional tone for everyone in the classroom.

On the other hand, some children are given names they don't really understand. In the book ***Little Eagle Lots of Owls,*** an old-time Native American story, a little Indian boy has a name "as long as it takes the moon to walk across the sky," says his grandfather, who decides to call him by the shortened form of "Little Eagle." To help the boy remember his full name, his grandfather sends him the gift of a strange creature sleeping in a basket. When the sun goes down it suddenly comes to life as three fat owls that had been huddling together—the second part of Little Eagle's name (Beaty, 1997).

As an extension activity to make this book meaningful, bring in a basketful of stuffed toy animals. Have children make up names for themselves according to what the basket contains when it is passed to them. Make name tags for each if the children like this game.

African American names often reflect the people's unique heritage. According to Faulkner (1994), "three-syllable names beginning with *La* for girls are popular because they are soft-sounding" (e.g., Lashandra, Latifah, or Latoya). Two-syllable names beginning with *Ja* "are chosen for boys because they are strong-sounding" (e.g., Jamal, Jamon, Jareem, or Jafta). Of course, many children are also named for someone in the family or for an African American sports hero, television personality, or historically famous person.

Three simple African stories about the little village boy named Jafta reflect his strong masculine name. Your youngest children may get a good feel for village life and African mothers and fathers as they identify with Jafta in ***Jafta, Jafta's Mother,*** and ***Jafta's Father.*** Afterward, the children may want to pretend to be Jafta, naming the various plastic African animals (lions, hippos, rhinos, elephants, zebras, and giraffes) available on your block center shelves (Beaty, 1997).

Social Environment

Child–Child Acceptance

Just as you and your coworkers are language models for the children, you are also behavior models. How you show your acceptance for each of the children makes a difference on how the children accept one another. Young children look toward you and the teaching staff when they first enter the classroom to see how you treat the other children. Most of their peers around them will be strangers to them. To a new child they all look different, no matter whether they come from the same race, culture, or background. They are, in fact, all different. All are unique individuals who have come from their own families and their own neighborhoods to be a part of this group.

Love Can Build a Bridge (Judd, 1999)

Margaret and Margarita (Reiser, 1993)

And to Think That We Thought That We'd Never Be Friends (Hoberman, 1999)

Young children show their acceptance of other children by the way they get along with them.

On the other hand, they are also all alike. They are all children with common bonds who have come to your program to grow and learn together. If you show your acceptance to each of these different youngsters, if you treat them with equal respect, then the other children should follow your lead by accepting one another.

Young children show their acceptance of other children by the way they get along with them. Do they play together? Talk together? Look at books together? Sit next to one another in group activities? Experience has shown that for young children to get along with peers in a classroom situation, they need to develop a feeling about their peers. This feeling does not arise from focusing on differences but from the children's ability to identify with or feel something in common with the other child. That feeling is *empathy:* the ability to feel as another child feels or to recognize how that child feels.

Empathy is one of the initial moral emotions that is shaped by the child's earliest interactions with other people. It then influences how the child himself will act toward others. As psychologist William Damon (1988) notes:

Young children feel the sting of injustice and the pull of empathy. . . . Wherever there is human discourse and interpersonal exchange there will follow rules of conduct, feelings of care, and sense of obligation. Children participate in social relations very early, practically at birth. Their moral thoughts and feelings are an inevitable consequence of these early relations and the others that will arise throughout life. (pp. 1–2)

Concern for Others

If you emphasize a concern for all the others in your classroom on a daily basis, children are sure to follow. Once they become aware of your values and expectations, most young children will try to please you by adapting their own behaviors to those you favor and acknowledge. What will they be? Showing sympathy and kindness? Helping and cooperating? Giving and sharing? Taking the perspective of another child? Hopefully, all of these, regardless of the children's race or culture.

Researchers have found, for example, that encouraging children to have a concern for others makes a big difference in children's attitude toward others and their development of empathy. In addition, "emphasizing the importance of children helping others whenever possible results in children undertaking more helping activities" (Grusec, Saas-Kortsaak, & Simultis, 1978).

Children like to follow the teacher's lead. Yet to make children aware of this concern for others, you will definitely have to take the initial lead by acknowledging any prosocial behavior you notice. "Oh, Kristen, thank you for sharing your toy with Mara. You're the kind of person who likes to help others." Or "I'm so happy to see the children in the dramatic play area taking turns with the new dress-up clothes. I can see that Tony knows how good it makes others feel when he takes turns with the new astronaut helmet." Comments like this are more important than most of us realize in helping children learn such caring behavior. You need to make them often.

Reading books featuring children of different races who help one another in need also emphasizes this concern. An excellent book to read is country singer Naomi Judd's ***Love Can Build a Bridge*** (1999) based on her song of the same name. In this story children of different races are shown, with one helping the other on every other page. The recipient of the help then helps someone else on the next page. Large realistic illustrations of each child show an Anglo-American girl giving part of her sandwich to a Hispanic boy, the Hispanic boy helping an African American boy who has hurt himself on a playground slide, this boy in turn visiting a little Asian girl in the hospital, and so on. A tape cassette of Judd's wonderful song is attached to the back cover for all to sing together.

Can your children look for and acknowledge helpful behaviors like this in their own lives? You might want to post a weekly chart listing helpful behaviors the children have noticed. Go over the listing with them from time to time and soon they may be "reading" it themselves.

The common denominator in Judd's book is *helping* and not *children of different races* helping. Factors other than race seem to make more of a difference in determining whom preschool children will accept or reject as friends or playmates. In fact, child development specialist Ramsey (1987) notes, "I found that, among children ages three through six, gender was a stronger determinant of friendship choice than was race" (p. 22).

Newcomers Becoming Accepted

Most teachers of preschool children agree with Ramsey. Girls of different races often band together in the dramatic play center to keep out a boy who tries to join them, no matter what his race. Boys, on the other hand, may try to prevent girls from entering the block center when they are building. But children of either gender or any race may find themselves rejected at first if they are newcomers to the program. It is not so much that the new child may look different in skin color or speak a different language. But often an outsider of any background may be shy or withdrawn at first. It is this behavior to which the other children respond, sometimes by rejection.

You may decide to ask one of the children who has displayed helping behaviors to help this newcomer become involved in a classroom activity and thus become accepted by some of the others. Or you may decide to help the child yourself by inviting her to join a small group while you read to them *Margaret and Margarita,* the simple story of Margaret, who speaks English, and Margarita, who speaks Spanish. They meet in the park and finally become friends as each girl says the same words in her own language. You will be able to pronounce the simple Spanish whether or not you are fluent in the language. Have a stuffed animal toy on hand for each of your listeners just as Margaret and Margarita do. Can the children play together with their toys after the story is finished, maybe even using some Spanish words?

If being rejected or having trouble getting along continue to be areas of conflict among the children, you might also read to small groups the humorous rhyming book *And to Think That We Thought That We'd Never Be Friends.* It starts with an African American brother and sister fighting over a game of croquet; next family members argue over which TV program to watch; the family next door keeps them awake by practicing their bassoon and tuba; a police officer comes to tell them they are all disturbing the peace; the uproar continues to grow with people of different cultures around the world until they are all marching in a great parade along with their friends and enemies. Hundreds and thousands join in, including elephants and whales, with every other page ending with "It's funny how quickly an argument ends…. And to think that we thought that we'd never be friends!"

Let your children look at the zany pictures as you read. Would they like to take the roles they see enacted and try their own hand at resolving the conflicts? Or you might try a role play using several different hand puppets. Ramsey (1991) believes, "Children's books are a primary vehicle for this kind of teaching. By engaging children in stories, we enable our young readers and listeners to empathize with different experiences. . . . When children role play situations and characters in a book, they learn how to perceive situations from a variety of perspectives and literally be 'in another person's shoes'" (pp. 168–169).

At the same time, children have the grand opportunity to listen and speak for the characters and about the situations they are experiencing. In this manner they acquire the words they need to express feelings, resolve conflicts, and get along with one another. Thus, the social environment of the classroom promotes early literacy in its own unique way.

Physical Environment

The physical arrangement of the classroom should speak to the needs of the children as they grow and develop physically, cognitively, socially, emotionally, creatively, and linguistically. Special learning centers should be arranged so that children can see them clearly and use them easily. Such centers should be filled with exciting materials appropriate to young children's developmental levels and learning styles. You may want to include some or all of the following in your program (see also Figure 2.1):

Dramatic play center	Manipulative/math center
Block building center	Science/discovery center
Book center	Computer center
Listening center	Large-motor center
Writing center	Woodworking center
Music center	Cooking center
Art center	Sensory table (water, sand, rice, etc.)

Focus on Early Literacy

Classrooms focusing on early literacy must include in each learning center equipment and materials to promote listening, speaking, reading, and writing. Early childhood educators often refer to such materials as "literacy props." They include signs, pencils and papers, labels, charts, logos, maps, magazines, books, chalk and chalkboards, tapes and tape recorders, children's print, notebooks, clipboards, posters, and many other print materials. Goldhaber et al. (1996/97) have found that "providing literacy props, facilitated by sensitive teacher guidance, is an especially effective means of supporting literacy development." They point out:

> Research also indicates that when given the opportunity, children use literacy props in much the same way they use oral language: to get what they need from others, to inform or communicate, to interact and to identify and express who they are. These findings are significant, for they suggest that teachers can use literacy props to influence both the amount and quality of children's literacy behavior. (p. 88)

Let's look at how a literacy-friendly classroom might be arranged.

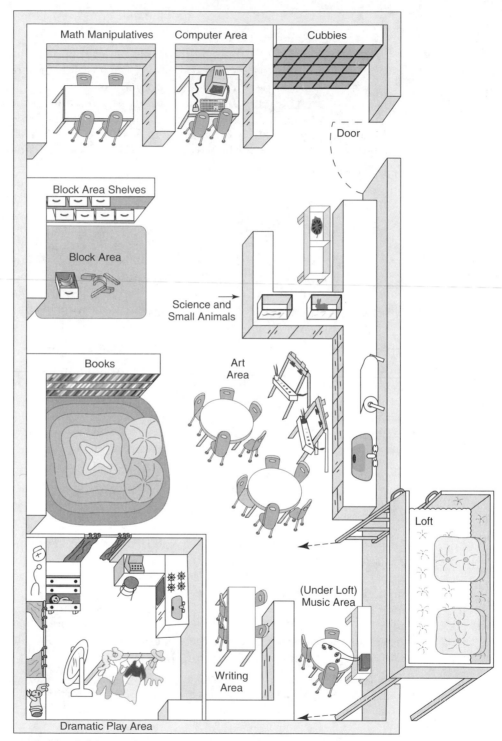

F I G U R E 2.1
Floor Plan

Dramatic Play Center

In addition to the child-size furniture such as table and chairs, stove and refrigerator, cupboards and sink, this center should also feature a print-rich environment with labels such as "chair," "table," "stove," "refrigerator," "cupboard," "sink," and "mirror" posted on them, a calendar on the wall, and appropriate multicultural posters or pictures mounted. When teachers are involved in the center, they should make note of the labels, pointing them out to the players, asking whether they know what they say, and asking them whether they wish to add new ones to new pieces of equipment.

Haircuts at Sleepy Sam's
(Strickland, 1998)
Saturday at The New You
(Barber, 1994)
I Love My Hair (Tarpley, 1998)

In case the dramatic play center becomes a barber shop, the barber chair can be labeled as well. A "barber's apron" can also be labeled and hung on a wall peg. Two toy telephones or cell phones can be available with an old telephone book or address directory with phone numbers placed near the phones for pretend calls. A pad and pencil for taking scribbled "messages" can be nearby. A sign-up clipboard with pencil attached can be hung at the entrance to the center waiting for "customers" to sign up for a turn with their initials or scribble writing.

What about cultural character props? Mount an American Indian dream catcher on the wall or an art calendar showing R. C. Gorman's wondrous prints of Navajo women. Hang a Mexican piñata from the ceiling at birthday time. Have a Guatemalan throw rug on the floor. Use woven baskets from Africa and Hopi pottery. Put chopsticks in with the plastic cutlery. Get travel posters from a travel agency to decorate the walls. A magazine holder full of back-issue travel magazines can stand next to the row of chairs set up for your "barber shop." Use your imagination!

Book-on-a-String in the Dramatic Play Center. Every learning center should also contain at least one sturdy string fastened to the wall and a large plastic kitchen clip at the other end to hold a "book-on-a-string": a cultural character picture book associated with the particular cultural play props in use in the center. Let's get books into every learning center, if we expect children to learn to love books and reading! When children are pretend-playing a barber shop theme, for instance, be sure to clip on a book such as **Haircuts at Sleepy Sam's.** If girls take over the barbershop or convert it to a unisex hair stylist shop, have a second book-on-a-string holding **Saturday at The New You** or **I Love My Hair.**

All three of these books feature African American children. You will be reading such books from time to time to small groups of children playing in the center, and the children can look at the books on their own afterward. If children have trouble releasing the book from the clip, show them how to hold the clip with one hand and pull the book out with the other. If you prefer not to use kitchen clips, then mount a large plastic bag on the wall for holding the book.

Missing the Point About Cultural Character Books. What if you have no African American children in your program? Then such books are even more important

Every learning center should contain at least one sturdy string fastened to the wall and a large plastic kitchen clip at the other end to hold a cultural character "book-on-a-string."

as an introduction to children of a different race involved in familiar situations just like your youngsters. Children do not have to be African Americans to appreciate these stories, just as television viewers do not have to be African Americans to enjoy a program featuring African American actors. Teachers often miss the point about cultural character books, thinking that they are useful only if the program serves multiethnic children. This is not the case. It is essential that your books include a wide variety of cultural characters so that all young children will become familiar with the wonderful multicultural array of people in America and the world. On the other hand, if your class does contain African American youngsters, then they will appreciate seeing children like themselves. As Ramsey (1987) notes, "Stories introduce children to unfamiliar people in a personalized and appealing fashion. By involving children with characters and situations that they can identify with, books increase children's appreciation of other ways of life and help them see unfamiliar people as individuals" (p. 69).

Literacy props such as books, signs, and writing materials are essential *in every learning center* if we want children to emerge into early reading and writing. As Bobys (2000) points out:

> Print is displayed in such a way that spontaneous literacy learning can occur. Materials that support children as readers and writers are available, and the teacher provides time for the children to experiment with reading and writing by engaging in literacy activities. Additionally, the teacher reads to the children on a daily basis and provides opportunities for the children to discuss, share, and respond to books in a variety of ways. (p. 17)

Block Building Center

In addition to containing a large selection of unit blocks placed lengthwise on shelves (not in bins), this center should also contain shelf space for a variety of building accessories such as small figures of people (of all races), animals (especially dinosaurs), small vehicles (including cars, trucks, construction vehicles, planes, and space vehicles), and dollhouse furniture for children's pretend play in the block center. Plastic aquarium tubing for pipes, string for wires, little traffic signs, pipe cleaners, and sticks can also be stored there for use in children's inventive building. Change or add to the accessories when a new learning theme is in use. Mount photos of buildings from field trips the children have taken and pictures of similar buildings from other countries.

Each accessory item or group of small items should be placed individually on shelf spaces so that child builders can see them clearly and return them to their space when they are finished. Cutouts mounted on shelves showing block shapes, vehicle shapes, and people and animal shapes are important for children to practice matching the items when they return them to their place on the shelves.

What about literacy skills in the block center? Be sure to label each of the shelf items with its name as well as its shape cutout. If you have several types of vehicles, mount a label for "trucks," "cars," "planes," and so forth, on the front of the shelf. Goldhaber et al. (1996/97) also suggest that teachers add a basket with index cards, masking tape, and markers so that children can create signs and labels for their structures. You may need to help with spelling words for signs unless children prefer their own scribble writing.

Book-on-a-String in the Block Center. Your book-on-a-string can contain a different book for every week or two depending on the types of buildings the children are making or the curriculum theme the class is following at the moment. Here are some examples:

City Buildings
Abuela—Hispanic Rosalba and her grandmother "fly" over New York City buildings.

Tar Beach—African American Cassie and family picnic on their apartment rooftop; she "flies" over New York City and George Washington Bridge.

Houses
Building a House—A multiethnic crew builds a house.

This Is My House—An African American boy, Japanese and Samoan children, a Saudi Arabian girl, and more show how their houses are built.

Bridges
Building a Bridge—Anglo-American Anna and Navajo Juanita meet on the first day of preschool and build a bridge together.

Roads
Road Builders—A multiethnic crew builds a road.

Book Center

Although you will be featuring books in every learning center of the classroom, the book center should be one of the most exciting learning centers in the class. Too often it is merely a set of shelves pushed back against the wall with little room for children to look at books comfortably. As a result, it is seldom used. Make your book center an exciting and inviting place to be in your literacy-friendly classroom. Have bookshelves pulled out from the wall forming two sides of the center and displaying books showing their covers. Put colorful cloth runners on top of the shelves and stand a pottery animal from Mexico on one and stuffed African animals or Maurice Sendak's *Wild Things* on the other. Tie a silver party balloon to either end of the shelves with colorful party streamers dangling here and there.

Place a comfortable couch against the wall between the shelves. Above the couch mount posters of culture character children reading books or dust jackets from the books you have on display. Some teachers prefer to string a clothesline across the wall above the couch with new books-on-a-string clipped to it. Be sure to have plenty of large plastic kitchen clips available. Be sure also to change your books at least once a month, adding new ones, putting away some of the old ones, but keeping out favorites. Variety keeps children coming back to this center. If nothing ever changes, children will ignore it.

Place soft carpeting and puffy pillows on the floor and a standing hat rack or puppet tree holding storytelling puppets or the hats of book characters (e.g., a Cat-in-the-Hat hat) on its pegs. Cooking supply stores stock hot pad gloves in the shapes of animals that make excellent hand puppets. Now, who can resist such a center? (See chapter 8 for more ideas.)

Listening Center

Listening centers are new to many preschool classrooms, but if you are serious about promoting early literacy, you should consider having a special center for listening and speaking. It could be set up as a little radio or TV studio, with a pretend microphone or inexpensive children's walkie-talkies for your "news reporters" to use. A tape recorder with a headset is important for children's recording and listening to each other's "news reports." This is the place for book tapes as well. You may want to include a jack box into which individual headsets can be plugged, along with a rack to store the headsets. Be sure to have the books on hand for every book tape you have out, and encourage listeners to turn the pages of the books as they hear the words being read.

Book-on-a-String in the Listening Center.

> ***Cock-a-Doodle-Doo! What Does It Sound Like to You?***—Voices of animals, sounds of trains, hammers, and dripping water are spoken differently in different languages.

Writing Center

Although you will not be teaching preschool children how to make letters and write words in a formal manner, some children will be emerging into writing naturally if you provide them with the tools and encouragement. Because writing is frequently done at a desk, you may want to provide a desk of some sort in the writing center. If it has pigeon holes and drawers, you can use them to store the tools of writing: pencils, felt-tip markers, pens, crayons, chalk, paper, notebooks, tablets, stationery, envelopes, stamp pads and stamps, blank postcards, and greeting cards.

Ask parents or a business to donate an old manual typewriter for the children's use. Toy typewriters do not work as well. The classroom computer and printer can be set up here if you choose not to have a separate computer center. This will then be the place for alphabet letters and games. Letters from sets of wooden, plastic, and magnetic letters can be matched. Children also like to find their own initials and trace around them.

Be sure to include individual mailboxes for everyone in the class, made from old shoeboxes or cereal boxes. Mount a bulletin board in the center for children to display their own "writing" products. Have maps or a globe in this center for children to find where their pretend letters might go. Mount picture postcards from different countries on the wall.

Book-on-a-String in the Writing Center.

> ***Like Me and You***—Children who live all over the world send pen pal letters to their friends in different countries as illustrated by this Raffi song in story form.

Music Center

Children also learn to speak through chanting and singing, so be sure your music center also contains a record player, tape recorder, or CD player along with music tapes, records, CDs, and headsets. Records, tapes, and CDs should not, however, be the extent of music in the classroom. Children need opportunities to make their own music while playing rhythm instruments from many cultures, as well as drums, flutes, xylophones, keyboards, ukuleles, and guitars. Instrument shelves or pegboards should be labeled like block shelves, with the instruments placed or hung next to cutouts of their shapes. Have posters of people from other cultures playing musical instruments. Keep sign-up pads and pencils here, too, if children need to take turns using instruments or equipment.

A colorful picture book illustrating a familiar song should also be kept in the music center as a book-on-a-string; change the selection from time to time just as you do the books in the other learning centers.

Book-on-a-String in the Music Center.

> *The Seals on the Bus*—Sung to the tune of the familiar "The Wheels on the Bus Go Round and Round," this book illustrates a wonderfully wacky bus full of raucous tigers roaring, geese honking, seals errping, and people going "help, help, help."

Art Center

The art center should be set up so that children can use it independently on a daily basis. Teacher-directed art activities can be carried out on tables scattered around the room, but keep the art center a self-directing place for children. Easels can be set up ahead of time with paper, paint, and chubby brushes at the ready. A table for flat painting can have materials laid out or be empty with materials on nearby shelves for children's easy selection and return. Have paper, paints, brushes, crayons, scissors, collage materials, clay, play dough, yarn, fabrics, stamping materials, glue, and glitter available for use throughout the year. These materials should also contain shelf labels just as your blocks and musical instruments do. If possible, set up the art center near a water source so children can rinse out brushes and wash their hands.

In case you wonder how art can promote early literacy, remember that using paint brushes, crayons, and markers leads to scribbling and writing. Also remember that young children draw pictures to communicate ideas even before they can write. What ideas do pictures from other cultures communicate? Have interesting art reproductions from other cultures on the wall, and talk to the children about them.

Book-on-a-String in the Art Center.

> *Sunpainters, Eclipse of the Navajo Sun*—Kii, a little Navajo boy, learns about the "children" who come and repaint the Earth during an eclipse of the sun. Kii helps by painting his own sun.

Manipulative/Math Center

Why call the math center "manipulative"? Because math is a manipulative skill for preschool children. These youngsters need to play and practice with concrete materials in sorting, classifying, and counting before they progress to abstract number symbols. To understand what "3" or "7" or "13" means, children need hands-on experiences with shape puzzles, counting blocks, animal dominoes, stacking pegboards, stringing beads, and sorting buttons. They should be able to compare sizes and shapes of shells or blocks or cylinders. They need to insert the correct pieces into concept puzzles, match the colors of beads, and sort shapes into matching holes.

Your manipulative/math center should contain all sorts of games, puzzles, and materials of varying difficulties, arranged on shelves or in plastic containers with name and picture labels. Cash registers, number beads, and counting frames can be added as the children progress in their skills. Or bring in counting games from other cultures such as an *okwe* board from Africa and counting seeds or a cowry shell game from the Pacific Islands. A simple balance scale, an abacus, rulers, and measuring tapes can add to the fun of exploring with numbers. And fun it is for young children. They have not yet developed "math phobia," and they won't, if you keep this center an exciting and fun place to investigate with a table or floor space for interacting with the items.

As for literacy skills, young math explorers will be developing finger strength for using writing tools as they pick up and insert beads and chips. Their eye–hand coordination will develop with their skill in making puzzles and sorting small items. Finally, they will learn that number symbols stand for amounts just as letter symbols stand for words. Don't forget to hang a counting book in this area—very important.

Book-on-a-String in the Manipulative/Math Center.
> ***Count Your Way through the Arab World***—illustrates the numbers 1 through 10 in Arabic.

Science/Discovery Center

Make this center just as exciting as all the rest. Give it space for children's experiments and collections, as well as the materials of science and discovery: magnifying glasses of various sizes, magnets and pieces of metal, children's binoculars and microscopes, fish nets, collection bags, tweezers, prisms, measuring devices such as a balance scale and wind-up ruler, several see-through plastic jars, and a sketch pad and pencil. An aquarium or terrarium can be placed here as well as a cage for a guinea pig, little white mouse, or garter snake. Signs and labels should be large and attractive. Have a table for problem solving with a sign that says, "How many inches will Rosa's bean plant grow this week? Measure it and see. Record your guess in the tape recorder." Include the bean plant, a tape measure, a tape recorder, and blank tape. One of the adult staff members may need to read the sign for interested children, but if you make it a picture sign with simple outline drawings of the plant, the tape measure, and the recorder, even nonliterate children may be able to figure it out.

Science discovery questions like these can be posed every week with materials on hand for children to figure out or guess the answers. "Which weighs more, the plastic egg roll or the taco?" or "Which of these items will float in the pan of water?" or "How many days before the snake sheds its skin? Make a guess." Be sure to have a book-on-a-string hanging in the center to go with the question of the week and another next to the aquarium or terrarium. Animal identification guides containing intriguing pictures are good for children to peruse.

Book-on-a-String in the Science/Discovery Center.
> ***Green Snake Ceremony***—Mary Greyfeather learns about her Native American heritage as well as protecting the environment when her grandparents take her on a hilarious hunt for a little green snake.
> ***My Visit to the Aquarium***—A dark-skinned boy describes his visit to a large city aquarium and all the wondrous aquatic creatures he sees.

Computer Center

The classroom computer and printer may be a part of the writing center, or they may stand alone. Either way they can be an important part of a literacy-friendly program. But be sure to have this equipment on a table low enough for children to see the monitor screen without craning their necks. They need to be able to see easily and become aware of the cause and effect that happens on the screen when they push down one key at a time. Place *two chairs* in front of the computer for two child operators at one time. Why two? Because in preschool, it is important for two children to work together when using the computer. Not only will they learn about taking turns, sharing, and problem solving, but they will find it necessary to talk. Thus, their conversation skills and vocabulary will show solid improvement—important skills for early literacy learning.

In addition, for every computer program in use, at least one activity should be on tap in one of the learning centers for integrating the abstract concepts viewed on the computer screen with the concrete materials of the preschool classroom. Young children learn best from hands-on manipulation of real things: blocks, books, toy vehicles, food items, and dress-up clothes. But computers can help children apply more abstract ideas in other areas of the classroom.

If the software in use is an alphabet program, have wooden or magnetic alphabet letters on hand for matching or tracing around or creating a name. Have an alphabet book-on-a-string available as well. It is best to have one piece of software at a time in use until all of the children become comfortable using it on their own. When you change to a new program, also change the book and learning center activity.

Book-on-a-String in the Computer Center.
> ***The Calypso Alphabet***—Each page shows lively Caribbean children illustrating one of their customs according to the letter and word shown (e.g., "P for pan. Beat this steel drum.")

Large-Motor Center

Preschool programs need to provide some indoor space for climbing, sliding, jumping, crawling, lifting, and balancing. An indoor wooden climber may be the best piece of equipment if you have room for only one. Many sets contain a ladder for climbing and a slide for getting down. A built-in loft may also have a ladder and slide. Molded plastic sliding equipment is popular in some programs; others prefer giant plastic waffle blocks with tunnels and slides. A crawl-through fabric tunnel can be brought out during large-motor activity time, as well as a balance beam or a small trampoline with a hand-hold for safety.

How can you make this center literacy-friendly? Be sure to label the various pieces of equipment. Also include a book-on-a-string that will promote a certain large-motor skill—for example, jumping—with cultural children as characters.

Book-on-a-String in the Large-Motor Center.
> ***Moon Jump***—Cayal, an East Indian boy, jumps out of bed, into his bath, into his clothes, onto the sofa, and up and down all the way to school. Most of all he likes jumping on his parents' bed. One night he jumps so high he goes all the way up to the moon. How high can your children jump on mats or a trampoline?

Woodworking Center

Boys and girls love to pound. Thus, a woodworking center is a must in a preschool classroom. Pounding with a hammer teaches children excellent eye–hand coordination, a necessary development before they can hold a writing tool and write with ease, as well as being an essential prereading skill in order for a reader's eyes to follow the words on a page. Preschoolers also learn to express their creativity in the wooden things they make, and they may even use the pounding as an acceptable means of venting frustration.

If you cannot afford a workbench, use tree stumps. Place them on a thick carpet to absorb the noise. Hang woodworking tools (hammers, vises, saws, and goggles) on a nearby pegboard with outlined pictures of the tools and their labeled names. Have a box of wood scraps, ceiling tiles, and pieces of Styrofoam and leather for pounding through, or let children pound nails into the stumps themselves to make interesting designs. Keep nails of various sizes in covered plastic containers. If there is only room for two children at a time in this center, mount a sign with the numeral 2 or two stick figures on it to show how many are allowed.

Book-on-a-String in the Woodworking Center.
> ***Building a House***—A multiethnic crew of workers uses various tools to build a house.

Cooking Center

The purpose for cooking with children in preschool is not to teach young children how to cook but instead to provide an excellent means for promoting development such as eye–hand coordination and small-muscle strength, as well as for learning cause and effect, prereading skills, sequencing, measuring, and nutrition. Peeling shells from hard-boiled eggs, scraping carrots, dicing potatoes, and turning the handle of food mills and grinders strengthens finger, arm, and hand muscles. Children's intense interest in food and food preparation provides the motivation for learning, and your ingenuity can supply the activities.

Your cooking center may be a temporary setup on a classroom table or a more permanent one on a counter near an electrical outlet. A microwave oven, a toaster oven, or an electric fry pan or wok can supply the heat if your safety and insurance regulations permit hot cooking. Otherwise, make salads, vegetable snacks and dips, and fruit desserts.

To make this center literacy-friendly, once again hang the cooking tools and utensils on labeled pegboards or on shelves where children can see what is available and return them later to their spots. Use a large, simply illustrated recipe chart for each food you prepare written in a sequence of steps that the children can follow as you read them to the "cooks." Have illustrated multicultural cookbooks in this center for the children to look at as well.

Don't forget your book-on-a-string that you will be changing for each new food you prepare. Because your program features a cultural character approach, the children's cooking experiences should include foods from a variety of cultures along with picture storybooks to illustrate them.

Book-on-a-String in the Cooking Center

> ***Dumpling Soup***—Every New Year's Eve all of Marisa's Hawaiian, Japanese, and Korean aunties, uncles, and cousins go to Grandma's house in Honolulu for dumpling soup. Marisa tells the story of the first time she tries to make dumplings.

Sensory Table

Not so long ago this activity area was called the "water" or "sand" table. Now, because so many other materials are used in it, it is better known as a "sensory table." In addition to water or sand, teachers also fill the table with Styrofoam packing peanuts, oatmeal, cornmeal, rice, and even dirt. Rather than filling the table to the brim, it is more effective to put in it no more than a few inches of material to prevent spills.

Plastic play aprons should be available on nearby hooks. Safety goggles should be used with sand or dirt. Accessories for use in the table should be kept on labeled shelves nearby. For water play, have plastic bottles, squirters, egg-beaters, and straws on hand for a few weeks, and then change to little boats and plastic fish, whales, and dolphins. For sand play, have shovels and buckets, sifters, hoppers, and other sand toys, later changing to little vehicles and people figures, or animals and dinosaurs. Your book-on-a-string should reflect what is going on in the sensory table.

Book-on-a-String near the Sensory Table

> ***Alejandro's Gift***—Alejandro, an old Hispanic man who lives by himself in the desert, is lonely until he learns to dig and fill a water hole for the desert animals. Soon he has the company of quail, coyotes, rabbits, badgers, mule deer, ground squirrels, and mourning doves, and he is lonely no longer.

Learning Center Checklist

Using a learning center checklist (see Figure 2.2) helps the teaching staff set up a new classroom with appropriate activity areas or to assess the present arrangement to make sure all the activity areas are included. Since the physical arrangement of a preschool classroom is the structure for an early literacy cultural character curriculum, you will want to arrange your room carefully, knowing that space, materials and activities can make a difference in your children's learning. As Kendall (1996) notes:

> Just as a curriculum reflects the system of values of its creator and the culture of the children in the classroom, curriculum materials reflect the attitudes of the person or people who choose materials. The pictures on the walls, the books on the shelves, the dolls in the dramatic play area, and the tapes in the music area in a classroom designed by a teacher committed to a multicultural approach will all reflect the values and belief systems of a diverse, multicultural community. (p. 111)

In the chapters to follow, specific cultural materials and books for each of the learning centers are described according to the cultural character themes being employed.

Learning Center Checklist

Classroom _____   _____   _____Date_____

1. Organize DRAMATIC PLAY CENTER to contain:

_____Appropriate equipment, furniture, and accessories, labeled
_____Male and female dress-up clothes, cultural outfits, and prop boxes
_____Clothes arranged for easy selection and return, labeled
_____Full-length mirror
_____Dolls of different skin colors
_____Language props such as two telephones
_____Literacy props such as telephone directory, pads, pencils, magazines, clipboard
_____Appropriate cultural character book-on-a-string

2. Organize BLOCK BUILDING CENTER to contain:

_____Blocks stored lengthwise on shelves, labeled
_____Enough blocks for building large structures
_____Small multicultural figures, trucks, and other appropriate accessories, labeled
_____Shelves marked with symbols of blocks and accessories
_____Photos of buildings and field trips
_____Basket of index cards and markers for making signs and labels
_____Appropriate cultural character book-on-a-string

FIGURE 2.2
Learning Center Checklist

3. Organize BOOK CENTER to contain:

_____Cultural character books on shelves at children's height, covers visible
_____Books in good condition
_____Puppets, culture character dolls, hats, and other book extension objects, labeled
_____Pillows, cushions, and comfortable chairs
_____Posters or books-on-strings

4. Organize LISTENING CENTER to contain:

_____Radio or TV studio props
_____Tape recorder, tapes, with headsets, jack box
_____Book tapes and books
_____Appropriate cultural character book-on-a-string

5. Organize WRITING CENTER to contain:

_____Desk to write on and to store writing supplies
_____Pens, pencils, markers, chalk, and chalkboard, labeled
_____Paper, pads, notebooks, file cards, and envelopes
_____Ruler, stapler, scissors, hole punch, and paper clips
_____Rubber stamps and pad, peel-off stickers, and stamps
_____Typewriter and/or computer
_____Sets of alphabet letters
_____Individual mailboxes
_____Appropriate cultural character book-on-a-string

6. Organize MUSIC CENTER to contain:

_____Sound- and rhythm-producing instruments and materials
_____Tape recorder, tapes, and headsets (or record player and records)
_____Electronic keyboard
_____Strumming instruments, from different cultures
_____Percussion instruments (drums, xylophones)
_____Movement props (scarves, ribbons, bells, streamers)
_____Appropriate cultural character book-on-a-string

7. Organize ART CENTER to contain:

_____Easels and tables set up for daily use
_____Paper, paints, brushes, crayons, scissors, and collage materials on nearby shelves, labeled
_____Clay, play dough, yarn, fabrics, glue, glitter, and stamping materials available
_____Cultural art materials available (feathers, willow wands, weaving, beads)
_____Appropriate cultural pictures and art reproductions on walls
_____Appropriate cultural character book-on-a-string

8. Organize MANIPULATIVE/MATH CENTER to contain:

_____Tables, floor space; nearby materials on shelves, labeled
_____Puzzles, table blocks, geoboards, pegboards, stacking cubes, sorting and matching games
_____Shape, color, counting, and number games (some multicultural)
_____Cash register, abacus, balance, measuring tools, giant calculator

FIGURE 2.2

Continued.

_____Necessary parts and pieces not missing from games and puzzles
_____Appropriate cultural character book-on-a-string

9. Organize SCIENCE/DISCOVERY CENTER to contain:

_____Animal, fish, snake, or insect pets (aquarium, terrarium), labeled
_____Plants and seed-growing experiments
_____Children's collections, science kits, labeled
_____Magnifying glasses, magnets, binoculars, child microscope, measuring tools, labeled
_____Collecting tools, nets, tweezers, sketch pads, labels, plastic containers
_____Appropriate cultural character book-on-a-string

10. Organize COMPUTER CENTER to contain:

_____Computer, monitor, keyboard on low table with two chairs in front
_____Printer and paper
_____Several appropriate software programs, labeled
_____Games, puzzles, materials to extend each program
_____Appropriate cultural character book-on-a-string

11. Organize LARGE-MOTOR CENTER to contain:

_____Climbing equipment (bars, ladder, climber, slide, tunnel, loft), labeled
_____Balancing equipment (balance beam, balance board, blocks)
_____Jumping equipment (inflated mat, trampoline)
_____Children's basketball net and balls
_____Wooden riding vehicles, wagons, labeled
_____Appropriate cultural character book-on-a-string

12. Organize WOODWORKING CENTER to contain:

_____Usable pounding, sawing tools and safety goggles
_____Labeled tool storage shelves or pegboard
_____Woodworking table or stumps, vise
_____Wood scraps, ceiling tiles, and nails
_____Appropriate cultural character book-on-a-string

13. Organize COOKING CENTER to contain:

_____Knives, large spoons, beaters, scrapers, and food mill, labeled
_____Bowls, pans, measuring cups, and spoons, stored and labeled
_____Microwave or toaster oven, blender, electric fry pan, hot plate
_____Multicultural cookbooks and food posters
_____Large homemade recipe charts
_____Appropriate cultural character book-on-a-string

14. Organize SENSORY TABLE to contain:

_____Children's water play aprons and safety goggles
_____Squeeze bottles, basters, plastic toys, and egg beaters, stored and labeled
_____Shovels, sifters, sand toys, small vehicles, people figures, stored and labeled
_____Appropriate cultural character book-on-a-string

SUMMARY

Chapter 2 discusses brain research that describes language development in preschool children when a "window of opportunity" for language occurs in the developing brain. A child-friendly emotional environment with teacher acceptance of all children and their languages is an essential element in stimulating language development. Empathy toward others is the most important aspect of the preschool social environment with children learning to accept one another. The physical arrangement of the classroom can then support early literacy development by being partitioned into learning centers complete with cultural character books to lead children into exciting literacy activities.

LEARNING ACTIVITIES

1. Describe how the development of the brain in young children makes it imperative that language-learning activities take place in preschool. What should these activities be? Carry out one of the activities in your classroom as described in the text. Report the results.
2. How would you describe the ideal emotional environment of a preschool classroom? How can a teacher or staff member show acceptance of every child? Carry out one of the text activities described to show acceptance while supporting language learning.
3. Why is it important for young children to learn empathy toward others? How can children learn to get along with others in your room? Use one of the books described with one child or a small group who need help in getting along. Report the results.
4. Use the Learning Center Checklist (Figure 2.2) to assess the present arrangement of your classroom. What changes will you need to make in each learning center to create an early literacy/multicultural environment? Make these changes and report on the results as they affect your children.
5. Put appropriate cultural character books-on-a-string in five of the learning centers. What books did you choose? How will you use them with the children? Try one and report the results.

REFERENCES

Beaty, J. J. (1997). *Building bridges with multicultural picture books.* Upper Saddle River, NJ: Merrill/Prentice Hall.

Bobys, A. R. (2000).What does emerging literacy look like? *Young Children, 55*(4), 16–22.

Briggs, D. (1970). *Your child's self-esteem.* New York: Doubleday.

Browne, G., Howard, J., & Pitts, M. (1984). *Culture and children.* Austin: Texas Department of Human Resources.

Damon, W. (1988). *The moral child: Nurturing children's natural moral growth.* New York: Free Press.

Faulkner, B. (1994). *What to name your African-American baby.* New York: St. Martin's.

Goldhaber, J., Lipson, M., Sortino, S., & Daniels, P. (1996/97). Books in the sand box? Markers in the blocks? Expanding the child's world of literacy. *Childhood Education, 73*(2), 88–91.

Grusec, J. P., Saas-Kortsaak, & Simultis. (1978). The role of example and moral exhortation in the training of altruism. *Child Development, 49,* 920–923.

Healy, J. M. (1990). *Endangered minds.* New York: Simon & Schuster.

Kendall, F. E. (1996). *Diversity in the classroom: New approaches to the education of young children (2nd ed.).* New York: Teachers College Press.

Kontos, S., & Wilcox-Herzog, A. (1997). Teacher's interactions with children: Why are they so important? *Young Children, 52*(2), 4–12.

Kosnik, C. (1993). Everyone is a V. I. P. in this class. *Young Children, 49*(1), 32–37.

Kotulak, R. (1996). *Inside the brain.* Kansas City: Andrews & McMeel.

Lapp, D., Flood, J., & Roser, N. (2000). Still standing: Timeless strategies for teaching the language arts. In D. S. Strickland & I. M. Morrow (Eds.) *Beginning reading and writing* (pp. 183–193). New York: Teachers College Press.

Newberger, J. (1997). New brain development research—A wonderful window of opportunity for building public support for early childhood education. *Young Children, 52*(4), 4–9.

Ramsey, P. (1987). *Teaching and learning in a diverse world: Multicultural education for young children.* New York: Teachers College Press.

Ramsey, P. (1991). *Making friends in school: Promoting peer relationships in early childhood.* New York: Teachers College Press.

Simmons, T., & Sheehan, R. (1997, February 16). Brain research manifests importance of first years. *The News and Observer* [on line]. http://www.nando.net/nao/2little2late/stories/day1-main.html

Willis, C. (1997). *Your child's brain: Food for thought.* Little Rock, AR: Southern Early Childhood Association.

SUGGESTED READINGS

Barnet, A. B., & Barnet, R. J. (1998). *The youngest minds: Parenting and genes in the development of intellect and emotion.* New York: Touchstone.

Beaty, J. J. (1999). *Prosocial guidance for the preschool child.* Upper Saddle River, NJ: Merrill/Prentice Hall.

Beaty, J. J. (2000). *Skills for preschool teachers.* Upper Saddle River, NJ: Merrill/Prentice Hall.

De Gaetano, Y., Williams, L. R., & Volk, D. (1998). *Kaleidoscope: A multicultural approach for the primary school classroom.* Upper Saddle River, NJ: Merrill/Prentice Hall.

De Melendez, W. R., & Ostertag, V. (1997). *Teaching young children in multicultural classrooms: Issues, concepts, and strategies.* Albany, NY: Delmar.

Hernandez, H. (2001). *Multicultural education: A teacher's guide to link context, process, and content.* Upper Saddle River, NJ: Merrill/Prentice Hall.

Isbell, R. (2001). *Early learning environments that work*. Beltsville, MD: Gryphon House.

King, E. W., Chipman, M., & Cruz-Janzen, M. (1994). *Educating young children in a diverse society*. Boston: Allyn & Bacon.

Lindsey, G. (1998/99). Brain research and implications for early childhood education. *Childhood Education, 75*(2), 97–100.

Morrow, L. M. (1990). Preparing the classroom environment to promote literacy development. *Early Childhood Research Quarterly, 5*(4), 537–554.

Morrow, L., & Rand, M. (1991). Promoting literacy during play by designing early childhood classroom environments. *The Reading Teacher, 44*(6), 396–402.

Neuman, S. B., & Roskos, K. (1990). Play, print, and purpose: Enriching play environments for literacy development. *The Reading Teacher, 44*(3), 214–221.

Neuman, S. B., & Roskos, K. (1991). The influence of literacy enriched play centers on preschoolers' conceptions of the function of print. In J. F. Christie (Ed.), *Play and literacy development* (pp. 167–187). Albany: State University of New York Press.

Neuman, S. B., & Roskos, K. (1992). Literacy objects as cultural tools: Effects on children's literacy behaviors. *Reading Research Quarterly, 27*(3), 203–225.

Norton, D. E. (2001). *Multicultural children's literature: Through the eyes of many children*. Upper Saddle River, NJ: Merrill/Prentice Hall.

Pratt, L., & Beaty, J. J. (1999). *Transcultural children's literature*. Upper Saddle River, NJ: Merrill/Prentice Hall.

Puckett, M., Marshall, C. S., & Davis, R. (1999). Examining the emergence of brain development research: The promises and the perils. *Childhood Education, 76*(1), 8–12.

Vukelich, C. (1994). Effects of play intervention on young children's reading of environmental print. *Early Childhood Research Quarterly, 9*(2), 153–170.

West, L. S., & Egley, E. H. (1998). Children get more than a hamburger: Using labels and logos to enhance literacy. *Dimensions of Early Childhood, 26*(3 & 4), 43–46.

CHILDREN'S BOOKS

Agard, J. (1989). *The calypso alphabet*. New York: Holt.

Albert, R. E. (1994). *Alejandro's gift*. San Francisco: Chronicle.

Aliki. (1991). *My visit to the aquarium*. New York: HarperCollins.

Ashley, B. (1991). *Cleversticks*. New York: Crown.

Barber, B. E. (1994). *Saturday at The New You*. New York: Lee & Low.

Barton, B. (1981). *Building a house*. New York, Greenwillow.

Begaye, L. S., & Tracy, L. (1993). *Building a bridge*. Flagstaff, AZ: Rising Moon.

Dorros, A. (1991). *Abuela*. New York: Dutton.

Dorros, A. (1992). *This is my house*. New York: Scholastic.

Gage, A. G. (1996). *Pascual's magic pictures*. Minneapolis: Carolrhoda.

Edmiston, J. (1993). *Little Eagle Lots of Owls*. Boston: Houghton Mifflin.

Haskins, J. (1991). *Count your way through the Arab world*. Minneapolis: Carolrhoda.

Hennessy, B. G. (1994). *Road builders*. New York: Viking.

Hoberman, M. A. (1999). *And to think that we thought that we'd never be friends*. New York: Crown.

Hort, L. (2000). *The seals on the bus*. New York: Holt.

Judd, N. (1999). *Love can build a bridge*. New York: HarperCollins.

Lewin, H. (1981a). *Jafta*. Minneapolis: Carolrhoda.

Lewin, H. (1981b). *Jafta's father*. Minneapolis: Carolrhoda.

Lewis, H. (1981c). *Jafta's mother*. Minneapolis: Carolrhoda.

Matura, M. (1989). *Moon jump*. New York: Knopf.

Raffi. (1985). *Like me and you*. New York: Crown.

Rattigan, J. K. (1993). *Dumpling soup*. Boston: Little, Brown.

Reiser, L. (1993). *Margaret and Margarita*. New York: Greenwillow.

Ringgold, F. (1991). *Tar beach*. New York: Crown.

Robinson, M. (1993). *Cock-a-doodle-doo! What does it sound like to you?* New York: Workman.

Strickland, M. R. (1998). *Haircuts at Sleepy Sam's*. Honesdale, PA: Boyds Mills.

Tarpley, N. A. (1998). *I love my hair!* Boston: Little, Brown.

Tomoika, C. (1992). *Rise and shine, Mariko-chan!* New York: Scholastic.

Tompert, A. (1988). *Will you come back for me?* Morton Grove, IL: Whitman.

Vertreace, M. M. (1993). *Kelly in the mirror*. Morton Grove, IL: Whitman.

Watkins, S. (1995). *Green snake ceremony*. Tulsa, OK: Council Oak Books.

Whiteborne, B. (1994). *Sunpainters: Eclipse of the Navajo sun*. Flagstaff, AZ: Northland.

SOUNDS OF THE LANGUAGE: RHYME, RHYTHM, AND SONG

MUSIC AS A NATURAL LANGUAGE

CHANTING AS A PRELUDE TO SINGING

SOUND MAKING, SINGING, AND SONG STORYBOOKS

MUSIC AS A NATURAL LANGUAGE

Music is a natural "language" that crosses cultural barriers for children and speaks to them in tones they can quickly relate to. Sing or play a song in the classroom, and instantly you will have everyone's attention. Waltz around the room in a toe-tapping rhythm, and children will be up on their feet following you. Play a few chords on a guitar or keyboard, and everyone will crowd around to take a turn.

For children ages 3 to 5, music seems to be even more effective than words. Children perk up and listen when teachers sing greeting songs, give directions with music, or play musical games for a transition between activities. Are you having problems getting children to pick up the blocks during cleanup time? Sing them a challenge like this to the tune of "London Bridge":

> Who can pick the blocks up now,
>
> blocks up now, blocks up now?
>
> Who can pick the blocks up now,
>
> before I finish singing? (repeat)

Why do songs seem to work better than words? Perhaps it is the melody children respond to, with its happy tones that sound like fun rather than a difficult chore. Maybe it is the rhythm that resonates with children's own internal heartbeats or breathing. Or maybe children are simply glad the teacher is cheerful enough to sing today. Whatever the reason, teachers of young children know that music makes a difference in the classroom. It is as if music is a natural language that young children respond to more excitedly than they do to spoken language. Snyder (1997) tells us, "Beginning four and one-half months before birth, and continuing throughout life, music is an essential human way of thinking and communicating about the world. It has existed since before language, and exists in every culture" (p. 165). Snyder goes on to say, "There is evidence that music is pre-literate, emerging before word language, and actually encompassing word language through common expressive features of pitch, duration, stress, tone, color, dynamics, tempo, and phrase, and sometimes use of words" (p. 166).

The early years are the critical time period for the brain's musical center to develop, just as word language development occurs before age 6. Young children must have early exposure to both music and words in order for these music and language centers of the brain to develop. Thus, it is crucial that early childhood programs provide appropriate experiences and interactions with music and words for all the children.

Researcher Howard Gardner (1983) identifies "musical intelligence" as one of his seven "multiple intelligences" (i.e., a person's way of knowing and communicating about the world). Children's emotional response to music seems to stimulate brain development and motivate critical thinking. But can musical activities actually help young children emerge into literacy?

They can if they are geared to young children's interests and development. Children learn best about the sounds of the spoken language through sound and word games, nursery rhymes, chants, songs, finger plays, and rhythmic activities. *Phonemic awareness* (i.e., a child's understanding that speech is composed of words, syllables, and sounds) seems to be rooted in children's singing, rhyming, skipping, and word games. As noted by the National Association for the Education of Young Children (NAEYC) in its position statement on learning to read and write (1998), "Researchers found that three-year-old children's knowledge of nursery rhymes specifically related to their more abstract phonological knowledge later on. Engaging children in choral readings or rhymes and rhythms allows them to associate the symbols with the sounds they hear in these words" (p. 34).

Music and the Brain

As brain research continues in the field of *neuropsychology,* we are learning more and more amazing facts about the importance of music as a tool for learning. As Davies (2000) reports:

> Music synchronizes the right and left hemispheres of the brain. Researchers report that the left hemisphere analyzes the structure of music, while the right hemisphere focuses on the melody. The hemispheres of the brain work together when emotions are stimulated, attention focused, and motivation heightened. Rhythm acts as a hook for capturing attention and stimulating interest. Once a person is motivated and actively involved, learning is optimized. Electroencephalogram tests reveal that music alters brain waves, making the brain more receptive to learning. (p. 148)

How can this happen in a preschool classroom? It all comes down to the emotions, strange as it seems. As Greenspan (1997) found in his study *The Growth of the Mind and the Endangered Origins of Intelligence,* it is emotions, not cognitive stimulation, that serve as the mind's primary architect.

> The new and for many, startling notion—that emotion has an integral, and perhaps the most crucial, role in shaping the intellect—has already begun to change how we assess infants and young children....We suggest that babies' emotional exchanges with their caregivers, rather than their ability to fit pegs into holes or find beads under cups, should become the primary measuring rod of developmental and intellectual competence. (p. 9)

Greenspan also notes, "In brain-imaging studies, practicing a musical instrument has been seen to produce additional neural connections in the cortex for frequently used fingers" (p. 8).

Music and Emotions

Music, first, has an emotional appeal. Walk into a preschool classroom where music is playing and you may suddenly feel happier, lighter, and more alive. A smile is certain to cross your face when you see the children smiling. You may note that the sensitive teacher has also picked up this positive emotional feeling and is beginning to move around the room clapping her hands to the rhythm of the background music. Soon a few children leave their learning centers and join her in a conga line around the room. When the record ends, everyone stops, laughs for a moment, and then returns to their learning centers smiling, chattering, and with a renewed interest in the activities. As Davies (2000) points out: "music's power to evoke emotions also enhances learning." When there is a heightened emotional involvement in learning, a stronger neural connection is created in the brain, which then makes it easier to remember things. "The rhyme, rhythm, and repetition of music make it easier to remember facts. Music captures our attention and balances repetition with novelty, which in turn facilitates retention" (p. 152).

Davies has also found that playing background music while reading books to children enhances the story. Try it and see. Bring a tape recorder and some of your multicultural musical tapes into the book center, and play them as you read. Try to set the mood of the story with the mood of the music. Another day, see how much children remember of the story and its characters. Did the music seem to help their retention?

No wonder that the neuroscientist Frank Wilson, who has registered brain scans of children as they perform certain tasks, reports that when children read words, the language center of the brain lights up on his scanner. But when they read music, the entire brain lights up like a Christmas tree (Snyder, 1997, p. 168)! With this kind of evidence, can any early childhood educator not include the natural language of music in the classroom on a daily basis?

CHANTING AS A PRELUDE TO SINGING

Even teachers who cannot carry a tune can engage children with musical sounds and rhythms through chanting. According to Buchoff (1994), "A chant is any group of words that is recited with a lively beat. Through chanting, all children speak together in unison. They learn the importance of clear and expressive pronunciation as their voices combine to make the message of the chant come alive" (p. 26). Because children recite chants over and over, they learn to say unfamiliar words as they learn the pleasure of voicing rhymes in a rhythmical way. Children who speak nonstandard English, shy children, and even those who are learning English as a second language can be successful in such group chants.

Many of the children may have already heard chants previously if they have heard spectators at sporting events doing *cheers* in unison. They know how peppy and lively a cheer makes everyone feel. A team wants to rush right out and win the game. Now you have the opportunity to bring such enthusiasm into the classroom with chants as a fun way to use and hear our language and as a prelude to singing such verses. Cheers are one type of chant. Jump rope rhymes are another type. But teachers engaged in the cultural character ap-

Even teachers who do not sing can engage children with musical sounds and rhythms through chanting.

proach of using children's picture books will want to draw on the books for their chanting activities.

Chants from Cultural Character Picture Books

Choose cultural character books having words that rhyme or sentences in rhythm, and look for sentences or phrases that are repeated. The titles of these predictable books often give you a clue. For example, ***And to Think That We Thought That We'd Never Be Friends*** is a rhythmical title that is repeated frequently:

> It's funny how quickly an argument ends,
>
> And to think that we thought that we'd never be friends!

This multicultural musical rumpus, also described in chapter 1, is written in verse with the last two lines of each rhyming episode repeating the title. Toward the end, the lines change, saying:

> For music is magic, it soothes and it mends,
>
> And to think that we thought that we'd never be friends!

And to Think That We Thought That We'd Never Be Friends (Hoberman, 1999)
Twist with a Burger, Jitter with a Bug (Lowery, 1995)
There Was an Old Lady Who Swallowed a Trout! (Sloat, 1998)
Beach Feet (Reiser, 1996)

Not only the words but the animated illustrations of individuals of different cultures playing every kind of instrument you can imagine will keep your children's attention to the end of the story. If you've read the book aloud with enthusiasm, the children will want you to read it again . . . and again. Good. Now you can engage them in chanting the last two lines of each rhyming episode together. Lead the chant when the time is right by swinging an arm in rhythm like a musical conductor. Children will love it and soon want to take turns being the chant conductor themselves.

Look for other multicultural books whose titles seem to indicate they would contain excellent chanting lines. A recent all-time favorite is **Twist with a Burger, Jitter with a Bug.** The entire story, with its large flashy cartoon illustrations of various cultural characters dancing, has a brief phrase at the top of each page, creating a toe-tapping chant:

> Dance a mambo,
>
> Snap to a rap,
>
> Put on your cleats and tap, tap, tap.

You will need to repeat the reading of this book a number of times before the children have learned the words to its verses. But don't wait till the end. Repeat the first verse over a few times and ask the children to join in. The idea of chanting is not to have children memorize verses (although many will do it anyway) but "to offer each child the opportunity to join with others and share the joy of language" (Buchoff, 1994, p. 29).

In **There Was an Old Lady Who Swallowed a Trout!** dazzling illustrations show on page after page a wonderful Native Alaskan old woman swallowing a trout, a salmon, an otter, a seal, a porpoise, a walrus, a whale, and finally the ocean. Each rhyming episode in this story ends with the lines

> That splished and splashed and thrashed about.
>
> It wanted out!

This structure is just perfect for your children to chant the last two lines in unison as you reach the end of each rhyming episode. Eventually, after hearing the story repeated a number of times, many of the children will learn most of the words, in addition to the last lines. Oh, yes, they will also want to chant about the Anglo-American old lady who swallowed a fly. Can they also make up a story featuring an African old lady swallowing African animals, or one featuring a Caribbean island old lady swallowing coral fish and ocean creatures, or a Hispanic old lady swallowing items from the classroom? What fun! What else can they think of? Don't forget always to include the children's ideas in all of the books you read together. As they dictate their stories, you can record them on a newsprint pad and try them out together to see whether they fit the appropriate rhythm and rhyme.

Beach Feet is a concept picture book, with no characters or story line but only *feet* and wonderfully descriptive words that lend themselves to chanting. If you don't have a real beach nearby, children can pretend to visit a beach either inside or outside the classroom after hearing this lively, rhythmical description of feet. Large horizontal illustrations stretching across two pages show all sorts of brown feet, white feet, crab claws, dog paws, and more. A simple rhyming phrase in large blue type follows a dog as it investigates "slimy, salty, sandy feet," or "furry, fancy, fiddle feet" across each page. Children's feet scrunch, squash, squish, and splash through the book in "sound words" youngsters love to repeat aloud.

Read this book to individuals or a child on each side of you at first so they can see the illustrations up close and get involved in counting the feet along with you. Repeat the words until everyone in the class has had a chance for an individual look at all the feet. Then invite groups of children to chant parts of the verses along with you: "one-two-three-feet; four-five-six-feet."

Now it is time for some foot games and rhymes of their own. Have children march around the room behind you single file, chanting as you go with words you or the children have made up: "My-feet, your-feet, his-feet, her-feet; giant-step-two-feet; tiptoe-three-feet," and so on.

If it is warm outside, barefoot children can step in a pan of water and make wet footprints on the sidewalk, or in a pan of paint and make colored footprints on newsprint. Bring in a bucket of seashells and let children line them up in a curving path to follow, counting each shell as they take a step—all the while chanting the simple rhyme. This is truly music without a melody that even non-musicians can sing!

Be sure to hang the book *Beach Feet* on a string in the music center or another center featuring a foot activity as suggested in chapter 1. You may be focusing on the theme "Who Am I?" Have the children do some of the feet chants they have enjoyed. Or you can read chants aloud from the book while they work.

Cultural and Literacy Concepts

By appealing to something all children are familiar with (their feet), this simple book has illustrated the cultural character concept that everyone has feet, although some are different looking than others. Its catchy rhymes have involved the children in chanting, moving to rhythm, and making up their own rhymes—important literacy concepts. And because the motivation for all of these activities comes from a cultural character book, children can dip into *Beach Feet* whenever they want and let its inspiration take them anywhere they choose.

Physical Movements to Chants

Be sure to wait until the children are able to maintain the appropriate rhythmic pattern while reciting the chant before you add physical responses. When you feel they can chant and move at the same time, still keeping the rhythm, you can add hand clapping, foot stomping, finger snapping, toe tapping, stick clicking, or other movement activities. Buchoff (1994) notes, "Chants naturally lend

When children can chant and move at the same time, you can have them keep time with rhythm instruments.

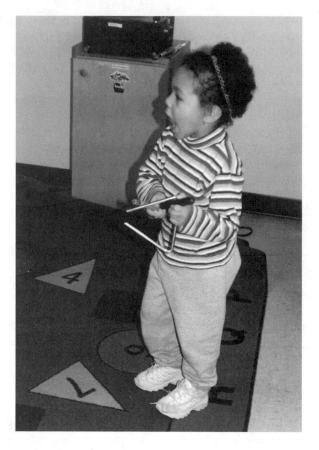

themselves to physical responses. Give children opportunities to experiment with the rhythm and tempo of the chant, and encourage them to try different actions. By varying the physical response, children have the opportunity to re-cite the same chant multiple times but with novel approaches" (p. 29).

Clapping to a beat is an important rhythmical accomplishment that not every preschool child learns immediately. Have them first practice clapping out the syllables of their names before they tackle chant clapping. Bren-da Par-ma-lee, for example, would be "clap-clap" (pause) "clap-clap-clap." Go around the group and have them clap out everyone's name. Once children can clap out the rhythm of chants, let them try clapping with their hands above their heads and swaying to the beat.

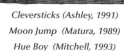

Cleversticks (Ashley, 1991)
Moon Jump (Matura, 1989)
Hue Boy (Mitchell, 1993)

Action Chants for Picture Book Characters

If you find that you love chanting as much as the children, you will want a few more new chants to enliven your program. This time, in-stead of taking the words of the chant from a book, make up your own simple chants about the children's favorite culture characters. Yes, you can do it! Did the children enjoy the story of *Cleversticks* (from chapter 2)? Read it again to yourself and think of simple actions you can have the character performing in what is called an "action chant." Try writing out a few lines. Can you think of words that will rhyme with different lines? What about this one:

> Cleversticks, click your sticks;
>
> Click them fast, click them slow,
>
> Click them high as 'round you go!

If the children enjoy that chant, they might want to add new verses such as "Clap your hands" and "Tap your feet." Be sure to print out each chant on a newsprint pad for later use. As children actually emerge into reading words, such written-down chants will help. Of course, some children will want to get up and perform the actions of the chant immediately. Because it is often difficult for the youngest children to do chanting and clicking sticks at the same time, have part of the class do the chanting while the rest perform the actions.

Another active cultural character is Cayal, the East Indian boy in *Moon Jump* who jumps to the moon. Can the children help you make up an action chant for him? Make it simple and repetitive—for example:

> Jump Cayal jump,
>
> Jump Cayal jump;
>
> Jump off the chairs,
>
> Jump up the stairs,
>
> Jump to the moon,
>
> But come back soon! (clap)

Once children can say this chant in rhythm, have them jump up and down in place, giving a loud clap at the end. If children enjoy particular books, then use your inventiveness to extend the stories with action chants for the children. *Hue Boy*, for example, tells the story of a little Caribbean boy who does not seem to grow "at all, at all." Your children can certainly identify with such a dilemma. They can also engage in the fun of exercising and stretching just as Hue Boy does in the book's large and striking illustrations if you make up a chant about it. First read the book to individuals and small groups so that everyone is familiar with the story and knows what the fruits and exercises look like. Then do action chants in which everyone stands in a circle to chant and imitate Hue Boy's and his neighbor Carlos's actions. You can make up your own chant or use the one that follows:

> Eat pumpkin soup, yum-yum,
>
> Eat mangoes and melons, mum-mum;
>
> Eat pineapples and sapodillas, sap-sap;

Eat craboos and cashews, rap-rap;

Eat guavas and tamarinds, tall-tall;

But Hue Boy doesn't grow at all, at all.

Once children know the chant, they can make up actions to go with the last two words. Then they will want to exercise with Hue Boy's neighbor, Carlos, to another action chant:

Arms up, arms down,

Arms up, arms down,

Arms right, arms left,

Arms right, arms left, str-r-retch!

Now stand up tall and measure all.

If your children enjoy this story and the action chants, consider doing this chant every few months and actually measuring each child afterward on his or her own height chart. To make the story itself more meaningful for the children, bring in some of the Caribbean fruits mentioned in the book for snack or lunch on measuring day. And be sure to play some reggae or calypso music during the chanting to give it a real island flavor. Hue Boy may be different from your children, but they should be able to identify with this island boy who has similar growth concerns.

Some other book characters you or the children may want to chant about include Pablo, the Hispanic boy with the birthday tree; Marisa, the Hawaiian girl who makes dumplings for the soup; Pascual, the Guatemalan boy with the camera; or Kelly, the African American girl who looks in the mirror. You may find other appropriate books in libraries or bookstores whose characters lend themselves to creative action chants. A fine collection of simple jump rope rhymes for chanting is the book *Anna Banana: 101 Jump-Rope Rhymes* (Cole, 1989).

Literacy Concept and Brain Research

Why are such action rhymes so important in the development of early literacy? Snyder (1997) has this to say:

> Rhymes and songs are the authentic literature of music language. Rhymes provide the rhythm of the mother tongue, the language they are learning to speak. . . . Steady beat activities that begin with bouncing on a knee or being rocked back and forth develop pathways in the brain that are not yet understood but appear to be essential for normal development and learning, *especially related to reading.* (pp. 169–170)

From such research, early childhood educators have come to understand the importance of including musical activities such as chanting, moving to a beat, and singing on a daily basis. Merely listening to recorded music is not the same. Children must participate in music by saying or singing words and moving to a beat in order for music to be an effective promoter of early literacy.

But these activities should be impromptu and not taught as a lesson. You yourself can clap while you are chanting, and some of the children may follow your lead. After a few rounds of clapping, you can start tapping on something with your hand to carry the beat. Children may pick up this sound-making game of yours and tap with their own hands or even their feet. This kind of music can occur anytime during the day, not just during a formal music period. Let's not make music formal—it should be fun. When children realize you are chanting and tapping because you enjoy it, they will want to participate, too.

Patterned Chants

Certain cultural character picture books are written in verses that do not necessarily rhyme but follow a rhythmic pattern. **Bein' with You This Way** is a lively action story set in a public park and narrated by an African American girl with beaded hair and a bright orange shirt. She gets everyone's attention by telling them to snap their fingers, tap their toes, and sing along with her. She then begins a cumulative chant as she marches around the playground pointing out the differences and similarities in the people she sees. She chants about straight hair and curly hair, big nose and little nose, brown eyes and blue eyes, thick arms and thin arms, light skin and dark skin that are different but the same. Alternate verses end with "Uh-huh!" Or "Ah-ha!"

Bein' with You This Way
(Nikola-Lisa, 1994)
The House That Jack Built
(Stow, 1992)
Miss Mary Mack (Hoberman, 1998)

Although the verses get longer as the chant continues, children soon understand that when a new phrase has been added, they must repeat all the original phrases in a cumulative fashion after they say the new one. As you reread this story, encourage children to join in the repetition. They especially love to shout out "Uh-huh!" or "Ah-ha!" at the ends of the verses. This is a patterned chant with words such as *hair*, *eyes*, *nose*, *arms*, and *skin* repeated in a pattern rather than a rhyming chant with words at the ends of lines in rhyme. Its catchy rhythm makes everyone want to clap hands or move to the beat.

Cultural Character Concept

This particular chant is an expansion of the important concept presented in **Beach Feet:** that we humans are all different but still the same. *Multicultural education for preschool children stresses this focus on our common bonds as human beings, even though we may have different characteristics.* Your activities should focus on such likenesses rather than our differences. Differences should be accepted in a matter-of-fact manner—even celebrated, as in this book—but it is our likeness to one another that is the most important fact. We are truly different but the same.

Children enjoy trying to find themselves in the illustration of this book. When you read it to individuals, have them look through the pages one at a time to choose which child they would like to be. When you come to that page in your reading aloud of the story, be sure to make mention of that child by name (e.g., "just like Maria" or "just like Mark"). Children respond best to activities that involve them personally. Whenever books have a number of characters like this, be sure to have children choose one to be themselves.

Literacy Concept

Don't forget to read this book again and again to individuals and small groups. Hang it on a book-on-string line in the music center where the youngsters can enjoy the illustrations on their own and then bring the book over to you to read aloud. If they have participated in the chant, they will come to know every word by heart, so try not to skip any. Some may even be able to tell you the whole story. Is such memorization appropriate? you may wonder. Jalongo and Ribblett (1997) have this to say about it: "Not so long ago, reading teachers looked upon children's memorization of a favorite book as unconnected to 'real' reading. Educators now know, based on emergent literacy research, that an important breakthrough in the literacy process occurs when a child knows a few books so well that she can tell if any portion of the text has been skipped or altered" (p. 15).

The House That Jack Built is a traditional cumulative old English folk story about the man "all tattered and torn" and "the maiden all forlorn" but located in a lush Caribbean setting with palm trees, tropical flowers, and brown-skinned people. Children listeners soon pick up the pattern of adding a new line but repeating each of the old lines in the order they occur. The rhythm is so catchy that youngsters can't help repeating the lines after hearing them a few times. What wonderful new words they will be hearing and repeating: "tattered and torn," "all forlorn." Can they figure out their meanings?

Miss Mary Mack is a traditional jump rope rhyme in picture book form as a rhyming and patterned chant. In this instance Mary Mack is a little Anglo-American girl, but her friends in the back yard where the story takes place are a cultural character throng. It is the Fourth of July and they all have gathered for a barbecue as well as to see the elephant jump the fence for fifty cents. If you remember the verse, he jumped so high, he reached the sky and didn't come back till the Fourth of July.

Chanters repeat the last word of every line three times. Children love to play this game of saying Mary's name as *Mary Mack, Mack, Mack*, which rhymes with *black, black, black*—just as *sky, sky, sky* rhymes with *July, July, July*. Get the idea? The author has extended the traditional jump rope rhyme with added stanzas to make a hilarious story as the elephant falls so hard, hard, hard, he makes a hole deep enough for a swimming pool in Mary's _____, _____, _____. When you first read the book, let the children guess the rhyming words they will soon be chanting.

Children love to chant the repeated words, clapping as they do. A simple tune can also be sung, as illustrated on an end page. Expect to hear words in triplicate for all kinds of situations in the classroom for the next few days if your children, children, children catch the rhyme bug from Mary. You may want to extend this idea with jumping activities by the children. Who wants to be the elephant who jumps over a low block fence they have built, while everyone else chants the verse? What about having some other animals try their skill at jumping? Have the children invent their own chants about these experiences, while you record them on a newsprint pad for later use.

Brain Research

Snyder (1997) discusses the importance of such patterns for brain processing, storing, and understanding new information: "Music education from the earliest years focuses on recognition and construction of large and small patterns. Because, as mentioned before, music is preliterate and aural, it becomes a perfect pre-reading tool for understanding language patterns before symbolic codes are introduced" (p. 167).

   Such new research helps us to understand why children involved in nursery verses and jump rope rhymes are more successful later on in learning to read. We must remember, however, to give children opportunities to repeat chants many times before we can expect them to say them by themselves. Repetition like this is a part of a self-taught pattern all young children follow as they acquire new learning. Hart (1983) believes that all brain processing seeks and stores *patterns of behavior*. These patterns help the brain process and understand new information. Because music, or in this case chanting, is patterns of sound, such activities are excellent brain development tools for young children. In other words, whether or not you can sing with children, be sure to chant with them!

SOUND MAKING, SINGING, AND SONG STORYBOOKS

Sound Making

Sound making has long been a natural part of young children's lives. In their playful exploration of their environment they hit objects, drop things, bang materials, and jangle things, making all kinds of interesting sounds. If the sound pleases them they repeat it. Sometimes it turns into music, as Snyder (1997) notes: "Exploration of sound potential through striking objects is fascinating early play. Two- and 3-year-olds instinctively compose their own songs constantly throughout the day in the course of play" (p. 157).

   Set up the music center for this sound exploration to take place before you introduce rhythm instruments. Put out a table full of potential sound makers—cricket clickers, empty bandage boxes, pebbles, empty margarine tubs, sticks, stones, nails, gourds, spoons, sandpaper, and anything else you can think of that might make an interesting sound. Have children record their sounds on a blank cassette tape, to be played back and discussed. Later play an instrumental tape with a beat and see whether anyone can keep time to the beat with the sounds they make.

Another time put out several empty glass jars and spoons. Fill each jar with graduated amounts of water and have children make sounds by tapping the jars. What will happen if more water is added to each jar? Less water? Have each child guess and then try it to find out.

Sound Words

Cock-a-Doodle-Doo! What Does It Sound Like to You? (Robinson, 1993)
Hush! A Thai Lullaby (Ho, 1996)
Baby-O (Carlstrom, 1992)

Because music is patterns of sound just as language is, young children need to experience sounds in all their varieties to emerge into musical and language literacy. Can words found in cultural character books help children do this? We seldom think of words in terms of sound, but young children do. They are intrigued by any strange or funny sounds around them. When such sounds come from words read in books, they are simply delighted and will want to hear the story over and over again—just for its funny word or phrase. As Snyder (1997) notes, "Young children are natural sound tinkerers. They begin by imitating environmental sounds, then elaborate upon them through invention and improvisation. When parents, caretakers, and teachers reinforce these communications, they continue to flourish and develop. However, they are frequently ignored or discouraged rather than elaborated on" (p. 167).

It is up to you to keep this sound exploration going. Jot down what words children think are funny on a file card of early literacy accomplishments you should be keeping for each child. Then make a fuss over the neat words the children have discovered. What other words can they tell you that sound like that? Children quickly pick up what teachers want from them, as well as what teachers seem to ignore. If we want children to pay attention to sound words, then we must do the same. Look at your collection of cultural character picture books to see whether any contain interesting sound words.

In *Cock-a-Doodle-Doo! What Does It Sound Like to You?* large double-page collage pictures show animals like the rooster saying "kee-kree-ree-kee" in Spain and "koh-keh-koh-koh" in Japan. Dogs bark "guv-guv" in Greece, "wo-wo" in China, and "how-how" in India. Frogs croak "kroo-kroo" in Africa, "gedo gedo" in Japan, and "kwok kwok" in Germany. What do your children think of that? Do any of these words make your children laugh? Jot them down on their cards.

If the children enjoy this story, set up your barnyard animal figures from the block center on a table, and ask a few children from the small group you are working with to be from a different country and the others to be from the

United States. Have them try to make the sounds for each of the animals as their country's language does. When they know the sounds well, have them change sides. Be sure to take time out to laugh!

Hush! A Thai Lullaby is a simple song sung by a mother to her "sleeping" baby as she notices various animals making their sounds around her thatched house. The animal sounds alert the worried mother, making her repeat her shushing verse for each animal she spies. But baby is not asleep and climbs unnoticed out of its hammock to follow the action. Read this story to one or two children at a time so they can see what is happening. What do they think about sounds like "tuk-ghaa, tuk-ghaa," for a long-tailed lizard, "jeed-jeed" for a fat gray mouse, "op-op, op-op" for a bright green frog, "uut-uut, uut-uut," for a muddy pig, "jiak-jiak, jiak-jiak" for a loose-limbed monkey, "maau, maau" for an old water buffalo, or "hoom-praa, hoom-praa" for a great big elephant?

Let each child comment on the illustrations that show a house, country, and animals quite different from their own. Can your listeners find the baby hiding somewhere on each two-page spread? Can they repeat any of the sounds? What sounds do they think this child's mother might make to keep the baby from waking?

When you read the story to a small group, have them close their eyes and listen for a few minutes afterward to the environmental sounds in the classroom. What do they hear? An aquarium bubbling, footsteps in the hall, the tick of a clock, the sound of an air conditioner, other children shuffling around, blocks tumbling down, coughs and sneezes, whispering or giggling? This story also makes a fine lullaby at naptime. Read it in a whispery or singsong voice with the lights off, the curtains closed, and everyone stretched out on cots.

Baby-O is a joyous song or chant repeated in this story by three generations of a Caribbean island family as they prepare their products for a ride to market in a jitney bus called Baby-O. Baby tries to catch the chickens to the sound of "chuka chuka." Mama scrubs clothes in a big tin tub to the sound of "wusha wusha." Brother rolls his toy trucks down the road to "toma toma." Pappy (grandpa) digs weeds and gathers vegetables with the sound of "kongada kongada." "Pika pika" is the sound of mangoes falling from the tree for Sister-O. Grasses swish with a "plesh plesh" sound for Granny as she weaves baskets. Papa catches fish with nets going "dippa dippa." When the jitney finally appears, they pile their produce aboard and all ride to town (Beaty, 1997).

Once again this is a story for one or two children sitting close to the reader. Let each choose to be one of the characters, and when you repeat the story, have them make the sound for their character. Which sound is their favorite? Some children like Pappy's "kongada" best. Would they like to make up their own sounds and substitute them when the time comes in the story? When enough other children have had a chance to be the sound makers, have a parade around the room with the children making their sounds as they take a pretend ride in the jitney.

Playing Rhythm Instruments

Max Found Two Sticks (Pinkney, 1994)
One Smiling Grandma (Linden, 1992)
Turtle Island ABC (Hausman, 1994)
The Singing Man (Medearis, 1994)
Red Bird (Mitchell, 1996)

It is the makers of music who enjoy it most. When young children find they can make their own music by playing an instrument, they often take part in musical activities they had avoided previously. You may be surprised to learn that the musical instruments young children can explore actually fall into the same categories as those used by professional musicians: sound makers, rhythm instruments, melody instruments, and harmony instruments. Simple sound makers children can strike or shake include the following:

Pots and pans

Glasses with water

Seed pods, gourds

Cans with seeds

Rhythm spoons

Multicultural rhythm instruments may include these:

Agogo bells (Africa)

Ankle/wrist bells (Native American)

Balaphon xylophone (West Africa)

Cactus rain sticks (Chile)

Coconut shells and strikers (Caribbean)

Den den drum (Japan)

Djembe tone drum (West Africa)

Floor tom-tom (Native American)

Steel drum (Trinidad)

Wood guiro and scratcher (Mexico)

Wood maracas (Cuba)

Zulu marimba/thumb piano (Africa)

Multicultural instruments like these can be ordered from Lakeshore Learning Materials, 2695 E. Dominguez Street, PO Box 6261, Carson, California 90749 ([800]421-5354). Traditional rhythm instruments also include these:

Brass cymbals	Tone blocks
Finger cymbals	Sand blocks
Handle castanets	Rhythm sticks
Hand tom-toms	Triangles
Jingle clogs	Tambourines
Maracas	Bongo drums

Cultural character books featuring some of these instruments can be the motivating factors for children to participate in musical sound making while at the same time experiencing early literacy activities. In **Max Found Two Sticks,** Max, an African American city boy, finds two sticks that have been blown off a tree and uses them to tap out a beat on his doorstep. When his mother comes home from shopping, she sees Max tapping on the bottom of his grandfather's window-cleaning bucket. Next, he taps out his beat on the hat boxes his mother has brought. Then he uses empty soda bottles from the boys next door. Finally, as he taps out his beat on the garbage can in front of his apartment building, a marching band comes by. The last drummer in line spies Max beating his drum and tosses him his spare set of drumsticks. Max catches them without missing a beat (Beaty, 1997).

As you read this book to the children, you will want to repeat the sound words of Max's tapping several times, having the youngsters join in when they can: "pat, pat-tat"; "putter-putter"; "tippy-tip, tat-tat"; "ding, dong, ding." Next comes the fun of making drum music like Max did. Can the children find sticks to use? What about pencils, or paintbrushes, or chopsticks? Let each child tap out a beat that you record on a cassette. Play them back when everyone has finished. It is not only the sounds themselves that are intriguing, you will find, but also the pattern of the sounds—in other words, the rhythm or beat. Becoming familiar with such sound patterns is an important ingredient for children's learning of language patterns.

Bring in sticks or tappers for everyone and have them tap out the beat when you read other books with a beat, such as **Beach Feet, Bein' with You This Way**, **Miss Mary Mack**, **Hush!** or **Baby-O.** Tape-record the stories and their accompanying sounds, and let children play them back. Can they change the beat when you read the story again? This activity works best with small groups in the music center. If the sounds become too loud, have the children use chopsticks.

Children also learn rhythm by tapping to tapes or records, such as Hap Palmer's *Rhythms on Parade* with its hand claps, finger snaps, and rhythm band sounds; Ella Jenkins's *And One and Two* with its rhythmic songs for children to clap and tap with; or *Rhythm Stick Fun* with lively music from Japan, Puerto Rico, West Africa, and more.

Cultural Character Drums

Drums come in all sizes and shapes: bongos, double bongos, hand bongos, hand tom-toms, Indian tom toms, snare drums, tambourines, and paddle drums like the Japanese "den den," to name a few. Some are meant to be played with the hands, others with one or two sticks. Talk to the children about each kind of drum and the people who use them as part of their culture. Have them pretend to be a cultural character themselves.

You may find illustrations of drums from different cultures in ABC or counting books. For instance, in the Caribbean counting book **One Smiling**

Bring in drums and sticks for everyone to tap out a beat when you read books with sound patterns in their words.

Grandma, the number 4 is brilliantly illustrated as "Four steel drums tapping out the beat." In the Native American alphabet book ***Turtle Island ABC,*** the letter *D* stands for *drum,* with a simple illustration of an Indian drum and descriptive paragraph.

Drums also appear in picture storybooks of other cultures. In the African folktale ***The Singing Man,*** the young man Banzar becomes a musician who plays the flute and sings, as he accompanies the old man who plays an *omele* drum. Although the story is too long for most preschool children, the realistic illustrations show a number of *omele* shoulder drums being played with strikers by African villagers in colorful garments.

In ***Red Bird,*** a contemporary Native American story, Katie and her family leave the city every September and drive to Delaware for the Nanticoke Pow-wow where they celebrate their heritage through chanting, drumming, and dancing. Katie becomes Red Bird and the drumbeat becomes her heartbeat as she dons her crimson shawl for the shawl dance. Drummers sit around a huge ground tom-tom pounding out the beat and chanting the song.

Making Drums and Rhythm Instruments

Once children get involved in drum beats and rhythm making, they will soon want their own personal drum or rhythm instrument. Simple shakers can be made from paper towel tubes by placing a few beans and pebbles inside and taping them shut securely. Children can have fun painting their shakers in the colors they see in Willie's story. Simple drums can be made from inverted round waste baskets, empty round gallon ice cream cartons, oatmeal boxes, or coffee cans. Have parents save cardboard tubes and empty containers of every kind for your instrument making. Children can paint or decorate their own instrument like those from the books or in their own designs.

Drums and other rhythm instruments in preschool should be treated as real instruments, not toys. If all the children march around banging as loud as they can on their instruments, they are making noise, not music, and drowning out the sounds of individual instruments and their rhythm. Instead, you should introduce each rhythm instrument separately with suggestions on how to use it properly. Then children can try out each one, listening for the sounds it makes and comparing one instrument with another. Achilles (1999) suggests that children with physical disabilities join the fun by using a paddle drum with a handle that they can twist to make the drum beats. She notes, "Children love to explore the drum, discovering how to play fast and slow, loud and soft; having drum conversations with their friends; and accompanying their own movements" (p. 24).

On days when you read these books about drumming, you can play records or tapes from different cultures such as *Fiesta Musical* (songs from Puerto Rico, Cuba, Mexico, and more), *Waves of Wonder* (folk songs, ballads, raggae, rap, tango and more), *Let's Get the Rhythm of the Band* (African American music from talking drums of Africa to rap), or *Multicultural Rhythm Stick Fun* (music from Japan, Vietnam, West Africa, Puerto Rico, and more). Have children first clap to the rhythms, then play drums or rhythm sticks. Not only will children have fun making music, but they should also make the connection that books and stories can be associated with music and fun.

Playing Melody Instruments

Melody instruments for young children include toy horns, flutes, ocarinas, tonettes, tone bells, xylophones, and sometimes the *kalimba*, an African thumb piano. Horn-type instruments are of course played by blowing with the mouth, tone bells and xylophones with hammers, and the kalimba with the thumb. Blowing through an instrument to make a sound is often a new and exciting experience for preschool children. You can lead them into such cultural character literacy activities through children's books like the ones already mentioned or others you may own.

Willie Jerome (Duncan, 1995)
Love Flute (Goble, 1992)
The Bravest Flute (Grifalconi, 1994)
Charlie Parker Played Be Bop
(Raschka, 1992)
An Island Christmas (Joseph, 1992)

After you read **Willie Jerome,** about an African American boy who plays the trumpet from the top of his apartment roof, have the children make a blowing instrument with their fists. Can they pretend their balled-up fist is a trumpet as they blow sounds through it like Willie Jerome? You can demonstrate. Have them try making high sounds and low sounds. How long can they hold one tone before taking a breath? Can they play a real song on their trumpets? Will their "neighbors" in the room think they are just like Willie Jerome, making noise, not music? What happens when they clap a hand back and forth over the end of their fist trumpet as they make a sound? Put on a tape of jazz trumpet music, and have them make their own trumpet sounds along with it. Invite a school trumpet player to visit the class and demonstrate.

Another day have the children make their own "tooter" trumpets with paper towel tubes painted any color they want. Put tape around the ends to keep the cardboard firm and the paint from peeling off. Be sure you have enough tubes for everyone before you introduce this activity. For health's sake, have each child initial his tube. Then ask them to blow through only their own tubes so they won't pass germs around and to put the tubes in their cubbies when they're finished. As they blow a long tone through their tubes, have them clap a hand open and shut over the end of the tube to see how it sounds, just like they did over their fists. You will want to tape-record their trumpet playing, first individually and then as a group.

The *Love Flute* story comes from a plains Indian folktale about the first love flute that was given to a shy young man by the Elk People to play for the one he loves. You may need to "read the pictures" rather than the words of the text, as it is long for 3-year-olds. Afterward have someone bring in an Indian five-hole wooden flute and demonstrate how it works. Play a tape of a famous Native American flutist such as Carlos Nakai (tape cassette, *Canyon Trilogy*), and have the children close their eyes as you read the story again. Can they see in their mind's eye the shy young Indian following his arrow to the woods where the Elk Men gave him the flute? Can they see the red-headed woodpecker? How does the flute music make them feel?

In *The Bravest Flute* a Mayan Indian boy from a mountain village in Guatemala has been chosen to lead the annual parade down the mountainside to the town square on New Year's Day, playing his bamboo flute nonstop all the way. He has a bass drum strapped to his back that a drummer pounds as they proceed. When he finally reaches the square, he is ready to collapse, but suddenly a wonderful silver flute is thrust into his hands. The widow of the old master flutist has given him her husband's flute, and the sweetest music he has ever heard comes out of it as he blows (Pratt & Beaty, 1999, p. 171).

You may also need to "read the pictures" of this folktalelike story, because the text is long for preschool children. If the children like it, have them fall in line behind one another, each with a musical instrument, and let one with a "flute" lead the parade around the room. You may even want to celebrate the New Year this way in your class.

Whether or not the children have heard of the famous African American jazz saxophone player Charlie Parker, they will love this simply written, wonderfully illustrated book *Charlie Parker Played Be Bop.* How can the words and pictures in a book represent jazz music? Open this book and be astounded by the riffs and runs of be-bopping shoes, lollipops, and bus stops! Boppitty, bibbitty, bang! Children are soon caught up in the zany word-sounds and pic-

Children can have the fun of playing along with jazz saxophone music after you have read Charlie Parker Played Be Bop.

tures—just the kind of playing around with sounds that they do themselves. Play a tape of jazz saxophone music to set the mood. Children can have the fun of playing along with the music if they make their own saxophones from long wrapping-paper tubes painted yellow like Charlie's sax. Tape around the outside of the blowing end to keep it firm. Again, be sure to have children mark the tubes with their own initials and remember not to blow through other children's tubes.

Girls play instruments, too, although you may be hard-pressed to find a young children's picture book that shows this. Here is one. In **An Island Christmas** Rosie helps her family on the West Indian island of Trinidad prepare for Christmas, and then she enjoys a *parang* band of wandering men playing saxophone and guitars. She and her brother Ragboy join in playing on glasses of water with two spoons. On Christmas morning, Rosie finds a wonderful present from her daddy under the tree: a steel drum of her own, and she wakes the house playing "pom de dum dum pom pom!"

Playing Harmony Instruments

Harmony instruments for young children include the autoharp, accordion, banjo, electric keyboard, guitar, harmonica, and ukulele. When you read cultural character picture books featuring one of these harmony instruments, be sure to bring in a real instrument for the children to handle and try out. Try to find someone who plays such an instrument to give a demonstration. **The Banza,** for instance,

The Banza (Wolkstein, 1981)

Music, Music for Everyone (Williams, 1984)

Old Cotton Blues (England, 1998)

is a Haitian folktale about a magic banjo. Perhaps a music store can provide you with a banjo, and maybe even a player. Sometimes senior citizen centers have members who play such "old-time" instruments who would enjoy getting involved with an early childhood program like yours.

Although *The Banza* does not include human players, children love to follow the illustrations of the little goat named Cabree and little tiger named Teegra who become best friends and romp together in a wonderful jungle of featherlike palm trees with pink and blue vegetation. When Teegra leaves to go home to his family, he gives Cabree a banza, a magic banjo that will protect him if he plays it with his heart. Later, when 10 fierce tigers corner the little goat, Cabree begins playing the banza with all his heart. Suddenly out of his mouth comes a ferocious song about eating 10 fat tigers. The frightened tigers disappear into the jungle two by two, until only the chief tiger is left. Cabree promises to let him go if he takes a message to Teegra saying that today Cabree's heart and the banza are one.

Play Caribbean island music such as *Smilin' Island of Song* or *Reggae for Kids* while reading this story. Would your youngsters like to make their own banzas? Have everyone save shoe boxes for your class, and when you have enough, the children can paint them in the Caribbean colors shown in the book. You should be the one to cut a hole in the cover, tape the cover tightly onto the box, cut notches at both ends, and string two or three rubber bands around the box lengthwise for the banjo strings. You can purchase long rubber bands the right length in an office supply store. Would the children like to have a heart on their banza like Cabree does? Help them to fold a paper in two, cut half a heart shape (like a candy cane), and open it into a whole heart. Then they can paint the heart and paste it to their banzas. A long narrow piece of cardboard taped to the box can serve as the neck. Now the children can strum along with the music, just like Cabree.

Music, Music for Everyone is another story too long for most preschool children. You can first read it to yourself and then tell it to the children, showing them the illustrations. It is important to share a book like this when most of the other cultural character books about instrument playing feature boys. This one shows four cultural character girls who make music with bongos, a violin, an accordion, and a flute. The girls play for a special anniversary party in their backyard with people from the neighborhood attending. After you read this story, have the children play the various instruments they have made with taped music from various cultures playing in the background.

Old Cotton Blues tells a simple, poignant, beautifully illustrated story of an African American boy Dexter who wants very badly to play blues music on the clarinet like his adult neighbor Johnny Cotton, but Dexter's mama cannot afford to buy him a clarinet. When Johnny Cotton finds out, he gives Dexter his own father's silver Mississippi harp, a harmonica, and encourages him to learn to play. His first sounds come out "mingle-mangle mishamasha music," but he soon learns how to play the Old Cotton Blues. Bring in several small harmonicas for your children to play as well. Children love blowing on harmonicas for the good sounds they make. Show them how to blow and draw for different sounds, but let them find out how to play high and low at either end of the instrument. (Be sure to clean off the harmonicas afterward with wet wipes, to prevent the spread of germs.)

Singing

After children have mastered chanting, they will want to move on to singing. You can help them make the transition by singing some of the chants with them. It's not that difficult. **Miss Mary Mack,** a simple repetitious song, has its musical notes written on a front end page. If you can't read the music or carry a tune, now is the time to use an audiotape such as Ella Jenkins's *Adventures in Rhythm*, which includes the Mary Mack song.

Miss Mary Mack (Hoberman, 1998)

My Mama Sings (Peterson, 1994)

The Singing Man (Medearis, 1994)

Northern Lullaby (Carlstrom, 1992)

The Old Man Who Loved to Sing (Winch, 1996)

Literacy Concept

By now you have probably learned from the children that singing is as natural to them as talking. Singing is one of the common bonds that runs through all cultures and all peoples. Cultural character books about songs and singing can help to reinforce this concept, creating a bridge between cultures and a connection between singing and speaking. Once again we need to keep in mind what Moravcik (2000) tells us: "Music and language have similar roots. First vocalizations are the precursors of song and musical understanding just as they are the precursors of speech and language. We know there is a critical phase for the development of language, and it seems logical that the abilities to sing and to respond musically have their roots in early childhood experiences" (p. 27).

In **My Mama Sings** the story is told by an African American boy who lives with his mother and their black-and-white cat, Great-Aunt Gretna. He loves the songs Mama makes up when winter is over and in summer when it's too hot to sleep. In the fall, when they stamp through piles of leaves, Mama's songs have a clicking rhythm she makes with her tongue, sounding like a cricket. (Can your listeners make it?) In winter Mama whistles a tune. But one day when everything goes wrong, Mama stops singing. Then the boy has to make up his own song and sing it to Mama to help lift her spirits. When she finally sings it back to him, he knows she is feeling good again.

Brain Research

Davies (2000) has more to say about the emotions evoked by music:

Music's power to evoke emotions also enhances learning. Everything we learn contains a context of feeling, no matter how subtle. It might generate interest, boredom, anxiety, happiness, or anger. These feeling-tones serve as the brain's

82

system for coding and filing information. Music heightens emotional involvement in learning. This heightened involvement creates a stronger neural connection, which in turn makes it easier to remember information. Music helps us store and retrieve rich, multisensory memories. (p. 149)

When someone seems grumpy and out-of-sorts, you might hold the child on your lap and chant or sing over and over a simple name song you make up: "Raphael, Raphael, very soon you will feel well." Another time make up a new greeting song with each child's name in it and sing it in the morning when they arrive. For example, to the tune of "Lazy Mary, Will You Get Up" sing "Rhonda Ripley, will you come in," naming children in the group as each arrives. The ones already there can join in or clap.

Can children make up their own songs like the boy in **My Mama Sings**? If you listen closely, you may hear some of them singing made-up songs just under their breath. Would they like to tape-record them? Once one child has put her song on tape, the others are sure to try it, too. Then they can play their songs for everyone when it seems appropriate.

The previously mentioned book **The Singing Man** is a long but lovely West African folktale about a young man named Banzar who wants to become a musician. The village elders do not accept his choice of an occupation because he will not be growing yams to fill the belly or making crafts to fill the pocket, so they ask him to leave. Banzar takes his flute and sets off. One day he meets Sholo, a blind man with an omele drum who is a "praise singer," going from village to village composing songs to honor the chief and his ancestors.

Sholo takes Banzar along and shows him how to make a living as a praise singer. After Sholo passes away, Banzar carries on his tradition of singing the history of their people. When the king of Lagos hears Banzar play and sing, he honors him by giving him a house, money, and servants. When Banzar finally returns to his own village to play for the chief, he reveals himself and then gives money and gifts to his family. Now the people say, "Yams fill the belly and trade fills the pockets, but music fills the heart."

Read this long story to yourself and then shorten it for your children by telling it as you turn the pages to show them the realistic illustrations in the vibrant colors of Africa. Would your children like to become "praise singers" like Banzar and Sholo? Have them sing words about another child to a familiar tune like "Twinkle, Twinkle Little Star," while other children beat on the drums they have made.

I know Joshua. He can climb so high.

Watch him climbing up to the sky.

You can adapt many nursery songs and rhymes for your praise singers:

"Here We Go Round the Mulberry Bush"

"London Bridge Is Falling Down"

"This Old Man, He Plays One"

"Row, Row, Row Your Boat"

"Hickory Dickory Dock"

"Three Blind Mice"

"Mary Had a Little Lamb"

"Old MacDonald Had a Farm"

Or they might sing words to the tune of "Sing a Song of Sixpence":

Do you know Maria?

She can count to twenty.

She knows how to whistle.

Her best friend is Jenny.

It will be up to you to make up many of the words to the praise songs, but have the children help, too. Such activities help to reinforce children's ability to recognize and make up rhyming words. Be sure to have a song for everyone. Nobody wants to feel left out. If children want to sing songs from Africa and elsewhere bring in Ella Jenkins's album *Multicultural Children's Songs* with chants, songs, and rhythms from many cultures or the *Children of the World* album with songs, dances, rhythms, and games from Africa, Mexico, Puerto Rico, Russia, China, and Japan, and more (Lakeshore Learning Materials, phone: [800]421-5354).

Northern Lullaby, a Native American lullaby, is a goodnight song sung to Papa Star, Mama Moon, Grandpa Mountain, Grandma River, Great Moose Uncle, Auntie Willow, Cousins Beaver and Deer Mouse, and a host of other northern animals as they go to sleep on a winter's night. Large, stylized paintings in the colors of the Northern Lights, against a black, snow-sprinkled sky, dwarf the little cabin in the corner of each page. In the cabin a Native American baby sleeps peacefully in a deer hide blanket, as shown on the last page. Can the children sing go-to-sleep songs for objects in the room when the lights are dim and they are lying on their cots ready to take a nap?

Have the children join in quietly as you point to objects around the room. When you have finished naming the toys and equipment, start with the children, naming each one in your whispery voice. How many children will be asleep before your lullaby is finished? Another time play the cassette *Native American Lullabies: Under the Green Corn Moon* (1998), Silver Wave Records, PO Box 7943, Boulder, Colorado 80306 (phone: [800]745-9283). This is an outstanding collection of lullabies sung by Native singers (Aztec, Kiowa, Taos Pueblo, Navajo, Cheyenne, Oneida, Hopi, Pawnee, Souix, and others), sung in their own languages.

The Old Man Who Loved to Sing is about an Australian man who lived by himself in a valley far from the city where he could sing all day long. When he wasn't singing, he whistled; and when he wasn't whistling, he played music on an old wind-up gramophone as loud as he could. All the animals in his valley came around to hear him: the echidnas and wombats and bandicoots, the platypuses and koalas and kangaroos. But as he grew older, he began forgetting things, and one day he forgot to sing. So the kangaroos began beating their tails in the dust; the frogs joined in with their own harmony, and soon the birds burst into song: the kookaburras and parakeets and lyrebirds. But finally the loudest song of all came from the old man when he remembered.

Children love to scrutinize the marvelous illustrations of the animals that look something like animals they are familiar with, but somehow different. They may not know what the old man or the animals sounded like in their singing, but most will be eager to reenact this story, taking all the parts. Have children pick out which animal they would like to be and help them to make a headband with animal ears for each to wear. Several children can play the part of the old man and begin singing a song they know. You can point to the child animal characters one by one and have them join in with a whistling, braying, hooting, chirping, howling, or clacking sound of their own. Can animals be cultural characters? Why not? You may need to bring in a book or two about Australia's creatures so your children can find out more, such as *Kylie's Concert* about a singing koala, *Little New Kangaroo* about Australian animals, or *Whose Chick Is That?* about Australian birds (Pratt & Beaty, 1999).

Song Storybooks

Literacy Concept

Wheels on the Bus
(Raffi, 1988)

One of the most effective ways of making a connection between singing, a right brain activity, and reading, a left brain activity, is through song storybooks. Song storybooks are picture books that illustrate the words of a familiar song that most children already know, such as "Old MacDonald Had a Farm," "Itsy Bitsy Spider," or "This Old Man." More books of this nature are being published annually by publishers who are aware of young children's natural emergence into literacy. They understand that children who already know the words of a song will more readily be able to recognize these words when they are written in a book. Jalongo and Ribblett (1997), however, have something quite different to say about young children's initial literacy learning:

> Whether a young child is mastering language or learning music, the foundation is the same: enjoyment. Just as a young child's inauguration into the world of music is not learning to read musical notation, a young child's introduction to literacy with print is not learning to decode words....Thus, experts recommend that teachers connect music with literature as a pathway to expressive, meaningful experiences. (p. 16)

Are they saying that preschool children should have *fun* with reading and music? Yes. Absolutely. Children should start by *playing* with words and music. It is the enjoyment of the activity that will carry them over to the eventual learning. Song storybooks can do that. As Jalongo and Ribblett (1997) continue,

"When children participate in read aloud/sing aloud sessions with song picture books, they are involved in authentic, holistic literacy experiences, rather than task-focused instruction that breaks up reading into discrete skills" (p. 16). Such books entice children into singing/reading by building on their familiarity with the words and their catchy rhymes, repetition, and predictable structures. When the song storybooks include cultural characters, another dimension is added to children's acquisition of early literacy.

In Raffi's "Songs to Read" book ***Wheels on the Bus,*** his bus goes put-putting through a French village where people wearing berets and kerchiefs board it carrying eggs, chickens, and babies. The Raffi musical cassette *Rise and Shine* contains this song if children want to hear it played. It may be more fun for them to follow along on the pages if they sing it themselves or drive a "puppet bus" down the streets of the village. (Order from *Sing & Play* Raffi Song Kits by Lakeshore Learning Materials; phone: [800]421-5354.) Instead of purchasing commercial materials, you may decide to duplicate pages of the book, cut out the characters, mount them on cardboard and sandpaper (or Velcro), and have children place the characters on a homemade felt board or flannelboard when they make their appearance in the story. Keep the book-on-a-string in the music center along with the cassette and cardboard characters for the children's creative use afterward.

Integrating Cultural Character Music Books into the Curriculum

After you have acquired some of the cultural character music books suggested in this chapter, you will want to integrate some of them into the entire curriculum, not just the music center. If you are pursuing the curriculum topic "Caring for Ourselves" (mentioned in chapter 1), which you then break down into several subtopics starting with "Who am I?" you will want to look over your entire collection to find which books best represent this subtopic. You will be looking for books in which your children can identify with the main character and his situation. Of the 36 books described in this chapter, here are some that meet that criterion:

Red Bird (Mitchell, 1996)

Powwow (Ancona, 1993)

Iktomi and the Buzzard
(Goble, 1994)

Moon Jump	*Bein' with You This Way*	*Willie Jerome*
Hue Boy	*Red Bird*	*Powwow*
Iktomi and the Buzzard		

Teachers find that extension activity lists such as *Using Cultural Character Picture Books* shown in Figure 3.1 are helpful in curriculum planning, not only for the current year but also for using particular books in the future. You may want to fill out a list like this for several of the books you have chosen to see which one fits best into your present learning centers or for your curriculum needs. The book ***Red Bird*** has been chosen as an example, and the extension activity list has been filled out as shown in Figure 3.2.

USING CULTURAL CHARACTER PICTURE BOOKS

Title: _____

EXTENSION ACTIVITIES

Dramatic play _____

Block play _____

Water play _____

Woodworking _____

Songs, chants, instruments _____

Creative movement, dance _____

Large motor _____

Manipulatives _____

Cooking _____

Crafts _____

Painting, drawing _____

Storytelling _____

Story writing, dictation _____

Letters, labels, journals, signs _____

Games _____

Puppets _____

Other _____

(Permission is granted by the publisher to reproduce this checklist for evaluation and record keeping.)

FIGURE 3.1

Extension Activity List: Using Cultural Character Picture Books

You may want to begin by reading the book **Red Bird** to a small group at a time in the book center. They will want to sit close to see the illustrations. Because it is a long story for preschoolers, read the story to yourself first and then read aloud only a sentence or two from every page, filling in the rest by telling them what else is happening. Can any listeners identify with Katie as she takes the "regalia" out of a trunk and begins packing for the trip to the powwow? Have any of them traveled in a car pulling a camping trailer? When the story arrives at

USING CULTURAL CHARACTER PICTURE BOOKS

Title: Red Bird

EXTENSION ACTIVITIES

Dramatic play   Pretend to camp out at a powwow (view video: "Within the Circle")

Block play   Make dance stage for cone puppets

Water play   Make paper boat "canoes" and float them

Woodworking   Make drumsticks, drums

Songs, chants, instruments   Play drums to Indian drumming, chanting tapes

Creative movement, dance   Join in round dance

Large motor   Join in round dance

Manipulatives   String beads to wear

Cooking   Make fry bread

Crafts   Make headbands

Painting, drawing   Finger paint to sounds of drumming

Storytelling   Tell more "Iktomi" stories

Story writing, dictation   Record stories on cassette player

Letters, labels, journals, signs   Keep daily journal

Games

Puppets   Make paper "cone puppet" dancers

Other   Go outside for "bird watching"; look for cardinal red bird and others

FIGURE 3.2
Extension Activity List For *Red Bird*

the powwow grounds, it is time to play a tape of American Indian drumming and chanting in the background. How does this music make the children feel? What is it that makes Katie turn into Red Bird? How does Katie change back to herself when the powwow is finished?

When using books like **Red Bird** with non-Indian children, it is important to show respect for native peoples. "We are still here," they declare, and their traditions are still alive and well throughout Indian country. Intertribal powwows

Do present Native peoples as appropriate role models with whom a Native child can identify.

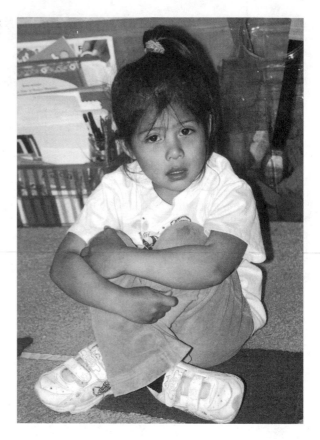

are held almost every weekend somewhere in Indian country. They may be social powwows, benefit powwows, or contest powwows, and everyone is invited. But only tribal members and contestants participate in the singing, drumming, and dancing or in the wearing of the gorgeous and flamboyant regalia. The back cover of the Indian children's book catalog *Oyate* lists important do's and don'ts for teachers, regarding the presentation of Indian culture in the classroom:

> **Do** present Native peoples as appropriate role models with whom a Native child can identify.
>
> **Don't** single out Native children and ask them to describe their traditions or culture.
>
> **Do** look for books written and illustrated by Native people.
>
> **Don't** use ABC books that have "I is for Indian" or "E is for Eskimo" or counting books that count Indians.
>
> **Do** make sure you know the history of Native peoples, past and present before you present it.

Don't use storybooks that show non-Native children "playing Indian."

Do avoid arts and crafts that trivialize Native dress, dance, or ceremony.

Don't use picture books by non-Native authors that show animals dressed as Indians.

Do use materials which show the continuity of Native societies, with traditional values and spiritual beliefs connected to the present.

Don't have children dress as Indians with paper-bag costumes or paper feather headdresses, doing war whoops.

Do present Native peoples as separate from each other with unique cultures, languages, spiritual beliefs.

Don't make charts about "the gifts Indians gave us."

Do invite Native community members to the classroom (but not as entertainers).

Don't use books that show Native people as savages, primitive people, or tribal people now extinct.

Do talk about the lives of Native people in the present.

You can have children make drums or use classroom drums and play them to the beat of Native American drumming and chanting tapes, such as *Caddo Tribal Dances* or *Round Dance Songs of Taos Pueblo, Vol. 1* (Indian House, PO Box 472, Taos, NM 87571). Bring in a book such as ***Powwow*** with its authentic color photos of dancers and dances from the Crow Fair. It is the story of the boy Anthony, who is a traditional dancer. Talk to the children about the reasons for the old dances and the differences of four of the main types of dances seen at today's powwows: traditional, fancy, grass, and jingle-dress. Everyone can join in for the last dance: the Round Dance. Or play a flute tape such as Carlos Nakai's lovely *Canyon Trilogy* (Canyon Records Productions, Inc., 4143 N. 16th Street, Phoenix, AZ 85016).

Because many (or most) children may never have seen a powwow, you may want to order the impressive video *Within the Circle* (Cool Runnings Production, PO Box 3564, Window Rock, AZ 86515) and play at least the first part showing the exciting Grand Entry procession in which all of the dancers in regalia enter the dance circle; then the Tiny Tots group "Ironwood Singers" in which preschool girls dance in fancy shawls or jingle dresses, and boys in grass or fancy outfits.

Later read ***Iktomi and the Buzzard,*** one of the humorous Sioux trickster tales, in which Iktomi in his Eagle Dance outfit is on the way to the powwow when he tries to get Buzzard to help him cross the river without getting his regalia wet. Can they guess what happens? Depending on the children's interests, you may involve them in this topic for several days or even weeks.

Next you may want to feature African American ***Willie Jerome*** and his trumpet as the curriculum focus, filling out another extension activity list to help you plan the activities. Be sure to balance your cultural character activities with books featuring both boy and girl characters of different cultures. Your choice may depend on the topics you are pursuing, the field trips you are taking, the musical activities you want children to experience, or the expressed interests of the children.

SUMMARY

This chapter describes how music is a natural language that crosses cultural barriers and speaks to children in tones they can relate to. When teachers use musical directions children respond more promptly. When they use chants and rhythmical verses, children's excitement carries them into every learning center of the classroom. Chanting and singing help young children develop speaking and later reading skills. Because music and rhythm focus on recognizing and constructing patterns, they become important prereading tools for understanding language patterns, for learning new words, for brain processing, and for storing information.

Cultural character picture books can lead children to chanting, sound-word activities, instrument playing, and singing, as well as to important concepts about people from every culture being different but the same. As the cultural characters from these books make music through your readings, children listeners are motivated to try out their own sound-making, instrument-playing, chanting, and singing skills.

They may role-play the various book characters, thus learning how it feels to be from another culture, while the books themselves become favorites to be looked at again and again. Children who respond to music and rhythm like this become more linguistically aware, a powerful predictor of later reading success.

LEARNING ACTIVITIES

1. Explain why music is often more effective than words for preschool children. Use music as suggested for a pick-up activity, a transition, or a calming effect. Report the results.
2. Play musical mood music while reading a new story to a small group of children. Another day see how much children remember of the story and its characters. Try reading another new story without the background music. Do the children remember the story as well?
3. Do a chanting activity with the children comparing the two books *There Was an Old Lady Who Swallowed a Trout!* and *I Know an Old Lady Who Swallowed a Fly.* Which book did the children like better? Have them make up their own words to one of these chants.

4. Read one of the books featuring rhythm, melody, or harmony instruments. Have the children make one of the instruments described and play it.
5. Read *The Singing Man* and have the children become praise singers. Help each to make up a short praise song for another child to one of the tunes suggested.

REFERENCES

Achilles, E. (1999). Creating music environments in early childhood programs. *Young Children, 54*(1), 21–26.

Beaty, J. J. (1997). *Building bridges with multicultural picture books: For children 3 to 5.* Upper Saddle River, NJ: Merrill/Prentice Hall.

Buchoff, R. (1994). Joyful voices: Facilitating language growth through the rhythmic response to chants. *Young Children, 49*(4), 26–30.

Cole, J. (1989). *Anna Banana: 101 jump rope rhymes.* New York: Beech Tree Books (Morrow).

Davies, M. A. (2000). Learning . . . the beat goes on. *Childhood Education, 76*(3), 148–153.

Gardner, H. (1983). *Frames of mind: The theory of multiple intelligences.* New York: Basic Books.

Greenspan, S. I. (1997). *The growth of the mind and the endangered origins of intelligence.* Reading, MA: Addison-Wesley.

Jalongo, M. R., & Ribblett, D. M. (1997). Using song picture books to support emergent literacy. *Childhood Education, 74*(1), 15–28.

Moravcik, E. (2000). Music all the livelong day. *Young Children, 55*(4), 27–29.

National Association for the Education of Young Children (1998). Learning to read and write: Developmentally appropriate practices for young children. *Young Children, 53*(4), 30–46.

Pratt, L., & Beaty, J. J. (1999). *Transcultural children's literature.* Upper Saddle River, NJ: Merrill/Prentice Hall.

Snyder, S. (1997). Developing musical intelligence: Why and how. *Early Childhood Education Journal, 24*(3), 165–171.

SUGGESTED READINGS

Allen, J., McNeill, E., & Schnidlt, V. (1992). *Cultural awareness for children.* Menlo Park, CA: Addison-Wesley.

Braman, A. N. (2000). *Traditional Native American arts & activities.* New York: Wiley.

Bruce, J. B. (1995). *Whose chick is that?* N. P.: Kangaroo Press.

Crinklaw-Kiser, D. (1996). Integrating music with whole language through the Orff-Schulwerk Process. *Young Children, 51*(5), 15–21.

Hildebrandt, C. (1998). Creativity in music and early childhood. *Young Children, 53*(6), 60–74.

Honig, A. S. (1995). Singing with infants and toddlers. *Young Children, 50*(5), 72–78.

Jalongo, M. R. (1996). Using recorded music with young children: A guide for nonmusicians. *Young Children, 51*(5), 6–14.

James, A. R. (2000). When I listen to the music. *Young Children, 55*(3), 36–37.

Orozco, J.-L. (1994). *De colores and other Latin-American folk songs for children.* New York: Puffin.

Wolf, J. (1994). Singing with children is a cinch! *Young Children, 49*(4), 20–25.

Wolf, J. (2000). Sharing songs with children. *Young Children, 55*(2), 28–30.

CHILDREN'S BOOKS

Ancona, G. (1993). *Powwow.* San Diego: Harcourt Brace.

Ashley, B. (1991). *Cleversticks.* New York: Crown.

Carlstrom, N. W. (1992a). *Baby-O.* Boston: Little, Brown.

Carlstrom, N. W. (1992b). *Northern lullaby.* New York: Philomel.

Duncan, A. F. (1995). *Willie Jerome.* New York: Macmillan.

England, L. (1998). *The old cotton blues.* New York: Simon & Schuster.

Goble, P. (1994). *Iktomi and the buzzard.* New York: Orchard.

Goble, P. (1992). *Love flute.* New York: Bradbury.

Grifalconi, A. (1994). *The bravest flute.* Boston: Little, Brown.

Hausman, G. (1994). *Turtle Island ABC.* New York: HarperCollins.

Ho, M. (1996). *Hush! A Thai lullaby.* New York: Orchard.

Hoberman, M. A. (1999). *And to think that we thought that we'd never be friends.* New York: Crown.

Hoberman, M. A. (1998). *Miss Mary Mack.* Boston: Little, Brown.

Joseph, J. (1992). *An island Christmas.* New York: Clarion.

Linden, A. M. (1992). *One smiling grandma.* New York: Dial.

Lowery, L. (1995). *Twist with a burger, jitter with a bug.* Boston: Houghton Mifflin.

Matura, M. (1989). *Moon jump.* New York: Knopf.

Medearis, A. S. (1994). *The singing man.* New York: Holiday House.

Mitchell, R. (1993). *Hue boy.* New York: Dial.

Mitchell, R. (1996). *Red Bird.* New York: Lothrop, Lee, & Shepard.

Nikola-Lisa, W. (1994). *Bein' with you this way.* New York: Lee & Low.

Peterson, J. W. (1994). *My mama sings.* New York: HarperCollins.

Pinkney, B. (1994). *Max found two sticks.* New York: Simon & Schuster.

Raffi. (1985). *Like me and you.* New York: Crown.

Raffi. (1988). *Wheels on the bus.* New York: Crown.

Raschka, C. (1992). *Charlie Parker played be bop.* New York: Orchard.

Reiser, L. (1996). *Beach feet.* New York: Greenwillow.

Robinson, M. (1993). *Cock-a-doodle-doo! What does it sound like to you?* New York: Stewart, Tabori, & Chang.

Sheehan, P. (1993). *Kylie's concert.* Kansas City, MO: Marshmedia.

Sloat, R. (1998). *There was an old lady who swallowed a trout!* New York: Holt.

Stow, J. (1992). *The house that Jack built.* New York: Dial.

Westcott, N. B. (1980). *I know an old lady who swallowed a fly.* Boston: Houghton Mifflin.

Williams, V. B. (1984). *Music, music for everyone.* New York: Mulberry.

Winch, J. (1996). *The old man who loved to sing.* New York: Scholastic.

Wiseman, B. (1993). *Little new kangaroo.* New York: Clarion.

Wolkstein, D. (1981). *The banza.* New York: Dial.

CHAPTER 4

SOUNDS OF THE LANGUAGE: SPEAKING AND LISTENING

RECOGNIZING PRESCHOOL STAGES OF LANGUAGE PRODUCTION

PROVIDING OPPORTUNITIES FOR CONVERSATION

LISTENING TO STORY READING/STORYTELLING

RECOGNIZING PRESCHOOL STAGES OF LANGUAGE PRODUCTION

Visitors to modern early childhood classrooms are often surprised by the amount of verbal interchange going on. The classroom is abuzz with talking. Children are conversing with one another about the new guinea pig in the science center. Children are role-playing the story *Cleversticks* with real chopsticks in the dramatic play center. Children are building a block apartment with a black paper roof in the block center for the Cassie character doll from *Tar Beach*. It is not what you would call a quiet classroom.

Visitors used to traditional classrooms where children are taught to sit down, be quiet, and learn may not realize that the best way young children learn—especially learn to speak—is by speaking and that teachers who are aware of this fact set up their classrooms to promote as much oral language as possible. These are teachers who agree with Buchoff's (1994) belief that "[o]ral language is the foundation for all literary experiences in the classroom. Common sense and research show that children's success in reading and writing depends upon a solid background in the development of oral language skills" (p. 26).

But oral language is much more than the foundation for literacy success. It is the key to children's own development and learning in preschool. Novick (1999–2000) reports one teacher as saying, "Language becomes a way to support children's power—their ability to deal with a peer, with conflict, with sad or scary feelings. Words empower them to express themselves—to handle life" (p. 70).

Assessing Children's Language Production

How do children learn these skills? They have teachers who have taken time at the outset to assess the language production of each child and to set up activities to help children develop these skills. A simple language checklist is all it takes to observe every child and determine how he handles spoken language. Figure 4.1 can be copied onto a file card for every child, filled out by observers from the classroom team, and used to decide what learning activities to set up.

Teachers may find from their observations that some children can accomplish most, if not all, of the checklist items, while others may rarely speak at all. Such uncommunicative children may simply be immature in their development, or they may come from a non-English-speaking background and are just learning English as a second language. Others may be fluent speakers at home but silent at preschool until they become acclimated to the new situation they find themselves in.

In fact, teachers often find that young speakers, no matter what their language background or how fluent they are at home, may progress through several stages of language production before they become fluent speakers in the classroom. These stages are described in Figure 4.2.

☑ **Spoken Language Checklist**

_____Listens but does not speak

_____Gives single-word answers

_____Gives short-phrase responses

_____Does chanting and singing

_____Takes part in conversations

_____Speaks in expanded sentences

_____Asks questions

_____Can tell a story

FIGURE 4.1
Spoken Language Checklist

Source: From Beaty (2002, p. 299).

(Permission is granted by the publisher to reproduce this checklist for evaluation and record keeping.)

Preproduction Stage

Helping Uncommunicative Children

For some young children when they first enter a preschool classroom, their initial response may be silence. Not only do they find themselves in a strange new language environment, but the noisy activity of 18 or more peers may be overwhelming. They may withdraw into themselves at first and spend their time observing the others and listening to their conversations, rather than speaking. Your principal task as teacher, assistant, or volunteer in this case is to help such shy or uncommunicative children to feel comfortable in the classroom, rather than involving them in speaking.

Mice Squeak, We Speak
(De Paola, 1997)
Louie (Keats, 1975)

In the beginning, you can do the speaking as you greet them upon arrival, show them where to hang their outside clothing, and offer them an activity of their own to pursue. Maybe they would like to make a puzzle or look at a book. Perhaps they would prefer to join another child in the block center or at an art table. How else can you help these children to feel accepted and welcomed? What about reading a book to one child at a time?

De Paola's (1997) very simple book ***Mice Squeak, We Speak*** shows three children—an African American boy, an Anglo-American boy, and an Asian American girl—listening to the sounds each different animal makes on separate

Preproduction Stage

When children first enter a strange, new language environment, they often respond by being silent. Children who are learning English as a second language often concentrate on what is being said rather than trying to say anything.

Transition to Production

When children have settled in and become more comfortable, they often begin speaking by giving single-word answers to questions.

Early Production

Children may respond to questions and activities in short phrases. They may be able to engage in simple conversations and even do chants and singing.

Expansion of Production

Children speak in expanded sentences, ask questions, tell stories, and carry on extensive conversations.

FIGURE 4.2

Stages of Language Production in Preschool

Source: Adapted from Teaching and Learning in a Diverse World: Multicultural Education for Young Children *(pp. 157–158) by P. G. Ramsey, 1987, New York: Teachers College Press.*

pages (e.g., "Cats purr"; "Lions roar"). One by one the child characters interrupt by answering the animal sounds with a loud rhyming response, such as "Mice squeak" with "But I speak!" "Horses neigh" with "But I say!" and "Parrots squawk" with "But I talk!"

If your young child listener likes the story, read it again, and this time you make the sounds for the animals. Can your listener say a word for each child character who "speaks" or "says" or "talks"? Another time have hand puppets representing several of the animals. Put one on your hand, and when you come to the page where that animal makes its sound, have the puppet say the sound. Let your child listener choose a puppet, if she will, put it on her hand, and when you come to that animal's page, have the child make her puppet say the sound. Often children who are still too shy to speak for themselves will speak through a puppet, especially if the speaking seems to be fun or part of a story or a game.

Another day, if the child is still interested in the story, invite a second verbal child to listen to the story along with the uncommunicative child. Each of your two listeners can choose an animal puppet to make its sound. If this activity catches on, bring in other books with animal sounds that your uncommunicative children can make through their puppets.

An older book with engaging child characters is Ezra Jack Keats's (1975) ***Louie***, in which inner-city cultural children characters put on a puppet show with "cone puppets," and the little nonverbal boy Louie is so entranced he speaks his first words to one of the puppets: "Hello." Your children can use the book's puppet illustrations to help them design paper "cone puppet" animals for their own "hello's" in animal talk (puppet body: a paper teepee; puppet head: a round cutout or Styrofoam ball).

Make your activities simple and fun for uncommunicative children. If they do not feel comfortable enough to make animal sounds, they can listen while you make them or while the other child listeners make them. For children who are not yet up to speaking in the classroom, they can gain a great deal by listening to others speak. In fact, all the children can gain by building listening skills through books like this and their follow-up extension activities. Choose the cultural character books you intend to use carefully, as discussed in chapter 1, with the idea of extending their use into as many classroom learning centers as possible.

It may take the uncommunicative child many days or even weeks to feel at ease enough in the classroom to speak. Using pressure to get him to talk may, in fact, produce the opposite results. Instead, show the child you accept him as he is with smiles, hugs, words of welcome and encouragement. Invite him to participate in the classroom activities, but if he refuses, you must honor his reluctance. Sometimes making friends with one other child can help the uncommunicative child become involved. Sometimes you and the others just need to be patient.

Helping Non-English-Speaking Children

Be patient with the non-English-speaking child as well. Can someone on the teaching team speak her language? If not, perhaps a family member or a student who is learning the language can visit and do a bit of speaking. If no one who speaks the language is free during the day, have them make a tape in their language of everyday expressions to be played for all the children to hear and learn some new words. You can supply the tape recorder and tape for an overnight recording.

For children learning English as a second language, it was once believed that their parents should learn English and use it with them at home rather than their native language. This is no longer the case. As Ramsey (1987) notes, "Current research suggests that it is better for parents to continue to speak to their children in their home language. . . .The more skilled children are in their home languages, the more able they are to learn a second language" (p. 159).

Educators are finally beginning to recognize the value of home languages that are different from English and to promote rather than discourage their use by children and their parents. The National Association for the Education of Young Children (1996, pp. 4–12) has issued a position statement responding to

Teachers need to be patient with non-English-speaking children, accepting their home language and helping them make the transition to English.

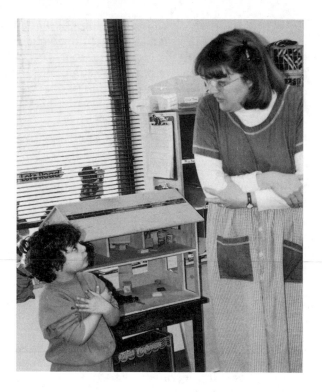

linguistic and cultural differences in early childhood education that includes some of the following recommendations:

1. Recognize that all children are cognitively, linguistically, and emotionally connected to the language and culture of their home.

2. Understand that without comprehensible input, second-language learning can be difficult.

3. Actively involve parents and families in the early learning program and setting.

4. Recognize that children can and will acquire the use of English even when their home language is used and respected.

5. Support and preserve home language usage.

Okagaki and Diamond (2000) report, "In 1991 38% of the three- to five-year-old preschoolers in our country who lived in homes in which a language other than English was the primary language participated in center-based early childhood programs." Kagan and Garcia estimated that by 2000, about five million preschoolers in the United States would be from families speaking a language other than English cited in Okagaki & Diamond (p. 77).

If the first language is Spanish for many of the children in your program, be sure to provide opportunities for all of the children to be exposed to the language in a natural manner. This does not mean you will be teaching Spanish.

Young children do not learn word meanings by having someone teach them; rather, they induce the meanings by hearing the words used in life experiences. Read books and sing songs in Spanish (see "Simple Picture Books in Spanish" at the end of the chapter). Do number games and dramatic play in Spanish. Children love to hear and say new words. Have their favorite chants and songs translated into Spanish. If you do not speak Spanish, invite a speaker from the children's families or a nearby high school or college. Your primary classroom language will still be English, but your use of some Spanish will not only help young Spanish speakers to make the transition to English but will also show respect for their home language.

Many Native American tribal groups are also promoting the use of the tribal languages in the preschool programs and Head Starts that their children attend. Picture books about Indian children written in English alongside the tribal language include those available from Oyate, 2702 Mathews Street, Berkeley, California 94702 (phone [510] 848-6700 for a catalog; see the list in the references section at the end of the chapter).

What if your program includes children who speak many different languages? Ramsey (1987, p. 160) describes a program attended by children of foreign students representing 15 different languages. The program rose to the occasion by requesting parents to help them make a book with simple sentences that the teachers needed to use in all 15 languages, such as "Your mother will be here soon," or "Do you need to go to the bathroom?" Then the parents and children enjoyed coaching the teachers on their pronunciation. This gave the foreign families who were having to experience daily their lack of expertise in English the opportunity to be the experts.

Acceptance of Ungrammatical Language

Are you also being careful to accept everyone's language in the classroom no matter how poorly it is pronounced or how ungrammatical it is? Language is a very personal thing, reflecting not only young children's differing stages of language development but also their families' backgrounds. Be especially careful not to correct a child's language. Telling him he is using a word wrong is a personal reproach against himself and his family. He will learn to correct himself when the time is right by hearing the word used correctly by you and others. In the meantime, uncommunicative children listen closely to how you deal with other speakers in the classroom. They need to hear you being accepting of everyone's speech.

Transition to Production

You will know when your formerly uncommunicative children have reached this stage of language production when they begin answering questions that you or the other children ask them. Have you noticed that they often start speaking by giving single-word answers

Mama, Do You Love Me? (Joose, 1991)

Yo! Yes? (Raschka, 1993)

to questions? When you recognize what is happening, be ready with some off-the-cuff question-and-answer games you can play with them. For instance, you might play a follow-the-leader game with several children, including reluctant speakers, in which you lead them around the room asking questions about objects you notice: "What do you see on top of the block shelf that is blue?" or "What has Carlos got hiding inside his garage?" or "What is Marta feeding her baby doll?" If they can't answer these questions themselves, can they ask Carlos or Marta for an answer? Make this a guessing game that is fun for all.

Cultural character picture books in which the characters ask a question are also excellent resources for children who are in this transitional stage to language production. In the vibrantly illustrated story **Mama, Do You Love Me?** a little Inuit girl challenges her mother with the title question, which her mother answers, "Yes, I do, Dear One." But this is not enough for the child, and she presses on with question after question ("How much?" "How long?" "What if . . . ?") to test the limits of her mother's love. For each question the girl asks, the daughter and mother are shown clothed on alternate pages in bright home-sewn dresses—a different one for every question. Each answer the mother gives involves the birds, mammals, and fish of the Arctic, some of them draped in colorful blankets as well.

Read this simple story to a few children at a time, including transition speakers, so they can see the pictures and try to put themselves in the same situation. How would they answer the questions if they were the mother? Next time you read the book, bring in some dresses in blue, purple, red, and green, and ask your listeners whether they can match the dresses in the book with the ones you have brought. Would they like to put them on and play the roles of mother and daughter? Bring several small blankets, too, and perhaps a fake fur cape, so that other children can pretend to be the animals as well. Let the children act out the parts as you read the story. Can one of the children wrap up in white as the polar bear, become "the meanest bear you ever saw," and scare the mother with his sharp teeth? You can reply simply in the mother's words of unconditional love for her daughter: "Still, inside the bear, you would be you, and I would love you." Reluctant players can watch and listen.

Cultural Character Concept

Not only does such a book give transition speakers numerous opportunities to develop their oral language by answering simple questions, but the book itself demonstrates the universal sentiment of mother love at its finest among people of a very different culture from mainstream America. All children can feel closer to these Native Alaskans of the north because of it. If you are prepared with props and dress-up clothes as suggested, some of your children may make this their favorite story by acting out the roles again and again. They may even make up their own game of Mama Do You Love Me? by asking and answering their own "what if I . . . ?" questions. For example, "What if I turned into a spider— would you still love me?"

Another way to help children to bring this story into their own lives is through dolls and puppets. An Inuit girl doll made to look exactly like the book character Dear One, holding her own little Inuit doll, is available commercially. Or children can pretend by using their own dolls. As you can see, this is not just another unit on Inuit life. Instead, the book and activities focus on a mother's love for her child, a common bond most of us share no matter where we live or which culture we come from. For children 3 to 5 years old, this is enough. They begin to understand that people who fish from boats called *umiaks* and wear snow boots called *mukluks* also have mothers who love them. For teachers of young children, this is a topic that can easily be incorporated into a unit on "the family," perhaps at the beginning of the year, as well as providing oral language practice for transition speakers any time.

A book that all children seem to enjoy and be able to repeat is **Yo! Yes?** a simple story with a huge picture of a child who is looking for a friend and one or two large words on each page. On one page is a picture of an African American boy who starts the story by saying, "Yo!" On the opposite page is a picture of an Anglo-American boy who responds at first with a hesitant "Yes?" Their simple one- or two-word conversation finally brings them together as friends. The book ends as it started, with a loud, "YO!" and "YES!" followed on the final page with a "YOW!" as the boys jump high together.

Have half of your group be one boy and say his words and the other half be the other boy and say his words. As you turn the pages, point to each group when it is their turn to speak in unison. If this book becomes a favorite, be prepared to have this conversation repeated in the classroom whenever children meet one another.

Early Production

Children who are at the early production stage of preschool language production often respond to questions in short phrases. They may be able to engage in simple conversations and may even be able to do chants and singing if they are comfortable in the classroom (see chapter 3). Second-language speakers may also have picked up enough English from the other children around them, so that they, too, will respond in short phrases and incomplete sentences. Be sure you accept any responses they give to your questions, whether in English, their home language, or gestures.

Is Your Mama a Llama?
(Guarino, 1989)
Does a Kangaroo Have a Mother, Too?
(Carle, 2000)

To help all the children develop their early production of language, you can use some of the strategies shown in Figure 4.3, "Teacher Strategies to Foster Language Production." You may already be using some of these natural responses as you listen closely to what beginning speakers are saying, and then add to or repeat their responses. In doing so, you validate what the child has said and encourage her to continue.

For example, if you ask Carla how she got to school this morning, and she answers, "Car," you can *expand* her answer by adding, "Oh, you came to school

---

1. **Expansion:** Respond to whatever a child says, but add a few more words to it.

2. **Extension:** Respond to a child's statement by adding more information to what was said.

3. **Repetition:** Repeat what the child says or what you as teacher have said.

4. **Parallel talk:** As you watch a child performing an action, you can describe aloud what she is doing.

5. **Self-talk:** As you perform an action, you can describe what you are doing.

6. **Vertical structuring:** After the child has said something, ask questions to encourage her to continue talking.

7. **Fill-in:** Structure what you say so that the child has to provide a word or words to complete your statement.

FIGURE 4.3

Teacher Strategies to Foster Language Production

Source: Adapted from "Conversing with Young Language Learners in the Classroom," by A. M. Kratcoski and K. B. Katz, 1998, Young Children, *53(3), 31.*

in a car this morning." To *extend* her answer, you might say "Yes, I saw the blue car you got out of." Or you might *repeat* her answer: "Yes, in a car." As you watch Carla playing at the water table, you might use *parallel* talk by describing aloud what she is doing: "Oh, Carla, I see you filling the squeeze bottle by holding it under water, squeezing it, and then letting go." You can become involved in the activity yourself, using *self-talk* to describe what you are doing: "See, I am filling another squeeze bottle the same way by holding it under water, squeezing it, and then letting go." If Carla now says, "Squeezing, squeezing," you can encourage her to continue talking through *vertical structuring* by asking a question: "Now what shall we do with our filled-up squeeze bottles?" If she answers by squirting the water into a cup instead of speaking, you can encourage her to use words through *fill-in*: "Yes, you are squirting the water into a _____."

You don't have to remember the names of each strategy to use them to encourage children's early production of language. These are descriptive terms to suggest strategies you might use with children. They may seem rather simple and perhaps even silly to an adult, but remember: young beginning speakers learn language by hearing it spoken around them. The more you can become involved in *what they are saying* and in helping them to expand their responses in this manner, the more they will pick up from you how words are pronounced and used.

Reading a picture book in which the main character asks a simple question is an excellent strategy to help young speakers with their early production of language.

If you don't understand the child's speech in the first place, try to pick up a word here and there and repeat it as an encouragement for her to continue speaking, rather than continually asking the child, "What did you say?" It often takes time for a teacher to become used to the different speech patterns and pronunciations of beginning speakers. The same is true for the children. They, too, may need time to get used to your spoken language. Be sure to speak slowly and clearly in simple sentences. You may also need to vary the tone of your voice to emphasize certain words.

Reading a picture book in which the main character asks a simple question is another excellent strategy to help young speakers with their early production of language. In **Is Your Mama a Llama?** a young llama goes around to various animals asking the title question. Each animal answers with the same simple words: "No, she is not," and then goes on to explain in rhyme what its mama is like. The llama then picks up the conversation, extending it in rhyme: "Oh," I said. "You are right about that. I think that your mama sounds more like a _____." Listeners must say the last word ("bat"), then turn the page to find out whether they are correct. They quickly catch on to what the fill-in word should be by seeing the illustration of the animal that is speaking, hearing the description of the animal's mother, and figuring out what rhymes with the last word in the llama's sentence (e.g., "bat" rhymes with "that").

In Carle's book **Does a Kangaroo Have a Mother, Too?** this question is asked to each animal without the aid of a character. The answer is in the same form for every animal (e.g., "Yes! A kangaroo has a mother: Just like me and you"). The opposite page shows an illustration of the animal and its baby. The title question is then asked once more about the next animal. Listeners must always turn the page for the answer. Although the story is much more simple than ***Is Your Mama a Llama?*** the youngest beginning speakers have a chance to repeat the same answer over and over, which may be necessary to get them started.

Both of these books support extension activities in various learning centers of the classroom if you have sets of little plastic animals (e.g., farm animals, zoo animals). After reading the books once or twice, let your listeners hold the various animals from the stories and answer the questions when it is their turn. Afterward put the animals in the block center, the sand or water tables, and the art center, and watch what happens. Children may pretend to be the animals and ask the title questions to other players. Advanced children may even paint an animal picture or model one in play dough. Can they make up a story about their animal?

Expansion of Production

On Mother's Lap (Scott, 1992)

Not Yet, Yvette (Ketteman, 1992)

Preschool children ages 3, 4, and 5 are at the ages when their speaking develops most rapidly. From the simple phrases they spoke earlier, they are suddenly able to expand into long, complex sentences. Even a month makes a difference, especially if other more advanced child speakers are a part of the group. Multiage grouping in preschool programs makes a great deal of sense if your goal is to improve children's speaking skills. The youngest speakers begin imitating the more mature speakers, while mature speakers have an opportunity to practice and improve their own speech. For this reason many preschools include children ages 3, 4, and 5 years together in the same class rather than segregating them into separate classrooms according to their age.

Just as beginning speakers can expand their language production through interaction with speakers more advanced than themselves, you need to use cultural character picture books a bit more advanced than the previous books discussed in this chapter with children whose language production is expanding. For instance, ***On Mother's Lap*** is a through-written story rather than a series of separate questions. Michael, a little Alaskan Native boy, wants to sit on his mother's lap and be rocked. But as he is rocked, Michael spies his toys around the room and asks Mother in simple sentences if they can be rocked, too. One by one he brings Dolly, Boat, his reindeer blanket, and his puppy. But when Baby cries and wants to be rocked, Michael says there isn't room. Mother replies, "Let's see," and soon they are all rocking together on Mother's lap—where there is always room.

Because this is a cumulative story with a new object being added every few pages, it also contains repetition. Once Michael is settled again with his new object, the story repeats: "Back and forth, back and forth they rocked." Soon your listeners should also be able to repeat this sentence themselves if you pause and give them a chance. Be sure to read this story at first to the individuals who need the language practice as determined by your initial observations.

If you have a rocking chair in the room, these children may eventually want to reenact the story with one child at a time "on Teacher's lap," rocking back and forth, but stopping to get their favorite toy as long as there is room. Thus, all your child actors will have another chance to use the language from the book just as Michael did.

Cultural Character Concept

Just as with the story *Mama, Do You Love Me?* here is another book that demonstrates mother love among people of a very different culture from mainstream America. All children can identify with Native Alaskan people who express this universal sentiment. Boys, especially, can appreciate the same unconditional love shown in *On Mother's Lap* as girls did in *Mama, Do You Love Me?* Since gender seems to be more significant than race to children of this age, as discussed in chapter 1, it is important for teachers to acquire a balance of cultural character books showing both boy and girl main characters.

In *Not Yet, Yvette* the main character is a young African American girl Yvette who is helping her father to arrange a surprise birthday party for her mother. Together they clean the house, bake a cake, buy presents, buy flowers, arrange the table, decorate the cake, decorate the room, and watch for Mother in rhyme. Almost every other minute impatient Yvette asks her father, "Is it time yet, Dad?" and he answers, "Not yet, Yvette. There's still more to do." Most children identify closely with someone like themselves who can't wait for an exciting event to happen. Whether this picture book character is of the same or a different race seems to make little outward difference. But if she happens to be of a different race, child listeners inwardly recognize yet another common bond they have with people from that race.

As children's language expands into more complex sentences, they enjoy contributing to the reading of such books as this by repeating Yvette's persistent question over and over. How many of them can recognize the proper place in the story to insert the next question as you read to them? Have one of the children be Yvette who asks the question at the proper time, and another be her father, who gives the repeated answer.

PROVIDING OPPORTUNITIES FOR CONVERSATION

The Basics of Communication

Young children's most important oral language-learning situations occur through the conversations they engage in or listen to with the children and adults around them. Most have already acquired the basics of communication as infants through their early interactions with parents and caregivers. Just as infants are predisposed to acquire language in a particular manner, they are also preprogrammed to extract and learn the rules of conversation naturally. Researchers have found that infants as young as 10 weeks are beginning to learn the behaviors necessary for conversation (Holzman, 1983). For example, to converse a speaker must first listen to what someone says, then respond, and finally pause for the other speaker to have a turn, before speaking again.

Mothers seem to be programmed the same way. They treat their baby's coos, cries, gestures, and babbling as meaningful contributions to a real conversation. When the baby reaches for her rattle and cries, the mother responds by handing it to her and saying, "Oh, you want your rattle. Here it is." The baby then shakes the rattle and smiles, looking at her mother for her next response. The mother then says, "Shake, shake your rattle. You like your nice rattle." The baby then shakes the rattle again and waits for another response. Thus, the rules for conversation are learned long before the child can speak (Beaty, 2002).

Speaking to infants should begin at birth or even before. Some parents think that because their baby cannot speak, it is not necessary for them to speak to the baby. Yet infants and young children learn to speak by hearing language spoken around them. Children coming to preschool from nonverbal families are at a greater disadvantage in learning language than those from highly verbal families.

Hart and Risley (1995) observed "a vast range in the amount the parent talked to the child [in 42 midwestern families], from a low of about 50 utterances per hour to a high of approximately 800 utterances per hour when the children were 11–18 months of age," resulting in important cumulative differences in children later on. They also found that "greater diversity in parents' language was associated with more rapid growth in children's vocabulary." Thus, some children may function at a lower level not because of any inherent cognitive limitations but because they have heard less language or less diverse language (cited in Okagaki & Diamond, 2000, pp. 77–78).

Teacher–Child Conversations

Your role as a teacher in an early literacy preschool program is to initiate daily conversations between yourself and each child in the class, as well as to set up opportunities for conversations among children. Be careful that the conversations you initiate are natural and not contrived—interesting for the children and not so-called "teaching situations." As Machado (1995) notes,

> Daily teacher-child conversations become amazingly easy when teachers focus on 'children's agenda.' Teachers defeat their purpose when the objective is always to teach, or add a new word to the children's vocabulary. The key is to identify the child's interests; words then become meaningful. (p. 269)

What are some of the things your children are interested in? Objects and activities that involve them personally are especially effective conversation topics. What about shoes or friends? Children's cultural character picture books featuring such topics can serve as motivators for ongoing conversations with children, as well as presenting interesting characters from different cultural backgrounds interacting with objects your children like.

Your role as a teacher in an early literacy program is to initiate daily conversations between yourself and each child in the class.

Conversations About Shoes

My Best Shoes shows a different cultural character on every page for each day of the week, using a different pair of shoes. On Monday an African American girl steps into high-laced shoes and twists back and forth. On Tuesday an Asian girl wears tap shoes to whirl and prance. On Wednesday an Anglo-American boy wears tennis shoes to skip and hop in a meadow. What are your children's favorite shoes? Do they see any shoes they especially like in this book? Read to individuals and small groups, and then start up a dialogue about shoes—the ones in the book or the ones they are wearing. Another day bring in a bag full of shoes after reading this book and have your listeners put them on and pretend to be the children in the story. Can they talk about why they chose certain shoes and how they felt wearing them? Uncommunicative children can listen to what others in your small listening group have to say and perhaps add a word or two of comment.

Fascinating conversations can arise from any book you read about shoes, since shoes seem to play such an important part in the lives of young children.

My Best Shoes (Burton, 1994)
New Shoes for Silvia (Hurwitz, 1993)

Have you noticed how they comment about their own shoes and those of others around them? **New Shoes for Silvia** takes place in a Central American town where Silvia receives a beautiful pair of red shoes from her Tia Rosita in North America. But the shoes are too big for her, and everyone in her family tells her to put them away until they fit her. Instead, Silvia uses them for doll beds, a two-car train, ox carts, containers for her shell collection, and finally for her own feet when they are big enough. What would your listeners do with shoes too big for them? Striking illustrations in each of these books can alert your children to differences in these people and their cultures yet also the common bonds all of them have regarding favorite objects like shoes (Pratt & Beaty, 1999).

Child–Child Conversations

Just as important for oral language learning as teacher–child conversations are the one-to-one conversations children have with one another. Teachers need to structure the classroom into learning centers where a few children at a time can interact or to set up situations that promote dialogues between the children. Child–child conversations may not happen frequently unless teachers are aware of their value. As Howard Shaughnessy, Sanger, and Hux (1998) note, "Regrettably, teachers in many classrooms do most of the talking, often communicating with 25 children simultaneously. This contrasts with the normal turn-taking flow of the one-to-one adult-to-child conversation prevalent in homes. Children have less opportunity to initiate conversations or discussions at school because the teacher too often controls the topic" (p. 35).

The reading of cultural character picture books to pairs of children can promote child–child conversations if teachers choose books featuring topics children are interested in, such as friends.

Conversations About Friends

I'm Calling Molly (Kurtz, 1990)
Jamaica and Brianna (Havill, 1993)

Conversations between two children about friends or friendships can be motivated when you read books about different cultural characters trying to find or maintain friendships. Read to two children at a time and then let them converse between themselves about what they think the characters should do or what they themselves would have done. After you have read the story more than once and the children are familiar with it, encourage your pairs of listeners to take the roles of the book characters and carry on their own conversations. You may want to look through the cultural character books discussed thus far to find two characters that converse with one another or use one of the books described here.

In **I'm Calling Molly** an African American boy Christopher phones Anglo-American Molly, his next-door neighbor, to ask her to come over and make gorilla stew. But Molly is busy making gorilla stew with Rebekah and won't come over. None of Christopher's numerous telephone calls to Molly work until

Rebekah's mom comes for her. Then Christopher does not need to call Molly, because Molly is calling him. Children enjoy pretending to be Christopher or Molly if you have a toy telephone for each of them to use. Encourage the callers to make up fantastic escapades to lure the other child over to their house, while the answerers make up just as outlandish excuses for not coming. If they can't think of any, you be the model.

In *Jamaica and Brianna* the friendship breaks down between the little African American girl Jamaica and her Asian American friend Brianna over the snow boots each must wear, not over their cultural differences. After reading this book, bring in several pairs of boots (including cowboy boots), and have the youngsters take on the roles of Jamaica and Brianna with plenty of conversation between them. How will they choose which boots to wear? Young children especially enjoy playing with shoes and boots as previously noted. Be sure to read this book to many pairs of children and give all of them, girls and boys alike, a chance to be Jamaica or Brianna and choose the boots. It is the boots, not the culture, that makes the difference to these children. And it is the boots that will often stimulate exciting dialogues between pairs of children.

Cover illustrations often give you a clue as to whether a book contains conversations. Books showing two children on the cover usually do. To decide on topics that will stimulate children's conversations, check out the "Topical Cultural Character Book Index" in appendix B with your children.

Cultural Character Books to Promote Conversations in Dramatic Play

Dramatic play for preschool children is completely different from formal dramatics in which children memorize lines and put on a play for others to enjoy. In preschool dramatic play children take on roles and do spontaneous pretending and speaking involving a theme or play situation that they have chosen. The "play" is for the actors themselves and not for an audience. The teacher's reading of a picture book with interesting cultural characters can be the stimulus for dramatic play situations in which the children's roles are based on characters from the book, and the "play" itself is based on either the plot of the story or an extension of that plot.

Going Home (Wild, 1993)

Tar Beach (Ringgold, 1991)

Bones, Bones, Dinosaur Bones (Barton, 1990)

If You Are a Hunter of Fossils (Baylor, 1980)

Dramatic play can take place in many different areas of the classroom. Children can take on pretend roles in the block center, the sand table, the music center, the large or small motor areas, and of course in the dramatic play center itself. As a stimulus for child–child conversations, Isenberg and Jalongo (1993) have this to say about dramatic play: "In dramatic play, younger children generate more verbal play and richer language than in any other setting, develop narrative competence by inventing stories that contain essential story elements, and display their knowledge of the functions of reading and writing" (p. 142).

Dramatic Play Center _____

This center is the location for much of the spontaneous pretending in most preschool classrooms. The center is most often set up as a kitchen with a child-size sink, refrigerator, stove, cupboards, table, and chairs. Some programs also set up a store with empty food containers from home on shelves, and a cash register for checkout on a table. Other possibilities can be a shoe store, a restaurant, a beauty/barber shop, or a doctor's clinic because children enjoy playing the roles of doctor and nurse. Youngsters are often frightened to visit the doctor and get a shot, so role play like this can be therapeutic, as well as an opportunity for a great deal of conversation among the players.

A picture book such as ***Going Home***, about a little Hispanic boy Hugo who is in a small children's hospital overlooking a zoo, can stimulate fine dramatic play while promoting a great deal of conversation. Hugo's female doctor and male nurse tell him that he'll be going home soon. Two other children, Simon and Nirmala, share Hugo's room. In the story Hugo hears animal noises from the zoo outside the window. He knows that the elephant is calling for him, so he puts on his "magic" slippers and slips away in his imagination for an exciting trip on the elephant's back across the African plains, which are illustrated in the book. The next time his family comes to visit, Hugo tells his little sister Cathy about his trip to Africa and gives her a paper elephant he has made.

In his next imaginary trip, Hugo follows a howler monkey through the Amazon jungle and afterward makes a monkey finger puppet for his sister. After his final trip to the Himalaya mountains on the back of a snow leopard, Hugo makes Cathy a leopard mask. Before he goes home, Hugo tells Simon and Nirmala the secret of the magic slippers so they, too, can journey to far off places while waiting for their parents to take them home. If the children like it, read the story over and over. Then ask them whether they would like to pretend to be Hugo and his friends.

You can set up your dramatic play center to look like a hospital room like Hugo's. Put three cots in a row with pairs of "magic slippers" under each cot. Hang animal posters on the wall. Put out doctor and nurse props such as stethoscopes and white shirts for doctors' and nurses' jackets. Bring in pajama tops for three children to wear over their clothes when they lie on the cots, pretending to be the children in the story. As you read the story, have the children on the cots close their eyes and try to imagine what Hugo sees on his trips.

Play a tape of animal sounds from a tropical rain forest cassette. Can the children imagine going on their own romp through the jungle with one of the animals they hear? Ask each one where they went on their pretend trip, and tape-record their answers. In the days to come, have everyone in class pretend to be Hugo and record the stories of their adventures. Some may want to act out the adventure they imagined with animal props such as animal masks or finger puppets. Leave Hugo's book in the dramatic play center for children to look at and pretend on their own.

Because Hugo's adventures in ***Going Home*** provide such good lead-ins to activities in several other learning centers, you may want to fill in an Extension Activity List. On the other hand, some teachers prefer to fill in a *curriculum web* of activities based on ***Going Home.***

Curriculum Web

Teachers can plan the entire curriculum for several weeks at a time around a cultural character book like ***Going Home*** if they brainstorm ideas with staff members and the children themselves by developing a *curriculum web* with Hugo's book at the center. Traditional curriculum planning seldom takes into account the children's on-the-spot interests. Yet children's burning interests are the best starting points for curriculum activities that promote children's conversations. Curriculum ideas from ***Going Home*** tend to sprout out in every direction, causing the teaching staff to jot them down on a curriculum web instead of a lesson plan. As you brainstorm together, you may come out with an open-ended curriculum web something like that shown in Figure 4.4.

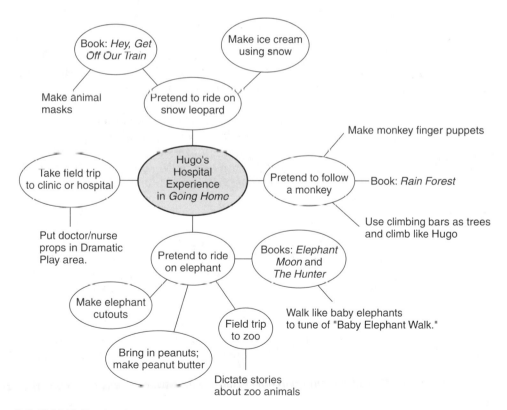

FIGURE 4.4
Curriculum Web for *Going Home*

How will these activities promote conversations? They will if you allow children to express their ideas during the brainstorming, as well as involving pairs of children in every activity so they can dialogue with one another. The Reggio Emilia preschools from Italy have become a model here in the United States for such verbal interactions, as noted by Cadwell and Fyfe (1997):

> A key component of the work in the Reggio Emilia preschools is dialogue— serious talk with children about their ideas about something of importance. . . . The teacher's role is to ask good, open-ended questions that stimulate children's thinking and provoke discussion—to facilitate, orchestrate, and gently guide so that the conversation does not stray too far from the subject, so that every child has a chance to participate, so that children consider the matter at hand with all their critical and creative thinking skills. (pp. 85–86)

When you create a curriculum from a cultural character picture book by including children in your on-the-spot planning, you are generating curriculum ideas where one thing leads to another. This is not the predetermined, carved-in-stone curriculum that most teachers are used to but an *emergent curriculum.* According to Jones and Nimmo (1994), "An emergent curriculum is a continuous revision process, an honest response to what is actually happening. Good teachers plan and let go. If you're paying attention to children, an accurate lesson plan can be written only after the fact" (p. 12).

Keep these activities going in each of the learning centers until all of the children get a chance to try them and repeat them as many times as they want. We realize that young children learn best by repeating activities and conversations over and over. They also learn more from activities that are personal, that focus on themselves. Pretending to be a book character like Hugo helps this to happen. If they are Hugo or Simon or Nirmala, they can almost feel what it is like to be in a hospital, or to hike through a jungle, or to ride on an elephant. Then they can talk about their adventures, learning to use the words they heard from the books, from you, and from each other.

Block Center

The block building area is another learning center where pretending can take place based on cultural character picture book themes. Your shelves of blocks and block play accessories will be pulled away from the wall and used to divide this area from the other learning centers, making it easy for children to choose and use independently. A flat carpet covering the floor makes it inviting for children to sit down and build. Blocks will be stored lengthwise on the shelves with cutout labels outlining the block shapes and mounted on each shelf, making it easy for children to see what is available and to return the blocks to their proper shelves during pickup.

Block accessories are important if we want children to build what they know about and do pretend play in this center. Accessories can include small cars, trucks, trains, planes, construction vehicles, and figures of people, including cultural families, community helpers and construction workers. Entire sets

The cultural character doll from Tar Beach *can invite children to participate in block building adventures.*

of block play people that include Anglo American, American Indian, Asian, African American, and Hispanic figures are available from educational supply houses (e.g., Constructive Playthings; phone: [800] 448-4115). Dollhouse furniture is also useful in children's buildings. Such small items can be stored in plastic bins with a picture label on the outside.

Other accessories can include traffic signs, plastic tubing, small boxes, and all kinds of animals: jungle, farm, forest, sea, zoo animals, and dinosaurs. Plastic animals from particular habitats—polar, mountain, desert, ocean, and grasslands—are also available. These are especially helpful in allowing children to create habitats that go along with those found in cultural character storybooks.

On the walls of the block center place colorful posters showing buildings, bridges, farms, zoos, airports, vehicles, construction sites, and so forth. Posters are available from educational supply houses and children's bookstores. Leave room for displaying photos of the children with their block buildings or on field trips. When you are reading particular books whose cultural characters can stimulate your children to do block building, be sure to mount the dust jacket from the book or a photocopy of the character on the wall of the block center.

Cultural Character Dolls

Now you are ready to have a book character invite children to participate in their building adventures. The picture book **Tar Beach** is an excellent starting place. A little African American girl Cassie is the main character and narrator of this story, the tale of her nighttime adventures on the black rooftop of her New York City apartment: her "tar beach." Whenever summer temperatures inside soar too high, her family and their neighbors retreat to the rooftop at night for a picnic. While the adults play cards, Cassie and her little brother lie on a mattress and look at the stars and the lights of the city surrounding them. But lying down does not satisfy

Cassie for long. Soon she is "flying" in her imagination above the George Washington Bridge, the Ice Cream Factory, and anywhere else she wants to go.

You will need a figure to represent Cassie. A Cassie doll is available from catalogs and stores that sell this book, or you can use a cloth doll or puppet from the cultural doll sets available at educational supply houses (e.g., Lakeshore Learning Materials; phone: [800] 421-5354; or Constructive Playthings; phone: [800] 448-4115). If you prefer to make your own paper doll Cassie figure, make a photocopy of her from the book, enlarge it to the size you want, and laminate it on a cardboard backing. To promote conversation, you need to have a character that talks. Dolls and puppets representing book characters can pretend to do this talking. Such cultural character dolls (sometimes called "persona dolls") also help to bring children back to the books as well as to extend the book experience through pretending with the dolls.

Whitney (1999), in her book *Kids Like Us: Using Persona Dolls in the Classroom,* has this to say about the dolls she uses, which can also be applied to the cultural character dolls this text uses:

> Kids Like Us dolls are special. They are not the same as the dolls found in the housekeeping area of many classrooms. Classroom dolls are usually babies, meant to be diapered and fed, and held as one's own baby in each child's imaginings. Kids Like Us dolls are not babies. They are the same age as your students. Each doll represents a real person and maintains its own identity. . . . They like hugs but do not want their hair pulled or their clothes taken off. The teacher sets the tone for this scenario of "real kids, just like us," and the children love to be part of it. (pp. 1–2)

To keep the children interested and involved in your cultural character dolls, you need to continue talking about Cassie, Hugo, and other book characters the children have come to know during the daily activities. For instance, you might say out on the playground, "How do you think Cassie would get to the top of the monkey bars?" Or during a discussion of an upcoming field trip: "Where do you think Hugo would take us on a field trip?" Book characters become real for young children. No matter what their culture, they become models the children may want to emulate. And because these characters often talk in the books and sometimes tell their own stories, children may try to do the same. As children's literature specialist Kiefer (1995) notes, "I found that picture books inspired imaginative experiences for children. Their language in response to picture books allowed them to participate in the imaginary world created by the author and artist or to create their own images. Younger children often 'chose' a character that they wanted to be as they read or looked through a book" (pp. 29–30).

Block people figures can also represent book characters. Any girl figure can represent Cassie whether or not you have a Cassie cultural doll. Bring your Cassie figure and the book **Tar Beach** over to the block area to read the book to a small group who have chosen to play with blocks during the free-choice period. Have a box of props with you to leave in the area after you have finished reading. Have Cassie pretend to read the story, since it is in the first person. If the children afterward would like to build Cassie's building and rooftop, tell them you will take their photo with their completed building later. Your props can include

> a square of black paper for the rooftop,
>
> a small rectangle of colored paper for Cassie's blanket,
>
> dollhouse furniture for the table and chairs, and
>
> figures of people representing the family and friends.

Pretend to be the Cassie doll yourself, showing the children the props and asking them how they would use them. Maybe they have better ideas on how to represent Cassie's tar beach. If some children prefer to build the George Washington Bridge, Cassie (you) might agree by helping them to cut out a blue river for their bridge to cross. Some children may even prefer to build the Ice Cream Factory. Will their buildings look like those in the book? No. Children's buildings tend to come from what they know, not what they see. Some children may not even be at the representational building stage. But if this is a group project, others will know how to "stack" and "bridge with blocks."

Cultural character dolls can also help you resolve racial discrimination problems such as Cassie's father encountered when he wanted to join the union. As Whitney (1999) notes, "Telling stories with your dolls will allow you to easily involve your students. . . . Being involved in discussions about stories enables each student to develop empathy and anti-bias attitudes. Doll stories are the perfect opportunity to gently correct incorrect beliefs or stereotypes your students may have picked up" (p. 5).

No matter what the outcome, Cassie's story should stimulate a lot of conversation. Listen to your children. If they are enthusiastic about constructing buildings like Cassie's, be prepared to follow up, perhaps by going on a field trip to a construction site or bridge, and by reading several other cultural character picture books about building, such as **Building a Bridge** (Begaye, 1993), **This Is My House** (Dorros, 1992), and **Road Builders** (Hennessy, 1994).

At some point you will want to brainstorm with the children and other staff members about extending this book into other areas of the classroom by creating a curriculum web for ***Tar Beach*** just as you did for Hugo's book, ***Going Home***. Figure 4.5 shows what one such web might look like.

How long you and your children spend on implementing these free-flowing plans depends on everyone's interests and enthusiasm. Involve as many classroom learning centers as appropriate as children pursue their ideas from Cassie's adventures on their own. At the same time, keep a record on cards of each child's accomplishments, especially their early literacy accomplishments in each of the classroom areas.

Accomplishment Cards

In a curriculum based on children and their accomplishments, evaluations should also be child based. Since a curriculum like this is ongoing and ever changing, the evaluation should also be ongoing. Be sure that staff members

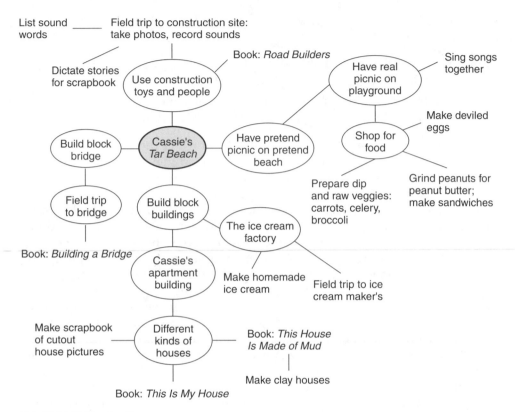

FIGURE 4.5

Curriculum Web for *Tar Beach*

observe and record the accomplishments of each individual child week by week. Individual children's cards can be kept in a pocket holder in each of the learning centers so that any staff member can add to them or start a new card whenever they observe an accomplishment (Beaty, 1997). What should they look for? Anything a child does in one of the areas of child development: social, emotional, physical, cognitive, language, or creative. Or if you are looking mainly for early literacy skills, then record any prereading, prewriting, speaking, or listening a child does.

Many programs use such cards in their weekly planning sessions to determine how things are progressing for the children and the curriculum. Changes in the plans for the following weeks make more sense when based on child observations like this. Filled-out cards are eventually kept in children's folders or portfolios. The accumulated cards can be used for conferences with parents, to share what their child is accomplishing. The dated cards also form the basis for developing an individual profile for every child in each area of child development.

Name: Ramon G.　　　　　　　　　　**Date:** 10/13
Learning Center: Block Center
Curriculum Web in Use: Cassie's *Tar Beach*

Built tall block tower every day.

Put toy figures of boys on his tower.

Made sign with his name for his building every day.*

Asked to have photo taken of his tower.*

Dictated story about his tower to student teacher.*

Looked at book *This Is My House* several times.*

Built cooperatively with Joel for the first time. (Good dialogue)*

*Early literacy accomplishments.

FIGURE 4.6
Accomplishment Card

In addition, the cards give the teaching staff an idea of how the learning centers are being used, and by whom. If few children are using the book center, for instance, the staff needs to consider making changes in the center to make it more attractive or useful. Figure 4.6 shows an example of an accomplishment card for Ramon (Dealy, 1997).

Sand Table

Any learning center of the classroom makes a good location for activities involving dramatic play dialogues about cultural picture book characters, depending on the theme or topic of the book. One classroom teacher chose the sand table to begin a project on dinosaurs because the children wanted to know what "extinct" meant. He felt that the sand table made an excellent exploration site for digging up extinct dinosaurs! Because children seem to love dinosaurs, such an activity could stimulate all kinds of discussion, conversation, and many spin-offs leading to other learning centers. Were there any cultural character picture books at his preschool children's level about searching for dinosaurs?

This teacher especially liked three simple concept books: ***Ten Terrible Dinosaurs***, a counting book; ***Dinosaur Roar!*** an opposites book; and ***Dinosaur Days***, a days-of-the-week book; as well as the storybook ***Sammy and the Dinosaurs***. These books showed wonderful dinosaurs but no digging. Then he found ***Bones, Bones, Dinosaur Bones*** with six cultural childlike characters who were diggers and assemblers of dinosaur bones, and he knew he had his lead-in book.

First the teacher buried 10 of the little plastic dinosaurs from his block center accessories in the sand table. Then he invited a small group of four children over to the sand table area where they all sat on the floor to hear the story *Bones, Bones, Dinosaur Bones* with a simple sentence of text on each double page: "We find them." "We dig them up." "We wrap them and pack them." The children were intrigued. Did they wonder what they were doing at the sand table instead of the book center? Not these children. They were used to being read to in all the different learning centers and seeing books-on-a-string everywhere in the classroom. This teacher realized it is important for children to connect reading to the world around them, and not just one location in the classroom. This particular story concluded with assembling the bones at a museum. Just as the children hoped, it was *Tyrannosaurus rex!*

Now it was the children's turn. Would they like to look for dinosaurs in the sand table? Of course! The teacher told them they could pretend to be "paleontologists" like the characters in the book and see what they could find. Big words like this intrigued the children, and soon 3-, 4-, and 5-year-old children were calling themselves "pa-le-on-TOL-o-gists." The teacher also provided them with props of little people figures and trucks from the block center and turned them loose. Conversations among the four children rose to an excited pitch as they dug.

Soon they had found all 10 dinosaurs and were reburying them, redigging them, and driving them around the sand table in the trucks. Finally the teacher asked them what kinds of dinosaurs they had found, and they began matching their dinosaurs with pictures in the book. Everyone had a chance to try pronouncing the "difficult" names of the dinosaurs.

Then it was the turn for the next group of four children to listen to the story and try their hand at digging and matching. Meanwhile, the teacher put out all of the dinosaur books he had obtained for children to look at in the book center, while he conducted the reading and digging operations for other groups at the sand table. Then everyone came together to brainstorm with the teaching staff ideas about what else they wanted to do with the topic "dinosaurs." Some children had already visited a dinosaur museum with their parents and wanted to go again with the class. Another thing they all agreed on was the need to create their own museum in the classroom and to make their own dinosaurs out of clay, play dough, or papier-mâché to be displayed in it. And the bones? One child brought in a science museum kit of dinosaur bones to be assembled.

Then the teacher found the book **If You Are a Hunter of Fossils** narrated as a first-person prose poem by an Indian girl who asks the listeners whether they are looking for fossils like she is. She then imagines a warm Cretaceous sea covering everything with the creatures swimming around that made the fossils. Finally she walks home with a fossil shell in her hand. The children loved the story and soon wanted to tell their own imaginary stories of the dinosaurs they had dug up in the sand table. And so it goes when children become enthusiastic with a hands-on activity that not only captivates their interest but also produces more excited conversations among children and teachers than anyone thought possible.

LISTENING TO STORY READING AND STORYTELLING

Children learn to speak by listening to the spoken language of those around them. They learn to read by listening to stories read to them. Such statements may be simplistic explanations for complex accomplishments, but nevertheless they are important beginning points in early literacy programs. Collins and Shaeffer (1997) call this "the look/listen" approach for learning to read: "The image of a young child enfolded in the arms of and being read to by a caring adult epitomizes the lap method, or look/listen approach. Not only does the experience support the child's growing sense of love and belonging, but it also lays the foundation for the beginnings of literacy" (p. 66).

Learning to Listen Through Story Reading

A Listening Environment

"Listening is the process used to convert spoken language and sound into meaning in the mind," says Jalongo (1996, p. 21). For this conversion to occur, children need to focus on what is being said and to filter out other extraneous sounds, noises, and distractions around them. In other words, teachers need to create a listening environment for book reading. This means the location of the reading needs to be away from noisy activities. The area needs to be comfortable for the small group you will read to. Have them sit on the floor on a soft rug or cushions. You need to join them at their eye level so they can see the book illustrations easily. Being too high above them or too far away breaks their attention and makes it more difficult for them to focus. Reading to individuals is different. You can sit in a chair and hold a child on your lap, or sit on a couch and have a child sit on either side of you.

Where Is Gah-Ning? (Munsch, 1994)
Carlos and the Squash Plant
(Stevens, 1993)
One of Three (Johnson, 1991)
The Other Way to Listen (Baylor, 1987)

Can't you read to the whole class at a time? Not if you want everyone's listening attention to focus on the story. Research finds that the children farthest

---

READING TO CHILDREN

1. Know your book well.
2. Make reading a personal experience.
3. Start with an attention-getting device.
4. Make your voice interesting.
5. Help children get involved through participation.
6. Talk about the story afterward.

from the book lose their attention. Furthermore, teachers seem to spend more time on trying to get and keep certain children's attention, while the rest of the group must wait. A small group or individuals are best for story reading in preschool. For a total group experience, *storytelling* works better. In kindergarten, reading for a total group can be appropriate.

Before Reading

Before you begin reading a book to the children, you must be well acquainted with the book yourself. Otherwise you may stumble over words and will not know important elements of the story that children should get involved with. You may not even know whether the story is appropriate for your children's age and listening level. What makes a book appropriate? For the youngest children, they need a character like themselves that they can relate to. They need a brief text full of action and repetition. You need to be able to turn the pages quickly and not stay on one illustration too long. The illustrations need to be eye-catching and interesting. If the text seems too long for your youngest children's attention but the character looks fascinating and the story is gripping, you may want to "read the pictures"—that is, tell what each illustration is depicting, instead of reading the too-long text.

As you familiarize yourself with the book ***Where Is Gah-Ning?*** you note that it is a humorous story about a strong-willed little Chinese Canadian girl who is determined to go by herself to Kapuskasing, a nearby town to go shopping. Her distraught father, a cook in a Chinese restaurant, is just as determined to stop her. But Gah-Ning starts out anyway, first on her bicycle, then on her roller blades, and finally with 300 balloons! Each time when her father rushes down the Trans-Canada Highway in his car until her finds her, he repeats the words "Don't go to Kapuskasing on your bicycle. Don't go to Kapuskasing on a bus. Don't go to Kapuskasing on a skateboard and don't go to Kapuskasing in a helicopter. Just don't go!"

You also note that the book is packed with exciting and colorful illustrations of Gah-Ning in her red, orange, yellow, and green clothes trailing bits of money, buttons, pieces of pine branches, and tiny toys as she zooms along. Is the text too long for 3-year-olds? It may seem to be until you realize that many of the pages are repetitions of the loud conversation the father has with Gah-Ning every time she takes off. You will also realize that children love the book and are captivated by the illustrations.

Make the reading of this book personal by reading it to a small group or one or two children at a time. They need to sit close to see the illustrations filled with tiny objects. And you need to be able to look up and direct comments or questions to each of them personally.

During Reading

The attention-getting device you start with will probably be the cover of the book showing the red-and-orange-clothed Gah-Ning on her bicycle pulling her little sister in her wagon with colored bits and pieces of objects fluttering every-where. Read children the title "Where Is Gah-Ning?" and then ask them where they think she may be going. Make your voice interesting as you read the con-versations between the characters, especially the father's with all of his ques-tions. If you have purchased a set of cultural character dolls from an educational supply company, choose the Asian doll to be Gah-Ning, and have the doll speak while you hold it, responding to the father's questions.

How can the children participate in the reading of this story? You may want to read it through the first time with no participation, other than one child hold-ing the Gah-Ning doll. If they like the story and want it read again, this time stop after every episode and ask them what they think Gah-Ning is going to do next.

After Reading

After the story is finished, talk about Gah-Ning's determination, her father's wor-ries, and the safety issues of riding a bike down the highway. Afterward let chil-dren play with the Gah-Ning doll, perhaps having it ride in a block center truck, or have them pretend to be Gah-Ning out on the playground. Do you have trikes they can ride and a balloon or two they can carry?

Be sure to talk about the story with the children after it is finished. Too many teachers put the book away as if that is all there is to story reading. *But just as important as the reading is the discussion of the book afterward,* another fine lis-tening activity. Talking about the characters helps to make them real. Talking about the story itself increases children's interest and understanding. In other words, reading a book to young children is just the beginning. Then you must talk about it and involve your listeners in talking about it as well. As the National Association for the Education of Young Children (1998) points out, "Children may talk about the pictures, retell the story, discuss their favorite actions, and request multiple rereadings. It is the talk that surrounds the storybook reading that gives it power, helping children to bridge what is in the story and their own lives" (p. 33).

If boys have trouble pretending to be Gah-Ning, a girl, they may like the next story better: ***Carlos and the Squash Plant***, the story of a little Hispanic boy who helps his father to raise vegetables in their field but hates to take a bath when he comes in dirty after work. His mother tells him that if he doesn't wash his ears, a squash plant will grow in them. But Carlos doesn't listen to his mother, and you know what happens. A squash plant actually begins growing out of his right ear, much to his embarrassment. He covers his head with his wide-brimmed straw hat and hopes nobody notices. By the end of the story, he finally washes his ears, and of course the plant shrinks away to nothing.

Large, colorful full-page illustrations of Carlos hold the children's atten-tion, but the text seems too long for many 3-year-olds. You may want to "read the pictures" to them, telling what happens rather than reading the words. Half the text on each page is in English and the other half in Spanish. You may want to have a Spanish speaker read along with you when you introduce this book. Have one of your boy culture dolls serve as the Carlos character, and let a boy listener

When you read One of Three *to a small listening group, have one of the children hold the cultural character doll they have chosen to represent "me."*

hold it while you read the story. Realistic cloth dolls with ethnic hair styles, skin colors, and bright clothing that reflect their heritage are exciting for both girls and boys to play with.

Culture Character Dolls to Facilitate Story Listening

The youngest children like dolls of any kind. Just as racial features do not seem to matter much in their choice of classroom playmates at this age, 3- and 4-year-olds will choose almost any doll to play with, no matter what their race or the doll's skin color. Five-year-olds begin to select more realistic dolls to go with the stories they are hearing. Such dolls bring children back to the storybooks again and again as indicated previously. Individuals may ask you to reread a story to them, or they may try to figure out what happens in the illustrations on their own, as they hold their doll character. Some of your boy listeners will be so attracted to the Carlos doll they may carry it around with them long after the story is finished. Caplan and Caplan (1974) say, "Dolls should be freely played with by boys without adult snickering or criticism. Homemaking play in childhood and housekeeping in adulthood require interchangeable participation of both female and male members of the family" (p. 224).

How can children participate in the reading of the Carlos book? Once they know the story, they can speak for Carlos every time he repeats his response to his mother's direction to take a bath before dinner—"Oh, Mama, do I have to?"—or when his mother repeatedly asks him if he took his bath—"Sí, Mama, I did." When you talk about this story afterward, ask the children if they think it was real. Can a squash plant really grow from someone's ear? Is everything we read in stories real?

This book is an excellent lead-in to planting squash seeds either inside in potting soil or outside in a garden. Cooking experiences can also be involved as Carlos eats sausages, cornmeal cakes, tortillas and honey, and calabacitas his mother cooks for him for breakfast or dinner. (A recipe for calabacitas appears on the last page.) Altogether **Carlos and the Squash Plant** is an excellent looking and listening experience.

The book **One of Three** has three inner-city African American sisters as characters: Eva, Nikki, and me. The "me" is the littlest of the sisters and also the narrator of the story. When you read this story to a small listening group, have one of the children hold the cultural character doll they have chosen to represent "me." If you have enough dolls you can have each of three listeners hold one. *One of Three* is a much simpler book than the previous two, with only one or two sentences on every other page describing what the three sisters like to do together in the city. Get your children's attention by asking them to guess who is Eva, Nikki, and me on the front cover. Whether or not your children are African Americans, they can easily identify with the sisters when they play together and then when they don't want the littlest sister tagging along. Afterward your listeners can extend the girls' adventures in your dramatic play center by playing with the "me" character doll, perhaps giving it a name.

Children's listening can be promoted as you read each of these books or any other books children may choose by setting *a specific purpose for the listening*. As Jalongo (1996), notes, "There is a useful distinction between listening *to* and listening *for* something" (p. 23). Children enjoy listening *to* a story being read, but you can enhance their listening skills by asking them to listen *for* something specific. For instance, in the Gah-Ning story, children can listen for the reason her father does not want her to go to Kapuskasing. In the Carlos story, children can listen for why squash was Carlos's favorite vegetable. In the one-of-three story, children can listen for what the little sister does when the two bigger sisters leave her behind.

Another Way to Listen

Many teachers also know of another way to teach listening skills: have children go outside to a quiet place, concentrate on one object, close their eyes, and listen. Take a small group at a time outside and first read to them **The Other Way to Listen** in which an Indian girl meets an old man who tells her he can hear the corn singing and a rock murmuring. She wants to learn how to listen like he does, but he tells her it takes a lot of practice and you have to have time. She tries and tries and finally cannot believe what she hears: "It came straight up from those dark shiny lava rocks humming. It moved around like the wind. It seemed to be the oldest sound in the world." Have the children concentrate on a natural object such as a tree or a bush or rock, close their eyes, and listen. Keep the silence as long as possible, and someone is sure to hear something. But perhaps, like the Indian girl, it won't be any sound you can explain, because it isn't made with words. "And that's all right, too."

Listening to Books on Tape

Another way to encourage listening to cultural character picture books is through audiocassettes: using headphones and a cassette recorder to hear the reading of a book. Your listening center can provide the headphones and cassette recorder while you provide the cassettes and copies of particular books. *It is absolutely essential that your children have access to the books themselves that are being read on the tapes* if it is your goal to bring children and books together. The book tape alone cannot perform this function. When children are able to see the actual pages of the book as they hear the story being read and to control the turning of a page when they hear the signal, they are experiencing more than a listening activity. They are also learning how a book works, an important prereading skill.

Headphones are essential to give each child the personal listening experience of hearing the story, as well as preventing the recorded story from disturbing other children. If you have several headphones available connected to a station junction box and then to the cassette recorder, it is possible to have several children listen to the same tape at once. In this case you will need several copies of the same book so each child can follow along as the cassette is being played. The reduced price of paperback copies makes it possible price-wise for programs to order more than one of each book. To make more books available to everyone, classrooms can also trade books.

Order both paperback books and tapes through a company such as Lectorum, "the best in children's literature in Spanish and English for grades pre-K–8." Phone for a catalogue: (800) 345-5946. Its address is 205 Chubb Avenue, Lyndhurst, New Jersey 07071-3520.

You can easily produce cassettes for books that have none available. Simply record your careful reading of the story onto a blank tape. As you turn each page, make a signal (e.g., tap a glass with a spoon) so that children following along will know when to turn the page. Obviously prereaders are not yet following the text and so need a signal of some kind to alert them to the page turning. When children are using the tapes on their own, check to see whether they can keep up with the recording by turning the pages.

Do not put all of your tapes and books out at once. This is not, of course, to be considered an entertainment center. Instead, place only a few of the tapes and books in the listening center, especially ones you are featuring or have featured in the curriculum. Keep a record of which children listen to which books. Do they finish the tapes? Find time to talk with them about their listening. What

Storytelling is different from story reading because the teller can concentrate on the audience and tailor the story to the children's attention span. Sometimes children also participate in the telling.

did they like about the story? Do they listen to the same story over and over? Since listening to books on tape is not the same or as personal as hearing them read by a teacher, be sure that you also read these books to individuals and small groups.

Learning to Listen Through Storytelling

Live storytelling is different from story reading in several significant ways: the teller does not read from a book but instead relates the story extemporaneously. The audience is more important than a book; therefore, the teller can concentrate on the listeners rather than on the words in a book. The teller's eyes are on the audience rather than on the pages of a book; thus, the attention of a large group is possible. Tellers are often more aware of their listeners' reactions than readers are, so they can tailor the story to children's attention span and interest. Tellers can make stories come alive with their body language, gestures, and facial expressions. Most tellers of stories are thus more animated than readers, and children love this. As Zeece (1997) points out, "They are able to shape stories to child and situation-specific needs and to their own personalities. . . . Eye contact is more intense and the resulting rapport captivates listeners and engages them in the storytelling process in unique and personal ways" (p. 39).

Coyote: A Trickster Tale from the American Southwest
(McDermott, 1994)
Juan Bobo Goes to Work
(Montes, 2000)

Storytellers obtain their stories from many sources: their own experiences, stories they have read, stories others have told, and stories they have made up, to name a few. As a storyteller in a preschool program, one of your best sources is the picture books in your book center. You will be learning the story by heart and telling it without the book, but afterward the children can look at the book and remember the story you told. In other words, *tales told from books bring children back to the books afterward.* Bringing children together with books is one of the chief goals of an early literacy program, you recall, and children appreciate the books even more when they recognize them as the source of your tale telling (Beaty, 1994).

Folktales

Folktales have long served the purpose of expressing the traditions, beliefs, and hopes of a culture. Oral tales often relate where the people came from or how they came to look the way they do. Such tales may describe the feats of folk heroes and tricks of wily animals, as well as the hopes and dreams of ordinary people. Today many of these traditional tales appear in children's picture books. Using such books with your children and their families not only helps your children to develop listening skills but also creates a cultural bond between school and home. As Hopson and Hopson (1993) point out, "Folktales, we think, demonstrate that whatever our skin color or cultural background, we share many if not all the same values that from the dawn of humankind have enabled civilization to progress. Offering stories is a subtle yet effective way of teaching children that the rainbow generation of the twenty-first century has much to appreciate, enjoy, and share" (p. 146).

This belief in the power of folktales can also be applied to establishing a contact with children's parents and families, so necessary in promoting early literacy. Make it a point to tell folktales from many cultures. Lend folktale picture books for children to take home and share with their families. When families realize you are interested in their culture, they may be willing to share folk stories that they know.

Have a weekly story time when you invite outside storytellers to share a story with the children. Invite family storytellers to have lunch in the program and then tell their story. You may want to start with humorous folk stories that feature animals as well as children tricksters.

Preparing for Storytelling

Coyote: A Trickster Tale from the American Southwest is a humorous animal tale in which the blue coyote is a trickster who gets tricked himself by a flock of crows when they try to teach him to fly. Read **Coyote** to yourself several times until you know what comes next. Then practice telling it to your own family or even to a mirror without using the book. You may want to make a brief outline of the incidents in the story to help you to remember them. For instance, the coyote tale has the following incidents:

Sticks nose into badger's hole. Gets bitten.

Tries to get a flaming red head like woodpecker. Fur catches on fire.

Looks for snake. Finds trouble.

Tries to fly with crows. Loses balance and falls.

Tries to fly again. Falls in water and dirt after crows take feathers back.

Telling the Story

Children will love hearing your tale if you make hand, arm, and head gestures for coyote's blundering actions. You will enjoy telling the story because of your children's rapt attention. You will not have to depend on the book or its illustrations to tell the story. Later children can look at the pictures in the book and laugh over the coyote's antics, which they already know so well from your telling of the story. You will realize how successful you have been when the youngsters beg you to "Tell it again, Teacher!" (Beaty, 1997).

Storytelling like this is best done for the total group. It is a good listening experience for all of them as they have their eyes glued on you and your gestures. Make your voice sound different for different characters. If your listeners seem restless, you can whisper to make them listen more closely. Folktales lend themselves to storytelling especially well because they often follow a formula of one incident leading to another, thus making it easier for a teller to remember.

In the story ***Juan Bobo Goes to Work***, a foolish boy disappoints his mother by bringing home his pay exactly the way he shouldn't. Jot down these incidents:

The farmer pays Juan a few coins for his work.

Juan puts the coins in his pocket, but they fall out through the holes.

The farmer pays Juan with a pail of milk for his work.

Juan pours the milk into a burlap sack, and it all drips out.

The grocer pays Juan a large hunk of cheese for his work.

Juan carries the cheese home on his head, but it all melts.

The grocer pays Juan a large ham for his work.

Juan ties the ham with a string and drags it home with dogs and cats following.

A rich man's sick daughter sees Juan and laughs so hard she is cured, and Juan is rewarded.

Tell your listeners to speak for Juan's mother when you raise your hand, saying, "Ay, Juan, What will I do with you?" You may want to act out this story yourself in the middle of your story circle of children, pretending to be Juan bringing home his "pay." Once the children know the story well enough, one of them can pretend to be Juan. Would one of them like to try telling the story, too?

If children want to hear certain stories over and over, they may enjoy telling the story themselves to a small group, the total group, or even to a few friends. Children who are shy about storytelling can have one of the cultural character dolls or puppets tell the story. Some children even like to have their doll tell a story to another doll! Let them make up their own stories about the characters if they choose. Tape-record children's storytelling so they can listen to it later.

Such stories not only develop listening skills but also build bridges between cultures. Such oral telling by you, the children, and their family members demonstrates to everyone the common bonds we all enjoy.

SUMMARY

This chapter discusses the development of speaking and listening skills, first by helping teachers assess children's spoken language; then by recognizing the four stages of language production demonstrated by preschool children. Activities from cultural character picture books help uncommunicative as well as non-English-speaking children to develop speaking skills. Conversations between teachers and children and children with other children are promoted, using such books as a stimulus. Pretend play in the dramatic play center, block center, and sand table also stimulates conversations when planned book activities are devised on curriculum webs. Children's literacy accomplishments are recorded on individual accomplishment cards. Finally, story reading, books on tape, and storytelling are presented in an environment that promotes listening skills.

LEARNING ACTIVITIES

1. Tell why it is necessary to assess children's spoken language skills at the beginning of the year, and describe how you would do it.
2. How would you help uncommunicative children to speak, and what could you do to help non-English-speaking children become verbal in English?
3. What opportunities for teacher–child and child–child conversation are present in your classroom? How can you promote such conversations using cultural character books? Try it and record the results.
4. Create a curriculum web focusing on one of the books discussed here, and use an idea from the web to stimulate conversation in one of the classroom learning centers. Record the results.
5. Have one of your cultural character dolls *tell* a story to the total group based on one of the books discussed here. Record the results.

REFERENCES

Beaty, J. J. (1994). *Picture book storytelling.* Fort Worth, TX: Harcourt.

Beaty, J. J. (1997). *Building bridges with multicultural picture books.* Upper Saddle River, NJ: Merrill/Prentice Hall.

Beaty, J. J. (2002). *Observing development of the young child.* Upper Saddle River, NJ: Merrill/Prentice Hall.

Buchoff, R. (1994). Joyful voices: Facilitating language growth through the rhythmic response to chants. *Young Children, 49*(4), 26–30.

Cadwell, L. B., & Fyfe, B. V. (1997) *Conversations with children.* In J. Hendrick, (Ed.), *First steps toward teaching the Reggio way.* Upper Saddle River, NJ: Merrill/Prentice Hall.

Caplan, F., & Caplan, T. (1974). *The power of play.* New York: Doubleday.

Collins, N. L., & Schaeffer, M. R. (1997). Look, listen, and learn to read. *Young Children, 52*(5), 65–68.

Holzman, M. (1983). *The language of children.* Upper Saddle River, NJ: Merrill/Prentice Hall.

Hopson, D. P., & Hopson, D. S. (1993). *Raising the rainbow generation: Teaching your children to be successful in a multicultural society.* New York: Simon & Schuster.

Howard, S., Shaughnessy, A., Sanger, D., & Hux, K. (1998). Let's talk! Language in early elementary classrooms. *Young Children, 53*(3), 34–39.

Isenberg, J. P., & Jalongo, M. R. (1993). *Creative expression and play in the early childhood curriculum.* Upper Saddle River, NJ: Merrill/Prentice Hall.

Jalongo, M. R. (1996). Teaching children to become better listeners. *Young Children, 51*(2), 21–26.

Jones, E., & Nimmo, J. (1994). *Emergent curriculum.* Washington, DC: National Association for the Education of Young Children.

Kiefer, B. Z. (1995). *The potential of picturebooks: From visual literacy to aesthetic understanding.* Upper Saddle River, NJ: Merrill/Prentice Hall.

Kratcoski, A. M., & Katz, K. B. (1998). Conversing with young language learners in the classroom. *Young children, 53*(3), 30–33.

Machado, J. M. (1995). *Early childhood experiences in language arts: Emerging literacy.* Albany, NY: Delmar.

National Association for the Education of Young Children. (1996). NAEYC position statement: Responding to linguistic and cultural diversity—recommendations for effective early childhood education. *Young Children, 51*(2), 4–12.

National Association for the Education of Young Children. (1998). Learning to read and write: Developmentally appropriate practices for young children. *Young Children, 53*(4), 30–46.

Novick, R. (1999–2000). Supporting early literacy development: Doing things with words in the real world. *Childhood Education, 76*(2), 70–75.

Okagaki, L., & Diamond, K. E. (2000). Responding to cultural and linguistic differences in the beliefs and practices of families with young children. *Young Children, 55*(3), 74–80.

Pratt, L., & Beaty, J. J. (1999). *Transcultural children's literature.* Upper Saddle River, NJ: Merrill/Prentice Hall.

Ramsey, P. G. (1987). *Teaching and learning in a diverse world: Multicultural education for young children.* New York: Teachers College Press.

Whitney, T. (1999). *Kids like us: Using persona dolls in the classroom.* St. Paul, MN: Redleaf

Zeece, P. D. (1997). Bringing books to life: Literature-based storytelling. *Early Childhood Education Journal, 25*(1), 39–43.

SUGGESTED READINGS

Cobb, J., & Rusher, A. (1996). "Grand conversations" with multicultural books. *Dimensions of Early Childhood, 24*(3), 5–10.

Garcia, E. E., & McLaughlin, B., (Eds.). (1995). *Meeting the challenge of linguistic and cultural diversity in early childhood education.* New York: Teachers College Press.

Genish, C., & Dyson, A. H. (1996). Ways of talking: Respecting differences. *Child Care Information Exchange, 110,* 43–46.

Karweit, N., & Wasik, B. (1996). The effects of story reading programs on literacy and language development of disadvantaged preschoolers. *Journal of Education for Students Placed at Risk, 1*(4), 319–348.

Kirk, E. W. (1998). My favorite day is "Story Day." *Young Children, 53*(6), 27–30.

Rioja-Cortez, M. (2001). It's all about talking: Oral language development in a bilingual classroom. *Dimensions of Early Childhood, 29*(1), 11–15.

Turner, T. N., & Oaks, T. (1997). Stories on the spot: Introducing students to impromptu storytelling. *Childhood Education, 73*(3), 154–157.

Wolf, D. P. (1996). Children's conversations: Why are they important? *Child Care Information Exchange, 110,* 40–42.

CHILDREN'S BOOKS

Ashley, B. (1991). *Cleversticks.* New York: Crown.

Barton, B. (1990). *Bones, bones, dinosaur bones.* New York: HarperCollins.

Baylor, B. (1980). *If you are a hunter of fossils.* New York: Simon & Schuster.

Baylor, B. (1987). *The other way to listen.* New York: Simon & Schuster.

Begaye, L. S. (1993). *Building a bridge.* Flagstaff, AZ: Rising Moon.

Buchanan, K. (1991). *This house is made of mud.* Flagstaff, AZ: Rising Moon.

Burton, M. R. (1994). *My best shoes.* New York: Tambourine.

Carle, E. (2000). *Does a kangaroo have a mother, too?* New York: HarperCollins.

Cowcher, H. (1988). *Rain forest.* New York: Farrar, Straus & Giroux.

DePaola, T. (1997). *Mice squeak. We speak.* New York: Putnam's.

Dorros, A. (1992). *This is my house.* New York: Scholastic.

Guarino, D. (1989). *Is your mama a llama?* New York: Scholastic.

Havill, J. (1993). *Jamaica and Brianna.* Boston: Houghton Mifflin.

Hennessy, B. G. (1994). *Road builders.* New York: Viking.

Hurwitz, J. (1993). *New shoes for Silvia.* New York: Morrow.

Johnson, A. (1991). *One of three.* New York: Orchard.

Joose, B. M. (1991). *Mama, do you love me?* San Francisco: Chronicle.

Keats, E. J. (1975). *Louie.* New York: Scholastic.

Ketteman, H. (1992). *Not yet, Yvette.* Morton Grove, IL: Whitman.

Kurtz, J. (1990). *I'm calling Molly.* Morton Grove, IL: Whitman.

Le Tord, B. (1993). *Elephant moon.* New York: Doubleday.

Manning, L. (1993). *Dinosaur days.* Mahwah, NJ: BridgeWater.

McDermott, G. (1994). *Coyote: A trickster tale from the American Southwest.* San Diego, CA: Harcourt Brace.

Montes, M. (2000). *Juan Bobo goes to work.* New York: HarperCollins.

Munsch, R. (1994). *Where is Gah-Ning?* Buffalo, NY: Firefly.

Raschka, C. (1993). *Yo! Yes?* New York: Orchard.

Ringgold, F. (1991). *Tar beach.* New York: Crown.

Scott, A. H. (1992). *On mother's lap.* New York: Clarion.

Stevens, J. R. (1993). *Carlos and the squash plant.* Flagstaff, AZ: Rising Moon.

Stickland, P., (1997). *Ten terrible dinosaurs.* New York: Dutton.

Stickland, P., & Stickland, H. (1994). *Dinosaur roar!* New York: Dutton.

Wild, M. (1993). *Going home.* New York: Scholastic.

Whybrow, I. (1999). *Sammy and the dinosaurs.* New York: Orchard.

SIMPLE PICTURE BOOKS IN SPANISH

The paperback books here are from Scholastic, PO Box 7502, Jefferson City, MO 65102; phone: (800) 724-6527. An asterisk indicates that Big Books are also available.

Carle, E. *La oruga muy hambrienta (The Very Hungry Caterpillar)* RZM43105*

Franco, B. *Beto y Pedro* RZM29306

Freeman, D. *Corduroy* RZM44194

Keats, E. J. *Un dia de nieve (The Snowy Day)* RZM93772*

Krauss, R. *La semilla de zanahoria (The Carrot Seed)* RZM45092*

Levin, J. *Ayudar (Helping)* RMZ29365*

McQueen, L. *La gallinita roja (The Little Red Hen)* RZM44927

Nikola-Lisa, W. *Llega la noche (Night Is Coming)* RZM46220

Rey, H. A. *Jorge el curioso en el hospital (Curious George Goes to the Hospital)* RZM47113

Sendak, M. *Donde viven los monstruos (Where the Wild Things Are)* RZM9005213

Tafuri, N. *Has visto a mi patito? (Have You Seen My Duckling?)* RZM45152*

Tello, J. *Amalia y sus primera tortillas (The New Batch)* RZM29381*

PICTURE BOOKS IN NATIVE AMERICAN LANGUAGES

Order from Oyate, 2702 Mathews Street, Berkeley, CA 94702; phone: (510) 848-6700.

Ahenakew, F. (1990). *Wisahkecahk flies to the moon.* (In Cree and English)

Children of La Loche (1990). *Bryon through the seasons.* (In Navajo and English)

Cutland, B. (1999). *The little duck.* (In Cree and English)

Keeshig-Tobias, L. (1996). *Emma and the trees.* (In Ojibway and English)

Thompson, S. (1994). *Cheryl's Potlach.* (In Navajo and English)

PART 3

EMERGENT WRITING

Children can discover how to write if adults stimulate and encourage them to do so. Writing, the act of expressing thoughts by means of written symbols, is a mysterious process. No one understands exactly how we learn to do it, but it appears that we learn to write at least as much by discovering as by being taught. Learning to write is largely an act of discovery.

Temple, Nathan, & Burris (1993)

DEVELOPING EYE–HAND COORDINATION

STRENGTHENING EYE–HAND COORDINATION THROUGH THREE-DIMENSIONAL ART ACTIVITIES

STRENGTHENING EYE–HAND COORDINATION THROUGH COOKING ACTIVITIES

STRENGTHENING EYE–HAND COORDINATION THROUGH WOODWORKING ACTIVITIES

STRENGTHENING EYE–HAND COORDINATION THROUGH THREE-DIMENSIONAL ART ACTIVITIES

For young children to make writing marks with a writing implement, they need to have the finger strength to hold the implement, the small-motor control to direct movements of the implement, and coordination between vision and hand movements to make the implement do what they want. This calls for eye–hand coordination, an ability that develops through maturity and strengthening of the fine muscles of the fingers, hand, wrist, and arm, as well as practice using a variety of implements.

Many activities in most preschool learning centers are set up to provide such practice: manipulating blocks in the block center; sorting and stacking items in the manipulative center; painting with brushes in the art center; using a computer keyboard and mouse in the computer center; using rhythm instruments in the music center; using squeeze bottles in the water table; as well as making puzzles, using a tape recorder, inserting pegs in a peg board, and using a paper punch to count items, to name a few.

This chapter focuses on three learning centers in particular that provide finger-strengthening activities especially conducive to promoting the eye–hand coordination needed for learning to write: the art center, the cooking area, and the woodworking center.

As Schickedanz (1999) notes, "Fine motor development involves the skillful use of the fingers in manipulating different objects." She goes on to say:

> As long as the movement of the writing or drawing tool comes from movement of the muscle in the upper arm, the marks the child makes will be relatively large and crude due to the great distance between the pivot and the point of the writing tool—the child is unable to control the movements very well. When the child holds the writing tool in her fingers, the point of control is much closer to the end of the writing tool, and the child is able to make smaller marks. Making controlled movements and precise lines is usually difficult for many young children, given their fine motor limitations. (p. 112)

Assessing Children's Eye–Hand Coordination

It is crucial that preschool children have many experiences with various sizes, shapes, and weights of finger-held objects that they must manipulate or move. Their success in controlling these items strengthens their muscles and sets the stage for their eventual success in controlling writing implements. Because a class of preschool children is at various levels of maturity and experience in using such items, it is necessary to determine where each child stands in his eye–hand coordination at the beginning of the year. Using an observation checklist such as the one in Figure 5.1 helps teachers and staff make such de-

✓ **Eye-Hand Coordination Checklist**
_____ Cuts with scissors
_____ Cuts with a knife
_____ Strings beads
_____ Weaves, twists materials
_____ Molds play dough, mud, clay
_____ Stirs batter with large implement
_____ Handles cooking tools (egg beater, etc.)
_____ Pours liquids without spilling
_____ Pounds nails with hammer
_____ Holds, uses writing implements

(Permission is granted by the publisher to reproduce this checklist for evaluation and record keeping.)

FIGURE 5.1
Eye–Hand Coordination Checklist

terminations. Copy the results onto file cards for each child, and use them to decide what learning activities to set up.

Three-Dimensional Art Activities

Three-dimensional art activities give young children excellent practice in strengthening the small muscles and in developing eye–hand coordination. They can include paper cutting, bead stringing, weaving, simple sewing, quilting, twisting materials, and molding play dough, mud, and clay. As an art form, three-dimensional materials also have a unique place in the development of children's creativity. Edwards (1997) notes, "Three-dimensional art provides children with a multitude of possibilities for making complex shapes from a main body of materials. Unlike painting, which is only seen, three-dimensional art can be touched, felt, and viewed from a variety of perspectives" (p. 201).

Best of all, these activities can tie in with the cultural character approach endorsed by this text. Anglo-American people, Hispanic people, American Indian people, Asian people, African people, Caribbean people, Pacific islanders, and many others all practice three-dimensional art as a part of their cultures. To put children in touch with such activities puts our children in touch with these cultures. We remember Boute and McCormick's (1992) affirmation: "Multicultural ideas are 'caught' rather than 'taught'; that is, multicultural attitudes are developed through everyday experiences rather than formal lessons. Multicultural ideas and activities, therefore, should be thoroughly integrated throughout all activities every day—not only in fragmented units" (p. 140).

As noted previously, we have found that story reading from cultural character picture books is one of the best lead-ins to cultural activities in every learning center of the classroom during every day of the year. Once again, it is up to teachers, of course, to choose books that will excite their children's interest in pursing three-dimensional art activities because the cultural characters they hear about are engaged in them. The chapters of this text will continue to provide cultural character book examples currently available for teachers' integration into an everyday curriculum. At the same time, a curriculum using such books can be focused on the development of early literacy among preschool children.

Cutting Paper with Scissors

Helping Beginners

Gilberto and the Wind (Ets, 1963)

Pablo's Tree (Mora, 1994)

Joseph Had a Little Overcoat (Taback, 1999)

Young children who have not used scissors before can learn with your help. First, you must provide *sharp* right-handed and left-handed scissors. Five-inch, blunt-end scissors with rubber handles are best for beginners. Pointed scissors are for older, experienced preschoolers and kindergartners. Show the children how to hold the scissors with their favored hand, and have them open and close them until they can do it easily. Then hold a narrow strip of paper taut between your two hands for the child to practice cutting in two.

As Cherry (1972) notes:

> Cutting looks easy. The child readily understands the principle of opening and closing the scissors, and he will frequently spend long periods of time trying to master the technique. Tiny, immature finger muscles are not so easily directed to move in the manner necessary to guide and control the opening and closing. The ability to control the arm muscles develops from the shoulder downward. It reaches the extremities only after the other parts of the arm and hand have developed. (p. 126)

If children are unable to make scissors work as they should, have them spend time playing with squeeze bottles in the water table or art center; with foam balls, sponge balls, or other squeezable balls in the large-motor center; and with snap blocks, strings of pop-end plastic blocks, and snapping or buttoning dressing frames in the manipulative center to strengthen their hand and finger muscles. When they have developed enough finger strength, let them practice cutting up scraps of paper. Try cutting the paper yourself to make sure it is easy to cut. Some paper is too thin or too thick. Poster paper and butcher paper are good for beginners.

A Cutting Table

Set up a cutting table for everyone's cutting practice. Put out several pairs of scissors along with different kinds of paper scraps and other items to cut: wallpa-

If children are unable to make scissors work the way they should, have them use squeeze bottles in the art center to strengthen their fingers.

per, old greeting cards, drinking straws. They can also cut up colored ribbons into small pieces for confetti. Once children have learned to control the scissors, have them cut out pictures from old magazines or catalogs. This requires cutting around the outside of a picture, another good practice. Have them start cutting around large pictures at first and then smaller ones. Accept anything they produce. At first they may inadvertently cut the pictures in two or leave large uneven borders. Eventually, with control they will be able to cut out fairly even pictures. Anything they produce can be pasted in a group scrapbook, as part of a collage, or in a personal scrapbook or journal.

Once the children have developed the skill of cutting out pictures, have them try tracing around objects with a crayon or marker onto colored construction paper and then cutting out their tracings. Can anyone do it? Have them start with large, easily traceable objects at first—for instance, unit blocks of different sizes and shapes, large round and square plastic covers, plastic dishes from the dramatic play center, a hand mirror, shoes. Help them, if necessary, by holding down the objects they are tracing. Ask them what else they would like to trace and cut out. Some will want to trace their hands, a much more difficult task in both the tracing and the cutting.

Keep the cutting tables going as long as the children show interest. As their cutting skill develops, challenge the children with smaller items to trace and cut out from file cards, wrapping paper, or stationery. Whatever the children produce can be mounted on paper of a contrasting color and displayed as a collage on the classroom walls. Be sure to date and have the children sign all of their work to show the progression of their eye–hand development. Later place it in individual assessment portfolios for parents, staff, and the children themselves to look at with pride. As Cherry (1972) notes, "Learning to use scissors is one of the important ego-building achievements of early childhood. The child discovers that scissors give him instant power to make changes in paper and other materials" (p.126).

Cultural Character Books as Lead-Ins

When children find they can use their cutting skills to make items that are a part of their favorite stories, they can't wait to get started. A good book to begin with is **Gilberto and the Wind**, the classic story of the little Hispanic boy Gilberto who challenges the wind to fly his kite, sail his toy boat, twirl his pinwheel, and blow his bubbles up into the sky. This is a book to read on a windy day when children can go outside like Gilberto and experience the wind face to face. Would they like to take a pinwheel outside with them? With your help they can make one.

They will need a square of paper ($8\frac{1}{2} \times 8\frac{1}{2}$) made from a typing sheet, a straight pin, and a drinking straw. Have them take the square of paper and fold it in two on the diagonal; then open it and fold it in two on the other diagonal. When they open the paper, they will see two diagonal fold lines across the paper running from one corner to the opposite one and crossing in the middle like an X. Now they must put a round small object (e.g., a nickel, penny, or bottle top) in the center of the paper where the folds cross and trace around it (with your help, if necessary.)

Now for the cutting. To make the arms of the pinwheel, they must cut very carefully along each fold line from the corner of the paper up to the line of the circle in the center, making four straight line cuts altogether, outlining four triangles attached at the center. If they cut too far into the circle at the center, the triangles of paper will become detached from the square and be unusable. They will need to fold and cut another square.

The last step requires your help, so work with only a small group of children at a time. Put the square of paper on the table. Take hold of the outside right-hand corner of each triangle one at a time and bend it over until its corner touches the center of the circle. Keep it held down with your finger until all four corners are touching the center of the circle (under your finger). You can easily see the shape of the pinwheel if you have bent (not folded) the arms into the center correctly. Finally, insert a straight pin through the four corners at the center of the paper and through one end of a drinking straw. Bend down the pointed end of the pin and tape it to the straw to keep the pinwheel attached. The pinwheel is now ready to be tried in the wind. First have the child who is holding it try to spin it by blowing at it like Gilberto does. If this works, she can go outside and try it in the wind. If the wind is too strong and blows the pinwheel apart, try making another one with stiffer paper, or wait for a gentler breeze.

As the first group of children is making the paper pinwheels, a different staff member can be reading the *Gilberto* story to a second small group. When the first group takes their pinwheels outside, the second group can begin making their pinwheels, while still a third group listens to the story. When the children return to the classroom, you may want to tape-record their stories about their own experiences with pinwheels and the wind. Would they like to hear the book story again and compare their experiences with Gilberto's? Keep the book on a string near the cutting table for the children to enjoy during the days to follow. Someone is sure to want to make one of the other items Gilberto plays with in the wind. How about a kite?

Small kites are simple to make by having children trace and cut around the kite-shape design you have drawn on poster board or stiff paper. Two or three long strips of thin paper can be cut out for a tail. Staple a length of string to the middle of the kite and the paper-strip tail to the back end. Children may want to paint or color their kites before testing them in the wind. Afterward they may want to hear their tape-recorded stories about their pinwheel experiences before tape-recording new stories about their kites in the wind. Even the older children should be able to identify with 3-year-old Gilberto. Gilberto was not always successful with his wind toys. Do any of your children have suggestions for what he should have done or what they would have done?

A Birthday Tree

Another story about a Hispanic boy, this one 5 years old, that can lead your children into cutting activities is **Pablo's Tree**, mentioned in chapter 1. It is a tender story about the close relationship between an adopted boy and his grandfather, Lito. After Pablo comes home as a baby, the grandfather buys a tree, plants it, and decorates it—with a different surprise every year on the boy's birthday. On this, his fifth birthday, Pablo goes with his mother to spend the night at Grandfather's to see the new birthday decorations and reminisce about his other four birthdays around the tree. For the pages of text that seem too long for your youngest children, simply skip over them or "read the pictures" (i.e., tell them what is happening in the pictures).

The story is an excellent lead-in to another paper-cutting project in which children make cut-paper decorations and hang them on their own "birthday tree" in the classroom. The tree can be a large tree mural on a bulletin board with the decorations stapled on, or a large bare tree branch set in a planter, or a real tree from a garden store. Leave the tree standing so that every time the children celebrate a birthday, you can read them this story and have them make new cut-out decorations to be hung on the tree in honor of the birthday child.

Bring in small colored napkins or doilies that the children can fold in two and then in two again. Have them cut out different shape holes in each side, cut off corners of the napkins, and then open them up into "snowflakes." Another

Children can cut out new decorations to hang on Pablo's Tree every time someone celebrates a birthday.

time curl over and tape two sides of the doilies together to make paper lanterns. What other ornamental shapes can the children create for other birthdays? As children become skilled cutters, bring in more difficult-to-cut paper such as colored foil for their decorations. Cut-paper birthday trees like this are a fine substitute for the often overused piñata. Don't forget to have the children reminisce each time about the earlier tree decorations made for their own birthdays. Some children are sure to request particular decorations when it is their turn.

Making Something Out of Nothing

An entirely different culture is featured in the book *Joseph Had a Little Overcoat*. Joseph is a Jewish farmer in an old-time village in Poland, and this story is based on the Yiddish folksong "I Had a Little Overcoat," which appears on the last page. Colorful folk-type characters populate the pages front to back with a simple line of yellow text at the top and Joseph in his many garments center-stage. "You can always make something out of nothing" is the moral of the tale, and Joseph demonstrates this by converting his old and worn overcoat first into a jacket, then a vest, then a scarf, then a necktie, then a handkerchief, then a button, and, finally, a book!

Children will want to sit close as your read this story to put their fingers into the cutout holes in the book pages or to guess what Joseph is going to make next. Read to individuals or two children at a time. Your listeners can then join in the act by tracing inside the clever cutout holes shown in every other page of the book onto sheets of wallpaper. Have them choose the wallpaper style they want, then put the sheet between the pages of the book, hold it still, and trace around the cutout of the jacket, the vest, the scarf, the necktie, the handkerchief, and finally the button to be used in a book of their own.

Can anyone trace and cut out such a tiny thing as a button? Can they then cut out their own tracings from the Joseph book and paste them onto blank pages of their own books they will be making? As you note, it takes practiced cutters to complete this fascinating task. You may need to help. Or ask the more skilled cutters to assist the beginners. Children may then want to dictate for you to write down their own stories about "making something out of nothing." And of course, everyone will want to sing the song. Amazing what one book can bring to children in a classroom that welcomes such creativity, isn't it? Listening, cutting, tracing, pasting, helping, book composing, singing, learning a moral, and identifying with another culture—all at the same time! Emergent literacy always gets a boost when teachers involve children in book extension activities like this.

Lakeshore (PO Box 6261, Carson, CA, 90749; phone: [800] 428-4414), the educational supply house with an exceptional selection of cultural character dolls and puppets, now also features a clever 21-inch Joseph-Had-a-Little-Overcoat storytelling doll with all the parts of the overcoat that come apart and can be put back together again. Children love dolls like this, taking off the coat and turning it into a jacket, a vest, a tie, a handkerchief, and a button over and over. They can use the doll to act out the story as you read it, make up their own version, or have the doll tell his own story.

Stringing Beads

Another excellent small-motor activity to help strengthen little fingers is bead stringing. Beads seem at first like such a simple item to deal with until you become involved in the creative and complex world of modern beading. As Reid (1997) notes on the flap of her children's book *A String of Beads*:

A String of Beads (Reid, 1997)

Two Pairs of Shoes (Sanderson, 1990)

White Bead Ceremony (Watkins, 1997)

> Counted, sorted, traded, worn—beads are pretty to look at and even more fun to handle. Find them at the seashore or in a pasta package. Mold them out of clay or dye them with food coloring. Combine them in a pattern or string them all the same. Ancient or new; store-bought or homemade; animal, vegetable, or mineral—beads are little pieces of the world that tell us their histories in fascinating fashion.

The girl who narrates the story *A String of Beads* along with her grandma is Anglo-American, while the children and people who fill the pages, making and wearing the beads, are from cultures as fascinating as the beads themselves. What is it that makes a small colorful roundish item a bead, your children may wonder? The girl tells us:

> "It's the hole that makes a bead a bead, isn't it?" I ask Grandma.
>
> "You bet," she says.

"When were beads invented?" I ask.

"Beads are as old as the hills," she answers.

"That means nobody knows," I say, and we both laugh.

Children seem to find it easy to follow stories like this consisting of a dialogue between two people. Large colorful illustrations against a black background make the characters in the story stand out as vividly as the beads. The girl and her grandma have fun sorting their beads first by color, then by shape. Then they talk about what the different kinds of beads are made of and how they were used by Native Americans and ancient Egyptians. But in the end it is the stringing of their own beads into necklaces, bracelets, and anklets that matters most, as well as the making of beads from pasta and clay. And who loves to wear all the things they make? Everybody!

Your manipulative center should be full of beads and bead-making materials when you read this story. Most preschools already have sorting materials such as buttons and small counters. Commercial wooden or plastic beads from educational supply companies come in all sorts of traditional shapes: disks, spheres, cylinders, cubes, spools, and ovals. Others called shape beads may be stars, cars, hearts, or butterflies. Still others may be transparent beads, number beads, or alphabet beads. Sizes range from jumbo and giant to tiny. To string them there are sturdy lacing cords as well as various-colored cotton bead laces with plastic tips for easy stringing.

This is where your bead-stringing activities should start. Let children experiment with the commercial beads in the manipulative center before making their own beads. They should put together and take apart beads of all sizes and shapes. The youngest children do best with large wooden beads, but let them try any that you have. Then, as you read or tell stories involving beads from cultural character books you can expand the bead experience into making beads and stringing them into necklaces or wrist or ankle bracelets that they can take home.

Indian Beads

Two Pairs of Shoes is a contemporary Indian story about a Cree girl whose blind grandmother makes her a beautiful pair of moccasins beaded with flower designs for her birthday. Do any of your children have moccasins with beaded designs? Outside of the Indian culture many beaded objects are machine made rather than handmade. What other wearing apparel is decorated with beaded designs? Sweaters? Belts? Children may want to bring in examples to share with the class. Because the tiny seed beads used for making these decorations are difficult for preschoolers to string, and the sharp needles used are not appropriate, it is better for children this age to admire these designs rather than trying to make them.

The book **White Bead Ceremony** tells the story of how Mary Greyfeather, a little Shawnee girl, gets her Native American name at a home ceremony where she is also given a white bead necklace. Lengthy pages of text make the story too long for preschoolers, but the plot is an important one for young children to hear, and the large, sensitive illustrations of a contemporary Indian family done with great humor, make this a fine book for reading the pictures. As the old women relatives gather in Mary's home to offer their suggestions for her name, it is discovered that the aunt who was to bring the white bead necklace cannot come because her car has broken down.

Grandma Greyfeather saves the day by stringing a hundred beautiful white buttons from Momma's button box onto a string of dental floss. Mary is given the name Wapapiyeshe, a horse-name meaning "white-necked, moving." Scattered throughout the story are illustrated cards containing Shawnee words with their English equivalents. Four pages of such cards at the end of the story can be cut out and played with so that anyone can learn some words in Shawnee.

Cultural Character Concept

Like many modern Indians, Mary's family lives the life of a contemporary American family in a modern home in town, while still maintaining its Shawnee traditions. It is important for educators to read books like this showing Indians wearing clothing and living in homes like most of the listeners do, while still respecting the old ways. Have your children talk about the idea of maintaining a family's culture. Does this happen in their families? As Indian educator Winona Sample (1993) notes:

> Teachers can enjoy teaching about Indians in a general manner, while respecting tribal differences and noting: "This is a Chippewa story," or "Some Navajo Indians live in hogans and some live in houses in the city." Keep the contemporary life style viewpoint in the forefront but bring in the past, which is still a part of Indian life. . . . Most Indian children live in two worlds: it is hoped that concerned adults will help them live in the best of both worlds. (p. 40)

Your children should enjoy stringing their own necklaces from a large container of buttons. They can sort out the buttons first by color, size or shape, if they want. Buttons can come from family sewing supplies or craft stores. Ask families to save or collect buttons, and then invite them to a button-stringing bee to help the children make necklaces. Beading has become such a popular craft that many cities have stores devoted solely to beads. If a bead store or craft shop is available, take your children on a field trip there, and let them select the beads they would like to string for their own necklaces or bracelets. Afterward they may want to find out what their beads are called by matching them with the ones in *A String of Beads* or in the adult book *The History of Beads* (Dubin, 1995) with its outstanding color photos of beads from 30,000 B.C. to the present.

Another day have children make their own beads. To make pasta beads purchase pasta in various shapes, four little bottles of food coloring (red, yellow, blue, green), four bottles of alcohol, and a quart jar with a lid. Fill the jar with pasta. Pour one bottle of food coloring into each bottle of alcohol and mix well. Pour a bottle of the colored alcohol over the pasta. Close the lid and shake until all the pasta is colored. Drain and save the colored liquid for the next batch. Spread out the pasta on newspapers to dry. Prepare other batches with the remaining colors and alcohol (Allen, McNeill, & Schmidt, 1992, p. 45).

Beads can also be simply made from drinking straws. Bring in several boxes of colored straws and have children cut them into piles of bead sizes for stringing. For strings use shoelaces, string, cord, or yarn. To string beads with cord, string, or yarn use a plastic yarn needle, or purchase bead laces with plastic tips.

Literacy Concept

How is bead stringing related to early literacy? It most directly involves helping children strengthen eye–hand coordination and the fine muscles of the hands and fingers needed for holding and using a writing implement and for turning the pages of a book. Inserting the end of a lacing string into bead after bead improves the perceptual/motor abilities of all young children. But as noted by Trawick-Smith(1997), "A great deal of variation in fine motor competence will exist among children in a typical child care or preschool setting. Some will require assistance, others little. . . . A 4-year-old can now skillfully use vision to guide hands in drawing. A 5-year-old can turn the pages of a small book while looking at pictures and print" (pp. 256–257).

Bead stringing and the other eye–hand experiences discussed in this chapter can benefit all of the children, whether or not they need the practice, since such activities also promote creativity as well as bringing children closer to the book characters from the various cultures they are becoming acquainted with. With some children there may be another cultural aspect to their fine motor development. As Trawick-Smith continues, "Identical fine motor abilities emerge in children of all cultures. However, the ways these skills are used in play or learning activities vary significantly. In cultures where writing and drawing are not common, for example, children are unlikely to learn a pencil grip or other fine motor activities which are common in the American preschool" (p. 258).

Quilting and Sewing

Luka's Quilt (Guback, 1994)
My Grandmother's Patchwork Quilt
(Bolton, 1994)

The idea of children actually making a quilt is one not usually considered as a three-dimensional art activity in preschool. But when an exceptionally fine cultural character picture book features quilt making as its theme, then preschool teachers need to take note and, if they favor the book, find a way to integrate some part of this activity into their curriculum. Such is the case with the book *Luka's Quilt*, the story of a little Hawaiian girl Luka and the traditional Hawaiian quilt her grandmother, Tutu, makes for her. Brilliant cut-paper collage art covers every page of the book, drawing the reader inexorably into the colorful Hawaiian island life of Luka and her family.

Luka picks out the green backing material for the quilt. Then she must wait patiently while Tutu covers the quilt completely with stylized cloth flowers. Luka, who thinks the flowers will be in the bright colors of their garden flowers, is crushed when she sees that the quilt flowers are all white. Tutu is hurt when she realizes that Luka does not like her quilt. After that, the two of them don't have much to say to one another when Tutu takes care of Luka while her parents are at work.

Then the two go on a picnic in the park where children are learning to make leis, Hawaiian flower necklaces. Luka is delighted. All of the other children string one kind of flower into a lovely lei, but Luka strings flowers of every kind into her lei. Tutu disapproves until she realizes it is Luka's necklace, not hers. Later Tutu surprises Luka by making a quilted cloth-flower lei of different colors just like the one Luka made from real flowers. Best of all, the two of them are friends again.

Traditional Hawaiian quilt designs are made of appliquéd whole cloth, often white, sewn onto a contrasting one-color cloth background. The intricate cutout designs, made to resemble stylized flowers from the tropical rain forest, somehow look like cut-paper snowflakes the children already know how to make. They are actually made in the same way. As noted by Zinn (1997), "Designs are cut from one piece of fabric that is folded in eighths. Generally two colors of cloth are used, one for the appliqued design and a contrasting value or hue for the background. Row after row of quilting stitches echo out from the appliquéd design like gentle ocean waves" (p. 119).

Hawaiian quilts are a blend of two cultural traditions: American quilt making and the ancient Hawaiian art of making *kapa* cloth from the inner bark of the paper mulberry tree. Your children can bring this cultural tradition into their classroom if they choose to make small "Hawaiian quilt" blankets for their doll beds out of colored burlap. Help them to measure their doll beds for the quilt size, to draw the size lines on the burlap with chalk; and to cut out the burlap along the lines. Then have the "quilt makers" fold squares of white paper (or another contrasting color) into fourths and cut it into "snowflake" designs as they did for *Pablo's Tree*. They can then sew their snowflakes onto the burlap with simple stitches using yarn and a yarn needle. One or two stitches should be enough to fasten the design to the "quilt," and you can help to tie off the yarn on the underside of the burlap.

How do they feel about their doll quilts compared to Luka's feeling about her quilt? To see exquisite colored photographs of real Hawaiian quilts as well as those made by the women of 25 different Indian nations, bring in the large adult book *To Honor and Comfort: Native Quilting Traditions* (MacDowell & Dewhurst, 1997). Can any of the children's families bring in a handmade quilt of their own? Can they tell a story about how it was made? Perhaps the children can respond by telling their own quilt-making stories and recording them on tape cassettes.

A Different Tradition

Another children's quilt book is **My Grandmother's Patchwork Quilt**, a story about a doll quilt the author's grandmother made when she was young. Every page shows a photo of one of the patches, cleverly sewn with a farm animal: rooster, dog, cat, sheep, goat, pig, goose, horse, cow, and owl. Although animal duplicating patches

Children can cut out patches from wallpaper samples and sew them to burlap with yarn.

come with this book, sewing like this is too advanced for most preschool children. They can make their own patches, however, for their own doll quilt using a piece of burlap cloth and wallpaper patches.

Again bring in several pieces of colored burlap cut to the size of doll quilts. You may need to fold under the borders and sew them so they won't unravel. Children who wish to create a quilt can cut out patches from different wallpaper samples (home improvement stores will give you wallpaper sample books to keep). Then thread a large plastic needle with colored yarn and show each child how to make a big stitch through the material that will sew their wallpaper patches to the burlap as you did with the Hawaiian quilt (Beaty, 1997).

Weaving

Abuela's Weave (Castenada, 1993)
The Goat in the Rug
(Blood & Link, 1990)

A different kind of "quilt" altogether is described in **Abuela's Weave**, the Guatemalan story of Esperanza and her grandmother Abuela. Abuela teaches her granddaughter to weave a beautiful traditional tapestry on a backstrap loom as your children will see in the brilliantly colored paintings of Mayan Indian village life. The story is written for somewhat older children, but yours can appreciate the sensitive illustrations of the girl and her grandmother, who take their woven work to market in the city as you tell the story or "read the pictures." Because Abuela has a birthmark on her face, some people will not buy her wares. But this time Esperanza herself sells everything because of the beauty of her elaborate weaving. Afterward, discuss with the children whether someone's looks should prevent people from buying their weaving.

Introduce children to weaving by having them practice the over-and-under concept with strips of colored paper or thick rug yarn to develop eye–hand coordination. A good beginning activity is using a paper plate cut with an odd number of slits that radiate like spokes out from the center. Knot one end of the yarn and catch it in a slit near the center of the plate. Then children can wind the yarn over and under the paper panels, pushing the yarn down firmly as they go. As they come around a second time, the yarn automatically alternates with the first row. Children can choose several different colors to make designs (Haskell, 1979, pp.62–63).

Later you can make a simple cardboard box loom by cutting an equal number of slots on opposite sides of an open box and stringing string or yarn across the open end of the box and around the slots. Then cut long narrow strips of colored construction paper, and have the children weave them over and under the strings across the top of the box, starting every other row above or below the first string. Be sure the strips of paper are pushed close to one another. When the weaving is finished, tape the vertical warp strings to the weft strips closest to the ends of the box so that the weaving can be removed from the loom.

Thick rug yarn can also be used instead of paper strips, with tongue depressors used as "weft sticks" to raise up every other warp string so the rug yarn can be passed through to the other side. Commercial weaving sets are also available (try Constructive Playthings, phone: [800] 448-4115).

A Different Kind of Weaving

For a different kind of weaving experience, bring in yarn and plastic berry baskets (have families save them for you). Thread several plastic yarn needles with yarn of different colors and tie the end of a strand to each basket. Then the child weavers must pull the yarn over and under through the plastic slats of the baskets. Show them how to pull each strand tightly before starting another round. Children can make their baskets as simple or elaborate as they want with different colors of yarn. It is not necessary for them to cover the whole basket with weaving—only as much as they want (Beaty, 1997).

The book **The Goat in the Rug** tells the story of how the Navajo weaver Glenmae weaves the wool from her goat Geraldine into a rug. It is a first-person story, or rather a first-goat story, narrated by the goat Geraldine. Every step of the process is simply described from a goat's perspective, including the gathering of wild plants to make colored dyes for the yarn. But of course Geraldine thinks these yummy plants are for her and so she eats them. Various plants from the Navajo country are illustrated, telling what colors of dye they produce. Children can be involved in dyeing their own yarn by boiling onion skins for brown or using Kool-Aid for pinks and purples (Booth, 1997, p. 81).

Cultural Character Concept

Children ages 3, 4, and 5 often have a difficult time understanding other cultures in other countries. They are still trying to figure out their own neighborhoods. Thus, it is not necessary or appropriate to "teach" preschoolers about the Navajos or about Guatemala. Instead, your focus should be on the book characters: Glenmae and Geraldine, or Abuela, the grandmother and Esperanza, the girl who tells that story. Although she is older than they are, they too can learn to weave, not Guatemalan-style, but in their own style, thus creating a bond between children from other countries.

Twisting Materials

Galimoto (Williams, 1990)
Dragonfly's Tale (Rodanas, 1991)
The Zunis (Flanagan, 1998)

Children in different cultures have often invented their own three-dimensional constructions. Can yours do the same? In the book ***Galimoto*** Kondo, a clever boy from Malawi, Africa, creates his own toys. This story concerns his search for the materials to make a *galimoto*, a "motor car" out of wires. Kondo's brother, Ufulu, laughs at him because he is too young to make such a toy car, and anyway he doesn't have enough wire. Off goes Kondo to trade his knife for more wire, to talk his uncle into giving him packing crate wire, and to scrounge wire from trash piles. Soon he has enough to make his galimoto—a fine truck. Tomorrow he may turn it into an ambulance or a helicopter.

How creative are your children? After hearing you tell this story, or reading the pictures because it may be too long for your youngest children to listen to every word, some of your older youngsters may want to construct with wire like Kondo. Bring in plenty of colored pipe cleaners (from craft stores, art shops, or educational supply houses), and let them get started. You will also need scissors for cutting the wire into smaller pieces if necessary and pencils for wrapping the wires into tubes. Children will also learn how to fasten wires together by twisting them, or taking them apart by untwisting them. Remember, for some children this is still a process and a time for manipulation of the material rather than making a product. A few may make a representational object, but most will be trying out a new art medium to see how it works.

Literacy Concept

Making such constructions from wire helps young children develop not only their creativity but also their small muscles and eye–hand coordination necessary for writing. As Jenkins (1980) notes, "Constructions are three-dimensional arrangements of materials, sometimes referred to as space designs. Children enjoy using some materials that offer resistance and that call for greater than usual physical effort. Here is the chance to offer children the stimulation of a variety of materials and the joy of making something from nothing" (p.167).

Dragonfly's Tale is a wonderfully illustrated Zuni Indian folktale about two powerful spirits, the White and Yellow Corn Maidens who watch over the Ashiwi pueblo's cornfields, and two young children, a boy and his sister, whose unselfish behavior saves their people. The story tells how the Ashiwi decide to show off their rich corn harvest one year by having a celebration in which they stage a mock battle using cornbread, biscuits, and balls of dough. The two Corn Maidens attend disguised as old women. No one will give them any food except the two children who offer them corn cakes drenched in honey. The Maidens decide to teach these selfish people a lesson by destroying their food and plants so that they must leave their village. Only the two children are left behind. The boy fashions a toy "butterfly" out of dry cornhusks to keep his sister happy. But the strange corn creature comes to life as the first "dragonfly" and flies off to get help from the Corn Maidens for the starving children. They are soon flooded with corn, beans, and squash and eventually help their returning people to respect nature's bounty and to share it. Pueblo people today still show this respect (Beaty, 1997).

Dragonfly's Tale is also a story too long for most preschoolers but easy to tell by "reading" the large wonderful pictures to a few children at a time sitting close to you. Be sure to have corn husks available so they can try twisting them into "corn creatures" afterward like the children in the story. This story can, of course, lead in many directions: planting corn, picking corn from a garden, husking corn, drying corn husks, and making "cornhusk dolls" or other creative inventions. Autumn is the time to bring in dried corn of various colors that you can hang by their husks for decorations. Using cornhusks in cooking experiences such as cornhusk-wrapped tamales is discussed later in the chapter under "Cooking with Corn."

If children are interested in knowing more about the Zuni people, a little children's book ***The Zunis*** is available full of lovely color photos of modern Zunis in traditional dress and ceremonies, showing their arts and crafts.

Molding Mud and Clay

Mud is one medium most young children love to play with. Playing with clay is probably the closest they may come to mud play, unless you bring in a pan of dirt and let children pour in enough water to make mud, or unless children play outside in a mud puddle or mud hole. In ***The Mud Family*** the girl Sosi is so upset with her ancient pueblo Indian family that she runs down to the pool of water on the canyon floor and makes her own family of people from the red mud. This family does not scold her, and there is no baby sister to bother her. Back

The Mud Family (James, 1994)
Pueblo Girls: Growing Up in Two
Worlds (Keegan, 1999)

home her pueblo family is worried because there is no rain, but they will not let Sosi dance for rain with them because she is too young. Finally, when all their water is gone and her family must move, Sosi has her mud girl dance for rain. The mud girl's rain dance is so successful that water roars down the canyon, sweeping away the mud family. Sosi's father saves her from being swept away, too, by snatching her up just in time, saying, "We are your family. You are my mud girl."

The children's picture book *Pueblo Girls: Growing Up in Two Worlds* (Keegan, 1999) contains large color photos showing two modern pueblo girls, 10-year-old Sonja Roybal and her 8-year-old sister Desiree who live today in the San Ildefonso Pueblo in New Mexico. The text is too long for most preschoolers, but the photos give a very clear idea of how modern Indian children live, wearing clothes like most Anglo-Americans, going to school, doing their homework on computers, playing basketball, practicing cheerleading, collecting Barbie dolls, but also learning to make clay pottery and feather headdresses, helping their grandmother to bake bread in an outdoor *horno* oven, and wearing traditional regalia to participate in the annual Corn Dance of their people.

Can your children relate in any way to growing up in two worlds? These sisters claim to have the best of both worlds. Would your children like to make a picture book of their own world by cutting out and pasting in a scrapbook pictures from magazines as well as photos of themselves to tell their story?

Also give your children the experience of working with their hands in a substance other than the usual play dough. They may not be at the stage of actually making mud dolls like Sosi, but they will enjoy the tactile experience of moving a substance like clay or mud with the fingers and shaping it into something different from what it started out to be. Pottery clay can be purchased ready mixed, but it dries out easily. Store it in an airtight container or a plastic bag with a damp sponge to keep it moist (Beaty, 1997).

Give children a lump of clay and have them work it with their hands. Because it is denser than dough and more difficult to work, keep encouraging them to squeeze and twist it, punch and poke it until it does what they want—a wonderful small-motor exercise for their fingers. According to Koster (1999), "When teachers are ready to introduce children to hands-on experiences with clay, they will put away the playdough and other modeling materials. The wet, cold, stiff clay does not compete well with these other soft, malleable materials that leave the hands clean. . . . A water-play table makes a good place for the children to work" (p. 20).

Children ages 4 and above can learn to make simple forms by rolling out the clay into hot-dog shapes or poking a finger into it and making a bowl. When they are finished molding it, they can set their shapes out to dry, but it may take a week or two. The clay mud on their hands will easily come off in water or will brush off after it dries. As Koster (1999) continues, "Children need many opportunities to poke and push and model in three dimensions. Playdough is fine, but clay is real! Clay speaks to a basic need in all of us to touch the earth and play in its life-giving soil. Clay and children belong together!" (p. 22).

STRENGTHENING EYE–HAND COORINATION THROUGH COOKING ACTIVITIES

Moving from the art center over to the cooking center brings us into another exceptional classroom area for promoting small-motor development and eye-hand coordination, as well as numerous opportunities for promoting prewriting and prereading skills. Because all foods are cultural in that they have originated from a particular culture, foods are one of the simplest ways to focus on children's common bonds of eating while celebrating their cultural differences of eating special foods. As Dahl (1998) points out, "Cooking can include gingerbread people, tortillas, wontons, waffles, fry bread, challah, hoe cakes, bagels, pasta, hush puppies, latkes, fortune cookies, and bread from scratch, to name just a few recipes. Each of these foods can be used in connection with other projects to make a multicultural experience. Who can separate food from its culture and its people?" (p. 82).

Young children are fascinated with food. When they are not gobbling down their own meals or snacks, they are watching like hawks as other children eat. Early childhood educators need to take cues like this from children. Their fascination with eating and food can be used to help promote their growth and development in several areas.

Children's cooking in the classroom promotes the small-motor skills of stirring, grinding, squeezing, mashing, peeling, cutting, grating, sifting, pouring, and rolling out dough. Their "reading" of recipe charts promotes prereading skills. The tasks of serving, sharing, waiting a turn, cleaning up, and helping one another promotes social skills. Making their own snacks, setting their own tables, and pouring their own drinks help preschool children develop a positive self-image. And the eating of nutritious foods develops healthful habits.

Cooking with Rice

By now your children may recognize that when you read them a new picture book, you are planning to introduce an exciting new activity with new storybook characters for them to meet. How delighted they will be when you begin bringing in books that focus on foods. (Be sure to check for food allergies before children eat any of these foods.)

Everybody Cooks Rice (Dooley, 1991)
How My Parents Learned to Eat
(Friedman, 1984)
Yoko (Wells, 1998)
Halmoni and the Picnic (Choi, 1993)

Be sure to have rice ready for cooking when you read ***Everybody Cooks Rice***. In this story big sister Carry, an Anglo-American girl, is sent out to find her little brother Anthony and bring him home for supper. She knows where to look for him because Anthony is a "moocher" who likes to visit their multicultural neighbors' houses and sample their dinners. But which neighbors? Carry begins with Mrs. D next door, who is from Barbados, but Anthony is not there. So Carry eats a small cup of rice and black-eyed peas while Mrs. D tells stories about Barbados people swimming even in December. Carry is soon working her way around the neighborhood, looking for Anthony but instead finding delicious rice dishes to sample. She returns home, empty-handed but full-stomached, to find Anthony there in their own kitchen. At the end of this remarkable rice expedition are recipes you can make with your children week by week:

Mrs. D's "Black-eyed Peas and Rice" (Barbados)

The Diazes' "Tumeric Rice with Pigeon Peas" (Puerto Rico)

Tam's "Nuoc Cham" (Vietnam)

Mrs. Tran's "Fried Rice" (Vietnam)

Rajit's "Biryani" (India)

Mrs. Hua's "Tofu with Vegetables" (China)

Madame Bleu's "Rice and Beans" (Haiti)

Great-Grandmother's "Risi e Bisi" (Northern Italy)

Literacy Concept

Put each recipe on a large newsprint sheet, oaktag, or an experience chart for the children to follow as they add the ingredients. They may not read the words but can follow along with your help if you make simple line drawings showing measurements (teaspoons, cups, etc.). Recipe charts like this are an excellent prereading experience for the children. As Dahl (1998) notes:

> For prekindergarten children, drawings with words and numbers can be used to help children understand the recipe. This is a good warm-up activity for reading in kindergarten or the primary grades. Many books, both for preschool children and elementary age, talk about food and cooking. These books are displayed in our library area for the children to look at. If we can find a book that applies to our specific cooking experience, we read it at circle time before we begin to cook. (p. 81)

Before you start preparing any of these recipes, be sure to read the book pages in *Everybody Cooks Rice* that describe what Carry experiences at the house where the particular rice dish is being prepared. You may want to use one of your character dolls to represent Carry and have her tell the story herself to a small group. It is important for the children to get a close-up view of the illustrations showing multicultural families in ordinary neighborhood kitchens preparing their native dishes. Your children should feel at ease with these folks from different cultures who cook food in such familiar surroundings.

Everyone in the Hua's house eats with chopsticks. Can your children do the same? Have they been practicing after hearing the story *Cleversticks* in earlier chapters? If not, better read *Cleversticks* again and let them practice first with cracker or cookie pieces before trying rice. Keep the rice sticky so they can pick it up in a clump. How well can you do it?

A book older children will enjoy is *How My Parents Learned to Eat* told in the first person by a girl who sometimes eats with chopsticks and sometimes with a knife and fork. Her father met her mother in Japan when he was a young American sailor and she was a Japanese high school girl. They both had to learn to eat with each other's utensils. Your children can pretend to be the characters in their favorite rice stories if you keep several pairs of chopsticks in the dramatic play center along with dishes and other cooking utensils. Using chopsticks is excellent finger exercise for prewriting children.

In the book *Yoko* the characters are all taking animals who represent children in preschool. Yoko is a little Japanese kitten girl who brings to school a lunch of her favorite sushi rice rolls with crisp cucumber, pink shrimp, green seaweed, and tasty tuna tucked into each one. The other children make fun of her lunch saying "yuck-o-rama!" The teacher decides to solve the problem by having an International Food Day at which everyone brings a dish from a foreign country and everyone has to try a bite of everything. Still nobody tries Yoko's sushi until hungry Timothy takes a chance. He loves it and polishes off the rest. Next day Yoko and Timothy push their desks together at lunchtime and open a restaurant.

If you read this book, be prepared to have an International Food Day at your preschool, or at least a day when you bring in sushi for everyone to sample. Have your listeners talk about their favorite foods as well. But be sure to ask them how they would feel if others made fun of their lunches.

Halmoni and the Picnic, a New York City story for older children, tells the tale of Yummi's Korean grandmother who comes to Yummi's class in Central Park bringing enough of the traditional Korean food *kimbap* for everyone. Young children can enjoy this story as you read the pictures.

Cultural Character Concept

This story not only uses the theme of food to contribute to children's cultural perspective but also serves to illustrate the type of family–school cooperation that you should try to achieve for your class. Do you show that you like a child's family member, just as Mrs. Nolan likes Yummi's grandmother even though she looks and acts so different? Does the family member endorse the preschool program even though it is so different from the home, as Yummi's grandmother does? Children breathe a sigh of relief when they see mutual respect and acceptance between adults at home and in school.

Invite a member of an Asian (or other) family to your class to help prepare a recipe of their own. If no one is free to come during the day, perhaps the family could send a favorite recipe for you to prepare. The importance of a family's endorsement of the school and the school's endorsement of their families may make the difference between a child's own success or failure in their schooling to come. "Knowing that her family and her school agree on who she is supposed to be simplifies the child's evolving self-image struggles" (Greenberg, 1998, p. 63).

Cooking with Corn

Children from Hispanic backgrounds may have relatives who have originally come to the United States from Cuba, Puerto Rico, Mexico, or any of the Latin American countries. The children themselves may have migrated to this country and still enjoy eating the special foods created by their people. For some children that food may be Mexican tamales, corn flour dough with spicy meat inside, cooked in corn husk wrappers.

Too Many Tamales (Soto, 1993)
Carlos and the Cornfield
(Stevens, 1995)

Too Many Tamales tells the tale of Maria and her parents, who are making tamales in preparation for a party. Maria's mother takes off her wedding ring when she and Maria are kneading the dough, but then the phone rings. Marie tries on the ring for a moment, but then forgets about it as she kneads the dough. Later when her cousins arrive for the party she is horrified to remember the missing ring. It must be in the tamales! She has her cousins eat the entire platter of tamales, very carefully, but no ring appears. (Unbeknownst to Maria, her mother had previously found the ring and put it on.) So everyone must remake a big batch of tamales.

Cultural Character Concept

This story should motivate a great deal of conversation about your children's past experiences in preparing food for a party. It should also lead to the children's actual cultural food preparation in the classroom. You can buy prepared tortillas and the fixings and make tacos. Or invite a Hispanic family member to help the children make tamales. Or you can purchase canned tamales and heat them in a microwave oven or covered frypan. At some point children should experience actually kneading dough the way Maria does, even if it is only play-dough. Afterward read **Too Many Tamales** again so the youngsters can see a cultural character in the illustrations doing the same thing they are doing. In this way children experience the common bonds all of us share in cooking food, while celebrating the differences in the types of food we enjoy.

International Food Day activities should be followed up in the days to come with dramatic play activities in which children pretend to prepare and eat international foods. Whenever you read any of these books, hang them on a book-on-a-string in the dramatic play center, and have international plastic foods available. Lakeshore Learning Materials (phone: [800] 421-5354) offers a Mexican Food Set with plastic tacos, bolillo, beans, rice, tortilla, chili pepper, and a serving of flan; a Japanese Food Set with eight pieces of sushi with ginger, wasabi, and a serving tray; and a Chinese Food Set with a steamer, three kinds of dumplings, rice, stir-fry beef, two egg rolls, a moon cake, and a bun. Don't forget to supply several pairs of chopsticks.

Carlos and the Cornfield is a second book in the Carlos series with both English and Spanish text on a page. Again, you may want to "read the pictures" as the text is rather long for preschoolers. Once again Carlos finds himself working in his father's field, this time to plant corn rather than squash. His father will pay him five dollars to plant the corn, but it has to be done very carefully with three kernels of corn in each hole. Carlos intends to spend the money for a pocket knife he has seen in the village store. The job is long and tiresome for Carlos, so he begins putting more than three corn seeds in each hole, first four, then five, then six, then a handful. When the corn sprouts Carlos is alarmed to see many rows with no corn, so he returns his knife for the money, buys more corn, and replants the empty rows. Later when his mother serves them blue corn pancakes Carlos finds that the corn he purchased turned out to be blue corn rather than yellow corn, and his laziness has been discovered.

Talk to your children about the different colors of corn, but then be sure to make cornmeal pancakes from the recipe in the Carlos book or from the cleverly corn-shaped book Totally Corn Cookbook (Siegel & Gillingham, 1994). Give

Have children exercise their finger power rolling out dough, flipping pancakes, and using food mills.

everyone a chance to flip over a pancake when it is ready. Children love to try flipping a "flapjack," a wonderful small-motor exercise.

Children can also exercise their finger power with cooking utensils such as food mills, melon ballers, egg beaters, and all sorts of grinding, squeezing, and cranking types of implements. The old-fashioned hand tools of Great-grandma's kitchen can often be found in flea markets. Keep some of these items in your dramatic play center for pretending or on the shelves of your manipulative center for small-motor practice, but also in the cooking center for use when children are helping to do real cooking.

STRENGTHENING EYE–HAND COORDINATION THROUGH WOODWORKING ACTIVITIES

Woodworking requires greater strength of arm, wrist, and fingers than any of the previous activities discussed in this chapter. It also requires the most precise eye–hand coordination of any discussed. Thus, working with wood can be the ultimate experience for helping young children to develop these prewriting skills. Yet fewer preschool programs include woodworking as a part of their curriculum than almost any other activity. Why is that?

We can conjecture that preschool teachers, the majority of whom are women, may see woodworking as a man's specialty. If this is the case, they may have little experience using hammers, saws, sandpaper, or drills. Or, as Andrews

(1997) notes, "If a teacher has never worked with wood, the thought of using hammers and saws with little children can seem scary. But with careful planning, teachers can find the woodworking area a pleasant and rewarding experience" (p. 29).

Just as with cooking, young children like woodworking because it is a real activity, not play, and uses real implements, not toy ones. Andrews (1997) addresses this need, saying, "Children want the real thing. They like using real telephones, real tape dispensers, real tools—often labeled 'too difficult' or 'for when you get bigger.' This urge to use real objects and materials justifies a woodworking center in the early childhood classroom" (p. 29).

Hammering

This Is My House (Dorros, 1992)

Abuela (Dorros, 1991)

Isla (Dorros, 1995)

Hammers, Nails, Planks, and Paint (Jackson, 1994)

Building a House (Barton, 1981)

Rather than starting with a full-fledged woodworking center including a workbench and shelves full of tools, why not begin simply with hammering? Hammering gives even the youngest children the same eye–hand coordination experiences as fully equipped centers. Locate your center in a corner to cut down on noise, in a space of at least three feet by five feet for two children. Bring in two tree stumps, two hammers of different sizes, and two boxes of 1¼-inch roofing nails. Put thick towels or carpeting on the floor under the stumps to cut down on noise. Cross sections of stumps can also be used on a sturdy table. Place each cross section on a piece of thick material such as a sample carpet square to absorb the noise.

Nails go into stump wood more easily than into boards; and roofing nails with their large heads, are easier for children to hit accurately. Small adult hammers are more efficient and safer for children than toy hammers, which do not have the necessary heft or head size to drive in nails easily. Children are more likely to hit their fingers trying to use ineffective toy hammers. Having two adult claw hammers of different weights gives youngsters the chance to experiment, to see which one works better for them. Every child who does woodworking needs to wear safety goggles, and they love to.

What is the point of the pounding? you may ask. For preschool children the process is more important than the product. Both boys and girls love to pound. When they have covered the top of a tree stump completely, you can saw off a two-inch slice and let them go at the stump top again. At first their hammering of nails is random, but later, especially for older children, they may begin to create their initials or other designs with the nail heads (Leithead, 1996, p. 12).

Cultural Character Concept

What about a cultural character picture book to get your children started? **This Is My House** shows an African American boy narrator telling how his house was built by his grandfather, who is now pounding on new roof shingles. Every two pages shows children of a different culture telling about their houses in English, but with the words "This is my house" also in their own language. Some of the houses have walls of stone, wood, mud, grass, or even paper. They are located

Both boys and girls love to pound, an excellent eye–hand coordination activity. When the top of the stump is covered with nails, saw off a slice and start all over.

in Bolivia, Egypt, Hong Kong, Indonesia, Japan, Mali, Mexico, and Mongolia, to name a few countries. Your children may want to start a scrapbook of various kinds of houses from photos brought in by the children, taken on field trips, or back issues of travel magazines. Can they make up stories to go along with their pictures?

Houses in the book *Abuela* are tall New York City buildings that the little Hispanic girl narrator Rosalba and her grandmother Abuela fly over like birds in their imagination. Through the windows of the buildings they see people eating, talking, phoning, and working. They even fly out to the Statue of Liberty in New York Harbor before returning to the city park where they started. Do any of your children live in apartment buildings like those Rosalba flies over? A cloth character doll Rosalba comes with some copies of this book. Or your children can choose a Hispanic puppet or doll from your cultural character collection to represent Rosalba. Have one of the children fly her over to the block center to see what constructions the children are making, and then fly her back to your small group at the woodworking center to report.

In the book *Isla* Rosalba and her grandmother have another imaginative flying adventure, this time to the island of Puerto Rico where Abuela was born. They fly over Puerto Rican forests, fields, and tiny towns until they come to the house of Rosalba's aunt, uncle, and cousin. Then they fly to a busy market town where they spin and dip over the town square entertaining the people below. Finally they fly to a big city where the buildings are taller, and then all the way back to New York City. Can one of your children speak through the Rosalba doll, telling what the houses and buildings are like in Puerto Rico? How are they different from New York City? Are any of the buildings in any of these places made of wood?

Hammers, Nails, Planks, and Paint shows a multicultural construction crew building an American house all the way from the architect's drawing to a family moving into the finished structure. Have children look at the book illustrations and pick out how many of the crew are actually doing hammering and what they are hammering. Even more hammerers appear in the simpler book *Building a House.*

As your children gain experience in woodworking, you may want to add a workbench to your center. These can be purchased or made from an old wooden kitchen table with the legs cut down. Other tools you may want can include a small steel backsaw, a miter box (saw holder that directs the blade), a vise mounted on the workbench or a C-clamp, and a egg-beater-type hand drill (Andrews, 1997, p. 30). Tools can be stored by hanging them on a wall-mounted pegboard on which the tools are outlined and labeled with their names, another prereading aid.

White pine or fir is best for hammering and sawing. Poplar, cedar, and spruce are also recommended. Young children can even learn to use sandpaper but have difficulty making it work unless it is securely fastened around an object they can hold onto such as a chalk eraser or a block of wood. Be sure to have adult supervision in the area whenever a saw, hammer, or drill is being used. Post safety rules in the center, and go over them with the children.

As children become accomplished woodworkers, they can actually make simple furniture and cars for the block center and boats for the water table. Most will just pound pieces of wood together because it is the process that intrigues them most of all. But Andrews (1997) adds, "Once you and the children become accustomed to using the tools and different types of wood, finished products will be a natural outcome of the joys of working with wood" (p. 31). Plus, holding a pencil and making marks where you want them in writing will become that much easier.

SAFETY RULES FOR WOODWORKING

1. Two children in work center at a time.
2. Wear goggles at all times.
3. Use only one tool at a time.
4. Use saw, hammer, or drill only when adult is present.
5. Return tools and materials to proper place when finished.
6. Sweep up sawdust and clean area when finished.

Source: Adapted from Andrews (1997, p. 31).

SUMMARY

This chapter has focused on helping young children strengthen their eye–hand coordination and finger dexterity to use writing implements through activities in the art center (cutting paper, stringing beads, quilting, sewing, weaving, molding mud and clay, and twisting wire and corn husks), in the cooking center using cooking implements to prepare rice and corn dishes, and in the woodworking center, using hammers and nails, saws and drills. Cultural book characters lead children into these activities as they read about the Hispanic boys Carlos and Gilberto, the American Indian girls Sosi and Mary Greyfeather, the Puerto Rican girl Rosalba, the Hawaiian girl Luka, the Anglo-American girl Carry, the African American girl Cassie, the Guatemalan girl Esperanza, the Japanese girl kitten Yoko, the Chinese boy Lin Sung, and the Korean girl Yummi.

LEARNING ACTIVITIES

1. What is eye–hand coordination, and why is it important in young children's development of writing skills? How would you assess it for each child? Try it and report the results.
2. Why are three-dimensional art activities especially effective in promoting children's eye–hand coordination? Give examples of some of these activities and the children's books you would use to lead children into involvement with the activities. Use one.
3. What are three different cultures featuring three-dimensional art that can be brought into the classroom through children's books to help children develop eye–hand coordination? Why is it important to use books with cultural characters for this?
4. How can cooking activities help children develop eye–hand coordination? What books can help children become involved in these activities? Try one and record what happens.
5. In what ways do woodworking activities help children develop eye–hand coordination? How would you set up a woodworking center to promote this development? Use a cultural character book as a lead-in to such an activity and record the results.

REFERENCES

Allen, J., McNeill, E., & Schmidt, V. (1992). *Cultural awareness for children.* Menlo Park, CA: Addison-Wesley.

Andrews, T. (1997). Woodworking: Winning from the beginning. *Texas Child Care, 21*(2), 28–33.

Beaty, J. J. (1997). *Building bridges with multicultural picture books.* Upper Saddle River, NJ: Merrill/Prentice Hall.

Booth, C. (1997). The fiber project: One teacher's adventure toward emergent curriculum. *Young Children, 52*(5), 79–85.

Boute, G. S., and McCormick, C. B. (1992). Authentic multicultural activities. *Childhood Education, 68*(3), 140–144.

Cherry, C. (1972). *Creative art for the developing child.* Belmont, CA: Fearon.

Dahl, K. (1990). Why cooking in the classroom? *Young Children, 53*(1), 81–83.

Dubin, L. S. (1995). *The history of beads.* New York: Abrahms.

Edwards, J. C. (1997). *The creative arts: A process approach for teachers and children.* Upper Saddle River, NJ: Merrill/Prentice Hall.

Greenberg, P. (1989). Parents as partners in young children's development and education: A new American fad? Why does it matter? *Young Children, 44*(4), 61–75.

Haskell, L. L. (1979). *Art in the early years.* Upper Saddle River, NJ: Merrill/Prentice Hall.

Jenkins, P. D. (1980). *Art for the fun of it.* Upper Saddle River, NJ: Merrill/Prentice Hall.

Koster, J. B. (1999). Clay for little fingers. *Young Children, 54*(2), 18–22.

Leithead, M. (1996). Happy hammering: A hammering activity center with built-in success. *Young Children, 51*(3), 12.

MacDowell, M. L., & Dewhurst, C. K. (Eds.). (1997). *To honor and comfort: Native quilting traditions.* Santa Fe: Museum of New Mexico Press.

Sample, W. (1993). The American Indian child. *Care Child Information Exchange, 3*, 39–40.

Schickedanz, J. (1999). *Much more than the ABCs: The early stages of reading and writing.* Washington, DC: National Association for the Education of Young Children.

Siegel, H., & Gillingham, K. (1994). *Totally corn cookbook.* Berkeley, CA: Celestial Arts.

Temple, C. A., Nathan, R. G., & Burris, N. A. (1993). *The beginnings of writing.* Boston: Allyn & Bacon.

Trawick-Smith, J. (1997). *Child development: A multicultural perspective.* Upper Saddle River, NJ: Merrill/Prentice Hall.

Zinn, E. (1997). The Hawaiian quilt research project. In M. L. MacDowell & C. K. Dewhurst (Eds.), *To honor and comfort: Native quilting traditions.* Santa Fe: Museum of New Mexico Press.

SUGGESTED READINGS

Braman, A. N. (2000). *Celebrating our heritage: Traditional Native American arts & activities.* New York: Wiley.

Cook, R. E., Tessier, A., & Klein, A. D. (1996). *Adapting early childhood curricula for children in inclusive settings.* Upper Saddle River, NJ: Merrill/Prentice Hall.

Flanagan, A. K. (1998). *The Pueblos,* New York: Children's Press.

Hedlund, A. L. (1994). Contemporary Navajo weaving: Thoughts that count. *Plateau Magazine of the Museum of Northern Arizona, 65*(1), 2–32.

Helm, J., Huebner, A., & Long, B. (2000). Quiltmaking: A perfect project for preschool and primary. *Young Children, 55*(3), 44–49.

Honigman, J. J., & Bhavnagri, N. P. (1998). Painting with scissors: Art education beyond production. *Childhood Education, 74*(4), 205–211.

Howell, N. M. (1999). Cooking up a learning community with corn, beans, and rice. *Young Children, 54*(5), 36–38.

Hughes, P. (1977). *Pueblo Indian cookbook*. Santa Fe: Museum of New Mexico.

Sosna, D. (2000). More about woodworking with young children, *Young Children, 55*(2), 38–39.

Thompson, D. (1981). *Easy woodstuff for kids*. Beltville, MD: Gryphon House.

CHILDREN'S BOOKS

Ashley, B. (1991). *Cleversticks*. New York: Crown.

Barton, B. (1981). *Building a house*. New York: Puffin.

Blood, C. L., & Link, M. (1990). *The goat in the rug*. New York: Aladdin.

Bolton, J. (1994). *My grandmother's patchwork quilt*. New York: Doubleday.

Castaneda, O. S. (1993). *Abuela's weave*. New York: Lee & Low.

Choi, S. N. (1993). *Halmoni and the picnic*. Boston: Houghton Mifflin.

Dooley, N. (1991). *Everybody cooks rice*. Minneapolis: Carolrhoda.

Dorros, A. (1991). *Abuela*. New York: Dutton.

Dorros, A. (1992). *This is my house*. New York: Scholastic.

Dorros, A. (1995). *Isla*. New York: Dutton.

Ets, M. H. (1963). *Gilberto and the wind*. New York: Viking.

Flanagan, A. K. (1998). *The Zunis*. New York: Children's Press.

Friedman, I. R. (1984). *How my parents learned to eat*. Boston: Houghton Mifflin.

Guback, G. (1994). *Luka's quilt*. New York: Greenwillow.

Jackson, T. C. (1994). *Hammers, nails, planks, and paint*. New York: Scholastic.

James, B. (1994). *The mud family*. New York: Dutton's.

Keegan, M. (1999). *Pueblo girls: Growing up in two worlds*. Santa Fe: Clear Light.

Mora, P. (1994). *Pablo's tree*. New York: Macmillan.

Reid, M. S. (1997). *A string of beads*. New York: Viking.

Rodanas, K. (1991). *Dragonfly's tale*. New York: Clarion.

Sanderson, E. (1990). *Two pairs of shoes*. Berkeley, CA: Oyate.

Soto, G. (1993). *Too many tamales*. New York: Putnam's.

Stevens, J. R. (1995). *Carlos and the cornfield*. Flagstaff, AZ: Rising Moon.

Taback, S. (1999). *Joseph had a little overcoat*. New York: Viking.

Watkins, S. (1997). *White bead ceremony*. Tulsa, OK: Council Oak Books.

Wells, R. (1998). *Yoko*. New York: Hyperion.

Williams, K. L. (1990). *Galimoto*. New York: Mulberry.

ART AS A NATURAL LANGUAGE

DEVELOPING DRAWING/WRITING SKILLS

DEVELOPING VISUAL REPRESENTATIONAL SKILLS

COMMUNICATING IDEAS THROUGH DRAWING

DEVELOPING DRAWING/WRITING SKILLS

Why should a chapter on young children's art development be included in a book on early writing? It is because art and writing come from a common urge to communicate that all humans possess. Like music, art also is a natural language, and preschool children treat it that way. They do not even differentiate drawing from writing in the beginning. Ferreiro and Teberosky (1982), in their classic book *Literacy before Schooling*, note, "In children's own first spontaneously produced graphic representations, drawing and writing are undifferentiated. Gradually some lines acquire forms like drawings, while others evolve towards imitations of the most salient characteristics of written language" (p. 52).

The 3 *Ms* of Playful Exploration

Most preschool programs spend a great deal of time involving children in art activities. In addition to the three-dimensional craft activities discussed in chapter 5, preschool art centers traditionally offer children some of the following painting and drawing opportunities on a daily basis: easel painting and flat painting, finger painting, drawing with crayons, markers, chalk, or squeeze bottles, or painting with tempera or water colors. But rather than creating a picture or a product, most preschoolers at first play around with the art medium they are using, just as they play around with blocks to see how they work before actually building with them. Early childhood specialists call this first stage of learning through play *manipulation*.

In art, children at an easel first play around with the materials, trying to get control of brushes and dripping paint. You will see beginners splash on color after color, sometimes covering a whole sheet with a single color or with all the colors, making a splotch that turns out brown. They are not painting a picture. They are "manipulating the medium" to find out how it works and what they can do with it.

Once they have learned how an art medium works, children start practicing their use of the medium spontaneously over and over in a second stage, called *mastery*. At the easel, they paint the same colors or scribbles again and again. At the collage table, they paste the same pieces on backing paper—maybe only one or two on each sheet—and then take another backing sheet and do it again and again. Once again we need to remember that they are not making a collage picture; they are mastering a process.

In the block center, children line up rows of blocks in flat "roads" or in vertical "walls" or in tall "towers" over and over before they learn (i.e., teach themselves) how to build a building. Watch to see what other activities children seem to repeat again and again in this mastery stage. It seems that young humans around the world are programmed to learn in this identical playful manner.

Finally, when children have had enough of this spontaneous, self-initiated practice (it may take days or weeks!), they progress to a third stage, called *meaning*, and begin to create art products that actually represent something—perhaps a person or animal or vehicle. Thus, young children use the so-called

Beginners at an easel at first play around with the materials, splashing on color after color. They are "manipulating the medium," not painting a picture.

"3 *Ms*"—manipulation, mastery, and meaning—in a self-imposed, playful exploration process whenever they encounter a new and unknown activity in their environment.

How long does it take for young children to progress through these spontaneous stages in drawing? you may wonder. It depends on how much previous drawing experience children have had at home, how many drawing materials were available to them, and how much support parents and family members gave them. As Seefeldt (1995) notes, "Preschoolers who have been deprived of a period of messing around with art materials, as too many in the United States who have been expected to produce an adult-pleasing product as toddlers, will require a great deal of time to mess around with art materials before they can use them to express ideas or feelings" (p. 42).

Instead, we must put out a variety of materials for children to select and use on their own in the art center: easels and paints, crayons and colored felt-tip pens, finger paints, glue, scissors, collage materials, colored construction paper,

Children's scribbles spontaneously take on shapes of circles, ovals, and squares as they begin to control what they draw.

white painting paper, and brushes of all kinds as a start. From research and observation of young children, we know that drawing skills develop over time in a predictable pattern, provided the youngsters are given the opportunity to pursue art on their own without a great deal of adult interference. Much of children's spontaneous art is directed toward the *process* of learning to draw or paint and not toward a *product* such as a completed picture or painting. Children show much more interest in the process of painting itself and not as much in what the final product looks like until they learn from adults that it is the product that most adults want from them.

Natural Stages of Drawing Development

Young children begin with scribbles as noted. Two- and 3-year-old children throughout the world scribble spontaneously. It gives them great pleasure to make marks of their own like this. Teachers and parents should encourage this beginning stage of drawing, just as they encourage infants to babble as a beginning stage of speaking. Between 2 and 4 years of age, children's scribbles spontaneously take on the shapes of circles, ovals, squares, triangles, and crosses, often scribbled on top of one another. At each stage they seem to practice their markings instinctively before moving on.

The next stage seems to occur when children concentrate on several shapes they like, perhaps circles or squares and crosses. Kellogg (1970), who studied children's scribbles around the world, notes that children next begin to combine some of their shapes, forming what Eastern religions call a *mandala*—that is, a circle or square with lines crossed over it—either a Greek cross (+) or a diagonal cross (×). Next comes the sun shape, although children do not call it a sun. It occurs naturally, almost as if the crossed lines of the mandala have leaked out over the edge of the circle, so children begin placing more radiating lines all around their circles and leaving the centers clear.

From mandalas and suns come humans. Somewhere between the ages of 4 and 5, children's designs around the world take the form of a person who seems to have evolved from the sun design they made earlier. The person is a circle or oval face with the "rays of the sun" evolved into hair, arms, and legs attached to this "sun-face-body" and is sometimes called by adults a "tadpole human." By age 4 or 5, children who have had this uninhibited practice also begin to make representational drawings of houses, trees, animals, and cars (see Figure 6.1). All of these figures are spontaneous and natural, not something that has been taught to the children. "Stick figures," on the other hand, seem to be an adult invention, and are not found in the natural scribblings of preschoolers.

At every stage it is important for you to accept children's artwork whether scribbles or pictures. You or they can display it attractively on backing paper or in frames, if they agree. Take photos of children painting at an easel for a personal scrapbook they are assembling. Be sure to date the work so you can follow an individual's natural development. When you talk with parents, share with them your knowledge about children's art development and how their own youngsters are progressing.

Uncontrolled Scribbles

Literacy Concept

Young children are able to make marks on a suitable surface very early in life. Some investigators have found children as young as 18 to 24 months interested and able to explore with a pencil or crayon. They tend to hold the implement in an immature grip known as a *fist grasp* in which the whole hand grips the implement and the arm is held above the writing surface. The hand is guided by muscles in the upper arm, resulting in large, rather crude marks. Only later after much experimenting and small-muscle development are they able to adopt a more mature grip, using the index and middle fingers and thumb to hold the implement, with the hand resting on the writing surface (Schickedanz, 1999, p. 112).

It is not up to you to teach children how to hold the crayon or pencil. They learn best through their own experimentation. Correcting them puts a damper on this natural learning process, and it really does not make them do it "your way" if they are not developmentally ready. All of the art activities described here are for children to practice on their own. Your role is to provide the materials and encouragement, and to read them the books that will lead them into the activities the book characters enjoy. Then they are on their own, pursuing new experiences at their own developmental level of manipulation, mastery, or meaning.

Nevertheless, these youngest children are greatly interested in the fact that their motions with the tool are making marks. They seem to follow these marks closely with their eyes and try to repeat them, not very successfully at first. Because they have little control over what they are doing, the marks appear somewhat scratchy and random, with no discernible pattern. As eye–hand coordination develops, their scribbles become controlled markings with repeated designs and patterns emerging.

1. *SCRIBBLE*
   UNCONTROLLED
   Marks made on paper for enjoyment. Child has little control of eye and hand movement. No pattern.
   CONTROLLED
   Control of eye and hand. Repeated design.
   NAMED SCRIBBLE
   Child tells you what s/he has drawn. May not be recognizable to adult.

2. *SHAPE AND DESIGN*
   Child makes shapes such as circles, squares, ovals, triangles. Child's muscle control is increasing and s/he is able to place shapes and designs wherever s/he wants.

3. *MANDALA*
   Child usually divides circle or square with lines.

   SUNS
   Formed from ovals, square or circle with short lines extending from the shape. The extending lines take many variations.

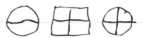

4. *RADIALS*
   Lines that radiate from a single point. Can be part of a mandala.

5. *HUMANS*
   Child uses SUN design and develops a face by adding human features. . . a "sun face".

   Child elongates several lines of the SUN design to create arms and legs.

6. *PICTORIALS*
   Child combines ALL stages to make recognizable designs or objects.

FIGURE 6.1

Stages of Art Development

Source: From *Skills for Preschool Teachers* (p. 184), by J. Beaty, 1996, Upper Saddle River, NJ: Merrill/Prentice Hall. Copyright 1996 by B. Helm. Reprinted with permission of B. Helm.

Encourage Scribbling

Most adults tend to disregard scribbles of all kinds as meaningless, certainly not something to be acknowledged and saved. They are, in fact, the impressive beginning stages of drawing/writing and should be regarded as such. Teachers need to encourage all scribbling by telling children how well they are working, by displaying pages of their scribbles on the art center bulletin board if they agree, and by encouraging them to try drawing with other implements. If they are scribbling with a crayon, they might want to try a felt-tip marker, an easier implement to use. Other activities can also give them practice.

Finger painting is one. Children can finger paint on butcher paper or on trays, even on tabletops, and later preserve their marks by making rubbings of their markings on sheets of paper placed over the marks. Cleaning off the tabletops later with water and small sponges that must be squeezed out is another method for strengthening children's hand and finger muscles. Cut the sponges to fit little hands. Trays of sand or salt can also be used for finger or stick scribbling.

Cherry's (1972) exciting activity of "arm dancing" on a long sheet of paper unrolled across the floor is especially helpful for beginners. After unrolling the paper on the floor, set out crayons at several intervals along its length for however many children will participate at one time. Have each child get down on the floor on his knees and use one of the crayons to do "arm dancing" to the music you will play on the recorder. When the music is turned on, tell them to pick up a crayon and begin moving it around on the paper to the music. Remind them to use their entire arm to "dance," not just their hand. After a few minutes change the music and have the children use a different crayon. Children of all ages tend to create the same large circular scribbles. Cherry also states, "Arm Dancing is an excellent developmental exercise. It is especially helpful for a child with visual or auditory perceptual difficulties" (p. 53).

Controlled Scribbles

Once children have developed hand control of a drawing/writing implement, they begin to make all kinds of scribbles. They may cover a paper with scribbles, place all of them at one side of the paper or another, or make a single scribble on one sheet of paper and do the same thing over and over again on other sheets. Are they wasting paper? Not at all. This is the spontaneous *mastery* phase of learning to handle a drawing/writing implement, and as much repetitive effort as necessary should be encouraged.

My Baby (Winter, 2001)
My Crayons Talk (Hubbard, 1996)

Easel Painting

What other media can your program provide to give children practice in scribbling? Easel painting for most young children starts out with paint scribbling using easel brushes. Children need to learn to control the brush and the dripping paint as previously noted, but then they are on their way to making pages of scribbles. You may want to thicken the paint to prevent drips by using less water when you mix the powder or by adding cornstarch to premixed paint. Be sure the brush is short enough for preschoolers to handle (a chubby brush), or else cut it down to their size. Be sure also to use large easel paper to give children room to do expansive scribbling, not 81/2 × 11 duplicating paper, which is too constricting. Any program wanting to encourage early writing and reading needs large unlined newsprint pads on hand. These can be used for easel painting as well as prewriting experiences. On the other hand, flat painting with watercolor paintboxes, small brushes, and tablet-size paper gives children additional practice dipping brushes into water to wet the watercolor before applying it to paper.

Chalk

My Baby (Winter, 2000)
My Crayons Talk (Hubbard, 1996)

Chalk is another excellent medium. Children can scribble on individual chalkboards with white or colored chalk. They also like to scribble on colored construction paper and even on fine-grained sandpaper. To give their scribblings a still different texture, try wetting the smooth paper first. Cherry (1972) suggests wetting paper with liquid starch to keep the chalk from rubbing off. Or children can dip dry chalk into sugar water, milk, or liquid starch and then draw with it (p. 61). Scribbling with wet or dry chalk on individual grocery bags is yet another satisfactory experience for children. Sidewalk chalk used outside on concrete or blacktop surfaces gives children even more exercise of arm and hand muscles.

Children of all ages seem to love chalk. If you have a large chalkboard in your room, be sure to keep chalk and erasers on hand. You will soon have scribbles of all kinds covering the surface. **My Baby,** a simple book about an African mother who paints a *bogolan* blanket for her baby, can evolve into a wonderful chalk experience for your children. After reading the story, ask who would like to paint a *bogolan* blanket for one of the dolls in the dramatic play center. Put out white chalk with water or liquid starch for dipping the chalk into as they make their designs—white scribbles for most preschoolers. They can choose black backing paper for the blanket or another dark color if they want. The book cover itself is bordered in black with white geometric designs which your oldest children may want to copy.

Cultural Character Concept

Why should you use an African book such as **My Baby** when few, if any, of the children will ever see such a blanket in real life? Once again, the use of a cultural character book that leads the children into activities promoting early literacy skills also leads them to understand that all people everywhere have common bonds. This African mother can help children realize that mothers of every cultural background make blankets for their babies. Do any of your children have baby blankets that their mother or grandmother may have made? Could they bring one to show the class? Are there any mothers or grandmothers who could come and demonstrate how they make a baby blanket?

The book My Baby *can lead children into a drawing/ scribbling activity with white chalk on black paper.*

Crayons

Do not neglect crayons. Sometimes programs purchase many of the newer kinds of drawing materials and forget about these time-tested drawing/writing tools. As Cherry (1972) notes:

> Crayons are wonderful tools for a child's first beginning scribbles. They are easy to manipulate and control. Using crayons leads to learning, growth, and development. Crayons are important in the development of writing skills. The child can practice moving his arm, wrist, and lower palm rhythmically on a table top or floor, as he pushes a crayon back and forth and round and round. This prepares him for writing where similar, but more controlled motions are necessary. (p. 46)

At first children should be given crayons large enough to be grasped with the whole hand. When they have developed better control of finger muscles, they can use regular-size crayons. It is better to keep crayons in an accessible plastic container, jar, or basket rather than a crayon box, where they need to be dumped out every use. Young children do not need all the available colors out at once. Six or eight of the large crayons in an individual container are enough to start with. A basket with a larger supply can be shared with several children at a table.

The simple humorous book *My Crayons Talk* shows a little Anglo girl shouting out rhyming verses about each of her person-size crayons as they color scribbles on the white pages or take off into the sky. Purple creates dots of purple bubble gum. Brown makes splotches of mud pies. Blue colors part of the sky and some cloud scribbles. Red roars out lion lines, shouting "No, do not go." Fill your crayon basket with these color crayons after reading this book. Place a long roll of white paper and a basket of crayons on a table for children to fill with their scribbles. When children realize they can unroll the paper and go on forever, they are quite willing to work nonstop. Afterward the paper scroll can be displayed along an entire wall as a border.

DEVELOPING VISUAL REPRESENTATIONAL SKILLS

Because many teachers do not make the connection between art and literacy, they may not see the need to help young children develop visual representational skills (i.e., art that represents things). Yet it is through drawing that writing emerges naturally. Neuman and Roskos (1993) point out:

> Out of scribble, around ages 3 to 6, children begin to figure out that these marks on paper can be signs of meaning. They now attempt to discover strategies for conveying an idea, a thought, or something they like to others. And like reading at this age, their notions of print and pictures overlap; just like a picture is seen conveying a narrative, so is a picture in writing thought of as symbolizing text. (p. 41)

Many American preschools and kindergartens have caught on to the idea that art and writing evolve from a common source, and they have thus encouraged children to do scribble writing and scribble drawing in both the art and writing centers. But it is the schools of Reggio Emilia in Italy that have based much of their curriculum on helping children develop their skills in visual representation in order to express their thoughts. As Houk (1997) notes:

> Reggio educators have long recognized that children have a far greater capacity than has been assumed to articulate their ideas through visual representation such as drawing. By giving young children the materials, tools, and skills to illustrate what they are thinking and observing at any stage of knowing, the teachers are empowering them to communicate with visual language before they can read and write. (p. 29)

In these schools, children's art products are not considered decorative pictures to be taken home at the end of the day but instead are viewed as a part of a *graphic language* the children are learning to express ideas. They are kept in the class for children to explore further and to add to, if necessary, as well as for children to "read" to themselves and others. Teachers tape-record children's comments and discussions of their work and transcribe them as documentation of the children's progress (Katz, 1993, p. 27).

Reggio teachers also do extra photocopying of children's drawings for the children to use in exploring several related ideas without having to redraw their pictures. For example, copies of a child's drawing of himself might later be worked on as the child explores different hair styles, favorite foods, or even family members. Although the teachers do not formally teach children how to draw, they do encourage and expect them to make their own natural visual representations of what they see. To accomplish this, the children need to develop observational skills.

Observational Skills

When we speak of observational skills, we normally refer to teachers observing children. In this instance, it is the children who learn to observe the things they want to find out about and learn to express their findings in the graphic language of drawing. *This will be a new concept for most American preschool teachers.* In the past we have not been so concerned with young children's prewriting attempts. We knew they would scribble first, although some young children never seemed to progress beyond the scribble stage. Others began to do "scribble writing," and still others printed a few letters and maybe their names. We let it happen—or not. We did not intervene to promote any sort of prewriting. But with the new ideas emerging from European programs such as those of Reggio Emilia, a number of American educators have changed their minds about not promoting prewriting skills. As Houk (1997) notes:

The Forest Has Eyes
(Doolittle & Maclay, 1998)
Brother Eagle, Sister Sky (Jeffers, 1991)
How Are You Peeling? Foods with
Moods (Freyman, 1999)
What Is Beautiful? (Avery, 1995)
Hats Off to Hair! (Kroll, 1995)
My Name Is Georgia (Winter, 1998)

> Reggio educators grasp the importance of giving children opportunities to communicate what they are thinking at any stage of knowing. Before they can read and write, children are encouraged to express their understandings in symbolic languages that they can use—drawing, painting, clay modeling, collage, performance, and so on. These are called "the hundred languages of children." (p. 34)

To express ideas in a symbolic language, children need to learn to observe things closely. For example, what is a person's face really like? What different things does it consist of? How is their face like Maria's or Monica's? How is it different? Houk (1997) notes that "the impact of visual training on a child's intellectual and creative growth is among the most innovative and challenging proposals [of this approach]." (p. 35). Loris Malaguzzi, one of the founders of the Reggio Emilia schools, described how children use their eyes as well as other senses to help identify, investigate, sort out, and think. He proposed that instruction in visual education be given to children at an early age, "to help them develop emotional maturity and sensitivity to the world around them, and free them from the limitations of passive perception, encouraged by television, that is so common in today's youngsters" (Houk, 1997, p. 36).

CHAPTER 6

Children are naturally curious, and this curiosity can be focused on objects of interest in their environment. Thus, teachers need to help children develop ways to investigate and make sense of objects about which they are curious. Children need to observe them closely, noting all of their characteristics. Then they need to be able to express what they observe in ways that they and others can understand. In this chapter we concentrate on drawing as a graphic language that helps children emerge naturally into writing.

Using Their Eyes

For young children to see an interesting person, object, or scene in all of its detail, they must use their eyes—that is, they must look. Of course, we exclaim, how else can a person see anything? But it is *how we look* and not what we look at that determines what we see. Do we look with curiosity? Are we looking for anything new or different about a person, object, or scene? Or when we look at one of them, do we simply see what we have always seen, our eyes sort of skipping over the details and giving us a general picture? For instance, do we see sadness, anger, or happiness in the eyes of the people we meet? Or do we simply see a person as she has always looked?

Young children already have the capacity to see details, even very small details. But when the adults around them pay little attention to the fine points about people, objects, or scenes, children soon learn to follow suit. It is time to reverse this unfortunate trend. If we want children to begin graphically representing the things that interest them, then we need to help them look with "seeing eyes," eyes that register even the more obscure details. Giving them the tools of observation and helping them use them can put children back on the track.

Books can also help. When you talk to small groups of children about using their eyes to discover things that are hidden, bring out the book **The Forest Has Eyes** with artist Bev Doolittle's clever scenes where American Indian faces and Indian eyes are hidden everywhere. Can your children find them? Start with the cover scene of a cowboy riding through a stream in a pine woods. There are at least four hidden Indian faces in the rocks of the stream and branches of the forest. As the author Elise Maclay states in the large-print introduction:

> Artists have magic eyes.
>
> They see hidden things,
>
> Things that look like other things.
>
> Things that happened long ago,
>
> Things that might happen tomorrow.

The poems that follow ask readers to find the answers to the questions they ask in the full-page illustrations accompanying each poem. Not always easy to do. Your children may turn out to be more perceptive than you!

If you do not have the previous book, read **Brother Eagle, Sister Sky** written in Chief Seattle's words telling that the Earth does not belong to us—we belong

The book The Forest Has Eyes *can lead youngsters into observing activities using binoculars or cardboard tube telescopes.*

to the Earth—and showing Indian children in the woods and lakes and mountains. The book ends with an Anglo-American family planting new trees on a cut-over meadow, hearing the words that they are merely a strand in the web of life. Whatever they do to the web, they do to themselves. Leaf through the book at first with the children. Do any of them see the Indian faces hidden in the lake on one page or in the rocks on the mountain or trees in the forest on another page? How many animals and birds can they identify on the end page? Children love the challenge of finding faces hidden in pictures. Are your eyes as sharp as theirs?

Now bring out your binoculars, telescope, microscope, and magnifying glasses. These can be toy tools, if you want, and need not be the expensive tools scientists use. Also have parents save bathroom tissue tubes, paper towel tubes, aluminum foil tubes, and wrapping paper tubes of all sizes for children's use in "spying" or focusing on an object. Or have children close one eye and look at an ant on the ground or a bird on a branch with the other eye through the hole they make with a closed fist. Now it is time to apply their observing skills in representational drawings.

Drawing a Human

When young children's drawing skill finally evolves naturally from scribbles to suns to people, we note that children everywhere draw their first humans the

All children everywhere draw similar-looking humans at first. Children may ask teachers to label their drawings.

same, as previously mentioned: a round or oval face that also serves as a body with lines protruding from either side as arms, sometimes with ball-like hands or line fingers radiating out at the end of the arms; with two lines protruding down from the face/body as legs; with two circles for eyes and sometimes a nose; and lines up from the top of the face/body for hair. Some draw a line across the long legs to form a body. If you ask children to draw a picture of themselves, this is what it looks like. A picture of their mother looks the same, but sometimes larger. Around the world young children draw their first humans like this.

As a teacher, you accept these drawings as the beginning of representational art and encourage them to continue producing it. Give them all sorts of drawing tools to choose from: crayons, markers, chalk, pencils, and paintbrushes. Can they draw other members of their families? You can label these drawings with the printed names the children give you, or have the children themselves label their own drawings with scribble writing. Be sure also to date these drawings to show the progression of their developing skills. Have children put the drawings in a manila envelope where they will keep their collection of "people pictures" for them to look at from time to time or add to if they want.

As a lead-in to one of your small group's first experiences in close people observation, you might read them ***What Is Beautiful?*** This is a simple story written in large colored words on every other page opposite the face of a person of a different culture, telling what one person thinks is beautiful about another person. For instance, Maryjean thinks Anglo David's ears are beautiful. A full-color picture of little David's face is shown on the opposite page. David thinks African American Angela's hair is beautiful, and so on. Beards, smiles, eyes, noses, mouths, and dimples are mentioned. On the last page is a round silvery paper mirror for each reader to look into and the words "What's beautiful about you?"

If you don't have a copy of ***What Is Beautiful?*** (or even if you do) but like the idea, then you should sit with a small group of children and go around the group asking each one to tell what they think is beautiful about the face of the person next to them. They will need to look closely at the person's face. After everyone (including you) has had a turn, pass around a hand mirror and have each one comment on what is beautiful about their own face in the mirror. This is a fine session to tape-record and play back later. If children start making comments on what they don't like, tell them, "We are talking about what is beautiful today."

As you note, this activity helps children focus their attention and begin to observe the details of their faces. The next step is for the children to record what they see. Because they are still at the egocentric stage of their development, their first visual representation activities should involve them. Set up several hand mirrors, and have children draw the picture of themselves that they see in the mirror. Give them as many sheets of paper as necessary, because children in the mastery stage of exploration will want to repeat their drawings. Such drawings may still take the form of the sun-face human they started with.

At this point do not instruct them to add hair or ears or a nose (if they haven't), although you can certainly ask them to look closely in the mirror again to see if they see any other feature of their face that they would want to add to their drawings. They may not want to. Or they may not see the missing details yet. This is a developmental sequence that takes time to accomplish. Give them all the time they need for this natural progression to take place without your instruction. It may take days—or weeks.

When you see that a few of the children are beginning to add more details to their face pictures, read to a small group ***Hats Off to Hair!***—a horizontal book showing the heads and hairstyles of three dozen children of different cultures with a simple rhyming verse embedded in every other page: "Rosie's long permed locks/resemble a lion./Crimps top off Jennifer,/dreadlocks for Ryan." The large, sensitive illustrations are intriguing to children, and they are soon interested in investigating their own hair. Bring out the hand mirrors again for a closer look. Is their hairstyle like any in the book? Can they draw a picture of themselves showing their hair? Can they make their hair look like one of the styles in the book? Be sure to clip ***Hats Off to Hair*** to an art center book-on-a-string for children to go back to whenever they want.

Once children begin observing things like their hair more closely, you can provide them with a simple tool for closer observation: one of the cardboard tissue tubes they can look through like a telescope. What do they see when they look at their hair in the mirror through a tube like this? Can they draw a picture of what they see? Do not expect accurate pictures from the children. They are still drawing what they know and not what they see. Some may still be in the scribble stage. But the more they practice, the better they will get. Accept all of their drawings as a progression sequence of their learning to observe and record details. Can you do it yourself? If you do not have a copy of **Hats Off to Hair!** have the children look at any of your cultural character books to see what hairstyles the characters wear.

What about drawing faces that express feelings? Have children look in the mirror and make a silly face. Talk with them about what detail makes their face look silly. Can they show that detail in a drawing? Have them make an angry face, a sad face, a happy face. Talk about the details that make faces express feelings. You may want to take photos of children's faces showing these expressions. Polaroid photos or digital camera photos produce instant pictures that children can look at while making their drawings. Isn't this copying? you may ask. No, they will not be reproducing the same face they see in the photo but making their own version of it. If the face features of a photo are too small, have children look at them through a magnifying glass. Using a photo copier or computer scanner will also enable you to enlarge any photos you take. Digital camera photos can also be enlarged and printed on computer printers.

Circular Drawings

From babyhood on, young children have first been attracted to circular or oval shapes because the first shape they see is their mother's round or oval face. Now is the time to send them off on a scavenger hunt around the classroom to see what toys and items they can find in the shape of a circle: ring toss rings, bubble-blowing wands, ladybug bean bags, plastic plates, pot and pan covers in the kitchen corner, plastic jar covers in the science center, wheels on vehicles, a circular rug, buttons and counters in the manipulative/math center, the magnetic letter O, and real and plastic foods—pancakes, cookies, crackers, and tortillas.

Can any of the children record on paper one of the circular objects that they have found? Normally we do not encourage children to copy objects in their art but just to draw creatively. This exercise is one that focuses on observation of a round object and then graphically representing the object. They are making a visual record of what they see rather than producing a creative drawing. Once again the youngest children may not be at the stage of visual representation. Still they may want to look at their object through one of the cardboard tubes and try to reproduce it on paper. Accept whatever the children draw. Date the drawing and label it as the children tell you, or let them scribble their own labels.

Work with one small group at a time so you will be able to talk with each one and listen to what they have to say. Have them look carefully at their object, turn it this way and that, and then add lines to their drawings if necessary. It is important to document what the children say about their drawings so that you will have a record of their levels of understanding. Do you wonder whether your 3s and 4s have the capability to do this kind of observing and recording through drawing? Let them try it. Katz (1993), who spent much time observing in the Reggio schools, comments that "many of us in the U.S. seriously underestimate preprimary school children's graphical representational capabilities and the quality of intellectual effort and growth it can stimulate" (p. 21).

If you have been encouraging the youngsters as they work their way through the controlled scribbling stage and into the drawing of shapes, mandalas, suns, and finally humans, they should be able to begin making graphic representations of objects they are interested in. Once children have become involved in observing and recording the round objects in their environment, this skill can be applied to any of the projects or activities going on in the classroom. It is always best to integrate as many activities as possible from each area of the classroom.

For instance, if the children are engaged in a project involving fruits and vegetables, you may be taking children on a field trip to a nearby market to purchase fruits or vegetables or visiting a fruit orchard or vegetable garden where they are produced. You may be preparing some of the fruit you have obtained, such as making applesauce or squeezing oranges if the children's interests lie in that direction. Plastic fruits and vegetables representing the ones you are investigating should be available in the dramatic play area where children may have set up a market. You may be singing songs about fruit, tossing fruit-shaped bean bags in the large motor center, counting and sorting plastic fruit counters in the manipulative/math center, dividing apples or melons into sections for snacks, blending oranges and bananas into a fruit drink, or planting seeds in the science center.

Round fruits are best at first if you want your preschool fruit explorers to record these activities graphically. Apples, oranges, lemons, cantaloupes, and tomatoes are the easiest for beginners to draw. Bring in the fruit, let them handle it and observe it closely, but also read them books with large clear pictures of the fruit you are featuring in the classroom to give children an artist's view of the real three-dimensional produce they are observing.

How Are You Peeling? Foods with Moods is a bizarre but fascinating book that has no human characters, only single fruits and vegetables that express their feelings through facial expressions added to real fruit pictures by the artist. Eyes are added, noses are the stem attachments, and mouths are drawn on a realistic picture of each fruit. The book opens with two large round oranges on opposite pages asking, "How are you feeling?" Next a pepper face asks, "Happy? Sad?" and on the opposite page a large round apple face asks, "Feeling blue? Feeling bad?" If children are drawing their own feeling faces by looking into mirrors, they should appreciate the faces of fruits expressing the same emotions. Bring in similar round fruits, and have children mark faces on them. Can they then draw the fruit they are looking at? For children who are at the representational drawing stage, they should be able and excited to make such funny round pictures. They may want to save them in a "How Are You Peeling?" book of their own.

Some children might prefer to draw flowers. They will probably start with a round sun shape and add petals around the outside or even the inside of the circle. They will want to hear the story of one of America's foremost artists, Georgia O'Keefe. *My Name Is Georgia* is appropriate for young children and may give them some exciting new ideas about drawing gigantic flowers. The original way she visualized what she painted changed the language of art for everyone.

By now you should be providing each child with a little sketch pad (unlined spiral notepad) and pencil for them to record what they are doing graphically. Keep extra sketch pads in the writing center for any of the children to use when they see something of interest they want to record. At some point you should talk with each of the children about what they have recorded and tape-record the conversation as documentation. Some children may want you to write on a page of their notepads what they dictate to you, while others may scribble their own notes. Even children who have not reached the representational stage of drawing should be given one of these notepads to scribble their graphic ideas in. Eventually the scribbles may become recognizable shapes and figures. Be sure to talk with these children as well, and comment on how diligently they are recording things.

Children Who Do Not Draw

Because preschool children are still in the early stages of learning to draw through self-discovery, you realize that you should not be imposing "art lessons" on any of them. If they want to try drawing a picture of their face by looking in a mirror, that should be a fun thing for them to do and not a lesson. Those who cannot or prefer not to draw faces should not be forced to try. Those who prefer to eat the round fruits rather than draw a picture of them should not be pushed into drawing. Just as you do not force children to sing or dance, you should not force children into art activities. Instead, offer them an invitation to participate in the drawing activities. If they do not accept, ask them what else they would prefer to do.

Your classroom should be full of exciting activities for children to choose from to follow their interests. Have activities available in every learning center for children to pursue on their own, or have staff members available to work with individuals while you read a fruit or mirror story to a small group. You will be repeating this story to other small groups that any children may choose to join on another day.

Literacy Concept

Children's picture books like the ones described in this text are important in and of themselves as a basis for emergent literacy, and thus should be read daily, whether or not the children want to follow the art extension activities you or they propose. As Kiefer (1995) notes, "Studying children's response to picture-books . . . has convinced me that picturebooks can and do provide children with purposeful talk, increase their literacy, deepen their response to books, and open up their awareness of art and aesthetics" (p. 41).

COMMUNICATING IDEAS THROUGH DRAWING

As we realize, many cultures focus on young children's development of art skills. It seems to be a common bond among us. But as adults, we also understand that most preschool children are not at a mature level of representational drawing during the preprimary years. They must go through the rather extended period of manipulating the medium, as noted, before they can begin to handle drawing tools with much skill. Nevertheless, some of the older children will want, and be able to communicate through drawing, even though it may be immature.

Part of their success with drawing tools may be due to their diligence in practicing the use of them, but part will also be due to *your recognition of their efforts and your expectations as a teacher that they can develop these skills if they practice*. Following the ideas presented in this chapter, you may find many more children ready and able to draw a simple picture.

People around the world draw pictures for any number of reasons: to tell a story, to illustrate a concept, to record information, or to give directions—to mention a few. At this point in young children's development of art skills, it may be possible for some of them to draw a simple picture that communicates an idea. In doing so, they may begin to understand that pictures like this can be symbols that stand for words.

Books as Lead-ins to Drawing Messages

Almost all early human societies have been involved in drawing pictures to communicate, especially cultures with no written language. Rock writing called *petroglyphs* or *pictographs* can be found in arid regions where dryness has preserved the circles, spirals, suns, stars, humans, mountain sheep, birds, bears, snakes, and other animals pecked or painted on flat rock surfaces and canyon walls by early people. Your children may be interested to hear stories about children like themselves who have been involved in discovering petroglyphs. If so, put these books in the writing center as a lead-in to "rock writing" activities.

Young Goat's Discovery (Tinus, 1994)
The Shepherd Boy (Franklin, 1994)
Native American Rock Art: Messages
from the Past (La Pierre, 1994)
Messages on Stones
(Stokes & Stokes, 1980)
Talking Walls (Knight, 1992)

Young Goat's Discovery is a contemporary American Indian story that takes place on the Navajo and Hopi Reservations in Arizona. In the story little Jeffrey follows his brother David as he leads a flock of sheep out to graze among the red rocks of a canyon. Young Goat trails behind every day, and David has to send Jeffrey out to bring him back. Jeffrey discovers that Young Goat has found a picture of a goat with long horns carved on the wall of a canyon. Jeffrey is intrigued and asks his father about it. His father calls it a petroglyph and sends him over to the library to find out more.

The Native American librarian reads a book about petroglyphs to Jeffrey and the other children. The book tells how the Hopi people carved pictures of animals on the rocks as hunting symbols long ago, and how the Hopi clans carved their clan animal symbol on special rocks every time they made the long journey to the bottom of the Grand Canyon for salt. After the reading, the children in the story visit a petroglyph site and draw petroglyph pictures of their own on paper, rocks, and play dough. This story is long for most preschoolers, so you may want to tell it in your own words or read the pictures. The entire book reflects the earth colors of the Southwest, with page backgrounds in a rich sandy tan, and illustrations of the rocks in reddish orange.

If your children are interested in making petroglyph drawings of their own, let them try making some in orange-red finger paint. On another day, take a rock-collecting field trip so that your children can bring back small, flat rocks to draw on with thick tempera paint. Can they make their own "clan marks," perhaps their own favorite animal? Children evolve naturally into drawing animals soon after they draw humans, as you may note from Figure 6.1. Their first animals are rather humanlike, only with body and head horizontal, four (or more) stick legs protruding down from the body, and the face looking human except for animal ears sticking out of the top. This is a "generic" animal that could be a cat, dog, goat, or anything.

Accept whatever marks the children make. Don't expect young children to be able to copy the petroglyphs shown in the book illustrations. Copying the artwork of others is not the point in preschool. Petroglyphs are simple stick and outline drawings. Some of the figures look decidedly like the children's art. Have children make some simple drawings of their own. Are they also trying to communicate something? Do they want to talk about it or have others guess what they are saying? Talking about what they are drawing is important both before and after the process is finished. As Oken-Wright (1998) notes:

> Language and drawing can come together in ways that enhance growth in representation. Talking about their pictures can help children remained focused as they draw, and it can help them extend the ideas about which they are drawing. When children talk about their pictures on a regular basis, their drawing becomes richer and is more likely to hold a story. (p. 77)

If the children's interest in petroglyphs continues, read them **The Shepherd Boy,** a simple contemporary story of Ben, a Navajo boy who cares for his father's sheep. Illustrations across double pages of this horizontal book are painted on clothlike texture showing the beauty of the surroundings, such as the red cliffs soaring high above Ben's *hogan* (house). Ben must search for a lost lamb over the rocks, down the wash, across the mesa, and into the canyon of the Old Ones, whose cliff dwellings and walls are covered with painted *pictographs*. Ben's dogs, White-Eye and No-Tail, help him track the missing lamb until he finds her in the canyon near the pictographs.

Talk with your small groups of listeners about the rock drawings they see in the book. Why do they think the people put them there? Do they think these drawings leave a message? What do they think they might be saying? Would the children like to make their own petroglyph messages? Have them choose dark backing paper and light marking tools (e.g., crayons, markers, finger paint). Can they pretend to be ancient people drawing a message? What will it say?

Don't forget to put out cultural character dolls when you read children these books. Ben and Jeffrey can be represented by dolls from the Multiethnic Dolls collection from Constructive Playthings (phone: [800] 448-4115), from the Community Kids Puppets from Demco (phone: [800] 356-1200), or from cloth dolls you have made. Have the dolls in the learning center where you read **The Shepherd Boy.** After reading the book, be sure to talk about it and introduce them to the Ben doll, the main character. Perhaps someone would like to take Ben to look for his lost sheep (toy) you have hidden somewhere in the room. Afterward, the child who finds it may want to tape-record the report of his and Ben's search.

These books also lend themselves to sand table experiences with toy animals and people from the block center accessories. Children who have made petroglyphs on rocks may want to bury their rocks in the sand table for the block animals and people to find. Again, this should be a child-initiated activity. You provide the materials, and then suggest to the children that they might like to have Ben and the animals look for petroglyphs in the sand table, your pretend western desert. If any children take your suggestion, listen in on their play, and afterward ask whether they would like to record it with a drawing in their notepads. You can tape record and later transcribe for them any messages they might want to tell.

Also place in your book center an adult book with good color photos of western rock art for children to look at. **Native American Rock Art: Messages from the Past** is a fine example, not only for the children to look at the pictures but also for the teacher to learn about this art, including petroglyph sites to visit in various states. **Messages on Stones** is a little paperback book showing black and white drawings of various types of petroglyphs: birds, designs, hands, headdresses, humans, and hunting.

Making a Talking Wall

Another book to broaden children's interest in messages on walls is **Talking Walls,** a nonfiction book showing child characters looking at Australian Aborigine rock art, cave art from Lascaux Cave in France, gigantic animals carved into cliffs near the Bay of Bengal in India, and the walls of Taos Pueblo in New Mexico, among other places. The front and back covers show children looking at ancient petroglyphs and Spanish inscriptions at El Moro Rock National Monument, New Mexico. If the children show an interest, you can tell them some of the stories that go along with each illustration. The book is for older children, but the large illustrations showing pictures of children from each of the cultures are sure to attract your own youngsters. They can see that rock writing is done by different people all over the world.

Someone may spot the Australian Aboriginal boy pointing to handprints on one of the walls. Do they remember the story about **The Mud Family** and Sosi from chapter 5 and how they stamped their handprints on the canyon wall as signatures? Would your children like to make their own handprints? There are several methods. They can dip their hands into a flat pan of tempera paint and stamp them on dark backing paper. To make it look more like rock art, use brown paper bags, cardboard, or brown wrapping paper for the backing. They can also trace around their hands and color in the outline. To make the prints look like aboriginal cave art, have the children hold their hands still against dark backing paper while you splatter-paint white water-soluble paint over them from a brush.

Children may also want to make their own "talking wall" in the classroom by drawing their petroglyph picture "message" on brown wrapping paper backing you have unrolled and fastened across a wall from the baseboard up to the height of the children. Place newspapers on the floor for protection. They can make their picture messages with fingers or brushes dipped in tempera paint. Those who want can stamp their signatures (handprints) next to their message. When the "talking wall" is finished, have each child tell the message she has drawn, or have the others guess what she has said in her pictures.

Listen to the children's own ideas as they become involved in creating messages with drawings. Some, of course, may not show much interest in rock art, especially if they do not live in the West. Can they create their own picture messages as if they have found a rock with pictures in their own backyards? Follow up on children's own ideas if it is appropriate. Your curriculum should always be flexible enough to include ideas from the children. They may take you in wonderful directions you never thought of. When children realize you are willing to incorporate their ideas into the classroom curriculum, they will surely be inspired to generate more.

Drawing Objects from Children's Environment

The Guinea Pig ABC (Duke, 1983)
Guinea Pigs Far and Near
(Duke, 1984)
I Love Guinea Pigs (King-Smith, 1994)

We usually do not think of drawing as a means for conducting research by children. But then we must wonder, how are they to record what they are finding out if they cannot write? Fox and Diffily (2000) have found, "Drawing gives children a concrete way to express what they have learned, and sets the stage for using words to represent objects and actions in formal writing. It is interrelated with writing, a relationship essential for emergent writers as they experiment with recording ideas on paper" (p. 4).

Curriculum Springboards

Classroom pets are often objects of great interest to children. Some children are so enthralled with these living creatures that they spend most of their time around them. One teacher found that her pudgy brown-and-white guinea pig, Whistler, was the star of the show for many weeks after she brought him in. The children named him because of the whistling noise he made every time they opened the kitchen refrigerator in the room next door to get him lettuce, cabbage leaves, or carrots. A few children wanted to spend the entire day getting him lettuce just to hear him whistle!

This teacher realized she had brought in a wonderful object of interest that could take the children in many directions in their learning, especially in their emergent literacy. She made sure her curriculum emerged from the children's strong interests that would engage them in activities in every learning center of the classroom. When she saw how important the guinea pig was to the children, she knew she had found another one of what she called "curriculum springboards." It was up to her to listen closely to what children were saying about the object, and then provide materials, space, and time for them to investigate it.

Her first move always was to find appropriate picture books at the children's level about the new object. Duke's **Guinea Pig ABC** and **Guinea Pigs Far and Near** were not storybooks with human characters as she would have liked, but their lively pictures of the pigs excited the children as they saw them bouncing through each page, illustrating one large-size alphabetical word at the bottom of the page.

It was not this teacher's intention to do any kind of formal teaching of reading or writing, but the children seemed as intrigued with the large words as they were the pictures of the guinea pigs. They loved seeing the first guinea pig's nightcap popping off when a second guinea pig's drumming made him wake up to the *A* word *Awake*. They thought it was silly that the *Clean* guinea pig scrubbed himself clean in a teapot and then went out on the next page and got himself all *Dirty* in the mud. Their favorite word was *Ferocious* for the guinea pig dressed up in a paper bag monster costume. You could hear this wonderful new word echoing through the classroom for days, and everyone wanted to make monster costumes for themselves out of grocery bags.

Several of the children decided to make their own guinea pig books, with a guinea pig on each page to illustrate a word of their own. The oval shape of the chubby pigs made them easy to draw, as you would expect. But most of their drawings still turned out to be a generic animal rather than a recognizable guinea pig. As the days went on, though, their illustrating skills increased, and some actually looked like a little guinea pig eating lettuce or a carrot.

But some of the young investigators were caught up short when the teacher brought in and read the book **I Love Guinea Pigs,** narrated by a man who knew all sorts of fascinating things about his own guinea pigs. His words made them laugh with the dreadful old saying "If you hold up a guinea pig by its tail, its eyes will drop out!" Then he wrote why that wasn't true: guinea pigs don't have tails! And they aren't really pigs! The children who had made books quickly got out their pencils (with erasers) and rubbed out the tails.

One boy, Randy, proudly showed his pig without a tail and told how he had "observed" Whistler with one of the class's cardboard "telescopes" and found out it didn't have a tail. Now everyone wanted to draw Whistler in their sketch pads. Children were going around "observing" the little animal through

Young children's first drawings of the classroom guinea pig turned out to be a generic animal with a tail.

cardboard tubes for days, hoping not to make another mistake in their drawings. But some children still had trouble making their drawings look anything like a guinea pig.

Children Who Have Trouble Drawing

Some children who have progressed to the human and animal stage of drawing may still have trouble making pictures come out the way they want them. They may try again and again, crumpling up their papers and throwing them away or even resorting to tears. Oken-Wright (1998) has something important to say about such children: "Children who don't draw comfortably may need a different set of conditions from those we are offering. They may need to learn to trust that they *can* make their ideas visible and that if they get stuck, a teacher will be there to help" (p. 77).

Help must be offered with care. To tell the child that her guinea pig looks "just fine," when it really doesn't, is negating the child's assessment of her work. The teacher might begin, instead, by engaging the child in conversation about what she thinks her guinea pig should look like. Do parts of her drawing look like that? She might show the child pictures of a guinea pig from one of the books they have been reading. Can she cover the head of a picture and just try to draw the body? What shape is it? An oval? Can she draw an oval? Healy (2001) tells us, "I feel that encouraging a child to think about the parts of what he wants to draw, if he has the skill and patience to draw simple shapes, helps him develop a technique he'll be able to use on his own" (p. 30).

Obviously, the teacher should not draw the picture for the child, nor should her help be for the purpose of making a better picture of a guinea pig. Instead, she should be *helping the child move forward when he gets stuck* (Oken-Wright, p. 77). It may be that the child needs to explore the pig's shape with three-dimensional materials such as play dough or clay before attempting drawing. One teacher even had a distraught child begin by making blank sketch books (cutting and stapling), before trying to do anything with drawing until she was comfortable.

As you can see, a teacher must also learn how to lead children forward in using art to communicate ideas, just as children are trying to do. In the end it is worth everyone's effort, for as Fox and Diffily (2000) point out:

> Children engaged in making art also refine their eye–hand coordination. As they add details to their work, consider placement of objects, and make pieces fit together, children learn to coordinate hand and finger movements with what they see before them. Coordinating these movements develops dexterity for many activities and influences the ability to form letters and to space words as children begin to write formally. (p. 4)

SUMMARY

This chapter discusses the stages of children's playful exploration: manipulation, mastery, and meaning (the 3 *M*s) that children use to teach themselves to paint, as well as the levels of drawing development children progress through. Ideas are presented for using cultural character picture books to help children progress through the scribble stage to the eventual drawing of humans and animals. Drawing pictures is viewed as a graphic language children can use to express ideas. It is thus necessary for them to develop observation skills to express themselves in the symbolic language of drawing. They learn to draw pictures of themselves by looking in a mirror and go on to drawing other circular and oval objects, such as fruit and even guinea pigs. The cultural character books discussed lead children into the past, when ancient people drew petroglyph messages on rocks, and back to the present, when such graphic language can be integrated into the children's learning centers. Teachers also learn how to help children who are having trouble drawing, so that they, too, may progress to actual writing when the time is right.

LEARNING ACTIVITIES

1. How can the 3 *M*s of playful exploration lead children into learning to draw? How would you help a child progress through these levels? Try it and record the results.
2. Why should children's scribbles be considered a serious part of art development? Tell how and why you would use a particular cultural character book with children who are involved in the scribble stage of art. Describe your experience.
3. Why are observation skills important in children's development of art as communication? Discuss in detail how you would use a cultural character book with children to promote this development.
4. How can learning about ancient rock art help preschool children develop their own communication through art? How would you help make rock art real and of great interest to children who have no access to such art? Try it and record the results.
5. Give a detailed discussion of how you would help a child who wants desperately to draw a particular picture but can't seem to do it. What was the result?

REFERENCES

Beaty, J. J. (1997). *Building bridges with multicultural picture books: For children 3–5*. Upper Saddle River, NJ: Merrill/Prentice Hall.

Cherry, C. (1972). *Creative art for the developing child*. Belmont, CA: Fearon.

Ferreiro, E., & Teberosky, A. (1982). *Literacy before schooling*. Portsmouth, NH: Heinemann.

Fox, J. E., & Diffily, D. (2000). Integrating the visual arts—Building young children's knowledge, skills and confidence. *Dimensions of Early Childhood, 29*(1), 3–10.

Healy, L. I. (2001). Applying theory to practice: Using developmentally appropriate strategies to help children draw. *Young Children, 56*(3), 28–30.

Houk, P. (1997). Lessons from an exhibition: Reflections of an art educator. In J. Hendrick (Ed.), *First steps toward teaching the Reggio way*. Upper Saddle River, NJ: Merrill/Prentice Hall.

Katz, L. (1993). What can we learn from Reggio Emilia? In C. Edwards, L. Gandini, & G. Forman (Eds.), *The hundred languages of children: The Reggio Emilia approach to early childhood education*. Norwood, NJ: Ablex.

Kellogg, R. (1970). *Analyzing children's art*. Palo Alto, CA: National Press Books.

Kiefer, B. Z. (1995). *The potential of picturebooks: From visual literacy to aesthetic understanding*. Upper Saddle River, NJ: Merrill/Prentice Hall.

Neuman, S. B., & Roskos, K. A. (1993). *Language and literacy learning in the early years*. Fort Worth, TX: Harcourt Brace.

Oken-Wright, P. (1998). Transition to writing: Drawing as a scaffold for emergent writers. *Young Children, 53*(2), 76–81.

Schickedanz, J. A. (1999). *Much more than the ABCs: The early stages of reading and writing*. Washington, DC: National Association for the Education of Young Children.

Seefeldt, C. (1995). Art—A serious work. *Young Children, 50*(3), 39–45.

SUGGESTED READINGS

Dyson, A. H. (1982). The emergence of visible language: Interrelationships between drawing and early writing. *Visible Language, 16,* 360–381.

Dyson, A. H. (2001). Writing and children's symbolic repertories: Development unhinged. In S. B. Neuman & D. K. Dickinson (Eds.), *Handbook of early literacy research.* New York: Guilford.

Edwards, L. C. (1997). *The creative arts: A process approach for teachers and children.* Upper Saddle River, NJ: Merrill/Prentice Hall.

Loughran, S. (2001). An artist among young artists: A lesson for teachers. *Childhood Education, 77*(4), 204–208.

Smith, N. R. (1993). *Experience and art: Teaching children to paint.* New York: Teachers College Press.

Strickland, D. S., & Morrow, L. M. (2001). *Beginning reading and writing.* New York: Teachers College Press.

Temple, C. A., Nathan, R. G., & Burris, N. A. (1993). *The beginnings of writing.* Boston: Allyn & Bacon.

Van Kraayenoord, C. E., & Paris, S. G. (1996). Story construction from a picture book: An assessment activity for young listeners. *Early Childhood Education Quarterly, 11,* 41–61.

CHILDREN'S BOOKS

Avery, M. W., and Avery, D. M. (1995). *What is beautiful?* Berkeley, CA: Tricycle.

Doolittle, B. (1998). *The forest has eyes.* Shelton, CT: Greenwich Workshop.

Duke, K. (1983). *The guinea pig ABC.* New York: Dutton.

Duke, K. (1984). *Guinea pigs far and near.* New York: Dutton.

Franklin, K. L. (1994). *The shepherd boy.* New York: Antheneum.

Freyman, S. (1999). *How are you peeling? Foods with moods.* New York: Scholastic.

Hubbard, P. (1996). *My crayons talk.* New York: Holt.

Jeffers, S. (1991). *Brother Eagle, Sister Sky.* New York: Dial.

King-Smith, D. (1994). *I love guinea pigs.* Cambridge, MA: Candlewick.

Knight, M. B. (1992). *Talking walls.* Gardiner, ME: Tilbury House.

Kroll, V. (1995). *Hats off to hair!* Watertown, MA: Charlesbridge.

La Pierre, Y. (1994). *Native American rock art: Messages from the past.* Charlestonville, VA: Thomasson-Grant & Lickle.

Stokes, W. M., & Stokes, W. L. (1980). *Messages on stones.* Salt Lake City, UT: Starstone.

Tinus, A. W. (1994). *Young goat's discovery.* Santa Fe, NM: Red Crane.

Winter, J. (1998). *My name is Georgia.* San Diego: Harcourt Brace.

Winter, J. (2000). *My baby.* New York: Farrar, Straus & Giroux.

7

BECOMING A WRITER

SCRIBBLING BECOMES WRITING

UNDERSTANDING ALPHABET LETTERS

WRITING TO COMMUNICATE

SCRIBBLING BECOMES WRITING

When children begin making scribbles that cover the middle of the paper and then make another row of linear scribbles underneath, they are beginning to differentiate between picture scribbles and writing scribbles. Sometimes they will pretend to read this pretend writing. Sometimes they will even bring their "picture" over to you and ask you to read what their picture is about. Because you know how to read and they don't, they assume you will be able to read their linear scribbles. You can tell them that you used to read that kind of writing, but now you have forgotten how, and maybe they can just tell you what it says about the picture.

What you do understand is that these children are now indicating by their linear scribbles that they recognize writing is different from drawing. Still, their lines of scribbles look nothing at all like letters or words. Learning to write is actually a complex and lengthy process that is much different from what logic tells us it ought to be. Temple, Nathan, and Burris (1993) describe it best by noting:

> Learning to write, it would seem, is nothing other than learning to make letters and to combine them into words. But studies of writing development have suggested that young children learn to write through a process that is quite the opposite. Rather than learning to write by mastering first the parts (letters) and then building up to the whole (written lines), it appears that children attend first to the whole and only much later to the parts. (p. 19)

All child development proceeds first from the general and then to the particular. In motor development, the large muscles develop before the small muscles. In drawing, children make generic humans lacking many details before they draw specific people with identifying characteristics. In writing, children first see the whole pattern and only later discern its specific parts (i. e., letters and words). Nor do they learn this process by being formally taught. Rather, they seem to extract through their own observations the broad general features of the writing system: that it is arranged in rows across a page and that it consists of loops, tall sticks, and connected lines that are repeated. Only later do children differentiate the finer features of the system: separate letters and words.

If no one teaches them, then how do they learn even this much about writing so early in life? Look around you. They are surrounded by the written word: in newspapers and magazines, in television advertising, on labels of food products, on boxes that toys come in, on covers of videotapes, on soft drink bottles, on letters in the mail, in the stories read to them, on store signs and stops signs, on car bumper stickers, on greeting cards, on fast-food packages, on cereal boxes, and on T-shirts. The printed word is everywhere. We call much of this writing *environmental print*. Davidson (1996) tells us:

> Children develop a holistic understanding that writing can communicate long before they can connect specific words with specific groupings of letters. Children's awareness of written language as a form of communication can be seen in many ways: when they ask someone what a sign says; when they know that a specific book always contains the same story; or when they make random marks and discuss what they are writing. (p. 87)

Some families, of course, encourage their children to print their own names at an early age. Some children have older brothers or sisters who bring home written material from school. Some children come from homes filled with the tools of writing: pencils, pens, markers, crayons, paper, and envelopes. Some children come from homes with computers that they are allowed to use. These children see family members engaged in writing or reading and try to become involved themselves.

Observing Children's Writing Behavior

Observe to discover which of your children do pretend writing, the first step in the writing process, which ones have progressed beyond this beginning, and which ones have not yet started. The "Preschool Writing Behaviors Checklist" in Figure 7.1 can help you determine where each child stands in his or her natural development of emergent writing. Remember that this is an observation tool and not a test. Do not force children to write, but observe what they are doing naturally. If they are doing nothing, it may be that you have not set up a writing center or have not provided interesting activities that invite them to try some kind of writing. It may take you several days or even weeks to complete the checklist. Once you know where children stand, you can help them progress from there in their natural emergence of the written word.

As you observe children by using the Preschool Writing Behaviors Checklist, you may note that some children seem to be stuck doing the same kind of

---

PRESCHOOL WRITING BEHAVIORS CHECKLIST

Child's Name   Age   Date

_____1. Makes writing-like scribbles in a line

_____2. Makes writing scribbles and drawing scribbles (or pictures) on same page

_____3. Makes a few mock letters in scribble writing

_____4. Makes more mock letters and fewer scribble marks in writing

_____5. Makes printed letters ("random letter writing")

_____6. Prints first name (letters not in order)

_____7. Prints first name (letters in order)

_____8. Uses writing skills to communicate

(Permission is granded by the published to reproduce this checklist for evaluation and record keeping.)

FIGURE 7.1
Preschool Writing Behaviors Checklist

scribbling or writing over and over. They fill page after page with lines of scribbles or with lists of words, or with the same imperfect letters. Do you remember the 3 *M*s of exploratory learning mentioned in chapter 6? Children who repeat lines of scribbles, mock writing, or lists of words are simply in the mastery stage of exploratory learning in which they repeat their new learnings over and over like a self-imposed practice routine. Do not stop them or try to get them to go on to something else. Be happy that they have progressed beyond the manipulative stage and are now at the mastery level in the natural sequence of their emergent writing. Show them acceptance by commending them for their hard work and encouraging them to continue.

Keep alert for the next level, the meaning stage of their emergent writing. What will it be? Perhaps they will start telling you what their scribbles or mock writing is meant to say. Or perhaps they will go on to printing real words. Most children progress through the three stages of manipulation, mastery, and meaning as they play around with learning this new skill. But they may not do it in the same manner as someone else or take the same amount of time.

In addition, most but not all children also progress through the same sequence as shown on the Preschool Writing Behaviors Checklist. Once they have control of their writing instrument, they begin to make writing-like scribbles resembling wavy lines going horizontally across a page or across the bottom of the easel paper. You understand that this means they seem to know about writing and what it looks like, and they are thus beginning their emergence as writers. If you are using the checklist, be sure to date each of the eight behaviors to give you an idea of how long it takes children to progress from one level to the next. You will know that children have reached the next level of emergence when they begin to add alphabet-like letters ("mock letters") to their lines of scribbles. When children begin to write mostly letters, they often believe that these letters can be read and may ask you to read them, as previously noted.

As young children create their own knowledge about writing, they will be extracting certain information from the writing they see around them that Marie Clay (1991), the New Zealand literacy educator, calls *principles* and *concepts* (see Figure 7.2). These principles are not something a child expresses or consciously knows about. These are the principles and concepts of the writing process as described by literacy educators to help *us* understand the process ourselves and to help us recognize what children understand about this process. It may be many weeks, months, or even years before a child comes to grips with all of these principles. Yet *it is not up to us to teach the writing process formally to preschool children or to push them forward in their progression*. The children themselves should be in charge of their natural emergence of literacy. Some will be quite advanced during their preschool years. Others may not really emerge until kindergarten or first grade. Teale and Yokota (2000) remind teachers, "Although children's acquisition of literacy can be described in general stages, children become literate at different rates and take a variety of paths to conventional reading and writing. Attempts to 'scope and sequence' instruction, such as those typical of reading readiness programs, do not take this developmental variation into account" (p. 5).

1. ***Recurring principle.*** Writing uses the same shapes again and again.

2. ***Generative principle.*** Writing consists of a limited number of letters from which you can generate a limitless amount of writing.

3. ***Sign concept.*** Print stands for something besides itself but does not look like the object it stands for.

4. ***Flexibility principle.*** The same letter form may be written in different ways, but the direction the letter faces is the same.

5. ***Page arrangement principle.*** English is usually written in lines of print from left to right and top to bottom on a page.

FIGURE 7.2

Principles and Concepts of Writing Extracted by Young Children

Source: Adapted from Clay (1975); Davidson (1996); Temple et al. (1993).

This natural emergent process was not even recognized by many educators as recently as 25 years ago. Thus, some child development specialists are now worried that preschool teachers, who are in a critical position for helping young children emerge into literacy, may not know how to do it. As Schrader and Hoffman (1987) note:

> When teachers are unfamiliar with current knowledge about the natural development of literacy in young children, they impose skill-oriented expectations and tasks on these youngsters—copying and tracing standard adult print, for example. Such activities not only are stressful for 3-, 4-, and 5-year-old children, but they do not afford children the opportunity to use their self-constructed knowledge in meaningful ways. (p. 13)

Role of the Teacher in Promoting Emergent Writing

Teachers should fill the children's environment with examples of written language and books. Signs and labels of all kinds should have a prominent place throughout the classroom. Teachers should also serve as models by doing a great deal of writing themselves in the presence of children. The use of observation checklists, accomplishment cards, notepads, and other writing objects by the staff should be visible daily and familiar to everyone. Finally, teachers should provide children with the tools of writing along with the time and encouragement to attempt the many writing activities they provide in the classroom.

A Letter to Amy (Keats, 1968)
Like Me and You (Raffi, 1994)

To encourage the children to practice writing, think of all the ways they can do it in your classroom. Having a writing center filled with all kinds of writing implements and activities is a good place to start.

Teachers should also serve as models by doing a great deal of writing themselves in the presence of the children.

Setting Up a Writing Center

A writing center is important in the classroom for a number of reasons. Its presence tells the children that they are encouraged to write and provides the tools and paper to do it. Because it takes time and practice for children to hold and manipulate a writing tool and then make marks on paper the way they want them to look, this center allows children to try it on their own. They can explore writing playfully just as they do objects in the other learning centers.

Fill the center with all kinds of writing tools (see Figure 7.3): markers, crayons, pens and pencils, chalk and chalkboards, magic slates and wooden pencils, stamp pads and alphabet letter stampers, peel-off letters, alphabet letters and games, alphabet books, typewriter, typing paper, pads, notebooks, stationery, envelopes, stamps, index cards, and post cards; also a stapler, hole punch, brads, scissors, pencil sharpener, and glue sticks. Locate your computer and printer here if you do not have a separate computer center.

Keep the materials in separate labeled plastic boxes on nearby shelves for easy access. Some classrooms use an old roll-top desk with pigeon holes and drawers for the writing materials. Others use an old school desk or two. A typewriter on a table needs one chair in front of it, while a computer works best with two chairs in front, so that two children can converse with one another about what they want to do, how they are going to do it, and what they see on the mon-

FIGURE 7.3

Materials for a Writing Center

Markers
Crayons
Pens
Pencils
Chalk and chalkboards
Wooden markers and magic slates
Fingerpaints
Salt or sand trays
Stamp pads and letter stampers
Peel-off letters
Alphabet letters and games
Alphabet books
Computer alphabet programs
Typing paper
Stationery and envelopes
Post cards
Canceled postal stamps
Pads
Notebooks
Index cards
Stapler
Hole punch and brads
Scissors
Pencil sharpener
Glue sticks
Plastic supply boxes
Mailboxes
Bulletin board

itor once they start, thus teaching themselves as they try out each program. They can also work out social problems such as what programs each wants to use, how to take turns using the different programs, and how to print off any letters or words they have typed. Kindergarten children, on the other hand, work best with one child at a time on the computer.

A newspaper office is yet another location where writing of all kinds takes place. If your class visits the local newspaper, they may want to set up their own newspaper office and pretend to be reporters and editors.

Or you might decide to make your writing center look like a business office with a Rolodex, appointment book, desk calendar, and telephone. If any of the parents work in an office, invite them to visit the classroom writing center and talk about how they do their own work. Or take a field trip to the parent's office, asking the children to observe and note what things in this office are different from the classroom "office." Can they make their classroom office more like a real one? Some observant children may return saying they want their own file cabinet, or desk lamp, or swivel office chair!

You might decide to make your writing center into a business office.

Another type of writing center is a pretend post office where children can write letters, greeting cards, and post cards and then mail them through a slot in a cardboard box or in individual mailboxes you and the children have made. After a field trip to a post office, it is important to set up a class post office so that children can follow up their trip, refining their ideas and playing the roles they saw enacted.

Reading Cultural Character Books

As you have done with other cultural character books, read ***A Letter to Amy*** to lead the children into a literacy activity—in this case, to the pretend post office. It tells the story of little Peter, the principal African American character in many of Keats's books, who writes a birthday invitation to his friend Amy and takes it outside in the rain to mail in a mailbox on the corner. The wind blows the letter out of his hands and he ends up knocking Amy down in his struggle to retrieve it. Amy runs off crying. Now will she come to his birthday party? A cloth 12-inch Peter doll character is available from DEMCO Kids & Things ([800]356-1200) to go with Keats's book ***Whistle for Willie.*** This is the same Peter character from ***A Letter to Amy,*** only with no yellow rain slicker and hat. Your children can help make a yellow rain cape for Peter from yellow construction paper and then can reenact the story as you read it. Use one of your other character dolls to represent Amy.

Like Me and You is a Raffi song put into book form. More than one cultural character is present. In fact, Janet, who starts the chain of pen pal letters, is from

England; Pierre, who receives it, is from France; Bonnie, who sends another letter, lives in Canada; Ahmed, who receives it, lives in Egypt; Moshe, who writes another letter, lives in Israel; and so on through Australia, China, Russia, Germany, India, Spain, and Colombia; also Japan, Chile, Pakistan, Italy, Ghana, Poland, Brazil, Iran, Paraguay, Kenya, Greece, and finally America. Would your children who are beginning to "write" letters like to send one to someone in another country? Whether or not they do, they all can sing the song about it at the back of the book. Once again they can see from a cultural character picture book that all children everywhere, whatever their culture or race, like to write and receive letters.

UNDERSTANDING ALPHABET LETTERS

To Teach or Not to Teach

There has long been a controversy over whether it is appropriate to teach young children the alphabet before they enter kindergarten. Those in favor tell how research suggests that knowledge of the alphabet is one of the best predictors of success in early reading. Those opposed point out that it is not developmentally appropriate to teach such skills to young children. Both sides seem to have missed the point. If you are following children's natural emergence into writing and reading that this text features, you understand that it is not the teachers but the children who teach themselves—not the alphabet, but *letters from the alphabet* that they find useful. As Neuman et al. (2000) point out, "And long before they go to school, young children can learn to spot letters important to them, such as the "S" of *Sesame Street* or the "z" of *zoo*, and begin to notice the general shape and length of familiar words" (p. 65).

Any "teaching" of the alphabet by the classroom staff tends to take place informally with small groups of children or with individuals, and it usually consists of the teacher pointing out names of letters the children are already using. It is not necessary for preschool children to learn by rote all 26 letters of the English alphabet in alphabetical order. That can come later in elementary school. What about the "Alphabet Song"? Let children sing it if they want, but you need to know it is not a letter-teaching device. In other words, children hear "elemenopee" as a single rhyming word, not the five separate letters: *L-M-N-O-P.*

Children's Names

How, then, can children learn the names and shapes of the letters they want to use? Look around you. The classroom should be full of environmental print *and* writing activities as previously suggested. Once you note that children have progressed in their natural development to the writing of mock letters and real letters, you can begin pointing this out to individuals. "Oh, Gilberto, you made an *L* in your writing, see! Yes, you did it again. Do you know that you have an *L* in your name? *G-I-L-B-E-R-T-O.* Gilberto."

The Day of Ahmed's Secret
(Heide & Gilliland, 1990)

As mentioned previously, young children learn best when the learning is personal. What is more personal than a child's name? You have been singing name songs, playing name games, reading books about characters with names, and sometimes substituting the child listener's name. Now is the time to make name cards for the children and to talk about the letters in children's names. As Green (1998) points out:

> Children acquire knowledge, including literacy concepts, at widely varied ages, of course. It may take as long as two or three years for some children to perfect the technique of writing their names. Patience is the key, for children become writers by writing. Consequently, the more opportunities children have to practice writing throughout the day, the more skilled they become; in addition, they will better understand the variety of ways writing is used in society. (p. 226)

You will soon find out that just because a child can print her name does not mean she knows the names of the letters in her name. But, as Green continues, "knowledge of all the letter names and forms is by no means a prerequisite to writing. Many children begin writing their names when they know only a few letter forms" (p. 226). You can help individuals by naming the letters in their names and pointing out similar letters in other words they see around the room. "Your name starts with the letter *G*, Gilberto. Can you find a *G* on the color chart on the wall behind you?" "You're right, Gilberto. You're pointing to the name for the color green, and green starts with a *G*. Can anybody else find the first letter of their name on our color chart?"

Sign-up Sheets

What other kinds of activities could you set up to encourage children to write their names? What about sign-up sheets? Attach a sign-up pad and pencil at the entrance to learning centers that limit the number of children who can use them at a time such as the woodworking center. You can have a list of numbered blank lines, and show the children how to sign their name on the line after the number. Then they can cross it off when they are finished. Children who are waiting their turns will then be next. Some children may already be able to print their initials or name, but others may say they don't know how to write. Encourage them to make a scribble signature. Most children can tell which scribble is theirs.

Other places for sign-up sheets include the following: for a turn at the computer, to use the typewriter, to use a book tape and head phones, to use the tape recorder, to use the trikes on the playground, in the dramatic play center for a turn to have their hair cut at the pretend hair stylist's, or to see the doctor at the pretend clinic. Some teachers have children write their names on a slip of paper and draw it out of a hat for taking turns with a new or favorite toy. Others have children sign out for books to be borrowed for home reading on a "library card."

At this point you may also encourage children to take their own attendance by "signing in" on a sign-up sheet when they arrive in the morning. As long as it is fun and not overwhelming for the youngsters, do lots of sign-up activities like this.

Children's names should already appear on their cubbies, on place cards that they put at the table for lunch, on their blankets for naptime, on their toothbrushes, on their science and art projects, and even on their block buildings. As they begin to recognize their names, they learn the first letter first and often confuse their name with another child's whose also begins with "their" first letter. Have them look closely at both names to see which is really theirs. Children generally see a whole word first before they recognize the separate letters. So Gilberto may at first confuse his written name with Gerald's.

Learning to write one's name is an important accomplishment for every child. Think of it: to be able to write your name is to be able to make your mark in the world! Be sure to read your children the Egyptian story **The Day of Ahmed's Secret** in which young Ahmed rides his donkey cart through the crowded streets of Cairo delivering fuel canisters to people with gas stoves, all the while hardly able to contain his excitement over the secret he will reveal to his family when the day is over. With its long text, you will probably want to "read the pictures," but try it and see. The sentences are short and so expressive. And what is Ahmed's wonderful secret? Against a dramatic black double-page background Ahmed takes out a pencil and writes his name in Arabic across a large white paper. "Look," he says "Look, I can write my name." And later he thinks to himself: "I think of my name now lasting longer than the sound of it, maybe even lasting, like the old buildings in the city, a thousand years" (Pratt & Beaty, 1999).

Ahmed's name does not look like the letters your children use in their names, but it shows them that people of different cultures often use different letters to write with from those of the English alphabet, just as the languages spoken by people of different cultures may be different from English. After reading Ahmed's story, be sure to fill your writing center with all the necessary paper and writing tools to encourage your own children to write their names. Give them cards with their names printed on, not so much to copy but just to look at as they make their own attempts at name writing. Names written with uppercase letters are acceptable in preschool. You may use lowercase letters if you choose, but it is not necessary at this time; they will learn lowercase letters in kindergarten. However, most alphabet books and computer programs do show lowercase as well as uppercase letters.

How do children learn to write their names, in the first place, you may wonder? As Green (1998) points out:

> Children's competence in name writing depends on fine motor control, an awareness of letter features (lines and shapes), and an understanding that letters are separate units. Novice writers must also understand that letters have names and certain formations, although knowledge of all the letter names and forms is by no means a prerequisite to writing. Many children begin writing their names when they know only a few letter forms. (pp. 226–227)

The first distinctive letter features children recognize are whether they are straight or curved. Round letters such as O or C are recognized first.

Recognizing Letters

In recognizing letters in names and words, children progress through a particular natural sequence just as they do in learning to make speech sounds. The first distinctive letter feature children seem to recognize is whether the letter is straight or curved. Letters that are round such as *O* and *C* are recognized first. Then letters with straight and curved lines such as *P* and *S* are noted. Next, curved letters with intersections such as *B* and *R* are distinguished from curved letters like *S* and *J* (Schickedanz, 1982, p. 311).

As children begin to print letters, their first attempts are often flawed. They make the same mistakes in writing letters that they do in recognizing letters: they overlook the letter's distinguishing features. As in other aspects of children's development, their emergence into written language proceeds from the general to the specific. Until they are able to perceive the finer distinctions in letters, they will have difficulty making letters that are accurate in all the details.

This difficulty will not stop them from trying. Nor is your pointing out their errors really productive, just as it is not productive in their development of spoken language. Let them practice on their own. In time their errors will become less frequent as they refine their perception of individual letters on their own.

Orientation of Letters

As children practice writing individual printed letters, you may wonder why they sometimes write them backward, on their sides, or even upside down. They may place the first letter of their name in the middle of the paper, and the other letters scattered here and there above, below, and to the side of their first letter. Can't they see what the letters look like on their name cards? Not at first. The problem, you might say, is a right-brain/left-brain perception problem of orientation in space. Most young children see things at first from a "right-brain perspective"—that is, letters not pointed in a particular direction or tied down to one horizontal line as in a "left-brain" or linear manner. To read and write in English, they must make the switch to the left-brain perspective, and for some, it takes longer than for others to get their orientation straight. Children often reverse letters even into the elementary grades. As Schickedanz (1986) notes:

> In much of children's early writing, vertical and horizontal are mixed . . . orientation of letters themselves is not consistent. Sometimes letters are reversed; sometimes they are placed upside down. These characteristics, plus a tendency to write in any direction—left to right, right to left, top to bottom, bottom to top—are all related. Until children understand that space can be organized in terms of coordinates, they do not select any consistent direction in which to place their writing. (p. 84)

Should you worry about these reversed letters and show children how to write them correctly? No. With practice and maturity, children resolve these problems themselves by the middle of grade 2. They are progressing as they should through the fascinating task of creating their own knowledge and emerging into writing. Your best strategy as a teacher is to fill the environment with words, letters, and occasions to write, as well as to accept all of the children's early attempts at writing. Or, as Wasik (2001) tells us, "It is important to expose them to the alphabet in ways that allow for success but do not allow for failure. In other words, young children should be exposed to letters in a natural, playful way rather than in a way that requires mastery (which develops later)" (p. 37).

If you provide alphabet blocks, wooden or plastic alphabet letters, or alphabet stampers and stamp pads, be sure to join in with children in their letter play from time to time. Because these letters can be turned every which way by the children, it is important to play games with children to help with their letter orientation. One game can be, how many letters can you line up so they face the right direction? If children reverse the letters, do not tell them they are wrong, but say, "You're close." Be sure to have a strip of alphabet letters mounted as a border in the learning center where children will be playing with loose letters like this, so they can see how letters are oriented.

C H A P T E R   7

Alphabet Books

Navajo ABC (Tapahonso & Schick, 1995)

K Is for Kiss Good Night: A Bedtime Alphabet (Sardegna, 1994)

Potluck (Shelby, 1991)

A few alphabet books are important additions to the writing area, but the question is, which ones? More and more new alphabet books are continually being published featuring foods, animals, funny rhymes, stories—you name it. This text with its cultural character approach recommends alphabet books featuring people of various cultures. Some books are simple with an object on every page, representing a letter. Some show several objects. Others feature "a day in the life of . . . ." with a phrase or sentence beginning with an alphabet letter and describing what happens on each page. Children are not as interested in alphabet books as they are in story picture books, but they will look at them with you if you give them opportunities to participate in the reading and finding things on the pages. They will look at them on their own only if the pictures grab their attention.

Choose books with exciting pictures and interesting words and actions. Once again, you remember that you are not teaching children the alphabet, but mostly bringing the names and shapes of letters to their attention. *Navajo ABC* is one of the simple books with a large upper and lower case letter at the top of each page along with a large picture of the object named. For example, *Bb Belt* shows a beautiful silver and leather concho belt. *Ff Fry bread* shows two Navajo women making fry bread outside over an open grill. The last page shows *Zz Zas*, the Navajo word for snow with a snow scene. As you look at the book with children, ask them what their own culture would show for a belt or bread or snow.

K Is for Kiss Good Night: A Bedtime Alphabet works very well as a naptime alphabet book in an all-day program. It shows horizontal scenes of children and parents from three families (African American, Asian American, and Anglo-American) getting ready for bed and finally falling to sleep. You can read the book to your children before naptime so they can see the beautifully sensitive pictures of mothers and fathers putting their children to bed: *A*, all ready for bed; *B*, breathing deep and slow; *C*, clock ticking quietly; *D*, dreams forming in my head. Read the book again slowly and quietly as the children lie on their cots waiting to fall asleep. This time do not show the pictures, but when you come to *K*, kiss good night, go around and lightly kiss each child on the cheek. Then finish the letters one by one in a whisper until you come to *Zzzz*, the end. This is a book the children like to look at afterward, not so much for the letters as for the lovely pictures of affectionate parents putting their children to bed.

The book *Potluck,* on the other hand, is a vivacious story in which two children, Alpha and Betty, decide to have a potluck, so they call up their friends and set their table for 31. Then come their alphabetic cultural friends with a marvelous array of alphabetic foods: Acton appears with asparagus soup. Ben brings bagels. Christine comes with carrot cake and corn on the cob. Don does dumplings. Your children's mouths will be watering before it is finished, and they will want you to arrange a real potluck. Would they also like to make a list of all the foods they can think of starting with some of the letters? They can dic-

Some teachers set the stage for using a computer by bringing in a typewriter.

tate while you write it on newsprint sheets. You may also want to bring in colored ads of foods, fruits, and vegetables from the newspaper, and let the children cut out a whole scrapbook of alphabetic foods of their own.

So, do alphabet books really teach alphabet letters to preschool children? Wasik (2001) has this to say about it:

> Alphabet books introduce the concept that the alphabet is comprised of a group of letters that all have different names and shapes. Children can see all the alphabet letters together. They can also hear that the letters have different names. With some alphabet books such as *Chicka Chicka Boom Boom* that tell a story about the letters, the children learn letters as if they were characters in the book. (p. 37)

Computer Alphabet Programs

Starting with a Typewriter

Some teachers set the stage for using the computer by starting with a typewriter. An adult's manual typewriter works better than a child's toy typewriter. The machine can be set up in the writing center on a low table with paper supplies nearby. You can help one child at a time put paper in the machine and then note how each one uses the typewriter in the beginning. Remember that these are preliterate children who explore new objects by playing around with them in the 3 *M* stages, as explained previously. They are not trying to type real words. After all, most of them do not know how to spell any words other than their names. And many do not even identify letters. In fact, most preschool children seem to get as much pleasure out of using the typewriter without paper as they do with paper.

Chicka Chicka Boom Boom
(Martin & Archambault, 1989)

Then what is the point of having a typewriter? you may ask. What are children supposed to be learning, if not to type words? Children will be teaching themselves that (a) to make letters and words with a typewriter, you must press keys on the keyboard; (b) that pressing one key at a time makes a letter appear (cause and effect); (c) that the letter appearing on the paper is the same one as on the key they pressed; (d) that pressing several keys at once jams the keys (incorrect operation); (e) that the shift key makes capital letters; (f) that the space bar makes spaces between the letters; (g) that turning the roller makes the line of type go up or down; (h) that the typewriter bell dings at the end of the line; (i) that pushing the return lever or moving the carriage starts a new line (Beaty, 1987).

In fact, most preschool children will not even absorb all of this learning. They will merely pretend with the typewriter, "piano-playing" the keys (pressing several at once)—thus, not being able to make it work at all. But because the typewriter keyboard is the same as a computer keyboard, using a typewriter keyboard first is a fine introduction to using the computer. On the other hand, children who are able to make the typewriter work for them get immense satisfaction out of typing their names and other familiar words.

Introducing Use of the Computer

Have the computer and printer placed on a low table near a wall outlet so that cords can be plugged in easily yet kept out of children's reach. Keep the monitor and keyboard close together, with the monitor at the children's eye level and not high above them. Children need to be able to see easily what happens when they press a key. Place two child-size chairs in front of the keyboard. Introduce the computer by gathering several children at a time around the machine while two children sit in the chairs. Name and point to the parts of the machine the children need to know: the keyboard, the monitor, the mouse, the printer. Show one of the seated children how to turn on the computer.

Start with a simple program such as an ABC program in which children must press one letter key at a time to make an animated letter scene appear. Let the children figure out how it works. Most young children's programs have oral instructions. It is best to use only one program at a time until everyone in the class understands how to use it. The adult in charge should give minimal instructions. If children ask you what to do, ask them what they think they should do, or suggest that they press a key and see what happens. Hitting the keys too hard or abusing the equipment is, of course, not in order. They should have learned to refrain from such behavior while using the typewriter. If they have forgotten, remind them.

Let the first group of children use the computer as soon as it has been introduced. Don't wait for the whole class to be introduced. Children need to apply their new knowledge immediately. The sooner they use it, the more comfortable they will be with the computer. It may take several times for most children to be comfortably familiar with this new device. Having two children use the computer at once promotes the social skills of turn taking, turn waiting, and helping one another figure out how to run the program. If you do it for

Having two children use the computer at once promotes the skills of turn taking and peer teaching.

them, they will miss out on this important peer-teaching/peer-learning process. They need to be able to explore their options freely and playfully to discover by trial and error how the computer works.

Have children sign up for turns to use the computer during the free-play period, or have them use one of the classroom self-regulating devices such as necklaces, name tags, or hooks and tags. Because the computer becomes one of the more popular classroom activities at first, having a sign-up sheet or self-regulating device makes it accessible to all who want to use it yet keeps it under the children's control. Occasionally you may have to ask two children to exchange turns with someone else when they have been using the computer overly long. Fairness generally prevails. When children understand that they are in control, they do not object to giving turns to others who are waiting. Do not regulate turns yourself at 5 minutes apiece, for example, or the children will never have time to teach themselves how to use the various programs.

Using Computer Alphabet Programs

There seem to be as many computer alphabet programs as there are alphabet books. However, many of the programs do not accompany alphabet books but stand on their own. The following alphabet CD-ROM programs are among those available from the Library Video Company (phone: [800] 843-3620):

Alphabet: Play with the ABCs

(Letters change to sound in acrobatic circus; based on book by Kveta Pacovska; Pre-K & up)

CD-ROM Suitcase Preschool (Includes *Chicka Chicka Boom Boom* CD-ROM)

(Includes 12 CD-ROM programs; pre-K–1)

Clifford Reading

(From Clifford, the Big Red Dog books; letter-sound recognition; read-aloud recording; pre-K–1)

Curious George Pre-K ABCs

(From Curious George books; letter names, shapes, initial sounds, letter pronunciation; pre-K–K)

Dr. Seuss's ABC

(From Dr. Seuss ABC book)

Fisher-Price Ready for School—Preschool

(Letter and number recognition; sorting; sequencing; listening; pre-K)

Jumpstart Preschool

(Letters, numbers, phonics, shapes, colors, motor skills; pre-K–K)

My First CD-ROM Preschool

(Multicultural parent support; letter recognition; counting; colors; sounds and rhymes; pre-K)

Reader Rabbit's Preschool

(Letters, numbers, patterns, and memory skills; games and music; pre-K–K)

Winnie the Pooh Preschool

(From Winnie the Pooh books; letter and number recognition; sequences; caring; sharing; pre-K)

Your class should not need more than one or two ABC computer programs at the most, since all of these CD-ROMs contain at least six individual programs within each disk. It is best if you preview the CD-ROM at a library or school resource center before purchasing it; but because this is often not possible, you can pick a program based on the children's interest in the characters or books involved. You will need to preview the CD-ROM yourself before using it with the children. Then complete the program set-up on your computer, set it at the menu screen, and let the children proceed from there. All of these programs have oral directions for your children to follow.

Each of the computer programs you decide to use should be integrated into the classroom curriculum either through cultural character picture books or through other learning center activities (e.g., art, puzzles, block building, manipulative games, music, writing). If the computer program is not a spin-off from a book, your children may want to make their own books based on one of the activities.

The alphabet book **Chicka Chicka Boom Boom** is often one of the children's favorites because of its catchy rhyming verse and the fact that alphabet letters are the characters. "A told B, and B told C, I'll meet you at the top of the coconut tree." Colorful alphabet letters against a white background scramble up a collage coconut tree ("Chicka chicka boom boom! Will there be enough room?") and then tumble down when it gets too crowded. Read the book to the children first before using the CD-ROM. In fact, it is best to reenact the story with three-dimensional alphabet letters. Have each child choose one of your loose alphabet letters and "climb it up the tree" when it is their turn. Of course, they love tumbling it down the best! This is an activity they will love repeating over and over. Have them choose a different letter every time.

What will you use for the coconut tree? It can be imaginary, or you can make your own alphabet tree by "planting" a broom or mop upside down in a bucket full of stones and sand, wrapping the handle loosely with brown burlap or cloth, and wrapping the mop or broom top with green crepe paper. Children can "climb" their letters up the tree, place them in the top, and shake them down when the time comes. You can also make an alphabet tree on a flannel board or purchase a free-standing 20-inch Activity Tree for *Chicka Chicka Boom Boom* with a set of 26 letters from Lakeshore Learning Materials (Phone: [800] 421-5354).

The CD-ROM *Chicka Chicka Boom Boom* uses animation, sound, video pictures of five cultural character children, a sing-along, and a read-aloud by Ray Charles in six activities to explore the story found in this book. Watch which alphabet letters the children press on the keyboard as they follow the directions in the alphabet identification program. They will also be learning the keyboard as they go. Do they explore the whole alphabet or return to a favorite letter again and again? One of their favorites is sure to be *V* as they watch and listen to a volcano explode.

When you use this CD-ROM, it is important to have the book available for children to look at afterward. Just as culture character dolls should lead children into book reading, so should computer programs lead children back to the book and into identifying and using letters in an integrated curriculum. Keep the book **Chicka Chicka Boom Boom** on a string in the computer center when this program is in use.

Cultural Character Alphabets

Cultural Character Concept

Once young children are familiar with some English alphabet letters, they are intrigued by the different kinds of letters used by other cultures and people. Rhoten and Lane (2001) suggest:

> The concept that there are many different alphabet systems can be introduced to young children using *Hieroglyphs from A to Z: A Rhyming Book with Ancient Egyptian Stencils for Kids.* Young children who know how to write their names may wish to try writing them in hieroglyphs using the stencils that come with the book. Hieroglyph rubber stamp sets can be ordered from most bookstores. (p. 43)

Hieroglyphs from A to Z: A Rhyming Book with Ancient Egyptian Stencils for Kids (der Manuelian, 1991)

At the Beach (Lee, 1994)

In the Snow (Lee, 1995)

Alef-bet: A Hebrew Alphabet (Edwards, 1992)

The Handmade Alphabet (Rankin, 1991)

Native American Sign Language (Olsen, 2001)

Hieroglyphics may not be used by contemporary Egyptians, but an ancient picture-type of writing is still used by millions of people. Xiao Ming, the Chinese boy in *At the Beach* shows readers how to write Chinese "characters" in the sand just as he is taught by his mother. She tells him how many of the characters are like pictures. He can remember the first character she draws, "person," because it looks like a person walking. The word *big* looks like a person stretching out his arms and legs. The pictures, characters, their meanings, and pronunciations appear on the end pages.

Xiao Ming follows his mother into a snowy forest in the companion book *In the Snow* to learn more Chinese characters by drawing them in the snow with a stick. These characters are a bit more complex than those in the previous book, and the text is longer, but if children want to try more Chinese writing continue reading this book. Are you really teaching the children to write in Chinese? Not at all. You are helping them become aware that all people write words, but some people write differently from others. Some children will want you to write the English word beside the Chinese character they are making. They can also practice both in the sand table or outside in the snow when the time is right. If you do not have a sand table, bring in some sand and spread it across small trays for the children to write and scribble in with their fingers. Salt can also be used. They can erase their writing easily by shaking the trays.

The book *Alef-bet: A Hebrew Alphabet* should also interest your beginning writers. Names of familiar objects and family activities are shown in Hebrew that children can try to write.

Your children may be surprised to learn that not everyone writes alphabet letters on paper. In fact, many hearing-impaired people use their hands to "sign" letters. The strikingly illustrated *The Handmade Alphabet* shows on its cover six hands of different sizes and skin colors doing signing. Inside large full-page pictures show each of these same hands making the manual alphabet sign for each of the letters from *A* to *Z*. For instance, a hand holding asparagus signs *A*. The picture for the letter *G* shows a hand in a glove signing that letter, while the picture for *K* shows a child holding toy keys. A large capital letter appears in the left-hand top corner of every page, but there is no text and the objects are not named.

As you show this book page by page to your small listening group, say the letter aloud and ask them to guess what object the hand sign stands for. Or say the name of the object aloud and ask them to say what the letter is. Can any children make the sign with one of their hands? It may not be easy for the youngest children. Older youngsters can place their hand next to the proper picture to check their success. Would any children like to learn to sign the first letter of their name? Put tracing paper over the appropriate hand picture and trace it for each child. Then mount it on cardboard and have them practice.

In the past many Native Americans used hand-sign language to communicate silently. Instead of signing letters, whole words were signed using the hands. Today elders of the Plains peoples and Pueblo peoples sometimes use sign language to emphasize a point or to tell the story dancers are illustrating by their movements. Your children may want to try using some of the hand signs in the book *Native American Sign Language*.

WRITING TO COMMUNICATE

A Process of Discovery

As we continue to learn more and more about how children become literate, we are often bewildered by our findings. The fact that young children can discover how to write by themselves if the adults around them stimulate and encourage them to do so is surprising enough. Then we have to admit, as Temple et al. (1993) tell us, "Writing, the act of expressing thought by means of written symbols, is a mysterious process. No one understands exactly how we learn to do it, but it appears that we learn to write at least as much by discovering how as by being taught. Learning to write is largely an act of discovery" (p. 2). But then we are confounded even more to learn that "[r]esearch and the experience of teaching and parenting have shown us a remarkable thing: Even when they are not taught about writing, most children make the same discoveries about it, in essentially the same order" (Temple et al., p. 2).

Why Write? (Moreton & Berger, 1999)

Writing Places (Chanko, 1999)

Thus, we have to conclude that learning to write is much like learning to speak: Children can develop it on their own given the proper support. And although this text discusses the development of oral language, writing, and reading in separate chapters, it is essential to understand that *all three of these processes occur at the same time* with children. Literacy educators Strickland and Morrow (2000) emphasize:

> Reading, writing, and oral language develop concurrently and interrelatedly rather than sequentially. Literacy develops within the framework of real-life activities in

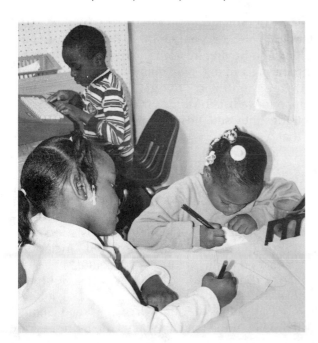

Learning to write is a process of discovery much like learning to speak. Children can emerge into writing on their own given the proper materials and support.

order to "get things done." Therefore, the meaningful or purposeful bases of early literacy are a critical part of learning to read and write and must be emphasized in the curriculum. Children learn written language through active engagement with their world, not merely by completing workbook activities or other types of academic exercises. (p. 5)

Furthermore, not all children teach themselves the basics of writing in exactly the same manner. The Preschool Writing Behaviors Checklist (Figure 7.1) at the beginning of the chapter shows a natural sequence of writing skills development that many children follow. Others may develop these same writing behaviors, but somewhat out of sequence. You realize that children's home background often makes a big difference in their preschool achievement. Children whose parents do a great deal of writing at home themselves, encourage their children to write, and provide a computer for their children have a head start over children who have never picked up a writing tool until they enter preschool. Your observations of the children's writing behaviors will help you understand where the children stand and how to help them progress in their development.

The simple book **Why Write?** shows a full page photo of a different cultural character on every page, often with a parent looking on. The photos illustrate children answering the question "Why write?"—to send a note, to send a message, to make a list, to make a card. The little book **Writing Places** uses the same format with photos of children illustrating some good writing places: a calendar, a board, a painting, and a computer.

In Dramatic Play

Making Lists

Bunny Cakes (Wells, 1997)

Warthogs in the Kitchen: A Sloppy Counting Book (Edwards, 1998)

Feast for 10 (Falwell, 1993)

Mcheshi Goes to the Market (Jacaranda Designs, 1991)

Think of all the pretending episodes your children create in the dramatic play center: selling and buying in stores, going shopping, eating in restaurants, preparing a meal, and many more. Can any of these situations involve the children in writing? Stores and shopping usually require buyers to make lists of things they want to buy. Sellers can make lists of things they sell. Restaurant servers can take an order of food items that a customer wants. To prepare a meal the cook can make a list of ingredients to be purchased, as well as making a recipe (a list of steps and ingredients) to prepare a certain food.

Obviously, your novice writers will not know how to spell most of the words involved, but with your support they can make lists with pretend as well as real words. Or they can use scribbles or pictures to substitute for words. You will find that certain children love to make lists and may prepare the same one over and over (in the mastery stage). Be sure to include a number of small pads with pencils attached in the dramatic play center.

Once again, picture books can lead your children into making lists for their pretend roles in dramatic play. Those who are not at the stage of printing letters can still be encouraged to communicate ideas through drawing. Read **Bunny Cakes** to two children at a time with one on either side of you so they can see the scribble writing and drawing of little bunny Max who wants to make Grandma an earthworm birthday cake, and the printing of big sister Ruby who is going to make Grandma an angel surprise cake with raspberry fluff icing. Max wants to help Ruby but he just seems to make a mess instead. He breaks the eggs accidentally, so Ruby sends him to the store to buy more. She writes *"EGGS"* on a piece of yellow notebook paper for the grocer. Max wants Red-Hot Marshmellow Squirters for his earthworm cake, so under the word *"EGGS"* he scribbles his message in red crayon. The grocer cannot read Max's writing so all he gets are eggs.

Next Max spills the milk, and Ruby sends him off again with a note that says "MILK". Max again scribbles his message under *"MILK"*, but all he gets is milk. Then he spills the flour and the same sequence occurs. Finally, Ruby puts Max out of the kitchen altogether while she finishes the cake. But she still needs a few more items from the store:

BIRTHDAY CANDLES

SILVER STARS

SUGAR HEARTS

BUTTERCREAM ROSES

Max looks at the list and has an idea: he *draws a picture* of the Red-Hot Marshmellow Squirters with his red crayon, and of course the grocer puts them in the bag. Afterward Grandma is so thrilled she doesn't know which cake to eat first!

Can your children make a list like Ruby and Max's? It may be fun for them to reenact the story as you read it. Can anyone print the word *"MILK"*? There are undoubtedly many who can scribble Max's message. A plush Max character doll is also available from DEMCO Kids & Things (phone: [800] 356-1200).

Recipe Charts

A real situation makes this kind of list writing even more valuable. Be ready to make a real birthday cake with the children if you have the baking facilities. Put up a large recipe chart with the ingredients listed and illustrated, for the children to follow. Talk to the children as they follow the steps on the recipe chart about "what comes next." One group of children who had completed every step in the birthday cake recipe except for the baking, were asked, "What do we do next?" They wanted to "put the candles on the cake," without understanding that baking the cake in the oven came next!

If children are reenacting the *Bunny Cakes* story, you can put the ingredients on a table or counter in a pretend store; then have children write down each ingredient they need as best they can, and get it from your store. Max, of course, should only pretend to break the eggs and spill the milk and flour! No matter what happens, be sure everyone has fun. As Klenk (2001) tells us, "Play-based literacy offers a much-needed reasonable response to the increasing expectations placed on young children (and their teachers) for literacy achievement. While these experiences do not hinge on formal instruction, they are authentic and purposeful" (p. 150).

Another hilarious cooking adventure is described in ***Warthogs in the Kitchen: A Sloppy Counting Book*** where eight peoplelike warthogs decide to make cupcakes. Each page shows the sloppy warthogs pouring ingredients into measuring cups and everywhere else in this absurd escapade. Because it is a counting book, a number appears at the bottom of each page along with a rhyming sentence describing the ingredient. A cupcake recipe for warthogs appears on the last page. If children are reenacting the story, be sure to prepare a large recipe chart showing the ingredients. Also read them the comical directions that go along with it. Does anyone want to copy the recipe? There is also a cupcake recipe for humans in case your children would like to bake up a batch.

In ***Feast for 10*** an African American mother takes her five children shopping in the grocery store to help her buy the ingredients for their "feast for 10." She does not carry a shopping list with her, but after reading the story to a small group, have them make their own list following the story:

2 pumpkins

3 chickens

5 kinds of beans

6 bunches of greens

7 dill pickles

8 tomatoes

9 potatoes

In ***Mcheshi Goes to the Market*** the little African girl Mcheshi invites readers to come along with her and her mother as they go shopping in an African open-air market. Your listeners can also make their own lists from this brilliantly illustrated story as little Mcheshi tries to help but manages to get into mischief. An English text is in red at the top of the page and in black in Kiswahili at the bottom. Does your children's market list look like this?

Shirt

Shoes

Chicken

Fruit

Vegetables

Eggs

Preschool children love to play store with a counter, a toy cash register, and money, along with items to sell. Empty bags from home come in handy, too, as do empty food containers. They may want to set up an open-air market in the dramatic play center with items of plastic fruits and vegetables for sale on the various tables and counter tops. Be sure to put up labels on each table telling what is for sale. One group of children turned its puppet theater into a store, and sold the puppets!

In the Writing Center

Writing Messages

Writing simple messages to others is another authentic writing experience many preschool children may enjoy. Teachers who are aware of children's writing skill development often set up various situations in which children have opportunities to write messages: a note to another child placed in his classroom mailbox; an invitation; an answer to another child's message; a note to others about a classroom project. These notes may be scribbles or mock writing, printing of a word or two, or writing combined with drawings. Children often want teachers to help them write, but you should encourage them to try it on their own at first.

Good Morning Franny, Good Night Franny (Hearn, 1984)
Jenny's Journey (Samton, 1991)
Click, Clack, Moo: Cows That Type (Cronin, 2000)
Families Are Different (Pellegrini, 1991)

Those who know some letters may invent their own spelling of words. Randy, a boy who loved to write messages, even put one on his block building at the end of the day: "PLS DNT NOK DN [a drawing of a house]; RANDY." Can you interpret this invented-spelling message? It says "Please don't knock down (drawing of a house)," signed Randy.

You realize that as Randy progresses in his development, he will begin to add a few more vowels to his spelling. It is not up to you to make the corrections. Other children may want to dictate their messages for you to write down and for them to copy. This is a real indication that they understand how writing represents spoken language. Be sure it is their message and not yours. They may not be able to copy your words accurately, but it is good practice for those who want to try. If children ask you how to spell a certain word, you may want to print it on a card for children to copy as best they can. Put a manila envelope in their cubbies to hold their word cards.

Hall (2000) suggests that teachers might want to get children started with message writing by having a daily message board with a written message on it from the teacher that asks for a response from the children as they arrive each day. The message board can be a large newsprint pad on an easel at the children's height with writing tools handy and plenty of room for the replies of any children who want to write. One teacher's message said, "I had a wonderful bike ride to school. How did you get to school?" The teacher will need to read the message, and then children who know how can print their reply. Others can scribble or even draw a picture. Replies are then read aloud by the children after everyone has arrived. Once children get the idea, more and more of them will "write" replies. Hall (2000) notes, "When children are just beginning their writing careers, or for some reason have limited experience writing, being able to write for a genuine communicative purpose can make all the difference to their perception of writing as a meaningful activity" (p. 360).

Writing with Chalk

Children also love to draw on the sidewalk with colored sidewalk chalk. Here is another opportunity for message writing. Let the vivacious city girl Franny lead your children into an exciting adventure in the park when you read the book *Good Morning Franny, Good Night Franny.* Franny tells how she took the elevator down to the street where she began zipping along so fast she knocked over the pigeon lady's cart by accident. Franny is in a wheelchair. A little Chinese girl, Ting, helps pick up the lady's scattered parcels, and starts a friendship with Franny. Ting speaks very little English, so Franny draws pictures and prints English words in the scrapbook Ting always carries with her. But the two girls always say "Good morning," when they meet in the park to play, and "Good night," when they leave the park at the end of the day. Then one day there is no Ting at the park. She and her family have moved away, but on the sidewalk she has left two written messages: "Good morning, Franny," at the entrance to the park, and "Good night, Franny," at the exit. Can your children think of a message they would like to write with chalk on the sidewalk outside their building?

Another cultural character story based on a message is *Jenny's Journey* about the African American, New York City girl Jenny who misses her island friend Maria so much she writes her a large colorful letter, saying, "Dear Maria, I miss you too. This is a picture of the boat I'll sail to visit you." The remainder of the book shows the imagined trip Jenny plans to take on her little boat sailing out of the harbor, across the ocean, past an ocean liner, through a chain of islands, through a terrible storm, and finally to Maria's island where she is waiting on a long pier for Jenny. Then the letter ends, "So don't feel lonely. (And someday I really will come to see you!!) Love, your friend, Jenny."

By now a few of your children may be able to write, draw, or scribble simple letters to their classmates to be mailed in the mailboxes in the writing center.

Typing Messages

What about *typing* a message? Some children in classrooms having a typewriter may become quite proficient at finding the right letter keys to press down, making letters on a sheet of paper that finally become words. They will surely appreciate the humorous imaginative story *Click Clack, Moo, Cows That Type.*

Farmer Brown can't believe his ears when he hears typing sounds coming from his barn. And he can't believe his eyes when he finds a message written by his cows: "Dear Farmer Brown, The barn is very cold at night. We'd like some electric blankets. Sincerely, The Cows." Somehow they had found an old typewriter in the barn. But electric blankets? "No way," says Farmer Brown. So the cows go on strike and leave another message: "Sorry. We're closed. No milk today."

Then the hens ask the cows to say they are cold too and want electric blankets. An angry Farmer Brown types his own reply demanding milk and eggs and saying no electric blankets. How does it all end? The cows finally exchange their typewriter for the blankets, giving the typewriter to the duck to take it back to Farmer Brown. But the machine doesn't quite make it back. Now the ducks are going, "Click, clack, quack." And they want a diving board in the pond!

Would your children like to reenact this story? Children can choose to be cows, hens, ducks, and Farmer Brown. Who can write a pretend message on the typewriter? No need to write out the whole message at this stage of your children's typing proficiency. If the children become excited about the idea, they could invent other versions of this story that include lions, tigers, and elephants typing messages to hunters.

Writing Stories

By now your children have been exposed to all sorts of stories, read by staff members, told by you, and looked at again and again by the children themselves in one of the classroom learning centers. Does this mean they know how to write a story of their own? Most do not, without a great deal of help from you, but some may be willing to try if the task seems interesting.

You might start the process by reading the book ***Families Are Different*** to a small group of listeners and talk about the little adopted Korean narrator Nico, as an author who is telling this story about herself and her adoptive Anglo family. Can any of the children be authors and write a story about themselves and their families like Nico did? Help them get started by making a journal book of their own to write in, by stapling together blank pages.

In *Families Are Different* Nico tells that she has a mother and father, a big sister and a dog; that her sister's name is Angelica; that they call her Angel, but she's no angel, and sometimes she drives Nico bonkers! Can any of your children make a story like this about their own families? DeGayner, a preschool teacher in Alaska, helped her children get started in the following way:

> Budding authors in this preschool had two options: They could draw and/or write their own stories and then read or tell them to an adult, or they could dictate them to an adult. Most of the preschoolers used pictures to represent their stories, sometimes adding a few letters, or letter-like forms. (Fields & DeGayner p. 131)

Most preschoolers begin the story-writing process this same way: by drawing pictures to tell the story as they did picture messages in chapter 6. You can then encourage them to tell the story about the pictures by writing it down in any way they can. After they have finished drawing their story, some of your budding authors may want to dictate their story to you and have you write it on the page with the drawing of their family. Others may try their hand at writing, perhaps with a few letters, or maybe an invented word or two. A few may ask you to write down a simple sentence like "This is my family," for them to copy under the picture they drew. Still others may scribble lines that look like cursive writing. If you ask them, they may be willing to share what they have written with the small group they are working with.

DeGayner found that "children must fully explore the belief that only pictures can tell stories before they can move on to exploring the ways to communicate with print" (Fields & DeGayner p. 131). But she also felt that these early stories were an essential link between her children's understandings of literacy and their future ability to read and write printed stories.

CHAPTER 7

After a Field Trip

My Visit to the Aquarium (Aliki, 1993)

Where Does the Trail Lead?
(Albert, 1991)

Famous Seaweed Soup (Martin, 1993)

After children return to the classroom from a field trip, teachers need to set up all sorts of follow-up activities to help them re-create what they experienced on their trip. Teachers need to find out what was meaningful to the children, and children need to make meanings of their own from their experience. Reading books, building with blocks, role-playing the trip in dramatic play or in the water or sand table, painting pictures or making three-dimensional art creations of things they experienced, and, of course, writing about the trip should ensue.

After a class visit to a nearby aquarium, it is important for children to hear a book such as **My Visit to the Aquarium,** the story of a little boy who visits an aquarium with his big brother and little sister. Beautifully illustrated pages transport readers into living aquatic surroundings as if they were there. Children of many cultures hurry from one exhibit to another, having the most fun at the tide pool where they can actually pick up live creatures. The narrator says he touched nearly everything except the crab. Can your children compare their own experience with the boy's in the book? What did they like the best? Was anything funny? Or scary?

Class-Dictated Stories and Lists

You will need to start an aquarium of your own in the classroom if there is none. In the meantime children will want to draw, paint, and model with play dough some of the creatures they encountered. This time start by writing down a class-dictated story on a large piece of newsprint for children to read together many times afterward. Individuals can write about their own adventures in their journals. Once again you may encounter mostly drawings to tell the story, but more children than ever may want to dictate to you their stories about the trip. One class painted a large mural of an underwater scene on paper across the wall, with everyone contributing and afterward signing their names under their work. Then they dictated a class story about the creatures in the mural for the teacher to write on the mounted mural paper.

Children near an ocean or beach may want to continue investigating this aquatic environment on another class field trip or with their parents. Afterward you might read **Where Does the Trail Lead?** in which an African American boy follows a trail along a beach encountering a lighthouse, a tide pool of periwinkles, gulls in flight, a ghost town of shanties and an old boat among the cattails—all beautifully illustrated in muted tones on scratchboard. You can start by listing the items the boy discovers. Children can make a second list of items they found during their own trips.

Or read the comical **Famous Seaweed Soup** in which the little Anglo-American girl Sara goes to the beach with her family and tries to involve them in helping her make her Famous Seaweed Soup. But nobody ever helps, so she repeats on every other page, "All right, I'll do it myself." And she does. Does anyone want to write down the recipe for Famous Seaweed Soup? Your list makers often laugh as they try to make it as stinky as possible:

Bay water

Crackly brown seaweed

Slimy green seaweed

Smelly horseshoe crab tail

Sandy seagull feather

Old clam shells

Most of the children, you will find, still do their best writing in pictures with a few letters placed here and there to represent a word and a scribbled line or two to represent a sentence. But as children listen to the stories told by their peers, as well as viewing their illustrated writing, they benefit in yet another way. As noted by Fields and DeGayner (2000) about the children in their class:

> They were able to experience different forms of children's writing and to consider how their peers treated print and story. When children are involved in writing and see others producing writing, they become more confident in their ability to partic- ipate in reading and writing events. Children's exploration of writing expands their knowledge of the conventions and functions that define reading and writing. (p. 132)

Calling children's early writing "scribbling" can often be a putdown, so some teachers instead use the term *personal script* for their initial efforts and *conventional script* for mature writing. As you work with children, encourag- ing them to write a story in their own way, it should become obvious that draw- ing, writing, and reading are, indeed, interconnected. Children should be encouraged to progress in all three skills as they teach themselves to emerge into literacy.

Summary

This chapter discusses how children evolve into writing through a natural process that is quite different from what one would expect. Instead of learning to make letters and then to combine them into words, children attend first to the whole (written lines), and only much later to the parts (letters and words). A Preschool Writing Behaviors Checklist is presented in order for teachers to ob- serve and record their children's writing progression. Teachers are warned not to teach the writing process formally to preschool children, but rather to encour- age them to emerge naturally through the books and activities furnished. A list of materials for the writing center is provided along with suggestions for furni- ture and arrangements. A discussion of how children learn alphabet letters with- out being taught is presented along with books and activities to promote children's name writing. The use of alphabet books and computer programs is also discussed. Writing to communicate is thus a process of discovery for children as books lead them to making lists in dramatic play, writing messages and stories in the writing center, and creating illustrated stories about field trips.

LEARNING ACTIVITIES

1. How does scribbling become writing for a young child? Discuss the natural process a child goes through in teaching himself to write. Collect samples of children's progression through this process and not how writing develops over time.
2. How would you set up and arrange a writing center in your classroom? What materials and equipment would you provide and why? How would you expect children to use the center? Observe and record different children's use of such a center.
3. How do children learn alphabet letters in a natural manner? Describe in detail what your role should be in assisting them. Carry out this role and report what happens.
4. How can children learn to use an alphabet computer program? How can such a program be integrated into the curriculum? Use such a program with children and report the results.
5. What kinds of writing might children do in the dramatic play center or after a field trip? Describe in detail how a cultural character picture book has helped them do this after a field trip you take with them.

REFERENCES

Beaty, J. J. (1987). *The computer as a paintbrush: Creative uses for the personal computer in the preschool classroom.* Upper Saddle River, NJ: Merrill/Prentice Hall.

Clay, M. M. (1991). *Becoming literate.* Portsmouth, NH: Heinemann.

Clay, M. M. (1975). *What did I write? Beginning writing behavior.* Portsmouth, NH: Heinemann.

Davidson, J. (1996). *Emergent literacy and dramatic play in early education.* Albany, NY: Delmar.

Fields, M. V., & DeGayner, B. (2000). Read my story. *Childhood Education, 76*(3), 130–135.

Green, C. R. (1998). This is my name. *Childhood Education, 74*(4), 226–231.

Hall, N. (2000). Interactive writing with children. *Childhood Education, 76*(6), 358–364.

Klenk, L. (2001). Playing with literacy in preschool classrooms. *Childhood Education, 77*(3), 150–157.

Neuman, S. B., Copple, C., & Bredekamp, S. (2000). *Learning to read and write.* Washington, DC: National Association for the Education of Young Children.

Pratt, L., & Beaty, J. J. (1999). *Transcultural children's literature.* Upper Saddle River, NJ: Merrill/Prentice Hall.

Rhoten, L., & Lane, M. (2001). More than the ABCs: The new alphabet books. *Young Children, 56*(1), 41–45.

Schickedanz, J. A. (1982). The acquisition of written language in young children. In B. Spodek (Ed.), *Handbook of research in early childhood education.* New York: Free Press.

Schickedanz, J. A. (1986). *More than the ABCs: The early stages of reading and writing.* Washington, DC: National Association for the Education of Young Children.

Schickedanz, J. A. (1999). *Much more than the ABCs: The early stages of reading and writing.* Washington, DC: National Association for the Education of Young Children.

Schrader, C. T., & Hoffman, S. (1987). Encouraging children's early writing efforts. *Day Care and Early Education, 15*(2), 9–13.

Strickland, D. S., & Morrow, L. M. (Eds.). (2000). *Beginning reading and writing.* New York: Teachers College Press.

Teale, W. H., & Yokota, J. (2000). Beginning reading and writing: Perspectives on instruction. In D. S. Strickland & L. M. Morrow (Eds.), *Beginning reading and writing.* New York: Teachers College Press.

Temple, C. A., Nathan, R. G., & Burris, N. A. (1993). *The beginnings of writing.* Boston: Allyn & Bacon.

Wasik, B. A. (2001). Teaching the alphabet to young children, *Young Children, 56*(1), 34–39.

SUGGESTED READINGS

Anderson, G. T. (2000). Computers in a developmentally appropriate curriculum. *Young Children, 55*(2), 90–93.

Bradley, D. H., & Pottle, P. R. (2001). Supporting emergent writers through on-the-spot conferencing and publishing. *Young Children, 56*(3), 20–27.

Dyson, A. H. (2001). Writing and children's symbolic repertoires: Development unhinged. In S. B. Neuman & D. K. Dickinson (Eds.), *Handbook of early literacy research.* New York: Guilford.

Fields, M. (1998). *Your child learns to read and write.* Olney, MD: Association for Childhood Education International.

Haugland, S. W. (2000). Early childhood classrooms in the 21st Century: Using computers to maximize learning. *Young Children, 55*(1), 12–18.

Miels, J. C. (2001). Abby Bear deserves to be heard: Setting early writers free. *Young Children, 56*(2), 36–41.

Neuman, S., & Roskos, K. (1997). Literacy knowledge in practice: Contexts of participation for young writers and readers. *Reading Research Quarterly, 32*(1), 10–32.

CHILDREN'S BOOKS

Albert, B. (1991). *Where does the trail lead?* New York: Simon & Schuster.

Aliki. (1993). *My visit to the aquarium.* New York: HarperCollins.

Chanko, P. (1999). *Writing places.* New York: Scholastic.

Cronin, D. (2000). *Click, clack, moo: Cows that type.* New York: Simon & Schuster.

Der Manuelian, P. (1991). *Hieroglyphs from A to Z: A rhyming book with ancient Egyptian stencils for kids.* Boston: Museum of Fine Arts.

Edwards, M. (1992). *Alef-bet: A Hebrew alphabet book.* New York: Lothrop, Lee & Shepard.

Edwards, P. D. (1998). *Warthogs in the kitchen: A sloppy counting book.* New York: Hyperion.

Falwell, C. (1993). *Feast for 10*. New York: Clarion.

Hearn, E. (1984). *Good morning Franny, Good night Franny*. Toronto: Woman's Press.

Heide, F. P., & Gilliland, J. H. (1990). *The day of Ahmed's secret*. New York: Lothrop, Lee, & Shepard.

Jacaranda Designs. (1991). *Mcheshi goes to the market*. Nairobi: Author.

Keats, E. J. (1968). *A letter to Amy*. New York: HarperCollins.

Lee, H. V. (1994). *At the beach*. New York: Holt.

Lee, H. V. (1995). *In the snow*. New York: Holt.

Martin, A. T. (1993). *Famous seaweed soup*. Morton Grove, IL: Whitman.

Martin, B., & Archambault, J. (1989). *Chicka chicka boom boom*. New York: Simon & Schuster.

Moreton, D., & Berger, S. (1999). *Why write?* New York Scholastic.

Olsen, M. (2001). *Native American sign language*. Mahwah, NJ: Troll Communications.

Pellegrini, N. (1991). *Families are different*. New York: Scholastic.

Raffi. (1994). *Like me and you*. New York: Crown.

Rankin, L. (1991). *The handmade alphabet*. New York: Dial.

Samton, S. W. (1991). *Jenny's journey*. New York: Viking.

Sardegna, J. (1994). *K is for kiss good night*. New York: Doubleday.

Shelby, S. (1991). *Potluck*. New York: Orchard.

Tapahonso, L., & Schick, E. (1995). *Navajo ABC*. New York: Simon & Schuster.

Wells, R. (1997). *Bunny cakes*. New York: Dial.

PART 4

EMERGENT READING

Children do not learn to read by magic. Rather, they learn by engaging with other, more accomplished readers around print. Caregivers and teachers play a critical role in promoting children's participation with books. They explain important concepts, encourage children's attention to meaningful events in stories, and involve them in using the information they are learning in dynamic ways that build connections beyond the printed page.

Neuman, Copple, and Bredekamp (2000)

HOW READING EMERGES

DEVELOPING A SENSE OF STORY

RETELLING STORIES FROM BOOKS

CHAPTER 8

DEVELOPING A SENSE OF STORY

Conventional versus Emergent Reading

A great deal has been written by reading educators about how young children learn to read. Much of this material applies to early elementary school children and describes what is known as "conventional reading." Schickedanz (1999) has this to say about it: "We say someone is reading when she is able to decode print in an unfamiliar book. Among reading scholars, this is called 'conventional reading.' A 'beginning reader' is one who reads conventionally but is still a novice" (p. 84).

An emphasis on conventional reading occurs in kindergarten, although emergent reading still persists there (which will be discussed in chapter 10, "Becoming a Reader"). This chapter describes only the early reading behaviors known as "emergent reading." Young children's reading behaviors can emerge naturally over the years through their use of print materials, their language and word play, their writing and knowledge of some words and alphabet letters, and especially their familiarity with particular picture books that have been read to them over and over. Their emergent reading, in other words, occurs with familiar rather than unfamiliar books.

These behaviors emerge over time from toddlerhood on, based on a child's experiences with books and reading. Such behaviors can be listed on a checklist like that in Figure 8.1, but they should not be considered developmental stages. Instead, they are mainly a progression of reading behaviors that many, but not all, preschool children may exhibit.

As with the writing and speaking checklists presented in earlier chapters, this checklist can help you to assess where each of your children stands as he or she begins to emerge into reading. If you decide to use the checklist, be sure you and other staff members use it informally as an observational tool, not a test. Many children may not exhibit any of the behaviors because they have not yet begun to emerge into reading. They should not be penalized or pushed forward by adults in the classroom or at home. If any children do seem to indicate these reading behaviors, however, you may want to keep track of their progress, using dated checklists like Figure 8.1 from time to time to help you follow their development and to help you provide appropriate activities to support it.

There is an additional purpose for presenting a checklist like this. It is to inform teachers about areas of preschool children's reading development they may not be aware of. This chapter discusses each of the items on the checklist as it presents information on children's emergence into reading.

Silly Sally (Wood, 1992)
Handa's Surprise (Browne, 1994)
Juan Bobo Goes to Work
(Montes, 2000)

A Sense of Story

Before young children can emerge into actual reading, they must first develop "a sense of story"—that stories are plotted narratives in which characters act in certain ways and events happen "because of" something in the story line. The youngest children do not view picture book stories in that manner. They seem to treat each page of a book as a sep-

---

PRESCHOOL READING BEHAVIORS CHECKLIST

Child's Name _____ Age _____ Date _____

Story Not Formed

1._____ Opens book and begins to babble or jabber as if reading ("book babble")

2._____ Attempts to retell what is in book through naming pictures ("picture naming")

3._____ Retells story as if each page of book is separate unit, not part of ongoing story

Story Formed

4._____ Tells story in sequence in own words, guided by pictures, ignores print

5._____ Uses pictures as cues in telling story, but seems to recognize print and avoids covering it with hand

6._____ Tells familiar story in sequence by reciting story words verbatim

7._____ Notices print on pages and asks what it says

8._____ Points to words of familiar story and says them while telling memorized story ("fingerpoint reading")

(Permission is granted by the publisher to reproduce this checklist for evaluation and record keeping.)

FIGURE 8.1

Preschool Reading Behaviors Checklist

Source: Based on information from Sulzby (1985) and Schickedanz (1999).

arate unit instead of as part of a whole story. This level of reading emergence is categorized as "story not formed," as described on the first three checklist items.

Little by little children's familiarity with picture storybooks helps them become aware of narrative structure. As Van Kraayenoord and Paris (1996) note:

> Picture books show that stories have settings, plots, and themes. Specifically, this knowledge is acquired through children's attention and understanding that characters' actions occur in different settings, that narratives comprise events in related sequences, that stories carry messages from authors, and that stories elicit cognitive and emotional responses. (p. 43)

Book Babble

The youngest children (e.g., toddlers of 1 to 2 years) who have been read to extensively at home and in child care programs may exhibit a behavior called "book babble." Sometimes when looking at a book by themselves, especially a favorite one, they begin to jabber away as if they were actually reading the

If your program does not have a staff member with time for reading daily to individuals, perhaps a volunteer such as a Foster Grandparent could come in on a daily basis.

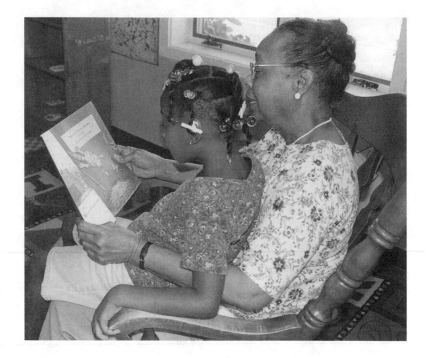

words. These are children who also may have done conversational babbling before they could speak, although book babble sounds more like reading than speaking (Schickedanz, 1999, p. 23). Babbling like this is practice reading, just as scribbling is practice writing.

Not all toddlers do book babbling. The babblers are often the children who have been read to many times, probably seated on the reader's lap so they can enjoy the warmth of being held close to a loving adult, and so they can see the book illustrations clearly. They, in turn, come to love books and the experience of being read to and so try to repeat it on their own, imitating the adult reader. As one 6-year-old told his younger brother, Mike, who was worried because he couldn't read, "Oh, Mike, don't worry. It's easy! You see, you just sit on Mom's lap and she reads you stories. Then you can read the words." As authors Collins and Shaeffer (1997) continue, "It's true! That's more or less what happens after an adult has read the same story over and over to a child sitting on her lap or cuddled up next to her. He studies the pictures, absorbs the words and cadences, notices the print, and progresses significantly toward being able to read" (p. 63).

Reading to Individuals

What does such information about book babble mean for preschool programs committed to the development of emergent literacy in their children? It does not mean you will expect children of preschool age to do book babbling (although a few may). It means you must make sure *individual children are read to by caring adults every day*, on and off throughout the day, especially from the books children have indicated are their favorites. You remember that book reading is the most important element in successful emergent literacy. If your program does not have a staff member with time for such an essential activity, perhaps a volunteer could come in on a daily basis. Check to see whether your area has a Foster Grandparents Program that could send a volunteer for reading to individual children. Other federal programs with volunteers who work with children include RSVP (Retired Senior Volunteer Program), Americore, VISTA, America Reads, and Learn and Serve. The children's own grandparents as volunteers are another source of picture book readers.

One of the favorite preschool books, especially for the youngest children, is **Silly Sally**, about the topsy-turvy red-headed medieval English maiden who proceeds through a field of golden buttercups: "Silly Sally went to town, walking backwards, upside down," meeting absurd animals all the way. The full-page illustrations, combined with the lilting cadence of a brief rhyming sentence at the bottom of each page, seem to captivate the attention of young listeners. This is a cumulative tale in which the accumulated actions of Sally and the pig that danced a jig, the dog that played leapfrog, the loon that sang a tune, and the sheep that fell asleep have to be released from sleep by Neddy Buttercup, walking forward, right side up, who tickles each of them in turn.

The youngest children want to hear the tale again and again, especially if the reader holds their rapt attention by "dancing the book" when the pig dances, "leapfrogging the book" when the dog jumps, falling asleep and snoring when Sally does (children love this), and doing all kinds of tickling of the child listener when Neddy Buttercup tickles the animals.

To the young child listener, each action on the various pages is an event separate from the rest of the story, as noted, because she has not yet developed a sense of story. It may still take months or even years of experience, maturity, and many book readings before she understands the narrative flow involved in the story line of a storybook. You can help this process along for children who have heard the story repeated numerous times by asking them to look for clues in the pictures as to what is going to happen next.

Each double-page illustration has the animals that Sally will meet partly concealed in a field of yellow buttercups in the order of their appearance. The pig's back, the dog's paws or feet, a part of the duck sticking out of the water, and even Neddy Buttercup asleep among the flowers off in the distance can be discovered by listeners with sharp eyes once they know the story well. And once Sally and her entourage arrive at the Medieval town, all of the town's diverse cultural characters join the ridiculous procession "walking backwards, upside down!"

Story Reenactments

Another way you can help children begin to develop this sense of story is through the impromptu dramatization of favorite stories, called *story reenactment*. For **Silly Sally** children can choose to be the characters of Sally, the pig, the dog, the loon, the sheep, and Neddy Buttercup while you do the reading of the story. Everybody else is the audience. It is perfectly acceptable to have more than one Sally or any other character at a time. Before you do story reenactment, the children need to be completely familiar with the story through repeated readings of it.

After the children choose which characters they want to be, turn the room into an imaginary field of buttercups with the various animals hiding discreetly behind furniture or room dividers, ready to pop out and perform their actions when Sally arrives at their positions as you read the story once more. Then they can join Sally and proceed along to the next character. At one point they will all need to collapse in a heap and fall asleep with loud snoring (they love this), until Neddy comes along and awakens each one through tickling. When they finally get to town, the rest of the class can join the procession winding through the room with Sally in the lead.

Dramatizing stories through story reenactment is different from the regular imaginary play that children do by themselves in the dramatic play center. It is more structured because the children will be following a prescribed story line from the book you read. But it is less structured than a traditional play in which children are chosen to take a role and must learn their lines. Story reenactment is for the children themselves and not for an outside audience. It can be performed immediately in an impromptu manner with no practicing. Children like pretending to be a character, not once but again and again. They even relish being the audience which is often directly involved in the action. Once again, it is the *process* of being involved that is important for the children, not the *product* of a polished performance (Beaty, 1994).

Just as children ask you to read the same story over and over, they will want to do the same reenactment again and again. If they do not ask you, you can ask them, because this repetition is important in their development of a "sense of story." Ishee and Goldhaber (1990) tell how their children performed *The Three Bears* 27 times in 4 days! They have this to say about repeat performances:

> This is the most important part. Many repetitions help children. For many children it is necessary to watch a play numerous times before making that first gesture of pretense within the play. For others, repetition allows an opportunity to elaborate and expand on the story as presented, to take on a variety of roles, and to assume major responsibility for a role. (p. 74)

After the children have performed the reenactment several times, ask them whether they would like to make headbands with animal ears or feathers to wear when they take on their roles. They can trade their headbands with someone else when they switch roles. Or they may simply want to wear a yarn necklace with the name of their character printed on a card. Perhaps children can also cut out yellow paper buttercups (even a yellow circle will do), to be distributed here and there around the room if this story becomes an important part of class activities. If you have no yellow paper, have the children paint yellow "buttercups" on white paper and cut them out.

Be sure to have the audience clap for each of the characters every time a reenactment is finished. Children love this. Then the characters can clap for the audience, too. Leave the book in the book center afterward to see what happens. Do any of the youngest children pick it up and pretend to read it?

A number of the picture books previously described can be reenacted like this, with you as the reader, especially if they are simple stories with (a) a folktale-like structure, (b) an engaging character who must perform a series of actions with other characters in an easily remembered sequence, and (c) a satisfying conclusion in which everything comes together.

Cultural Character Concept

Besides helping children develop a sense of story, such reenactments help to bring cultural characters to life for young children. They can actually step into the shoes of the characters and find out for themselves what it is like to be Handa, for example, the African girl who is taking her friend Akeyo a surprise basket of fruit in the story **Handa's Surprise.** Your child characters will be Handa, Akeyo, a monkey, an ostrich, a zebra, an elephant, a giraffe, an antelope, a parrot, and a billy goat. For props you will need a basket for Handa to carry, holding it on her head, seven plastic fruits from your dramatic play center for six of the animals to steal, and several real tangerines. The children who portray animals can make animal ears attached to headbands if they like. But it is not necessary for anyone to wear a costume in story reenactments unless they want to. Child animals can hide behind shelves and furniture waiting to sneak up behind Handa as she passes by and take one of the fruits. The child billy goat can put tangerines into Handa's empty basket after she passes. Then both Handa and Akeyo will be surprised at the end, and everyone, including the audience, can end up eating pieces of the tangerines.

Children can also learn what it is like to be the Puerto Rican boy Juan Bobo from **Juan Bobo Goes to Work,** described in chapter 4. The characters are Juan Bobo, his mother, Don Pepe the farmer, Señor Domingo the grocer, the rich man, and his daughter. For props Juan Bobo and the farmer can wear straw hats, and the grocer can wear an ordinary man's hat. The basket of beans, the coins, the bucket of milk, the burlap bag, the broom, the cheese, and the ham can be imaginary or not, whatever the children decide. As you read the story, the characters can act it out.

Picture Naming

Children who have had books read to them since babyhood will automatically attempt to retell what is in a familiar book by naming a picture on the page, rather than retelling the story in a sequential narrative. After all, adults who have been reading to them often point to the pictures that are being described in the stories. Adult readers also direct children's attention to the pictures in a book by talking about them and asking the children to find the picture showing a particular character or action. Thus, to young children, it is the picture that tells the story and not the text. And it is not an ongoing story that the pictures tell for most young children but separate incidents, often one to a page.

To young children, it is the pictures that tell the story, not the text.

Young children who are asked to retell the **Silly Sally** story will quickly name the animals involved on each page, talking about and pointing out "the pig dancing," "the dog leaping," or perhaps "making a somersault" (the child may stop for a moment to demonstrate his own somersault). Children do not demonstrate a sense of story that these animals are going down a path with Sally in order to get to town, that falling asleep is preventing them from getting to town, or that Neddy Buttercup saves the day by tickling them all awake.

Book Illustrations as Meaning Makers

But it is not the pictures in picture books that are preventing the youngest children from developing a "sense of story." Quite the opposite. *Children who naturally emerge into reading depend on the pictures in picture books to help them understand the stories.* At first they may think that each picture is a separate event not connected with an overall narrative, as noted. But eventually through experience with picture books, through book extension activities in the classroom, and through their own maturity of cognitive functions, they come to realize that there is a narrative flow throughout a book. And it is the illustrations that help them "make meaning" of the whole story.

Reading educators did not at first understand the function of pictures, believing that deciphering words was the key to learning to read. They were, of course, defining reading as "conventional reading" that was taught to children in elementary school. But when Ferreiro and Teberosky, pioneer researchers in emergent literacy from Argentina, published their findings in Spanish in 1979 and in English in 1982, educators around the world took notice. The two researchers had this to say:

> Reading is not deciphering. Until now, psychology and pedagogy have viewed the learning of reading as an inevitable mechanism of establishing correspondence between oral language and written language. Only recently have some authors begun to defend other positions, manifesting that reading is not equivalent to decoding letters into sounds, and so cannot be reduced strictly to deciphering. (p. 20)

Most current researchers now know that "emergent reading," like "emergent writing," *begins with pictures* that help children establish a basis for the meaning of the words they will eventually come to recognize. Then many researchers go on to say that when young children listen to stories being read to them over and over, they begin to construct a mental model of the elements of the story: the setting of a story, the attributes of certain characters, the order in which events occur, and how the story will eventually end. But these researchers still seem to be concerned mainly with the *listening* aspect of story reading. As Neuman and Roskos (1993) have noted, "This sense of story comes about by hearing stories, and by being read to on a regular basis. Perhaps no other finding in research is as well documented as the simple fact that reading regularly to young children significantly influences their understanding of what reading is all about as well as their later proficiency in reading" (p. 37).

This research is correct as far as it goes. But for young children, the books they are "hearing" are picture books—so, of course, they are also "seeing" the story. Why is this factor not recognized by many researchers? It is the pictures young children see along with the words they hear that help them to develop the sense of story. Picture book specialist Kiefer (1995), in her groundbreaking book *The Potential of Picturebooks: From Visual Literacy to Aesthetic Understanding*, feels it is unfortunate that "[e]xperts in the field of visual literacy have often neglected the potential of picture-books to develop visual literacy, just as reading and writing researchers have overlooked the opportunities for language and literacy learning provided by picturebooks" (p. 10).

But young children have not overlooked the pictures in picture books. For them, the pictures are the story. It is the pictures that give the words their meaning. When they begin to retell stories from books themselves, their words are guided by their individual interpretation of the pictures. As you have found, if you have assessed any children using the Preschool Reading Behaviors Checklist, the first five items of the children's progression through the reading behaviors involve using the pictures in the picture book to tell the story. Can pictures alone help children develop "the sense of story" necessary for them to emerge into reading?

One of the most effective ways to help children who have already listened to a story over and over develop a real "sense of story" is to illustrate the story with cutout pictures on a flannel board.

C H A P T E R   8

Telling Stories with Flannel Boards

Gilberto and the Wind (Ets, 1963)

Iktomi and the Buzzard (Goble, 1994)

The realization that emergent reading can occur in preschool children has brought about a renewed interest in the use of flannel boards or felt boards as a form of literacy meaning making. Whether or not teachers realize that placing the cutout characters and elements of a story on a flannel board has anything to do with their children's developing a "sense of story" makes no difference. Children enjoy the activity and that is enough. But reading educators like Short, Harris, and Fairchild (2001) know that "[r]epeated readings and tellings of familiar stories can help children learn grammar, elements of story such as plot and sequence, speaking and listening skills, and improve comprehension. Flannel board figures are visual reminders of a story's main characters, setting, and sequence of events" (p. 4).

Although some teachers use storytelling aprons that the story figures adhere to, using a board is best, so that the teller can step back from it, and the viewers can see distinctly "what happens next" in the story. Teachers need to be the ones who model the use of a flannel board the first time with a small group (not total group) of children seated in front of the board. Then the teacher should lay out the flannel board figures on a table in front of the board. As the teacher reads the already-familiar story, a second time *without showing children the book illustrations*, one of the children can find the first figure mentioned and place it on the left side of the board. As the reading continues, the second figure can be placed next to the first one, and so on across the board, left to right in sequence, as the story continues.

Another time the teacher can *tell* the story without the book and place the figures on the board herself. Always leave the book and figures on the table next to the flannel board, so that eventually the children can experiment with telling the story and placing the characters on the board themselves without adult help. In fact, they enjoy "being the teacher" and telling the story to their own small group of listeners. Their stories will often skip certain incidents or relate them out of order, because they have not yet developed the concept of sequencing, a left-brain skill, to any degree. With your prompting, most of them will eventually be able to tell "what comes next."

Flannel boards and their story figures can be purchased or made by the teacher. Commercial boards of various sizes can be ordered from Lakeshore Learning Materials (phone: [800] 421-5354) or Constructive Playthings (phone: [800] 448-4115). To make your own board simply glue a rectangular piece of flannel or felt to stiff cardboard. A freestanding flannel board can be placed on an easel or chalk tray, or you can glue the flannel to the side of a large carton to be placed on a table. Magnetic boards and figures are also available from Lakeshore.

The story figures can also be purchased from the aforementioned educational supply companies, along with their books, and kept in baggies or manila envelopes when not in use. But many teachers prefer to make their own figures by photocopying or scanning pages of the books they want to use, cutting out the figures, and laminating them or gluing them onto oaktag cardboard. They then cut out the figures from the cardboard and fasten an adhesive back-

Eventually children can experiment with trying to tell the story and placing the characters on the flannel board without adult help.

ing to each one (e.g., felt, sandpaper, or Velcro), so the figures will adhere to the flannel board but can be easily removed.

Simple books with large distinct pictures of their characters and events are the best ones to use for converting to flannel board stories. For instance, folktales with three distinct incidents or characters make it easy for children to follow the sequence of events, and reproduce them on a flannel board. Some of the books and storytelling figures available from Lakeshore include these:

The Very Hungry Caterpillar	*Silly Sally*
Brown Bear, Brown Bear, What do You See?	*Patrick's Dinosaurs*
There Was an Old Lady Who Swallowed a Fly	*Corduroy*

Lakeshore also has these books and magnetic storytelling figures:

Pancakes for Breakfast	*Love You Forever*
In a Small, Small Pond	*Are You My Mother?*

Flannel board storytelling figures from Constructive Playthings include the following:

Goldilocks and the Three Bears	*The Gingerbread Boy*
The Three Little Pigs	*The Little Red Hen*
The Three Billy Goats Gruff	*Jack and the Beanstalk*
Little Red Riding Hood	

But what about the cultural character books described in this text? Can any of them be converted to flannel board storytelling? Very easily. Simply make photocopies or scans of the desired pages, and cut out the characters and illustrated incidents of the story. Mount them as previously described, and use them with the children whenever you read the book. For instance, you might cut out the following characters and incidents from *Gilberto and the Wind*:

Gilberto and balloon at top of tree	Gilberto and sailboat
Gilberto and clothes on clothesline	Gilberto and pinwheel
Gilberto and umbrella	Gilberto blowing bubbles
Gilberto on gate	Gilberto raking leaves
Gilberto and kite	Gilberto in house
Gilberto and apple tree	Gilberto sleeping

From *Iktomi and the Buzzard*:

Iktomi doing Eagle Dance	Iktomi upside down in hollow tree
Buzzard	Woodpeckers in hole
Iktomi on buzzard's back	Girls through hole in tree
Iktomi's shadow on buzzard	Iktomi coming out of tree
Iktomi falling	Girls running away

Be sure to choose favorite stories. Once children know these stories well, have heard the teacher read them many times, and seen the teacher use the flannel board figures, they can try it themselves. At first, an adult will need to read the story while a child places the figures on the board. When children finally use the figures to make up their own stories, you will know their sense of story has arrived. Or, as Short et al. (2001), note, "Story retelling experiences provide opportunities for children to express their unique interpretations of stories while allowing the teacher to observe individual children's literacy development" (p. 5).

RETELLING STORIES FROM BOOKS

Practice Reading

You may have noticed that children who love to look at books and hear them read aloud sometimes engage in what is called "practice reading." (Book babble, described previously, is a kind of practice reading done by toddlers). According to Schickedanz (1999), there are two types of practice reading:

The first is reading along with an adult. In this kind of practice, the adult scaffolds [supports] the child's reading of the book. In the *scaffolded* experience the child participates, but the adult does as much of the work as necessary to keep things going. . . . The second type of practice is the *independent* retelling of a familiar story. In this kind of practice, a child reads a familiar storybook to herself, to an adult, another child, or a doll or stuffed animal. (pp. 71–72)

Be sure to choose favorite stories for flannel board storytelling so listeners can begin to develop a "sense of story."

Not all preschoolers are at the level of doing practice reading, but a few may be. They are the children who have been read to a great deal both at home and in preschool. They are the ones who love books and have certain favorites that they want to read over and over. When children read along with adults in the first type of practice reading, they are actually saying words they have memorized by hearing the adult read them again and again. After children have read along with adults repeatedly in the same book, they are able to say more of the words and eventually may be able to retell the entire story independently, guided by the pictures.

Predictable Books

Books that prompt children to read along with an adult like this are books that both children and adults love because of their catchy rhythms and the sound of their words. Children are often just as captivated by the pictures of their favorite human or animal characters, as they are with the rhyming and repeated words, or sequential pattern of episodes. These books are called "predictable books." As Schickedanz (1999) tells us, "Predictable books are designed to make their texts memorable. Their structure specifically encourages children to chime in as

---

CHOOSING PREDICTABLE CULTURAL CHARACTER BOOKS

TITLE_____

1. _____ Text has repetitive and rhyming words, lines, episodes.

2. _____ Text has a rhythmic cadence.

3. _____ Text has cumulative episodes.

4. _____ Text uses a sequential pattern (days, numbers, letters).

5. _____ Text is brief, fast-paced, and fun.

6. _____ Story features engaging human or animal cultural characters.

7. _____ Pictures clearly illustrate words, lines, episodes.

Other _____

_____

(Permission is granted by the publisher to reproduce this checklist for evaluation and record keeping.)

FIGURE 8.2
Choosing Predictable Cultural Character Books Checklist

an adult reads and helps them recall chunks of text during independent readings" (p. 73).

They are among the most effective picture books to promote children's independent retelling of stories. They are not only fun to hear but even more exciting for children to chime in when the teacher pauses in her reading. Their engaging illustrations describe what the text expresses in words. When children see and hear these stories read aloud over and over, they begin to remember what is coming next—what word, what line, or what episode. Thus, they begin to emerge into reading.

To select predictable books that support the cultural character approach featured in this text, the checklist "Choosing Predictable Cultural Character Books" (Figure 8.2) can be helpful.

A selection of the predictable books from this text fall into one or more of the categories from this checklist:

Repetitive and Rhyming Words, Lines, Episodes

Dinosaur Roar!   *Is Your Mama a Llama?*

Flower Garden   *Miss Mary Mack*

Hats Off to Hair!	*My Best Shoes*
Hush!	*Pigs in the Mud*
Silly Sally	*How Do Dinosaurs Say Good Night?*

Rhythmic Cadences

And to Think That We Thought That We'd Never Be Friends	*Miss Mary Mack*
Bein' with You This Way	*Twist with a Burger, Jitter with a Bug*
Chicka Chicka Boom Boom	*Louella Mae, She's Run Away!*
How Do Dinosaurs Say Goodnight?	*The Lady With the Alligator Purse*

Cumulative Episodes

Bein' with You This Way Fiddle-I-Fee	*I Know an Old Lady Who Swallowed a Fly*
The House That Jack Built	*Old MacDonald Had a Farm*
There Was an Old Lady Who Swallowed a Trout	*Shoes from Grandpa*

Sequential Patterns

One of Three	*My Best Shoes*
Dinosaur Days	*Ten Terrible Dinosaurs*
Feast for Ten	*Warthogs in the Kitchen*
It's Simple, Said Simon	

Using Predictable Books with Children

You may already know which of these predictable books you will want to reread with your children, because they are books both you and they already enjoy hearing over and over. As Neuman and Roskos (1993) tell us:

> Predictable books are ideal for promoting young children's active participation in story reading. . . . Read selections you love. Your positive attitude is infectious and will encourage children to actively participate in the readings. Start with books that have easily learned patterns, and then move on to books with more complex structures. (p. 237)

Some of these predictable books will appeal to the children because of their rhythm or rhyming. These are the ones most easily memorized by certain children who want to hear them over and over. Bright pictures on every page against a white background help

Dinosaur Roar! (Stickland, 1994)

How Do Dinosaurs Say Good Night? (Yolen, 2000)

Louella Mae, She's Run Away! (Alarcon, 1997)

Twist with a Burger, Jitter with a Bug (Lowery, 1995)

Shoes from Grandpa (Fox, 1989)

listeners see what's happening. A few large words at the bottom of the page will eventually (not at first) help these same children recognize it is the print that tells the story. You may have already noted that the chanting books from chapter 3 are listed among the predictable books, because of their rhyming and rhythmic texts.

One of the simplest books in the first category of predictable books with repetitive and rhyming words is **Dinosaur Roar!** Huge pictures of orange, purple, brown, green, and blue dinosaurs with attitudes lumber across double white pages in this horizontal book quickly catching the readers' attention. The dinosaurs demonstrate opposite actions reflected by two-word sentences at the bottom of each page. Children's favorite lines seem to be "Dinosaur fat, dinosaur tiny, dinosaur clean, dinosaur slimy." They want you to read this book again and again, just to hear the hilarious word *slimy*. And you also may begin hearing *slimy* throughout the day. For children who want to make their own dinosaur books after this, be sure to provide plenty of "slimy green paint." *Sweet* and *grumpy*, *spiky* and *lumpy* are also new words children relish hearing and saying. It won't be long before the dinosaur picture cues and repeated readings of this book give your most avid dinosaur fans the means for retelling this story on their own to anyone who will listen.

On the other hand, **How Do Dinosaurs Say Good Night?** is a more complex but still fascinating predictable book from the second category of books having rhythmic cadence. Its double page pictures show various huge dinosaurs in human bedrooms acting as if they are children who don't want to go to bed. At first their papas, shown as tiny cultural character men standing in the doorways and scratching their heads at their huge beasts, have no luck at all getting them to bed. Then it is the mamas' turn. Various cultural mamas try their luck. "How does a dinosaur say good night when Mama comes in to turn off the light?" Children love the words on the next two pages: "Does he mope, does he moan, does he sulk, does he sigh?" And then: "Does he fall on the top of his covers and cry?" It is you who should do the moping, moaning, sulking, sighing, and crying sounds at first, but soon your listeners will know enough to join in. Listen to see how your child story retellers handle that scene.

Cadence is also the most attractive aspect of **Louella Mae, She's Run Away!** It is a farm story with all kinds of Anglo-American Arkansas farm family characters and their animals joining in this riotous search for Louella Mae in verse form. Not only do the verses rhyme, but readers must turn the page to discover the last word of each rhyme:

> Has anyone seen her/
>
> Now where could she be?
>
> Go look in the
>
> Hollowed-out trunk of that. . . .

Children love guessing the answer (tree) before turning the page each time. The first time you read it to one or two children, you must swear them to secrecy about the surprise ending of the book: not only where they finally find Louella Mae (in the tub), but also who Louella Mae turns out to be (a pig with piglets!). Once everyone knows the secret they can shout out the answers to the page-turning words every time you reread the story.

But the all-time favorite cadence story for most preschool children could very well be ***Twist with a Burger, Jitter with a Bug***. Have a child on either side of you as you read it, so they can see the large colorful illustrations of cartoonlike cultural children moving to dance rhythms against a stark white background. The catchy cadence and witty words should cue everyone that this is going to be fun. Hispanic girls dancing a mambo like Carmen Miranda or an African American boy with a boom box, snapping to a rap, will have the children wishing they could also "put on your cleats and tap, tap, tap." Keep the pages turning quickly. If children like the story, they will want it read again—and again, especially to see and hear their favorite four pages: "Boogie in the bathtub/hula-hula dance/rumba if you wanna/in your underpants." At this point you'll probably have to stop for a moment and just let them laugh. Books should be fun like this, if we want children to want to learn to read. Afterward, put on a catchy record and let them "rumba if they wanna" around the reading center.

Bring in a pile of clothes for your reading of the cumulative tale ***Shoes from Grandpa*** after you have read the story to a number of children. An Australian grandpa starts the whole shebang by buying Jessie a new pair of red boots. Then every other member of her family has to join in by buying Jessie another article of clothing, starting with her Dad: "I'll buy you some socks from the local shops, to go with the shoes from Grandpa." Her mom buys her a skirt; her sister buys a sweater; her grandma buys a coat, her aunt knits a scarf; her brother finds a hat; and her uncle says:

> I'll buy you some mittens that are softer than kittens,
>
> To go with the hat you can put on like that,
>
> To go with the scarf that'll make us all laugh,
>
> To go with the coat you could wear on a boat. . . .

Until poor Jessie replies:

> You're all so kind that I hate to be mean,
>
> But please, would one of you buy me some jeans?

If the children want to join in the spirit of this story, choose someone to be Jessie, and have each of the others give her an article of clothing when their turn comes as all of you read the lines in unison. She doesn't have to put it on, only hold it, or let the others drape it over her. At the end someone can run in from across the room with the jeans. This story may be longer than the others, but if you reread it enough, some of the children will learn it by heart, and be able to read it or tell it along with you.

Retelling Stories with Cultural Character Dolls

Now that you understand the importance of rereading the children's favorite books in order for them to (a) develop a sense of story, (b) follow along in the book when you read the story; and (c) begin to memorize the words, it is time for some of them to have the fun of retelling the stories on their own. Some may be able to retell stories already just as they have done with flannel board stories, story reenactments, and predictable book stories. But for other children who enjoy playing with dolls, your cultural character dolls may be the key to involving them in retelling their favorite stories.

Here are some of the cultural character dolls available commercially for teachers to purchase:

African American girl doll for *One of Three* and *Flower Garden*

African American boy doll for *Hue Boy*, *Haircuts at Sleepy Sam's*, *Yo! Yes?* and *I'm Calling Molly*

Grace doll for *Amazing Grace*

Cassie doll for *Tar Beach*

Peter doll for *Whistle for Willie* and *A Letter to Amy*

Dear One doll for *Mama, Do You Love Me?*

Native American girl doll for *The Mud Family*, *Dragon Fly's Tale*, and *Building a Bridge*

She-Who-Is-Alone doll for *Legend of the Bluebonnet*

Native American boy doll for *The Shepherd Boy*

Asian girl doll for *Where Is Gah-Ning?*

Asian boy doll for Ling Sung in *Cleversticks*

Joseph doll for *Joseph Had a Little Overcoat*

Rosalba doll for *Abuela* and *Isla*

Hispanic boy doll for *Carlos and the Squash Plant*, *Carlos and the Corn Field*, *Gilberto and the Wind*, and *Pascual's Magic Pictures*

Anglo-American girl doll for Anna in *Building a Bridge* and Molly in *I'm Calling Molly*

Anglo-American boy doll for *Yo! Yes?* and *Sammy and the Dinosaurs*

Find dolls in bookstores, order multicultural doll puppets—try Community Kids Puppets by Treehuggers, from Demco Kids & Things (phone: [800] 356-1200), Multi-Ethnic Dolls (16 inches) or Preschool Pals Rag Dolls (18 inches) from Constructive Playthings (phone: [800] 448-4115)—or make your own dolls.

Cultural Character Concept

It is important to keep these dolls separate from the baby dolls in the dramatic play housekeeping center, as noted in chapter 4. These dolls are the cultural characters from books and should be treated as such. Most have names and particular temperaments. Have them on hand in the book center when their book is being looked at by the children or read to them by the staff. Otherwise, store

Some teachers make cut-out paper dolls from photocopies of book pages, because they understand how essential it is for children to become acquainted with children like themselves from other cultures.

them out of sight. When they are out, talk about them: how they acted in their story and what the children like about them. Would any of the children like to be their friend? Would any of the children like to visit them at home? Would any of the children like to tell their story? Sometimes a shy child will hide behind a cultural character doll to tell its story.

Because cultural character dolls like these are expensive, some teachers make cutout paper dolls from photocopies or scans of book pages. They then laminate the cutouts and use them like real dolls with the children, as previously noted. Teachers often spend their valuable time creating cultural character dolls like this because they understand how essential it is for their youngsters to become acquainted with children like them from other cultures who have stories to tell. Preschool children soon begin treating both the dolls and paper dolls as real children whom they come to know and enjoy playing with.

For each of the cultural character doll stories you have reread many times to the children, plan on having a retelling of the story by one of the children in your small listening group if anyone is able to. Accept whatever the child says in his retelling, even though incidents are omitted or mixed up. If a child prefers to have the doll character tell the story, hand him the doll and encourage him to tell the story for the doll just as if the doll is speaking. After the retellings, children often want to have the story read again. One preschool teacher who spends time daily on story readings and retellings as a springboard into prewriting, drawing, and other classroom activities, has this to say about rereadings:

> The children like to hear stories again and again. It is not just enjoyment that they are getting from these readings; they also are getting new meanings with each reading, learning more new words, and acquiring new patterns of language. . . . My expectation is always that after we have enjoyed reading a story together a number of times, I will hear echoes of the story as I listen to the children at play. Furthermore, as they commit to memory parts of the story they create the possibility of reading the book on their own in the library corner—even though they may not look at the print during those readings. (Campbell, 1998, p 136)

Tape-Recording Children's Retelling of Book Stories

Not all children have reached the level of being able to retell stories from the books you have read. In fact, not many children will reach this level if they have not had a great deal of experience with books and stories at home as well as in the preschool. As Morrow (1989) notes, "Retelling is not an easy task for children, but with practice they improve quickly" (p.114). If story retelling by children is an expectation of yours, and the children understand this, many more youngsters may attempt the retelling—especially if you have made the experience fun for them. Some may be shy about it. Others may want to do their retelling at an inappropriate time. For everyone involved, the self-recording of stories into a tape recorder may solve the problem. Children are then free to retell their stories as they want and when they want by telling them into a simple tape recorder you have taught them to use.

There is one rule they must follow: they must not rewind and listen to their story immediately after recording it. Instead, they should stop the tape recorder when they are finished and leave it for the next story reteller. Otherwise it is too easy to erase stories accidentally during the tape rewinding and subsequent recording. Tell them that all the stories will be listened to by the group later in the day. As Hall (1998) relates:

> The use of the tape recorder means that there is always an opportunity and a means for any child in the class to act as a storyteller without having to worry about standing up and being a public performer. The recording can later act as the performance and the shy child can listen along with all the other children when the collected stories are heard and commented on by the other class members. (p. 89)

Children's Retelling of Stories Using Print

Dinosaur Roar! (Stickland, 1994)

At some time during a child's listening to story rereadings, he will notice the print on the page and asks what it says–especially if the print is large and noticeable. The large print at the bottom of the pages of ***Dinosaur Roar!*** is a case in point. Children who are aware of print may want to know which word says their favorite word *slimy*, so they can laugh about it again and point to the green slime dripping from the dinosaur. By now you will probably be tracing your finger under the words on these pages as you read them. Does anyone notice that the last word on the last page, "scrunch!" is being eaten by a dinosaur sneaking around from the cover, and that the *h* is caught in its teeth?

It is up to the reader to get her listeners caught up in the emotions of the story, as well. If she sounds bored, the children will hardly listen. It will certainly not be a book they want to hear again. **Dinosaur Roar!** may be a simple book, but neither its words nor its pictures are boring unless the reader makes it so. As one preschool teacher points out:

> It is essential to bring excitement to the voice. Where there's something exciting in the book, change the intonation in your voice, show in your face that you're excited. Whisper the voice, yell the voice. . . . I like to read books that are colorful and short. . . . This book shows the children the concepts of strong and weak, high and low, big and small. I don't say, "Dinosaur roar." I say, "Dinosaur ROAR!!!" That stops the children right there. You can see right there that they can see it's going to be a fun book. (Meier, 2000, pp. 100–101)

The reading of a real book by a live person is, first and foremost, the best reading experience a preschool child can have. He feels the warmth of a caring adult as he sits on the teacher's lap or next to her. He hears her own natural voice directed toward him, making him feel good and important that the teacher is doing this for him. It is a personal experience that cannot be compared to the abstract experience of hearing a book on tape or seeing one on a computer monitor or on television. With a live reading the child can follow along with the teacher's words and the turning of the pages. He can ask the teacher about the pictures or the words in the book, and she will answer him. He can ask her to read it again, and she will do it. He can look at the book afterward and relive this enjoyable experience. This kind of book reading is a personal experience he will not soon forget. It is the best kind.

Cultural character books that teachers read to individuals and small groups should afterwards be followed up with the many extension activities as described in previous chapters. In this way not only will the child be involved in a multitude of learning activities based on a book he loves, but the child can pursue this learning on his own while the teacher is free to read the book again to other children.

Using Computer Cultural Character Book Programs

Using a computer book program based on a book the teacher has already read to the children is a possible follow-up, so long as it is treated as such and not as entertainment. The teacher should know the program well and have goals for the children in mind who will be using it. Most book CD-ROMs have several levels of use depending on the ages and abilities of the children. In addition to the book reading itself, there are various other activities as well. Teachers should try out all of them to decide which ones are developmentally appropriate for their children. Point-and-click activities on various pages of the books can be explored. Teachers should find ways to integrate such computer activities into the learning centers of the classroom, so that children have three-dimensional experiences with real materials and not just abstract pictures to learn from.

A few of the cultural character book computer CD-ROM programs available include the following, all from Library Video Company (phone: [800] 843-3620):

1. *Big Anthony's Mixed Up Magic* (WIN/MAC) 5R1007. Children can read Tomie dePaola's book or explore Strega Nona's wonderful world of Calabria, Italy. Includes games, adventures, activities, sing-alongs, music, and more. Grades pre-K–4.

The classic *Strega Nona* book about the Italian Grandmother Witch and her bumbling assistant Big Anthony can be ordered from Lectorum (phone: [800] 345-5946). Also available from this company are hardcover and paperback books in English and in Spanish, tape cassettes in English and in Spanish, VHS videotapes in English and in Spanish, and a Strega Nona doll.

When Anthony decides to cook spaghetti in Strega Nona's magic pot, he has no idea how much trouble he's going to cause. Luckily Strega Nona returns just in time to save the day.

2. *Madeline—European Adventures* (WIN) 5R1847. Children can take a train trip through Europe and encounter four learning adventures and six skill-building activity games that develop problem solving, logic and critical thinking skills. Grades pre-K–3.

The classic book *Madeline* by Ludwig Bemelmans can be ordered from Lectorum (phone: [800] 345-5946). Also available from this company are the Big Book in English and in Spanish, hard-cover and paperback books in Spanish, paperback book in English, tape cassette in English and in Spanish, and a Madeline doll.

Madeline, the youngest and most mischievous of the 12 little girls who live in Paris with Miss Clavel, has been a cherished character since this book was first published over 60 years ago. The translation of this classic story into Spanish preserves all the charm of the original.

3. *Why Mosquitoes Buzz in People's Ears* (WIN/MAC) 5R3934. A tall tale sets off a chain of mishaps through the jungle grapevine in this traditional story from Africa by Verna Aardema. Its illustrations come to life in animated sequences, with narration by James Earl Jones. The program teaches how to sequence events and recall main characters. Includes two CDs. Grades pre-K–2.

Hardcover books in English and Spanish can be ordered from Lectorum (phone: [800] 345-5946). Also available from this company are VHS videotapes in English and in Spanish, a paperback book in English, and a tape cassette in English.

A mosquito annoys the iguana, who frightens the python, who scares the rabbit, and now the whole jungle is in an uproar because the sun won't rise. The animals discuss the situation and decide to punish the mosquito.

These three books can be used with the oldest preschoolers, but they may be too difficult for the youngest children. The CD-ROM programs, on the other hand, are geared for children from preschool through second, third, and fourth grades with different levels of activities. Cultural character books like this are not as numerous on CD-ROMs as the commercial Disney books and books of other cartoon characters. But this should not prevent teachers from developing their own exciting book activities from material that is available, as well as the creative projects of their own and their children's inventions, as long as they remember: *all cultural character book activities should start with the reading of the book.*

A Project to Motivate Children's Retelling of Stories Using Print

It all began with the reading of the book ***Carlos and the Squash Plant*** in a preschool class in New Mexico near where the original Carlos story took place. The children loved the illustrations of people and places that looked like ones they were familiar with. They especially enjoyed the story of Carlos's strange problem about not washing after he came in from working in the vegetable garden, so that a squash plant started growing out of his ear. Among the extension activities the class liked the best was reenacting the Carlos story using straw sombreros of graduated sizes to cover the imaginary growing squash plant. Then they chose one of their cultural character dolls to be Carlos and one to be his mother. Two children at a time had the fun of reenacting the story with the dolls, especially the question and answer session every time Carlos came in from the garden:

Mother: Carlos, did you take your bath?

Carlos: "Sí, Mama."

But this was not the end of it. The children wanted to write their own story of Carlos and the hat. So the teacher set up a large newsprint pad on an easel and began writing down the ideas anyone wanted to offer. Here is what the first sheet of this brainstorming session looked like:

Story of Carlos and the Hat

Carlos buys a new hat

A cowboy hat

A baseball hat

A football hat (helmet)

Carlos finds a hat

It is his brother's lost hat

His brother wants it back

Carlos won't give it back

The children liked the idea of Carlos finding his brother's hat and so abandoned their original idea of his buying a hat. They talked about what would happen with Carlos and his brother's hat and how the story should end. Everyone wanted it to turn out all right for Carlos. The teacher could see that these children definitely had a sense of story that was about to go off in several directions, so she

*The teacher in this boy's
classroom took photos of
the children reenacting their
own story with character
dolls to illustrate the book
they had written.*

decided to start with a fresh sheet of newsprint for page one of their story "Carlos and the Baseball Hat." Here is how the story eventually turned out with ideas and words from the children, of course:

Carlos and the Baseball Hat

Page 1: Carlos loves hats.

Page 2: He likes his brother's baseball hat better than his hat.

Page 3: His brother Ramon says: "Carlos, you can't have my hat."

Page 4: His brother Ramon says, "Don't wear my hat when I am away in Dallas."

Page 5: Carlos wears Ramon's hat out in the garden.

Page 6: Carlos loses Ramon's hat.

Page 7: He looks everywhere but can't find the hat.

Page 8: Ramon comes back wearing a new Dallas Cowboys hat.

Page 9: Ramon says, "Carlos you can have my old hat."

Page 10: Carlos finds Ramon's old hat under a squash in the garden.

The End

The children loved the way their story turned out. Then Carlos didn't have to tell his brother a fib. They wanted the teacher to write it out on the computer in big print like she did some of their other stories. But this time they wanted it to be illustrated. And not just any pictures. They wanted "real" pictures, so she took photos of the children reenacting their own story using character dolls. Then she scanned the photos on the computer and typed the words of the story under each photo page. She printed off and stapled enough copies of the book for everyone to have one. It became the most popular book in their library center. And the Carlos doll was clipped to the book-on-a-string clip for anyone who wanted to reenact the story.

Not everyone could "read" (remember) the print, yet all but the youngest children could tell the story in their own words. The teacher could see that this was just the tip of the iceberg for these adventuresome youngsters. She got out their American Indian girl doll Sosi for **The Mud Family** and their Asian boy doll Ling Sung for **Cleversticks** to find out where these two cultural character dolls might lead them.

SUMMARY

The fascinating process of how reading emerges naturally is discussed in this chapter, from the book babble of toddlers to the story retelling that a few preschoolers eventually develop. Readers learn about this progression from a Preschool Reading Behaviors Checklist that illustrates how young children need to develop a sense of story before they realize that a book is more than a series of separate pictures. Story reenactments, telling stories with flannel boards, and using cultural character dolls helps children develop this story sense about the books they love. Especially important is the reading of predictable books whose lilting lines and rhyming words help some children retell and even memorize favorite stories, finally coming to the realization that it is the print on the pages and not the pictures that tells the story.

LEARNING ACTIVITIES

1. Describe the differences between emergent reading and conventional reading. What steps in the progression of emergent reading can you expect to occur in preschool? How can you help to bring this about? Observe several children using the Preschool Reading Behaviors Checklist, and report the results.

2. What is "a sense of story," and how can you help children to acquire it? Use one of the books discussed with three children, and describe their sense of story or lack of it, and how you would help them to progress.

3. Do a story reenactment with the children, and report what you think the children learned from it. Do the same with a flannel board retelling of a favorite story.

4. Why are predictable books among the most appropriate books for assisting preschool children to emerge into reading? Use three different predictable books from different categories several times with individuals or small groups of children and report the results.

5. Use one of the cultural character dolls and its book to prompt children's retelling of the story, and tape-record their version of it. Report the results.

REFERENCES

Beaty, J. J. (1994). *Picture book storytelling: Literature activities for young children.* Fort Worth, TX: Harcourt Brace.

Campbell, R. E. (1998). A day of literacy learning in a nursery classroom. In Campbell, R. E. (Ed.) *Facilitating preschool literacy* (pp. 131–142). Newark, DE: International Reading Association.

Collins, N. L. D., & Shaeffer, M. B. (1997). Look, listen, and learn to read. *Young Children, 52* (5), 65–68.

Ferreiro, E., & Teberosky, A. (1982). *Literacy before schooling.* Exeter, NH: Heinemann.

Hall, N. (1998). Young children as storytellers. In R. E. Campbell (Ed.), *Facilitating preschool literacy* (pp. 84–99). Newark, DE: International Reading Association.

Ishee, N., & Goldhaber, J. (1990). Story re-enactment: Let the play begin! *Young Children, 45* (3), 70–75.

Kiefer, B. Z. (1995). *The potential of picturebooks: From visual literacy to aesthetic understanding.* Upper Saddle River, NJ: Merrill/Prentice Hall.

Meier, D. R. (2000). *Scribble scrabble: Learning to read and write.* New York: Teachers College Press.

Morrow, L. M. (1989). *Literacy development in the early years: Helping children read and write.* Upper Saddle River, NJ: Merrill/Prentice Hall.

Neuman, S. B., & Roskos, K. A. (1993). *Language and literacy learning in the early years: An integrated approach.* Fort Worth, TX: Harcourt Brace.

Neuman, S. B., Copple, C., & Bredekamp, S. (2000). *Learning to read and write: Developmentally appropriate practices for young children.* Washington, DC: National Association for the Education of Young Children.

Schickedanz, J. A. (1999). *Much more than the ABCs: The early stages of reading and writing.* Washington, DC: National Association for the Education of Young Children.

Short, R. A., Harris, T. T., & Fairchild, S. H. (2001). Once upon a time: Telling stories with flannel boards. *Dimensions of Early Childhood, 29* (2), 3–9.

Sulzby, E. (1985). Children's emergent reading of favorite storybooks: A developmental study. *Reading Research Quarterly, 20* (4), 458–481.

Van Kraayenoord, C. E., & Paris, S. G. (1996). Story construction from a picture book: An assessment activity for young learners. *Early Childhood Research Quarterly, 11,* 41–61.

SUGGESTED READINGS

Brewster, J. C. (1997). Teaching young children to make picture books. *Early Childhood Education Journal, 25*(2), 113–117.

Clay, M. M. (1991). *Becoming literate: The construction of inner control.* Portsmouth, NH: Heinemann.

Fields, M. V., & Spangler, K. L. (1995). *Let's begin reading right: Developmentally appropriate beginning reading.* Upper Saddle River, NJ: Merrill/Prentice Hall.

Kirk, E. W. (1998). My favorite day is story day. *Young Children, 53*(6), 27–30.

Seefeldt, C., & Galper, A. (2001). *Active experience for active children: Literacy emerges.* Upper Saddle River, NJ: Merrill/Prentice Hall.

Strickland, D. S., & Morrow, L. M. (2000). *Beginning reading and writing.* New York: Teachers College Press.

Tompkins, G. E. (1997). *Literacy for the 21st century: A balanced approach.* Upper Saddle River, NJ: Merrill/Prentice Hall.

Zeece, P. D. (1997). Bringing books to life: Literature-based storytelling. *Early Childhood Education Journal, 25*(1), 39–43.

CHILDREN'S BOOKS

Alarcon, K. B. (1997). *Louella Mae, she's run away!* New York: Holt.

Aardema, V. (1975). *Why mosquitoes buzz in people's ears.* New York: Dial.

Bemelmans, L. (1977). *Madeline.* New York: Viking.

Browne, E. (1994). *Handa's surprise.* New York: Scholastic.

De Paola, T. (1975). *Strega Nona.* Upper Saddle River, NJ: Prentice Hall.

Ets, M. H. (1963). *Gilberto and the wind.* New York: Viking.

Fox, M. (1989). *Shoes from Grandpa.* New York: Orchard.

Goble, P. (1994). *Iktomi and the buzzard.* New York: Orchard.

Lowery, L. (1995). *Twist with a burger, jitter with a bug.* Boston: Houghton Mifflin.

Montes, M. (2000). *Juan Bobo goes to work.* New York: HarperCollins.

Stevens, J. R. (1993). *Carlos and the squash plant.* Flagstaff, AZ: Rising Moon.

Stickland, P., & Stickland, H. (1994). *Dinosaur roar!* New York: Dutton.

Wood, A. (1992). *Silly Sally.* San Diego, CA: Harcourt Brace.

Yolen, J. (2000). *How do dinosaurs say good night?* New York: Blue Sky.

HOME BOOK EXPERIENCE

FAMILY LITERACY

Busy preschool teachers who have kept their classrooms current with the best cultural character books, print materials, writing materials, tape recorders, dolls, puppets, dress-up clothes, and all sorts of literacy activities in block centers, music centers, art centers, manipulative/math centers, science centers, and dramatic play centers may wonder about the topic addressed in this chapter: home book experience. Does this mean that they, too, are responsible for early literacy development in children's homes, as well? Morrow and Paratore (1993) have this to say about it: "It is clear that if we do not attend to the home when we discuss literacy development, whatever strategies we carry out in school will never be completely successful. Schools need to view family literacy as part of the curriculum" (p.194).

Family literacy? What is that? Reading educators seem to use the expression as an umbrella term to include the role of the family in developing their children's literacy, as well as the numerous programs designed to help families support their own literacy (Tracey, 2000, p. 47). According to Tracey, "The connections that are established between students' home and school environments can dramatically affect their literacy learning."

Most preschool teachers are aware of the fact that reading to children both at school and in the home is essential to children's success in learning to read, but is there something more they should be aware of? In fact, a great deal more information needs to be exchanged between the home and preschool regarding children's emergent literacy needs. And it is up to the teacher to initiate this reciprocal flow.

PHYSICAL BOOK ENVIRONMENT

A physical environment that supports children's practice reading and practice writing activities is just as important in the home as it is in the preschool. Children need a place to keep their books and writing supplies: a desk and chair, a table and lamp, a bookstand, cupboard, drawers, storage boxes, or shelves—someplace that is easily accessible and available for their materials alone, if possible: a hook for their book bags from school, a book-on-a-string clip, or a puppet tree for character dolls and puppet storage. Plastic shelves and bins from discount stores can be snapped together for book corners in bedrooms or dens. Peel-off stickers or cutouts from catalogs make fine decorations. A cozy reading corner can contain a comfortable chair, couch, bean bag, pillows, or cushions.

As for the equipment and materials needed, a chalkboard, a bulletin board, a write-and-wipe lapboard, an easel, a tape recorder, a typewriter, and a computer would be ideal. Puzzles, word games, lotto cards, plastic or magnetic letters and board, stamp pads and stamps, notebooks, pads, diaries or journals, scissors, glue, tape, paper, and the tools of writing (pencils, markers, chalk,

Whatever families can afford for the support of their children's reading and writing experiences will deliver the message "We believe it is important for you to read and write at home."

crayons), and paint and paintbrushes, the same as those found in the preschool, are just as valuable in the home. But whatever families can afford or invent for the support of their children's book and writing experiences will deliver the important message that "We support what you are doing," and "We believe it is important for you to read and write at home."

It is possible to create reading and writing corners for next to no expense using cardboard cartons and bed pillows. Children can decorate cartons with old magazine or catalog cutouts. Books can be stored inside them. Bed pillows can be piled into a cozy nest for reading. Plastic bags from the supermarket can hang on hooks or nails to contain writing supplies. As a child's teacher you can send home suggestions, including children's own ideas, for assembling creative reading and writing spaces like this to fit the space or environment available. Worn-down pencils, chalk, or crayons that would normally be discarded by the program can be sent home in a baggie for any child wanting to start his own writing center. Start a monthly literacy newsletter with suggestions for creating and stocking a home literacy center.

Obtaining Books

Where will parents obtain the books for a home center? Duplicate paperback copies of classroom books should always be available for home lending. At the end of the year these by now well-worn books can be given to each of the children to keep. New paperback copies can be ordered for next year's classroom supplies just as you order art supplies. Parents and children can be encouraged to visit the library or bookmobile to borrow appropriate books on a weekly basis. A "Parents and Children at the Public Library" day can be scheduled at the beginning of the year as a field trip during which families can obtain library cards, as well as looking over the picture books available for borrowing.

Preschool classes located in public schools can set up a weekly schedule for their children to visit the school library to borrow books to take home. Children can make their own books at preschool for use at home. Classes, churches, schools, and parent groups can sponsor book fairs to raise money for purchasing books for both the classroom and the home. As Tracey (2000) points out, "A greater access to books corresponds positively with children's literacy development" (p. 49).

A magazine and book exchange can be set up in the classroom for parents to bring in and exchange back copies of appropriate adult-level magazines and paperback books for home use. Children need to see their parents engaged in borrowing and exchanging books and magazines, and in reading and writing activities as well. Health, education, nutrition, and child development pamphlets can be available for home use, too, when parents stop by the magazine exchange. A copy of this textbook can help parents become aware of the emergent reading and writing processes their children are engaged in.

For families who would like to purchase their own appropriate books for a minimal expense, they are obtainable in paperback ($3 to $6) from Scholastic and can be ordered through the child's preschool program. Cultural character books available from Scholastic are listed in appendix A.

A Print-Rich Environment

Signs (Canizares & Chanko, 1999)
The Signmaker's Assistant
(Arnold, 1992)

The importance of a "print-rich environment" in the home also needs to be stressed. Give out calendars at the beginning of each year with captioned scenes of interest to all. Labeled posters and pictures can be sent home. Ask parents and children to collect items with print on them such as cereal boxes, milk and juice cartons, bread wrappers, fast-food wrappers, clothing labels, shopping bag labels, toy packages, tickets, and whatever else appeals to them. Items with easily recognized logos are best. These can be sent to school where they will be cut out and laminated and then used for matching, categorizing, and guessing games. For example, in one such game children can sort out food labels, clothing labels, and drink labels. Envelopes or baggies with these logo game items and directions for playing the games can be sent home for children to play with and to demonstrate to the family what items they can read. As West and Egley (1998) point out:

Children get much more than a hamburger when they order at a favorite fast-food restaurant. They are increasingly able to construct meaning from their expanding world as they encounter symbols, signs, labels, and logos. Environmental print is one useful tool for families and teachers to use to help children learn to read. (p. 46)

The simple book *Signs* showing photos of outdoor signs with a rhyming text is a book children may want to take home to do practice reading. On the other hand, *The Signmaker's Assistant* is a humorous book with a much longer text that the teacher needs to read. It is too long for most of the youngest preschoolers unless they get caught up in the humor of the plot and the illustrations. Norman, the Anglo-American signmaker's assistant, notices that people do whatever signs say, so he decides to paint some signs of his own one day after work. His first sign, "No School Today," brings happiness to all the children. But his "Garbage Dump" sign posted at the supermarket brings outrage. When things in town get too confused because people follow his silly directions, Norman finally confesses with a big sign hung across the street saying he is sorry.

Parents should be talking to their children about the environmental print they see around them. Can children pick out the traffic signs they see on the way to school? Do they know what the signs say on the familiar buildings they pass? Can they help get out the food containers such as cereal boxes and cans of soup you name? Do parents include preschoolers when they look through mail-order catalogs? Parents need to stop and ask their youngsters what the familiar print around them says. All of this is wonderful prereading practice.

HOME READING

As discussed in chapter 8, at first children are dependent readers; that is, they depend on adults to read aloud to them. Once children have heard a simple story reread numerous times, they begin to memorize it and to join in as an adult reads. Gradually children link the story to the text with the aid of the pictures. These picture cues help the child to "read" the text. Finally, children learn to read an unfamiliar text independently (Spreadbury, 1998, p. 31).

A Beasty Story
(Martin, Jr., & Kellogg, 1998)

Reading to their children has traditionally been the most common book experience parents perform in the home, and perhaps the most valuable. A great deal of research supports this finding. Tracey (2000) reports that six factors have been discovered by such research to be positively related to children's literacy development:

1. The total number of words spoken by the child during the storybook reading
2. The total number of questions answered by the child
3. The number of questions asked by the child
4. The number of warm-up preparatory questions asked by the parent
5. The number of post-reading evaluative questions asked by the parent
6. The amount of positive reinforcement provided by the parent (p. 50)

It is obvious that story reading by parents should include more than only reading the words in the book. Just as with shared book reading in preschool, the home reader and child need to talk about the story before, during, and after the reading, for no matter what happens during the story reading session, it is important that the child listener participates. Oral language development is one of the immediate outcomes of individual reading with preschoolers, but as we know, success in later learning to read also follows. Research by Arnold and Whitehurst (1994) indicates, "Engaging the child in verbal interaction during storybook reading is the most powerful key to facilitating his or her literacy growth" (p. 120).

Tracey and others have several suggestions for parents to improve the quality of an individual reading experience. Although the suggestions can be applied to any book, a good example might be *A Beasty Story*, one of the children's favorites. A parent needs to do the following:

1. *Be sure to read the book yourself before using it with your child.* You will find as you look through this book that, unlike most books, every part of it from the front and back covers, the inside flap, the end pages (front and back), and the inside title page, adds to the story, so be sure to look at every page very carefully before you introduce the book to the child. You will also need to go over the plot episodes ahead of time, and to know what the surprise ending is about, in order to ask your child appropriate questions.

2. *Get your child to talk.* With this book you can start by showing her the scary but funny cover with four little mice and a strange beast with big yellow eyes. Read her the title of the book, *A Beasty Story,* and ask what she thinks it might be about. Open to the front end page and ask your child to look at the picture carefully while you read her the flap. Then ask her if she "dares," since the flap says, "Don't dare look ahead. . . ." As the story unfolds through the dark, dark house, you can ask her what she thinks each color word says. (It always rhymes with the sentence it is in and is printed in the color it represents; i.e., the word *red* is red in color.) Because this is a mystery story for preschoolers, each double page spread lends itself to your asking the listener, "What do you think will happen next?"

3. *Read the story with expression.* This is a story that also lends itself to making your voice sound mysterious, low, or whispery. Also read the words slo-o-o-o-w-ly. Children love it when the adults in their lives pretend like this.

4. *Help your child understand the story.* Can she see how this story is mysterious because it takes place in the dark? Is she scared of the beast that flies with yellow eyes? Does she understand how the beast goes into the fireplace and comes out the chimney? Preschoolers do not necessarily understand the connection between fireplaces and chimneys. Does she remember the truck on the front end page with the sign "Nick's Tricks and Hank's Pranks"? Does she remember the title page where the two little mice, Nick and Hank, inflate the balloons? Why does she think Nick and Hank played this trick? Who is the ghost in the bed? Does this scare her, or does she think it is funny? Is it something she would do?

5. *Praise your child.* What good things can you say about the child's participation in this story? How attentive she was? That you thought she asked good

questions? That she solved the mystery before the end of the book? Wasn't that great! Let her know how happy you are if she identifies a word or color or knows what will happen next.

6. *Relate the book to the child's life.* Talk to her about things like what it is like going out in the dark at night; why someone would carry a candle; why one of the mice (Silly) wrote down everything that happened. Because a parent knows whether her child is afraid of the dark, she can talk about it frankly, relating her child's feeling to that of the mice. What other kinds of things is the child scared of? Would this scare the mice?

7. *Wait for answers to the questions you ask.* After you ask a question, wait for the child to answer. Sometimes it takes preschoolers a long time to think of what they want to say.

8. *Point to the words when you read.* Even though the illustrations in this book are so spine-tingling that few youngsters pay attention to the text, it is still helpful for you to point to the large print at the top of each page as you read it.

9. *Read the book again if your child asks you to.* Most adults think they must read a different book every time. But most children want to hear the story again if they liked it the first time. It is important for children's understanding of new words, of the story plot, and of the illustrations to be able to hear and see the story many times. One reader also found another reason that young children want stories reread: they love already knowing what will happen next in the story (Bates & Bates, 1999, p. 13).

10. *Have fun!* Both parents and children should have fun in a story session like this. This is not a lesson, and of course **A Beasty Story** should not be taken seriously. If you find that one or the other of you is not having fun, try to determine why that is so, and try to change whatever is blocking the enjoyment of the reading. Some very sensitive children, for instance, may not like a story that includes any hint of scariness, while others love to be scared, even as a trick. As you choose stories, try to match them with your children's temperament.

Reading Books for Fun

To begin your home reading, you might try reading some of the cultural character books written purely for fun. Among the Scholastic paperback books in appendix A that your children will enjoy laughing over are these:

Dinosaur Roar! (animals)

Handa's Surprise (African)

Is Your Mama a Llama? (animals)

Jonathan and His Mama (African American)

Let's Eat! (Spanish)

Miss Mary Mack (Anglo-American)

Saturday Night at the Dinosaur

Stomp (animals)

Silly Sally (English)

Tikki, Tikki, Tembo (Chinese)

Some of these books also rhyme and thus make fine predictable books that children love to repeat. Soon the youngsters may be memorizing their texts and telling you the story.

The Father's Role

Most family involvement in story reading with their preschool children focuses on mother-child not father-child interactions. But young children, of course, delight in having their fathers read to them, too. Many fathers feel the same way about it but don't quite know how to get started. Ortiz, Stile, and Brown (1999) have this to say about involving fathers: "Teachers who wish to foster father–child literacy need to understand that in some cultures it is more traditional for fathers to engage in other types of activities with their young children, such as athletics. Thus attempts to foster father–child literacy activities may present quite a challenge" (p. 16).

A study of preschool literacy activities of 47 father–child pairs in southern New Mexico showed that many of the fathers did read storybooks to their children at night. Others engaged their children in reading road signs, logos on buildings, billboards, and other environmental print. One father read interactive children's stories on the Internet, and another helped his daughter spell words on the computer. Fathers in this study wanted their children to be ready for school. They also enjoyed the bonding that occurred with their children during reading sessions. Fathers who spoke English as a second language wanted their children to develop literacy skills at an early age (Ortiz et al., 1999, p. 17).

Ortiz et al. (1999) suggest that fathers who want to read with their children can start by reading informal material such as comic strips or television commercials to one child at a time. It is not necessary for whole families to gather together for this reading. Young children actually gain more doing reading on a one-to-one basis in the home, just as they do in the preschool. But be sure the child is enjoying this interaction. Don't make it a chore or a test. Both parent and child should have fun with home literacy activities, or children may become disillusioned with learning to read. Ortiz et al. also have this message for teachers:

> We feel that teachers of young children are in an excellent position to cultivate this largely untapped resource. For example, fathers who are already involved in literacy activities can be praised and then invited to model their techniques at the next parent night. Similarly, teachers can share materials, activities, and expectations with fathers who attend individual parent conferences. (p. 18)

With more single fathers caring for their young children than ever before, teachers may want to include in their newsletters literacy ideas that fathers and children can become involved with at home. They may want to learn what interests fathers have and send home read-aloud children's books that speak to those interests. And, of course, they will want to invite fathers to visit the preschool and share the books they and their youngsters enjoy with the other children.

Cultural Considerations

As teachers become more aware of the many cultures represented by children in their classes, they need to find ways to establish co-operative relationships between the school and home. Newsletters, parent conferences, and home visits may be a start but not always a successful one in this day of busy schedules and harried lifestyles. Teachers sometimes feel unprepared to communicate with parents who come from a different culture, speak a different language, and may have different goals for their children. Parents, on the other hand, sometimes feel awkward about visiting classrooms or inviting their child's teacher into their lives.

Families Are Different
(Pellegrini, 1991)

One way to overcome some of this initial reluctance on the part of both teachers and parents is to focus on the child, not on the program or the home. What is the child like? What are her interests at home and at school? How does she get along with others? What would her parents like to see her accomplish this year? Do they do any story reading with the child? Would they like to?

Face-to-face communication is best. It does not need to take place at formal conferences. When parents drop off or pick up their children is a fine time for an informal chat about what literacy activities the child did in preschool today, and the hope that she shows some of her accomplishments at home. When parents bring in back issues of magazines, empty food containers, and the plastic shopping bags they are asked to contribute, you can talk with them about how you are using these items in literacy activities. Does their child do anything like this at home? Would they like to watch what the children are doing at the moment in their practice writing or reading activities? Invite parents to stay as long as they want.

Cultural Differences in Story Reading

Teachers also need to be aware of the different ways mothers of diverse cultures read or play with toys with their preschool children. For instance, as Okagaki and Diamond (2000) point out, "While American mothers emphasized teaching their children about the objects in the world around them, the Japanese mothers focused on socializing their children's interpersonal skills" (p. 78). An Anglo-American mother would identify an object by name and talk about it, while a Japanese mother would involve her children in social interactions. For example: "Here! It's a vroom vroom. [car]." "I give it to you." "Now give it to me." "Yes! Thank you" (p. 78).

Some Chinese American parents, on the other hand, read to their children, but not in English. They preferred that their children hear English from a native speaker. They made regular trips to the library for books, but especially for book tapes for children to listen to at home. Huntsinger, Huntsinger, Ching, and Lee (2000), tell about another clever book reading arrangement:

One Chinese American mother hired a 10-year-old in the neighborhood to read stories to her three-year-old for an hour each day. The arrangement was mutually

When parents drop off or pick up their children is a fine time for an informal chat with the teacher about what literacy activities the child did in school today and what she likes to do at home.

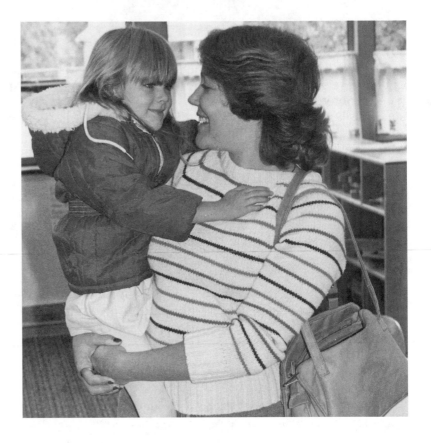

beneficial: the 10-year-old, who wanted to become an elementary school teacher, gained experience with children and the younger child became a fluent reader of English by age four. (p. 11)

Studies comparing story reading styles of low-income Hispanic, African American, and Anglo-American families found that children from all three cultural groups were exposed to literacy experiences throughout the day, contrary to the commonly held belief that children from low-income homes had little exposure to literacy, according to Vernon-Feagans, Hammer, Miccio, & Manlove (2001, p. 200). Nevertheless, many of the families were not accustomed to story reading aloud to children.

In rural African American homes, books were read out loud by adults to others in the family, and then the group discussed what was read. Children of all ages were expected to tell oral narratives using a storyteller's skill. In urban African American homes, mothers often labeled the pictures in picture books with little text and read the text in other books, but they did not engage in question asking. Children in Anglo-American families asked more questions, studies found, while children from African American families produced more spontaneous vocalizations. Hispanic families also read to their children but, like the

African American families, did not engage their children in question-asking routines. Research found, however, that most children from low-income homes and multicultural families are read to less frequently than Anglo middle-class children (Vernon-Feagans et al., 2001, p. 198). Bus (2001) concludes:

> Cultural and social variables influence the frequency and quality of book reading. It is likely that parents who are readers themselves are better able to engage their children in book reading. . . .When reading is not a source of pleasure to parents themselves, they may not know how to make book reading enjoyable and meaningful to them [their children]. It may also depend on their ability to create a close and intimate atmosphere in which to share books together. (p. 188)

The cultural character book *Families Are Different* narrated by the adopted Korean girl Nico described in chapter 7 supports this point of view as it takes readers through a number of families that Nico compares when she becomes uncomfortable because she looks so different from her own Anglo family members. Her mother tells Nico that "there are different kinds of families . . . that they are glued together with a special kind of glue called *love*." Nico finds this to be true as she looks around and sees nine familiar families more different within themselves than they are alike, and she decides, "Now I don't think I'm strange at all. I'm just like everyone else . . . I'm different."

Involving Families in Literacy Activities

It is up to you, of course, to use your imagination to find ways to involve families of diverse cultural backgrounds with preschool literacy activities. You could ask parents to share their child's favorite song in the home language. As Ogaki and Diamond (2000) note: "This also provides the child an opportunity to be an 'expert,' teaching classmates something that is familiar to him" (p. 79). Families might also provide copies of their children's favorite stories, and, of course, parents can be invited into the classroom to share a family activity with the other children. Ogaki and Diamond conclude, "Even in a classroom in which all children share a similar cultural, ethnic, and linguistic background, family experiences are different for each child. Providing children and families opportunities to share their own family cultures with other children is a way to bring a child's experiences from home into school" (p. 79).

PROGRAMS TO SUPPORT HOME READING

Lending Libraries and Book Backpack Programs

Most teachers soon find that their children want to be read to individually. Most research concludes that young children gain more from being read to individually than from group reading, not only in school but also at home. Thus, it may be up to the teacher to find ways of getting appropriate books into the home. Lending libraries and book backpack programs are two such methods that have proved successful. As Cohen (1997) notes, "It is one thing to explain to parents the benefits of reading aloud to children but quite another to provide them with the means of making it a favorite habit"(p. 69).

By developing a home lending library, the teacher can provide children's families with familiar books the children are already enjoying in school. Such books need to be the duplicates of books being used in the classroom so that you will not be lending out your only copy of a favorite book. Paperback book companies such as Scholastic ([800] 724-6527) include many of the cultural character books discussed in this text at extremely reasonable prices, ranging from under $3 to under $6. (See appendix A.)

Book pack programs from Scholastic for under $10 contain the book, an audiocassette of the book, and an activities sheet. Cultural character book pack programs from Scholastic include the following:

Abiyoyo (African)

Aunt Flossie's Hats (African American)

Bringing the Rain to Kapiti Plain (African)

Corduroy (African American)

Dancing with the Indians (African American and Indian)

Families Are Different (Korean and Anglo-American)

Jamaica's Find (African American)

Legend of the Bluebonnet (Native American)

Mama, Do You Love Me? (Native Alaskan)

Silly Sally (English)

Strega Nona (Italian)

Ten, Nine, Eight (African American)

Tikki Tikki Tembo (Chinese)

Ty's One-Man Band (African American)

What Mary-Jo Shared (African American)

The packs themselves can be made from simple baggies from the supermarket, or they can be purchased from discount stores or educational supply companies such as Lakeshore (phone: [800] 421-5354).

Some teachers also include cultural character cutouts from the books in each of the backpacks. These are made, as previously described, by cutting out the main characters from the dust jacket cover of the book or an inside page that has been duplicated, and laminating them. Such cutouts help children become better acquainted with the characters, thus motivating them to want to read or listen to books about these interesting multiethnic children who are like them but different. In addition, the characters become real for the children, just as the character dolls have, and soon they are making up their own stories about them.

Children can sign out for the books or backpacks and then return them in a week. This gives parents enough time to listen to and read the stories, as well as talking about them with the children. Also suggest to the parents that they ask the children to read the stories to them. Children will usually say, "I can't read." But have the parents tell the youngsters, "Yes, you can. You can read the pictures." Since these are familiar books, most children will delight in "reading" to their parents. Afterward, the parents can reread the book to them. Most

Some teachers include cultural character cutouts from the books they send home in backpacks for children to play with while they read about the characters.

children will want both experiences repeated, and you need to encourage parents to reread the stories as often as the children want them.

For parents not at ease in reading in English or in reading at all, they can listen to the tape and share it along with their children as they turn the book pages at the signal. Find out which families do not have cassette players and be sure to have little hand-held sets available whenever bookpacks are being taken home.

Meier (2000, p. 133) discusses several advantages for what he calls "the bookbag program":

1. Helps children develop a strong sense of self and independence in school literacy

2. Recognizes the respect that parents afford teachers and parents' interest in their children's happiness

3. Coordinates preschool literacy learning with kindergarten goals and practices

4. Recognizes and builds on the literacy teaching of entire families

5. Shows the variety of child-created literacy practices invented in children's homes

One parent commented, "I like the bookbag program because it gave the kids a sense of independence, and Akilah felt proud to have her own book come home. She took care of it, and she wanted to read it as soon as she got home. She wanted to read *her* book" (p. 133).

If an audiocassette is included in the backpack, children can also listen to it, but this should be a secondary experience for English speakers that teaches the children when to turn the page. Second-language speakers may want to listen to the tape first while looking at book pages. The most important part of the home/school book experience should be the reading by family members and their preschool children. Later children can play with the character cutouts, tracing them and coloring them in or making up new story adventures for them. Then when children return their book backpacks, they are free to borrow a new one.

Family Journals

When Harding (1996) started sending journals home, asking parents to write about what their children were doing at home with reading and saying she would reply, telling them what their children were doing at school with reading, most parents at first just wrote about their children. Later they began writing about their reading sessions at home. Not all of the families responded, just as many teachers found it difficult to reply to journal questions every time. Extensive communication was not necessary, most teachers who used journals concluded. But when exciting things happened with children and books, everyone wanted to know about it. As Harding notes, "Each child and each family is unique, with unique family life styles. Our classroom curriculum was being carried into the home and was valued by the children and their families" (p. 30).

Family Literacy Workshops

Some programs help parents to become involved with their children's reading at home through workshops held in the preschool. Children's mothers are often the primary participants, but some fathers and grandparents may attend. Meier (2000) discusses a series of family literacy workshops he has conducted. His goals (p. 119) include the following:

1. To increase dialogue about literacy among families
2. To introduce ways of reading with and to preschool-age children
3. To introduce a variety of high-quality multicultural children's literature
4. To discuss children's literacy development and cultural and linguistic diversity

Parents contribute questions about reading and writing with their children, such as wanting to know how often to read or about the appropriate content of books. Meier also asks participants to share things that work for them in their home reading. Book reading is demonstrated, showing enjoyable and effective ways to read out loud. His experience with Hispanic and African American participants is rewarding for all concerned. As he notes:

> Parents spoke with grace and sensitivity about what they wanted for their children's literacy education. Since some of the parents' children had left preschool or their preschool-age children had older siblings, the parents were also able to offer a long view of literacy education in preschool and beyond. This breadth of experience and knowledge about literacy enabled them to reflect on their own developmental journeys as parents and advocates for their children's education. (p. 121)

Because, as Tracey notes, "research suggests that engaging the child in verbal interaction during storybook reading is the most powerful key to facilitating his or her literacy growth," a number of family literacy workshops have

Some family literacy workshops teach family members how to get children to talk about their book during story reading.

been developed over the years to help parents learn how to involve their children verbally during story reading (p. 51).

Parents as Partners

Parents as Partners was designed to help low-income parents improve the way they share books with their children. The program uses live modeling as well as videotapes to help parents learn:

1. How to preview a book
2. How to relate a story to their children's lives
3. How to improve parent-child conversation during shared book reading. (Tracey, 2000, p. 51)

Another similar program reported by Tracey is a six-workshop series for low-income parents and children to help them improve their interactions during the reading of predictable books. Ideas presented include paired reading, choral reading, storytelling, readers' theater, and chanting, with a variety of follow-up activities for parents after each session.

Storymates

Storymates is a 9-week family literacy program that teaches school-age children, rather than parents, how to do shared reading with young children. School-age children learn through the modeling of high-quality read-alouds of 18 books chosen by the teachers. Follow-up activities are also included in the training.

Pairs of students practice the reading and activities with each other in the classroom. Afterward they take the books home and share them with younger siblings, relatives, and friends.

Three for the Road

This program uses backpacks to extend storybook reading into the home. Three carefully chosen books of increasing difficulty are included in each backpack, all on a single theme. Also included is a letter to parents with directions for using the materials, a response journal, writing and drawing materials, and hand puppets. Before children sign out the backpacks, teachers demonstrate the use of the materials with them. Children are free to use whichever book they are most comfortable with. After the materials have been used and returned, the children meet in groups to discuss the experience with the teacher (Tracey, 2000, p. 52).

Parents in the Classroom

Another common means of connecting home and school literacy activities involves inviting parents to participate in children's literacy learning in the school. A great many possible activities are available, including inviting parents to

- read books to children,
- assist with children's own reading and writing,
- take dictation from children as they make up stories, and
- tell stories about their own lives or cultural folktales.

Eldridge (2001) ties parent literacy activities in the classroom to inviting parents to share something of themselves, thus empowering the parents and creating in them "a sense of connection with classroom goals and their effects on the lives of their children." She continues by saying, "Teachers might invite parents to share a strength, hobby (playing guitar and singing), or vocation (firefighting, carpentry) with the class or schedule a surprise parent reader (children know that a parent will read to them, but they don't know who) each week" (p. 67).

Reading Together

More formalized in-school activities for parents include programs such as Reading Together, a large-scale in-school program for low-income parents in the Northeast in which parents themselves are not literate. According to Tracey (2000, p. 53), it involves first training community leaders to use prop boxes with small groups of children in the classroom. The prop boxes include books, play objects, chants, jingles, fingerplays, and blank writing books. Once the community leaders are comfortable using the materials with the children, they in turn recruit and train parent volunteers from the community to use the prop boxes for 30 to 45 minutes twice a week with small groups of parents in the community. Neuman (1995) reports, "Two years of implementing Reading Together have demonstrated that, despite poor economic circumstances, families in these communities continue to hold strong beliefs about the power of literature and its importance in their lives" (p. 128).

Whether parents attend workshops to learn how to read to their children or simply pick up a book and begin reading it, it is obvious that family literacy activities in the home and school have a large and important role to play in helping young children emerge into reading. As Tracey (2000) concludes:

> Children are profoundly affected by their literacy experiences at home. These experiences can be shaped in positive ways by educators who understand the role of the home literacy environment in children's literacy development and who strive to share valuable information about the home literacy environment with parents. . . . All educators are encouraged to become more informed about these critical connections and strategies for implementing them. All are invited to choose whatever ideas may work best to strengthen home-school connections as a part of their literacy programs. (p. 54)

SUMMARY

This chapter presents the idea that preschools need to view family literacy as a part of their curriculum. Children's early literacy activities in the preschool need to be supported and extended into the home. Not only should parents read with their children in an agreeable setting, but they should also support their children's literacy development with an attractive physical space equipped with necessary furniture, storage space, and writing tools. Sources for obtaining appropriate picture books for their children at home include the classroom lending library, the public library, and inexpensive paperback book sources such as Scholastic. Recognizing and identifying environmental print through matching and guessing games helps parents and children alike find meaning in logos and signs. Talking with children about the books being read before, during, and after the reading helps children understand them better. The father's role in literacy activities with his children is addressed, and cultural considerations that affect reading to children are also discussed. Programs to support home reading include book backpack programs and family literacy workshops, which may lead to parents reading to children in the preschool classroom.

LEARNING ACTIVITIES

1   What is "family literacy," and how does it support children's early literacy activities in the preschool classroom? Tell how your program supports a home/school book experience for its youngsters, and how successful it has been. Be specific. If you have no program, describe how you would start one.

2. Describe an ideal home physical book environment and tell how it is used. How do parents of your preschool children obtain books for home usage? What are some of their favorites? How can you help them obtain others? What ones would you suggest?

3. How is home reading carried out by parents of children in your program? How can you lend support to this process? What problems have parents encountered in carrying out home reading? How can you help them address such problems? If your parents are not doing home reading, describe how you would help them overcome any problems preventing home reading.

4. Choose one of the books from this text, and describe how you would encourage parents to apply each of the 10 suggestions Tracey has made to improve the quality of reading a book such as this to children.

5. Describe one of the parent reading programs in more detail, either one from this text or one being used in your community. How is it working? What suggestions would you make for improvement?

REFERENCES

Arnold, D. S., & Whitehurst, G. J. (1994). Accelerating language development through picture book reading: A summary of dialogic reading and its effects. In D. K. Dickinson (Ed.), *Bridges to literacy: Children, families, and schools*. Cambridge: Blackwell.

Bates, C., and Bates, R. (1999). Mother and daughter set out to promote literacy in a family child care home and a child care center. *Young Children, 54*(1), 12–15.

Bus, A. G. (2001). Joint caregiver–child storybook reading: A route to literacy development. In S. B. Neuman & D. K. Dickinson (Eds.), *Handbook of early literacy research* (pp. 179–191). New York: Guilford.

Cohen, L. E. (1997). How I developed my kindergarten book backpack program. *Young Children, 52*(3), 69–71.

Eldridge, D. (2001). Parent involvement: It's worth the effort. *Young Children, 56*(4), 65–69.

Harding, N. (1996). Family journals: The bridge from school to home and back again. *Young Children, 51*(2), 27–30.

Huntsinger, C. S., Huntsinger, P. R., Ching, W. D. & Lee, C. B. (2000). Understanding cultural contexts fosters sensitive caregiving of Chinese American children. *Young Children, 55*(6), 7–15.

Kaufman, H. O. (2001). Skills for working with all families. *Young Children, 56*(4), 81–83.

Meier, D. R. (2000). *Scribble scrabble learning to read and write: Success with diverse teachers, children, and families*. New York: Teachers College Press.

Morrow, L. M., & Paratore, J. (1993). Family literacy: Perspectives and practices. *The Reading Teacher, 47*(3), 194–200.

Neuman, S. B. (1995). Reading Together: A community-supported parent tutoring program. *The Reading Teacher, 47*(3), 194–200.

Okagaki, L., & Diamond, K. E. (2000). Responding to cultural and linguistic differences in the beliefs and practices of families with young children. *Young Children, 55*(3), 74–80.

Ortiz, R., Stile, S., & Brown, C. (1999). Early literacy activities of fathers: Reading and writing with young children. *Young Children, 54*(5), 16–18.

Spreadbury, J. (1998). Reading—It's a natural: Reading aloud to children in the home. In R. Campbell (Ed.), *Facilitating preschool literacy* (pp. 30–38). Newark, DE: International Reading Association.

Tracey, D. H. (2000). Enhancing literacy growth through home-school connections. In D. S. Strickland & L. M. Morrow (Eds.), *Beginning reading and writing* (pp. 46–57). New York: Teachers College Press.

Vernon-Feagans, L., Hammer, C. S., Miccio, A., & Manlove, E. (2001). Early language and literacy skills in low-income African American and Hispanic children. In S. B. Neuman & D. K. Dickinson (Eds.), *Handbook of early literacy research* (pp. 192–210). New York: Guilford.

West, L. S., & Egley, E. H. (1998). Children get more than a hamburger: Using labels and logos to enhance literacy. *Dimensions of Early Childhood, 26*(3&4), 43–46.

Suggested Readings

Morrow, L. M. (Ed.). (1995). *Family literacy connections in schools and communities.* Newark, DE: International Reading Association.

Risko, V. J., & Bromley, K. (2001). *Collaboration for diverse learners: Viewpoints and practices.* Newark, DE: International Reading Association.

Taylor, D. (1983). *Family literacy: Young children learning to read and write.* Westport, CT: Heinemann.

Thomas, A., Fazio, L., & Stiefelmeyer, B. L. (1999). *Families at school: A handbook for parents.* Newark, DE: International Reading Association.

Wasik, B. H., Dobbins, D. R., & Herrmann, S. (2001). Intergenerational family literacy: Concepts, research, and practice. In S. B. Neuman & D. K. Dickinson (Eds.), *Handbook of early literacy research* (pp. 444–458). New York: Guilford.

Weinberger, J. (1998). Young children's literacy experiences within the fabric of daily life. In R. Campbell (Ed.), *Facilitating preschool literacy* (pp. 39–50). Newark, DE: International Reading Association.

Children's Books

Arnold, T. (1992). *The signmaker's assistant.* New York: Dial.

Canizares, S., & Chanko, P. (1999). *Signs.* New York: Scholastic.

Martin, B., Jr., & Kellogg, S. (1998). *A beasty story.* San Diego: Harcourt, Brace.

Pellegrini, N. (1991). *Families are different.* New York: Scholastic.

BECOMING A READER

TRANSITION FROM PRESCHOOL TO KINDERGARTEN

KINDERGARTEN READING EXPECTATIONS

TYPES OF KINDERGARTEN READING INSTRUCTION

C H A P T E R   1 0

TRANSITION FROM PRESCHOOL TO KINDERGARTEN

In the previous chapters on literacy, much has been devoted to reading, writing, listening, and speaking in the preschool classroom. This chapter emphasizes reading as it emerges in kindergarten. Since the 19th century, kindergarten has been regarded as a child-centered place "where children could be nurtured and allowed to grow at their own pace" (Meyer, 2001, p. 161). Although this traditional perception and mission of kindergarten remain, there has been a relatively recent change in the kindergarten curriculum. Meyer (2001) asserts that the major factors largely responsible for shaping this change are: (a) societal demands, (b) misconceptions about how young children learn, (c) powerful commercial interests marketing educational materials often unsuitable for kindergarten-age children, and (d) the loss of trained teachers from districts and schools with declining enrollments. Thus, there appears to be an emerging dichotomy in what kindergarten is supposed to be and do. On the one hand, kindergarten is traditionally a place primarily to meet the needs of children as 5-year-olds. On the other hand, kindergarten is increasingly becoming a place that emphasizes the transition and preparation between preschool and elementary school (Graue, 2001).

Paralleling these two perspectives of what kindergarten is expected to be and do are divergent views of how literacy, in particular reading, should be taught. Reading in preschool is more child directed (emergent reading), whereas reading in the elementary school is more teacher directed (conventional reading). Consequently, with kindergarten being in the middle, one immediate problem arising is whether conventional reading should replace emergent reading when children enter kindergarten. Currently, emergent and conventional reading commonly coexist in the kindergarten class because of several factors, the foremost of which is what parents, teachers, administrators, state departments, and the general public expect kindergartners to accomplish as young readers by the end of the school year.

KINDERGARTEN READING EXPECTATIONS

What are some of the common expectations regarding what children should acquire in kindergarten? Here is a list of them and their associated definitions:

- *Book awareness and recognition.* An understanding about the nature of books, their organization, printed content, and purpose
- *Print awareness.* The recognition that print has specific properties and components, including directionality, words and letters, punctuation, linkages to speech and meaning, and illustrations
- *Alphabet knowledge.* The recognition of letters in isolation and within words

- *Phonemic awareness.* The understanding that speech consists of sequences of one or more distinct, individual sounds (phonemes)

- *Alphabetic principle.* The understanding that the sounds of speech can be represented by one or more symbols (letters) of an alphabet

- *Phonics.* The realization that specific printed symbols (letters) are related to certain spoken sounds (phonemes)

- *Word recognition.* Identifying and knowing frequently used or sight words

- *Making meaning.* The recognition that print and book pictures contain information and that reading is a way to get that information from the print

How these expectations are met depends on *how individual educators believe children acquire and develop literacy.* Some educators emphasize making meaning, as in a child-centered classroom of a preschool, while others focus on deciphering print, as in a teacher-directed classroom characteristic of some elementary schools.

Connection Between Story and Book

Rather than choosing between emphasizing meaning or emphasizing print to teach reading, a combination of the two is often used, depending on the children's stage of reading development at a particular time and within a particular reading situation. Thus, it is necessary to understand the children's stage of reading development, as noted in chapter 8, which focused on children developing a "sense of story." Here we look at children's book awareness and recognition—that is, making a connection between the story and the book it comes from. To an adult the story that the teacher reads obviously comes from the book she holds, but this fact is not necessarily clear to children listeners. At first they often see the adult reader, not the book, as the source of the story. This, of course, may happen in preschool as well as kindergarten.

Initial Focus on Meaning

Teachers reading stories can help children understand the purpose of books and thereby make the effort to read on their own. This serves to model reading behaviors. That is, children soon learn that reading is always accompanied by certain book-attending actions. As they listen to stories, they also come to see that the book is somehow a necessary prerequisite for story reading, but they may be unsure of the precise nature of that connection, strange as this may seem to an adult.

The realization that the book contains information and is the actual source of the story being read begins to sink in when children see that the pictures in the book depict certain aspects of the story they hear. The pictures and the spoken words seem to support one another to make the story seem more vivid and enjoyable. Picture books, therefore, can help children acquire an inkling that certain aspects of a story are in the book and, therefore, that books can bring enjoyment to them in the same way that the teacher's storytelling does.

Before this occurs children seem to think it is the teacher who is the source of the spoken story they are listening to. The teacher is the storyteller, the one who "knows" the story and retells it. Even though the teacher is holding the book, looking at it, and turning pages, the precise purpose of the book, beyond having pictures, may still be unclear.

Soon children notice and attend to each other's responses to the story they are listening to together. The teacher also responds to what the children say and do as they listen to the story. This ongoing feedback helps children validate their own constructions of and reactions to the story and confirms once again that the teacher is the story giver and that the book seems to have a supporting role, much like a prop.

After repeated story readings, however, children begin to make out a pattern. Namely, they notice that a story has a beginning, middle, and end. They may even observe that these parts of the story occur when the teacher handles the book in distinctive ways. The story starts when the teacher looks at the cover and then opens it. The middle of the story is associated with repeated page turning; the end, with closing the back cover of the book. This pattern of actions and events occurs essentially the same way every time the teacher reads the book. The once ambiguous connection between the story and the book begins to make sense.

The crucial breakthrough occurs when children realize that the story is really in the book rather than in the person who tells the story. They see that they too can tell the story by somehow "listening" to the book—that is, by reading the book. And reading the story, in turn, involves interacting with the print on the pages in the book.

Switch in Focus from Only Meaning to Print and Meaning

The children now understand that the teacher looks at the print while reading—it is the print that tells the teacher or anyone else how to read the story aloud. Confirmation of this hypothesis occurs when the teacher constantly looks at pages in the book, turns pages, points out words to the children, and says them. Moving from left to right across the page, from the top of a page to the bottom, and from the front of the first page in the book to the last page are perceived as important actions that must occur in the way modeled by the teacher. To the children, then, this recurring pattern of book-related actions is somehow involved in reading the story.

Thus, book awareness commences when children mimic these actions involved in reading a book; they go through the motions of reading. Concurrently, they become increasingly aware of the print on a page, vaguely realizing that it is in some way related to the story in the book. This awareness becomes evident when children ask what specific words "say" or mean. The children are now ready for the transition from only meaning-oriented instruction to print-and meaning-oriented learning. With the purpose of a book and its print finally clear to them, children begin to focus on print and use it as another way to "listen to" a story. They also learn to use the meaning of the story to construct and to validate their use of print, as well as to use print to confirm the meaning of what they are reading.

A Kindergarten Classroom

If you walk into a kindergarten and look around, much of what you see is similar to what you see in a preschool. Although there are larger tables and chairs, you will still notice many of the same picture books that you see in preschools. What is different is not so much the materials or even the arrangement of the classroom but rather how the materials are used. For instance, as a reader opens a picture book such as **Tiptoe into Kindergarten**, the two end pages depict very clearly and colorfully an entire floor plan of a kindergarten room with learning centers around the sides and all the equipment carefully labeled. The room could easily pass for a preschool classroom, principle differences being a teacher's desk, and two chalkboards. Other differences are not evident until the story unfolds.

Tiptoe into Kindergarten
(Rogers, 1999)

Preschool children enjoy hearing this story about the Anglo-American 3-year-old girl who goes with her mother and her kindergarten-age brother to spend the morning watching what the multicultural kindergarten children are doing, and then trying out the same things for herself. She watches the children at group time gathered around a large calendar. Then she tries to get involved in a reading group where the teacher is using a Big Book on an easel to teach reading. After the children practice making alphabet letters on the chalkboard, the little girl tries her hand at scribbling on the board. She watches children playing on the floor with blocks, number cards, and big dice and tries her skill at putting a puzzle together. She uses the bathroom, washes her hands, and then plays in the rice table. Singing songs and moving to jumpy rhythms come next. During snack time she tries painting at an easel, but soon she puts her head on a pillow and falls asleep.

Such a book is a fine lead-in to an end-of-the-year field trip to a kindergarten where preschool children can experience one of the classrooms they may enter in the fall. Such a real transition experience helps both children and teachers have a firsthand glimpse of the next step in the learning continuum.

How books are used in most kindergartens is chiefly determined by where children fall on the literacy acquisition and development continuum. Children range from simply learning to listen to story reading to reading independently. The position on the continuum, therefore, dictates the form of reading instruction that many teachers rely on.

TYPES OF KINDERGARTEN READING INSTRUCTION

Teachers select the forms of reading instruction that are most supportive of their children's reading acquisition and development at a particular time of the

The book Tiptoe into Kindergarten *is a fine lead-in for an end-of-the-year field trip to a kindergarten classroom.*

school year. For example, *read-alouds* and *shared reading* can work nicely when children first enter kindergarten, whereas *literature circles* and *reading workshops* are more helpful as the year progresses (see Table 10.1).

Read-Alouds

Somewhere in Africa
(Mennen & Daly, 1992)

Read-aloud is an instructional practice in which a teacher reads a story to a whole class, to a small group, or to an individual child. As commonly implemented in preschools, read-aloud is also appropriate for the kindergarten class.

According to Reutzel and Cooter (2000), the advantages of read-alouds for young readers include developing positive attitudes toward and enjoyment in reading, strengthening cognitive development, and instilling a sense of story structure and organization. Campbell (2001) identifies additional benefits that include developing vocabulary, implanting an aspiration to read, and learning about how print and books function.

As with most story reading formats, a kindergarten read-aloud can be organized into three stages: before the reading, during the reading, and after the reading.

Before the Reading

The first thing that needs to be done is to select a book that will interest the children and that can be read with enthusiasm. Carefully selecting the books is crucial for read-alouds as well as for all the other forms of reading instructions described on subsequent pages. High-quality stories and books enable young children to bring to new reading experiences what they already know, to better understand the characters and what they do and why, to make predictions and confirm them, and more generally to mine the stories they listen to for pieces of relevant information that they then try to fashion into something meaningful (Van Kraayenoord & Paris, 1996). Because pictures are as important as print at this early reading stage, they need to be a focus for the children's attention. After the book has been selected and previewed, begin the read-aloud.

To focus the children's attention and to increase interest, show them the front cover of the book and read the title. Think about ways you could use the cover and title to enhance in the children a sense of anticipation and eagerness to hear the story. For example, the cover of the book **Somewhere in Africa** shows a colorful picture of an African boy walking on a city sidewalk with a book under his arm, vehicles parked along the street, buildings across the street, and a red mountain in the background. You might begin by reading the title, "Somewhere in Africa," and mentioning that the boy's name is Ashraf. What do they think the story might be about? Is Ashraf "somewhere in Africa"? Where? How can they tell? Why do they think Ashraf is carrying a book under his arm? By now the children should be anxious to hear this story, to find out whether their predictions are correct.

During the Reading

A read-aloud involves much more than just reading the story. To keep the children attentive, read the story in an entertaining way with expression in your voice and on your face, show the pictures at the appropriate times, and make sure all the children can hear you and see the book. Pause to ask questions, invite comments, and positively acknowledge the children's responses. Additionally, encourage them to make predictions about what will happen next in the story and then continue reading far enough so they can find out whether their predictions approximate what happens in the story.

The first six pages of **Somewhere in Africa** tell and show where Ashraf does not live: not Africa where lions laze, or where crocodiles glide, or where zebras gallop. Before you turn the next page, ask where the children think Ashraf does live. Does anyone say, "In a city"? As you turn the page that shows Ashraf walking down a city street, the text tells that Ashraf lives in a city, confirming the prediction the children made.

TABLE 10.1

Types of Reading Instruction

Type of Reading	Definition	Goals	Grouping	Implementation
Read-alouds	• Teacher reads to children, who primarily listen to the story.	• Positive attitude toward reading and desire to read • Greater cognitive development • Better sense of story structure and organization • Increased vocabulary • Better understanding of how print and books work	• Whole class • Small group • Individual	• Teacher introduces book and then reads from it • Children may comment about what they hear and see • Optional follow-up discussion
Shared reading	• Teacher models reading to children, who are asked to comment extensively about the story they are listening to.	• Making meaning through partnership between children and teacher • Greater confidence in reading ability • More insight into how books are used • More reflection on story (plot, events, characters)	• Small groups	• Teacher selects book or Big Book and introduces it. • While reading book, teacher models reading and pauses to ask children for their questions, comments, and personal views. • Follow-up activities
Sustained silent reading (SSR)	• Children select books that they try to read or at least interact with in a reading-like manner.	• Better reading through regular practice • Recognition that reading is important • Progress toward independent reading • Enjoyment in reading alone • Learn about something from reading books	• Whole class	• Schedule SSR as a daily activity. • Explain to children the guidelines for SSR. • Children read their selected books. • Children may share their thoughts about what they read with each other and with the teacher.
Paired (partner) reading	• Two children help each other read or pretend to read a book.	• Recognition of reading as a form of communication • More practice reading orally and silently	• Two same-aged children	• Teacher pairs off children and schedules time for children to read together. • At scheduled time children engage in a particular activity, such as taking turns reading, asking each other questions, indicating what interests them most.
Independent reading	• Children read or pretend to read on their own without direct assistance from someone else.	• Greater personal control over and responsibility for reading • More progress toward independent reading • Enhanced confidence as a reader	• Individual	• Teacher schedules uninterrupted time and provides a place for children to read on their own. • Children select books they wish to read. • Children undertake follow-up activities related to what they read and participate in literature response group meeting.

Strategy	Description	Purpose	Grouping	Implementation
Buddy (supported) reading	• Older child tutors younger child in reading aloud.	• Reading improvement in older child • More practice reading for younger child	• Older child paired with a younger one	• Teacher identifies and prepares older child • Set up weekly reading sessions.
One-on-one	• Teacher, volunteer, or older child, who reads to a child, who can interrupt to ask questions, make comments, or otherwise respond to what he hears and sees.	• Improved reading in children experiencing difficulties in learning to read • Individualized instruction meeting specific needs	• Adult or one older child with one child	• Essentially implemented in the same way as read alouds
Supported reading	• Adult volunteer in class or parent at home tutors child in reading. Read-along cassettes and computer software used alone or by volunteer tutor to assist children as beginning readers.	• Individualized, extra instruction in class or at home • Reading instruction aided by educational technology	• Adult paired with one child	• Teacher contacts prospective volunteers or parents and provides training and provides supporting materials, such as prerecorded read-along tapes and CD-ROM programs
Guided reading	• Children read aloud from copies of same book while teacher guides them to effective cueing systems and reading strategies.	• Learn and practice reading strategies • Facilitate children's becoming independent readers • Follow up to read-alouds and shared reading	• Small group	• Group children by developmental levels. • Form reading groups. • Match groups with appropriate books. • Teacher models how to use cueing systems and reading strategies. • Through questions and comments, teacher directs children's attention to cueing systems and reading strategies, which they gradually apply to their reading.
Literature circles	• Small groups of children read copies of same trade or literature book and, under teacher supervision, discuss their thoughts, opinions, and feelings about what they have read.	• Critically thinking about a story • Expression of views, ideas, critiques about books • Individual and shared exploration of plot, characters, events, illustration	• Small group	• Select books that children are likely to be most interested in reading. • Teacher presents a "book talk" on selected books. • Let children select two preferred books and put those who have same preference into the same group. • Establish group's "rules" (meeting time, number of pages to read, etc.). • Teacher meets every day with one group to discuss assigned reading.
Reading workshop	• A comprehensive, systematic way to organize and integrate children's literature or basal readers into the classroom curriculum	• An adaptable framework and protocol for combining and coordinating key aspects of reading instruction	• Small group • Whole class	• Five phases: 1. Teacher-led sharing time 2. Minilessons for teaching reading skill and strategies 3. State of the class assessment that monitors student work and keeps them on task 4. Self-selected reading and response 5. Student sharing time

A word of caution: Asking too many questions can be distracting and interfere with the flow of the story and its meaning. As with any story reading, it is important to remember to alter continually how you read the book according to how the children react to the story.

After the Reading

When you finish reading the story, have the children either talk about the story or try to retell it in their own words. This gives them the chance to pull together the details of the story, to put the events into a meaningful sequence, recall the characters and overall plot, and to express their opinions about the story generally. These follow-up activities help to encourage children to express their ideas and ask questions about the book as well as to buttress their understanding and recollection of the setting, plot, events, and characters.

Teachers and children can make cutouts of cultural characters from photocopies of book pages and "me" puppets from photos of children.

Because ***Somewhere in Africa*** is a cultural character book with a new and fascinating cultural character for the children to meet, you may want to make a laminated cutout of Ashraf from a photocopy or dust jacket of the book cover. Use a Styrofoam or cardboard mount to have him stand upright, or wrap the cutout around a bathroom tissue tube to keep it upright. One teacher had the exciting idea of actually including each child in Ashraf's activities by having them make their own "me" paper puppets. She made photocopies of children's own photos, enlarging them to the same size as the Ashraf cutout, which were then cut out and glued onto cardboard tissue tubes. Now each listener could follow Ashraf through the city, stopping at store windows, walking past vendors, and dancing to the music of drummers and marimba players on his trek to the library. Children wanted to keep their "me" puppets on hand to be used with other book characters. If photos and character cutouts are small, they can be rolled into small tubes for finger puppets.

Shared Reading (Interactive Read-Alouds)

Shared reading relies on two interdependent, interacting instructional strategies. The first is teacher-modeled reading; the second involves children interacting with the teacher and with the reading process. The reasons for using shared reading stem from the cooperation between the teacher and children in extracting meaning from books in general and from the particular book being read together.

The Lady with the Alligator Purse
(Westcott, 1988)
It's Simple, Said Simon
(Hoberman, 2001)

Compared to read-alouds, shared reading emphasizes the importance that the teacher model how to read and that the children participate in the reading, see how books are used, and experience the power of language. Because children are actively taking part in shared reading, they can feel more confident as readers. Shared reading is similar to read-alouds but purposely encourages children to express more of their reactions to the story through comments, opinions, questions, and observations. During a shared reading, the teacher normally reads to a small group. This allows for a manageable amount of feedback while still supplying a sufficient variety of responses to which the children also may react. The teacher always is receptive to their feedback, which can be used to help gauge children's interest and comprehension and to ascertain what they remember about the story.

Typically, then, much of the time taken up by shared reading is spent by the teacher modeling how to read and by the children participating in that process and giving feedback.

Before Shared Reading

First and foremost, you should select appropriate books. Reutzel and Cooter (2000) enumerate key criteria for picking books (including some Big Books) suitable for shared reading. These attributes are general appeal and interest to children, obvious literary worth, engaging plot and characters, illustrations that support and complement the text; rhyme, rhythm, cumulative sequence, and repetition in the text; and predictability. Of these, predictability is probably the most important because it can facilitate the level and quality of the interaction between the children and the teacher while reading the story. An example of a good predictable book for shared reading is *The Lady with the Alligator Purse*, a humorous new version of a traditional jump rope rhyme.

During Shared Reading

The shared reading should be a scheduled part of the daily routine that children can count on. The reading usually begins with the teacher introducing the book to reinforce the children's desire to hear the story and to encourage them to think about and react to the story. This introduction also helps students tie the story into their prior knowledge and their recollections of other stories they have heard or read (Koskinen, Blum, Bisson, Phillips, Creamer, & Baker, 1999). As suggested by Reutzel and Cooter (2000), teachers can point out and explain certain things about a book, especially its title, the author, the publication date, the front and back covers, the pages in between, and the illustrations. Although you may know several ways to get children primed to listen and react to a story, two in particular are usually successful. The first involves reading and commenting about parts of the book (e.g., title and cover illustrations) in a playful or humorous way. *The Lady with the Alligator Purse* is surely humorous enough for such an introduction. Why are Miss Lucy, Tiny Tim, his sister, the dog, and the cat so wide mouthed and surprised looking as they watch the lady opening her alligator purse on the book cover? Does anyone notice that the purse is really a whole alligator who seems to be looking up and smiling? This relaxed and lighthearted introduction may entice the children to ponder what they perhaps already know about the book and to use that knowledge and their prior experiences to check the veracity of what the teacher says and shows concerning the book.

In the second approach, teachers may move their hands to connect the text visually to any accompanying illustrations (e.g., picture cues). The teacher may read the first page with her finger under the words "Miss Lucy had a baby. His name was Tiny Tim." She then moves her finger from the name "Tiny Tim" straight down to the picture of Tiny Tim all tangled up in the yarn he is playing with. Hand gestures like this can continue throughout the reading, serving as a natural and effective way to assist the children to focus on the print (e.g., letters, spaces between words, punctuation), to take note of the directionality of the book and its reading (e.g., left to right, top to bottom, first page to last), and to connect the print on the pages to illustrations and more generally to meaning.

While hand gesturing, the teacher needs to read the book in a lively and entertaining way. If she is reading from a Big Book on an easel, she has her hands free to use two imaginary phones at once in a hysterical manner when "Miss Lucy called the doctor. Miss Lucy called the nurse. Miss Lucy called the lady with the alligator purse." What can her gestures be when the doctor prescribes "penicillin," the nurse intones, "castor oil," but the lady with the alligator purse pronounces "pizza" and proceeds to remove one box of pizza after another out of the seemingly bottomless alligator purse?

Cumulatively these actions of teacher-led shared reading present a compelling model of how to use words and language structures, necessary prerequisites for development of independent reading in young children (Koskinen et. al., 1999).

Pausing at various points during the reading, the children are invited to articulate what they think about the illustrations and what was read. While reading individual words (e.g., graphophonic and language cues), teachers should briefly pause for commas, pause longer for periods, and use voice inflexions to signal questions and exclamations. Teachers can also pose questions about the story and ask the children to predict what happens next and what certain characters will do (e.g., meaning cues). In this story the children can chime in with the words "the lady with the alligator purse" every time after "the nurse" is mentioned. Also teachers need to prompt the children to confirm whether their guesses approximated the actual story. As children become increasingly active participants in shared reading, more time needs to be directed toward helping them use the aforementioned cuing systems that readers learn to rely on.

Cues Available to Young Readers

Young readers can use picture, meaning, language, and graphophonemic cues.

- *Picture cues.* As noted in chapter 8, one of the most readily available cues for young children reading picture books are the pictures themselves. They visualize, highlight, and augment the meaning of printed words in the story.

- *Meaning cues.* These cues include the meaning that the print conveys, the meaning that pictures or graphics communicate, and the use of prior knowledge.

- *Language cues.* These cues are based on the syntax of the English language, which is embodied in our everyday speech. Even though children may not know the specific parts of speech or be able to analyze a sentence grammatically, they do have an inherent feel of what is grammatically acceptable and what is not. This basic understanding of language helps guide young readers in their reading.

- *Graphophonemic cues.* These are frequently referred to as phonic cues and are used in unison with the other available cues. As efficient readers scan across the print, they usually read the initial consonants of words, and, depending on the amount of information gleaned, they promptly make predictions about the meaning of what they read.

Stressing exposure to the cueing systems can be helpful in two situations. First, after the children have heard repeated readings of a single book and have remembered much of it, they can mimic fluent reading strategies and, with the teacher's guidance, try to apply some of the cuing systems that are available by trying to read themselves. Second, benefiting from numerous shared readings, children will be better able to transfer to unfamiliar books some of the reading strategies and skills they have experienced, practiced, and assimilated with familiar books.

After the Shared Reading

After the reading ends, class discussion typically begins. Children at this point often will want to comment about their favorite episodes of the story, expressing their views of the book, plot, and characters. They may even describe personal experiences that are similar to or different from those in the story. Children often recall their predictions about the story and discuss what they found to be surprising, expected, funny, or wonderful. Frequently one child's comments elicit remarks from classmates. In addition to discussing the meaning of the story, children can make their own predictable Big Books and engage in several other activities that connect the story reading to specific cueing systems. For example, they can point to words in the story they want to add to a "word wall" they are making on a sheet of newsprint across the wall. Their selected words can then lead to more follow-up activities, such as building sight vocabulary, strengthening alphabet recognition, and practicing rhymes.

Children love to make up their own rhyming stories about Miss Lucy, Tiny Tim, and the lady with the alligator purse who always saves the day, no matter how outrageous her solutions. Children who are beginning to make representational drawings may be able to illustrate these stories. As children begin to recognize words, have them try to identify the name cards of the other children and the labels they see in the classroom. Can they be "word detectives"? When a word becomes their own (i.e., one they can identify regularly), print it for them on a card for their "Word Detective Cards" envelope. Neuman, Copple, and Bredekamp (2000) tell us, "Encourage children to figure out the meaning of the print they see—on a sign or a T-shirt or in a greeting card, magazine, or book—using their repertoire of known letters and cues such as word length. Challenge them to make educated guesses—to be 'print detectives' " (p. 65).

It's Simple, Said Simon is a predictable book with a sequential pattern rather than rhyming in which an East Indian boy proceeds through a series of repeated episodes, meeting a dog that challenges him to growl, a cat that challenges him to stretch, and a horse that challenges him to jump, which he does with ease, saying, "It's simple, said Simon." Finally he meets a tiger and the three challenges get more serious, since the tiger proposes to eat Simon. Now Simon has to perform each challenge three times until they are loud enough, long enough, and high enough to satisfy the tiger. As you and your listeners should note, the words get larger, longer, and higher, too. Can they find the print that says a really loud growl, a really long stretch, and a really high jump? Simon, of course, jumps off the tiger's back into the river and swims home. Your kindergarten listeners will eventually make *growl*, *stretch*, and *jump* into their words, too.

Sustained Silent Reading

Sustained silent reading (SSR) is known by several names; Be a Reader (BEAR) and Drop Everything and Read (DEAR) are two of them. Sustained silent reading

Sustained silent reading affords children opportunities to "play" the role of reader on their own with their favorite read-aloud book.

should be an integral part of every reading program and a natural successor to read-alouds. This is because children need to have a regular time to read books they have picked out themselves. During SSR, everyone in class reads, including the teacher, which bolsters the impression that reading is important.

Initially, sustained silent reading affords children opportunities to "play" the role of reader on their own with their favorite read-aloud books. It is important to let the children choose which books they want to read from those that are available. Doing so helps foster greater independence, motivation, enjoyment, and feelings satisfaction as they learn to read (Meyer, 2001). The children pattern their reading behaviors, with varying degrees of realism, after those of the teacher whom they have observed and listened to numerous times during read-alouds and shared reading.

SSR at first is frequently a blend of silent reading and audible oral reading. Initially children tend to vocalize as they pretend to read the text and pictures and intersperse their "reading" with personal remarks to themselves. SSR over time gradually bridges the divide between read-alouds and shared reading on the one hand and the full-fledged independent reading that children eventually achieve on the other.

Moreover, sustained silent reading has other reading-related purposes, which include practicing the "moves" of reading, finding enjoyment in reading by oneself, and perhaps even learning something interesting from the books they read.

To be successful, SSR requires careful planning. A definite period of time must be set aside each day for SSR. Usually this amounts to 10 to 15 minutes each day initially and then grows to 20 to 30 minutes as the end of the year approaches. Because they will be more or less on their own during each SSR, teachers need to prepare the children for what is expected of them. Specifically, the children need to know that they can select the books they want to read. They are also reminded to remain on task throughout their silent reading, to read by themselves, and not to intrude on others as they read. After SSR ends, teachers may have the children gather together and talk about what they read.

Paired Reading

Paired (or *partner*) *reading* involves two children from the same class and, therefore, roughly the same age working together. The essential dynamic of paired reading is two children reading or, in the case of the younger ones, at least trying to read to one another.

The benefits of paired reading result largely from the mutually reinforcing activities of cooperative "reading" and listening. In this way both children can gain a keener awareness of reading as communication and the distinct roles of reader and listener. The interaction between the two children can be varied from session to session to infuse the activity with novelty and anticipation. The children could, for example, take turns reading from a book and helping each other make sense of it as needed, or both could read from the same book and then ask one another questions or talk about their favorite parts or characters. From the mutual interactions inherent in paired reading, children can acquire more experience reading both orally and silently and thinking about what they read.

Setting up paired reading simply entails pairing off children, scheduling reading sessions, providing a setting and appropriate reading materials, and devising a range of activities to vary as paired readings unfold.

Independent Reading

Initially kindergartners may not be able to read in the conventional sense. Nonetheless, concerted effort should be made to encourage children to interact individually with books in whatever ways (e.g., "read" the pictures, pretend to read) they can, given where they are in becoming readers. The hallmarks of independent reading are, as you might expect, independence, control, and, by implication, a child's growing maturity and personal satisfaction as a reader. This form of reading brings to center stage regular silent (usually) uninterrupted reading for a designated period of time. Follow-up activities based on what was read may occur.

The major reason for independent reading is that children eventually will become independent readers. These practice solo "voyages" with books can help nurture the child's confidence and transition from a beginning reader to a competent, independent one.

To actualize independent reading, the teacher has to ensure ready access to a varied library of books that appeal to children. It is crucial for children to choose the books they want to read. A place and time also have to be arranged that will permit an adequate period of uninterrupted reading. Based on what the children read, the teacher can assign or assist children in selecting projects that build on the independent reading session (e.g., drawing a picture of themselves with their favorite cultural character in the story). Alternatively, the teacher can provide the children with opportunities to share with others their independent reading experiences.

Buddy Reading

Buddy reading, sometimes called *cross-age tutoring,* is similar to paired reading, but the buddies are several grade levels apart. During buddy reading, older children volunteer to read aloud one-to-one to younger children at a particular time. Sometimes the reading buddy is an adult from the community or from a local college.

Everyone benefits from buddy reading. For the older reading buddies, the practice they get prereading the book for a particular session can improve their own reading. For the community volunteer, the experience can be personally rewarding. The younger child clearly benefits from the additional time spent listening to someone read aloud, someone with whom the child perhaps may more readily identify and wish to emulate. As Henriques (1997) explains:

> A meta-analysis on cross-age tutoring shows that when older children work with young children, both tend to make significant gains in achievement and show improved attitudes toward school. . . . This activity has good potential for getting students who are at risk off to a good start in reading and writing and, at the same time, improving the tutors' reading skills. (p. 43)

Putting buddy reading into action is straightforward. First, the teacher selects potential volunteers based on their maturity and recommendations from teacher or referrals from the community. The individuals chosen to be buddies are briefed about why their help is important, how to present a book, and how to interact with their younger buddies.

One-to-One

One-to-one reading closely resembles both buddy reading and paired reading. The crucial distinction between those two forms and one-to-one reading is the individualized nature of the latter. Whereas everyone in a class participates in buddy reading or paired reading, perhaps only one or a few children actually participate in one-to-one reading. One-to-one reading is designed primarily for those children who need extra help in learning to read. The teacher, a volunteer, an older child, or perhaps a caregiver is the child's personal tutor in one-to-one reading.

One-to-one reading is generally easy to set up. Once a tutor is selected, then regular sessions can be scheduled. The specific needs of a child for help learning to read determine what transpires during any given session. In some cases the child may only need to practice reading more or to be read to, whereas other children may need help to improve retelling and comprehension. Regardless of which of these scenarios exists in a given situation, one-to-one reading can provide the child with individualized reading instruction that focuses on improving various skills, strategies, and confidence needed to become an independent reader.

Supported Reading

As its name implies, *supported reading* also relies on adult (parent) and child volunteers to work one-to-one in providing supplemental reading instruction either in the classroom or commonly in the child's home. Cassette players playing read-aloud tapes and computers running commercial educational software on CD-ROMs also can contribute significantly to supported reading in the classroom. These electronic aides for reading instruction are most appropriate for children in the earliest stages of learning to read.

Take-home books are frequently associated with supported reading, and they can assist parents or caregivers who wish to help their child at home in learning to read. With commercially available predictable books serving as models, teachers can produce their own leveled take-home books, which children take home along with suggested response activities and other materials (Richgels & Wold, 1998).

Guided Reading

Throughout a *guided* or *directed reading*, the teacher works with a small group of children (usually six) to focus and direct their interactions with a book. The children follow along in their own copies of that same book, which they attempt to read or otherwise refer to when necessary (e.g., when listening to the teacher read, commenting about pictures, answering questions). If the children are relatively young, the teacher typically has read the book the previous day, perhaps as a read-aloud or shared reading, so that the children will be generally familiar with it during the guided reading session.

The prime objective of guided reading is advancing the development of independent readers by supporting them to actively reflect on what they hear and possibly read. More specifically, guided reading encourages them to ask questions, make comments, share their ideas and opinions, and relate the story to their own experiences. Teachers may begin a guided reading by trying to find out from the children what they already know that may be relevant to what they will read. This groundwork and input help the children relate what they will learn to what they already know, thereby expanding their knowledge base (National Council of Teachers of English [NCTE], 2001). With guided reading as a model, children can more effectively and efficiently assimilate information gleaned from books as they become independent readers.

Besides reading the story (at least in part), the teacher tries to lead the children to predict how the story will unfold, what the characters will do, and then show ways they can verify their predictions. It is important that the teacher explains that the print in their books has the information they need to confirm their predictions, finding out whether their understanding of the story makes sense, and making corrections when it does not. Guided reading, then, can be an effective way to assist children to become independent readers.

Guided reading involves several stages with variations possible in every one. Generally the teacher selects a book for which a suitable number of copies are available. This book should be one that the children can read successfully but find a bit challenging. The guided reading group is formed and a meeting time and place are set. If the book is unfamiliar to the children, the teacher begins a session by reading the title and skimming through the book to get its overall gist. The children then may be asked to read a few of the words they encounter while scanning the book. After this preparatory phase, the teacher listens to the children as they read portions of the book in turn. At appropriate times, the teacher directs the children's attention to the print and illustrations as a basis for predicting, assessing, and confirming meaning and for making corrections to maintain the meaning that emerges from the book.

Literature Circles

In a sense, a *literature circle* is a specialized form of guided reading. The key distinction is that literature circles generally focus on books as bodies of information with certain literary qualities rather than on discovering and refining reading skills and strategies for extracting that information. The teacher's primary role is to work with a small group of children who each have copies of the same book. In the context of the group or circle, the children read a story and are urged to think continually about the content of the story, critique it, and explore it through discussion of plot, characters, setting, and the like.

At the Crossroads
(Isadora, 1991)

The underlying purpose of literature circles is to afford children the experience to go beyond the prerequisite process of reading (e.g., identifying words, predicting, and confirming meaning) to participate in thoughtfully shared reflection and discussion of the book or story read for its own sake. This dimension of reading is vitally important in full-fledged, independent reading.

Setting up literature circles and using them productively begins with the selection of good books—books that have strongly expressed literary qualities. Formation of the groups follows along with scheduling a regular time and place for discussing these books. The actual reading is assigned to children to do usually at home. Children initially may need prompting to sustain a meaningful discussion of the assigned reading, but over time they become more willing to offer their thoughts, opinions, observations, and questions for discussion. If properly implemented, literature circles help children become not only better readers but also equally important "critics" of what they read.

To adapt literature circles to kindergarteners, initially the children will express their views and attitudes and opinions about the intrinsic worth of stories that are read to them and the illustrations they see. For example, did they like the story? Was it funny? Was it sad or scary? Is it like another story they have seen or read? Children can also elaborate on their characterizations of the story with discussions of why they think one way or another about that story.

For example, *At the Crossroads* is a joyous story of six South African settlement children awaiting the imminent return of their fathers from ten months of working in the mines. "Our fathers are coming home! Our fathers are coming home!" they shout, and sing, and drum as they rush to the crossroads to wait for them. Large, realistic, double-page illustrations portray in water color the life in the settlement: at home, at school, at the water tap, making homemade instruments, and, finally, waiting alone in the dark under a blood red moon for their fathers' truck to arrive.

After you have read this book to a small group and they have seen the pictures, talk with them about the story. Did they like it? What did they like about it? What did they think about the children in the story? Could they tell how these children felt about their lives in the settlement? How? Would they like to do any of the things these children did on that special day? Would they be afraid waiting all night alone on the hill? Listen closely to your children's replies and let this lead you in the continued discussion of this story. Later they may want to make cutouts of these characters and continue their story.

Reading Workshop

Old MacDonald Had a Farm
(Rounds, 1989)

Fiddle-I-Fee: A Farmyard Song for the
Very Young (Sweets, 1992)

Skip to My Lou (Westcott, 1989)

The Very Busy Spider (Carle, 1984)

Pigs in the Mud in the Middle of the
Rud (Plourde, 1997)

Louella Mae, She's Run Away!
(Alarcon, 1997)

Click, Clack, Moo Cows That Type
(Cronin, 2000)

According to Reutzel and Cooter (2000), the *reading workshop* is a comprehensive way to incorporate children's literature or basal stories into classroom reading programs. They describe the reading workshop as having five steps: (a) sharing time, (b) minilessons, (c) state of the class, (d) self-selected reading and response, and (e) student sharing time.

Beginning with *sharing time*, the teacher reads aloud to the children to initiate interest in a genre of children's literature. This is followed by *minilessons* that are relatively brief, small-group or whole-class instructional sessions for teaching specific reading skills and strategies that a group or the entire class needs to work on. The teacher then assesses the *state of the class* by determining what and how well the students are learning those skills and strategies. If necessary, guidance and support are provided to assist children in their efforts. The next step is *self-selected reading*, during which the children have extensive time to practice what they have learned and to complete their logs, projects, diaries, and other assigned activities. *Student sharing time*, the final step, wraps up the workshop with a culminating activity in which the children come back together as a class to talk about what they have been reading, learning, and working on.

The reading workshop format described earlier can be adapted for kindergarten (Bryan, 1999). Careful consideration, however, must be given to the length of time that young readers will spend on a given activity and on the workshop as a whole. Thus, the duration of the individual components of a workshop depend on the children's level of maturity, their prior school experiences, and their motivation to complete the planned workshop activities. If these precautions are taken, then teachers can be reasonably confident that the interactions with students during a reading workshop can be productive, that the diverse needs of beginning readers can be attended to, and that meaningful opportunities for expressing and sharing their opinions and ideas about stories and books can occur.

One kindergarten teacher who was becoming very nervous about being able to help all his children with their wide range of reading abilities and so little time to work with individuals who needed help, decided to try a reading workshop. His class contained children who were readers, children who had very little letter recognition, and children who were at emerging reading levels and needed direct instruction to nurture continued growth.

He decided to place a selection of emergent reader books in several plastic baskets for children to choose from. Some were familiar books they had read together, others were books new to the children. All of them focused on a special theme: the farmyard and farm animals. (See books listed at the head of this section.) All of them were lighthearted, predictable books full of fun rhymes and rhythms. Several were written versions of songs the children knew. Every day he read one of these books to the class during shared reading. Then the children had to select one of these familiar books to read by themselves and one other book of their choice from the classroom library. He gave each child a gallon-size plastic baggie to use as a shopping bag for their books.

After shared reading, the teacher used cutout characters from the book he was reading to be placed on a large flannel board for retelling of the story. The characters in all of the books mentioned happened to be Anglo-American, so he asked the children to find a cutout character from a different culture to introduce to the farm characters. Children selected cultural book characters they already knew from a basket of finger puppet cultural characters they had made. During the self-selected reading time, the teacher worked with individuals who needed help with their reading or their letters. Some of the more advanced readers wanted to make up stories about their cultural characters meeting the farm characters they were reading about. This prompted the teacher to bring in several personal cassette players, which he placed in the children's shopping bags. Later they could play back any stories they recorded during the student sharing time. Altogether this reading workshop was a highly successful experience for everyone, and the class kept it going for a number of weeks (Bryan, 1999).

It is vital that as children steadily progress toward independent reading during kindergarten, cultural characters should accompany them every step of the way.

Cultural Characters in Kindergarten

As we have seen, the encounters with cultural characters that occur in preschool can continue and broaden throughout kindergarten. It is vital that as children steadily progress toward independent reading during kindergarten, cultural characters should accompany them every step of the way. Wham, Barnhart, and Cook (1996) assert that multicultural literature may be a powerful force in leading children to "broader levels of awareness and understanding of diverse groups" (p. 6). Thus, teachers have a responsibility to incorporate into the curriculum multicultural literature with all its enriching and fascinating cultural characters.

Table 10–2 lists the cultural characters presented in this text along with their books. The books described here are used as examples of cultural character books you may want to include in your library. Other similar books can serve just as well. Appendix A contains a list of cultural character paperback books available from Scholastic. Because new books come on the market annually you may want to phone for current catalogs from the publishers listed in chapter 1. As you prepare to read these books to children, be thinking of activities the cultural characters might invite your children to carry out that will promote early literacy. The activities described in this text are models for activities you and your children can create. Table 10–3 lists literacy activities the cultural characters from the books in this text were engaged in.

TABLE 10.2
Cultural Characters in Text

Name	Culture	Book	Chapter
Suki	Asian	*Will You Come Back for Me?*	1
Hue Boy	Caribbean	*Hue Boy*	1
Anna	Anglo-American	*Building a Bridge*	1
Juanita	Navajo	*Building a Bridge*	1
Ling Sung	Chinese	*Cleversticks*	1, 2, 3
Pablo	Hispanic	*Pablo's Tree*	1, 5
Susan	Anglo-American	*Susan Laughs*	1
Mariko-Chan	Japanese	*Rise and Shine, Mariko Chan*	2
Pascual	Guatemalan	*Pascual's Magic Pictures*	2
Kelly	African American	*Kelly in the Mirror*	2
Little Eagle	Native American	*Little Eagle, Lots of Owls*	2
Jafta	African	*Jafta*	2
Margaret	Anglo-American	*Margaret and Margarita*	2
Margarita	Hispanic	*Margaret and Margarita*	2
Mark, Randy, me	African American	*Haircuts at Sleepy Sam's*	2
Shauna	African American	*Saturday at The New You*	2
Keyana	African American	*I Love My Hair*	2
Kii	Navajo	*Sunpainters, Eclipse of the Navajo Sun*	2
Mary Greyfeather	Shawnee	*Green Snake Ceremony*	2
		White Bead Ceremony	5
Cayal	East Indian	*Moon Jump*	2, 3
Mary Mack	Anglo-American	*Miss Mary Mack*	3
Girl	African American	*Bein' with You This Way*	3
Max	African American	*Max Found Two Sticks*	3
Katie	Native American	*Red Bird*	3
Iktomi	Sioux	*Iktomi and the Buzzard*	3
Willie Jerome	African American	*Willie Jerome*	3
Guatemalan boy	Mayan	*The Bravest Flute*	3
Rosie	Trinidad	*An Island Christmas*	3
Banzar	African	*The Singing Man*	3
Louie	Hispanic	*Louie*	4
Dear One	Native Alaskan	*Mama, Do You Love Me?*	4
Michael	Native Alaskan	*On Mother's Lap*	4
Yvette	African American	*Not Yet, Yvette*	4
Silvia	Hispanic	*New Shoes for Silvia*	4
Christopher	African American	*I'm Calling Molly*	4
Molly	Anglo-American	*I'm Calling Molly*	4
Jamaica	African American	*Jamaica and Brianna*	4
Brianna	Asian	*Jamaica and Brianna*	4
Hugo	Hispanic	*Going Home*	4
Cassie	African American	*Tar Beach*	4
Girl	Native American	*If You Are a Hunter of Fossils*	4
Gah-Ning	Chinese	*Where is Gah-Ning?*	4
Carlos	Hispanic	*Carlos and the Squash Plant*	4, 8
		Carlos and the Corn Field	5
Eva, Nikki, me	African American	*One of Three*	4
Juan Bobo	Puerto Rican	*Juan Bobo Goes to Work*	4, 8
Gilberto	Hispanic	*Gilberto and the Wind*	5, 8
Joseph	Polish	*Joseph Had a Little Coat*	5

TABLE 10.2 Continued

Name	Culture	Book	Chapter
Girl	Anglo-American	*A String of Beads*	5
Girl	Cree Indian	*Two Pairs of Shoes*	5
Luka	Hawaiian	*Luka's Quilt*	5
Esperanza	Guatemalan	*Abuela's Weave*	5
Glenmae	Navajo	*The Goat in the Rug*	5
Kondo	African	*Galimoto*	5
Boy and girl	Zuni Indian	*The Dragonfly's Tale*	5
Sosi	Pueblo Indian	*The Mud Family*	5, 6
Sonja and Desiree	Pueblo Indian	*Pueblo Girls*	5
Carry	Anglo-American	*Everybody Cooks Rice*	5
Girl	Japanese American	*How My Parents Learned to Eat*	5
Yoko	Japanese	*Yoko*	5
Yummi	Korean	*Halmoni and the Picnic*	5
Maria	Hispanic	*Too Many Tamales*	5
Rosalba	Hispanic	*Abuela*	5
Mother	African	*My Baby*	5
Girl	Anglo-American	*My Crayons Talk*	5
Jeffrey	Navajo	*Young Goat's Discovery*	6
Ben	Navajo	*The Shepherd Boy*	6
Peter	African American	*A Letter to Amy*	7
Ahmed	Egyptian	*The Day of Ahmed's Secret*	7
Xiao Ming	Chinese	*At the Beach; In the Snow*	7
Mcheshi	African	*Mcheshi Goes to the Market*	7
Franny	Anglo-American	*Good Morning Franny, Good Night Franny*	7
Ting	Chinese	*Good Morning Franny, Good Night Franny*	7
Jenny	African-American	*Jenny's Journey*	7
Nico	Korean	*Families Are Different*	7, 9
Boy	African American	*Where Does the Trail Lead?*	7
Sara	Anglo-American	*Famous Seaweed Soup*	7
Sally	English	*Silly Sally*	8
Handa	African	*Handa's Surprise*	8
Jessie	Australian	*Shoes from Grandpa*	8
Madeline	French	*Madeline*	8
Strega Nona	Italian	*Strega Nona*	8
Big Anthony	Italian	*Strega Nona*	8
Norman	Anglo-American	*The Signmaker's Assistant*	9
Ashraf	African	*Somewhere in Africa*	10
Miss Lucy	Anglo-American	*The Lady with the Alligator Purse*	10
Simon	East Indian	*It's Simple, Said Simon*	10
Zola et al.	African	*At the Crossroads*	10

TABLE 10.3
Cultural Character Literacy Activities

Name	Activity	Learning Center
Mariko-chan	Greetings (speaking)	Dramatic play
Cleversticks	Chopsticks (eye–hand)	Dramatic play
Pascual	Photos (puzzle)	Manipulative
Kelly	Mirror (self-concept)	Book
Little Eagle	Name (writing, speaking)	Writing
Jafta	Name (speaking)	Book
Margaret, Margarita	Conversation	Book
Randy, Mark, me	Conversation; sign-up	Dramatic play
Shauna, Keyana	Conversation	Dramatic play
Kii	Sun Painting	Art
Alejandro	Watering pets	Science
Cayal	Jumping	Large motor
Hue Boy	Measuring, recording	Math
Mary Mack	Chanting (repetition, rhythm)	Music
Max	Drumming (rhythm)	Music
Katie	Dancing (rhythm)	Music
Willie Jerome	Playing instrument (rhythm, sound)	Music
Rosie	Drumming (rhythm)	Music
Dexter	Playing harmonica (rhythm, sound)	Music
Banzar	Singing (rhythm, rhyme)	Music
Louie	Puppet (speaking)	Book
Dear One	Questioning	Dramatic play
Michael	Questioning	Dramatic play
Yvette	Questioning	Dramatic play
Silvia	Conversation	Dramatic play
Christopher, Molly	Phone conversation	Dramatic play
Jamaica, Brianna	Conversation	Dramatic play
Hugo	Conversation	Dramatic play
Cassie	Conversation	Block
Sammy	Conversation	Sand table
Gah-Ning	Conversation (listening)	Book
Carlos	Dictating story	Writing
Juan Bobo	Listening to mother	Book
Gilberto	Making pinwheel (eye–hand)	Art
Pablo	Cutting decorations (eye–hand)	Art
Joseph	Tracing, cutting (eye–hand)	Art
Mary Greyfeather	Stringing beads (eye–hand)	Art
Luka	Making Quilt (eye–hand)	Art
Esperanza	Weaving (eye–hand)	Art
Glenmae	Weaving (eye–hand)	Art

CHAPTER 10

TABLE 10.3   Continued

Name	Activity	Learning Center
Kondo	Twisting wire (eye–hand)	Art
Sosi	Molding mud, clay (eye–hand)	Art
Carry	Cooking rice (eye–hand)	Cooking
Yoko	Cooking rice (eye–hand)	Cooking
Maria	Cooking tamales (eye–hand)	Cooking
Carlos	Making cornmeal pancakes	Cooking
Rosalba	Making houses	Block, woodworking
Jeffrey, Ben	Writing petroglyphs	Writing
Peter	Writing letter	Writing
Ahmed	Writing name	Writing
Xiao Ming	Writing Chinese characters	Writing
Max, Ruby	Making grocery list	Cooking
Mcheshi	Making shopping list	Dramatic play
Franny, Ting	Writing on sidewalk with chalk	Outside
Jenny	Writing letter	Writing
Nico	Writing story	Writing
Sara	Writing Soup ingredients	Cooking
Sally	Story reenactment	Dramatic play
Handra	Story reenactment	Dramatic play
Gilberto	Flannelboard story	Book
Iktomi	Flannelboard story	Book
Jessie	Retelling story	Book
Norman	Making signs	Writing
Ashraf	Making "me" puppets	Art
Miss Lucy	Making up stories	Writing
Simon	Finding new words	Book
Zola et al.	Continuing their story	Book

SUMMARY

The crucial transition from preschool to kindergarten is affected by a range of expectations that impinge on young children's efforts to further their progress in learning to read. These expectations, voiced by educators, parents, and society, include book and print awareness, alphabet knowledge, phonemic awareness, phonics, and meaning making. This chapter examines how these and other expectations influence the process of becoming a reader in kindergarten and the instructional techniques that commonly support and guide that process. Beginning with read-alouds and progressing to independent reading, children in kindergarten, along with their cultural character book friends, gradually move from primarily teacher-directed, print- and meaning-centered forms of reading instruction to more self-directed, independent learning.

LEARNING ACTIVITIES

1. Compare how read-alouds and shared reading assist children in becoming readers.
2. Describe the benefits that two nonfluent readers would have by participating in paired or partner reading.
3. Using one cultural character book, list the multiple ways the book could be used for developing shared reading follow-up activities.
4. Using three different cultural character books, describe how each would be introduced to children in the context of a read-aloud, a shared reading, and a guided reading activity.
5. Describe how to adapt literature circles and reading workshops to the kindergarten classroom. How would young readers benefit from these experiences?

REFERENCES

Bryan, J. W. (1999). Readers' workshops in a kindergarten classroom. *Reading Teacher*, 52(5), 538–540.

Campbell, R. (2001). *Read alouds with young children*. Newark, DE. International Reading Association.

Graue, E. (2001). What's going on in the children's garden? Kindergarten today. *Young Children*, 56(4), 67–73.

Henriques, M. E. (1997). Increasing literacy among kindergartners through cross-age training. *Young Children*, 52(4), 42–47.

Koskinen, P. S., Blum, I. H., Bisson, S. A., Phillips, S. M., Creamer, T. S., & Baker, T. K. (1999). Shared reading, books, and audiotapes: Supporting diverse students in school and at home. *Reading Teacher*, 52(5), 430–444.

Meyer, J. (2001). The child-centered kindergarten: A position paper. *Childhood Education*, 77(3), 161–167.

National Council of Teachers of English. (2001). Elementary school practices: NCTE guidelines and position statements. Available on-line at http://www.ncte.org/positions/elem.html.

Neuman, S. B., Copple, C., & Bredekamp, S. (2000). *Learning to read and write*. Washington, DC: National Association for the Education of Young Children.

Neuman, S. B., & Roskos, K. A. (1993). *Language and learning in the early years*. Fort Worth, TX: Harcourt Brace.

Routzol, D. R., & Cooter, R. D. (2000). *Teaching children to read: Putting the pieces together*. Upper Saddle River, NJ: Merrill/Prentice Hall.

Richgels, D. J., & Wold, L. S. (1998). Literacy on the road: Backpacking partnerships between school and home. *Reading Teacher*, 52(1), 18–29.

Van Kraayenoord, C. E., & Paris, S. G. (1996). Story construction from a picture book: An assessment activity for young learners. *Early Childhood Research Quarterly, 11*, 41–61.

Wham, M.A., Barnhart, J., & Cook, G. (1996). Enhancing multicultural awareness through the storybook reading experience. *Journal of Research and Development in Education, 30*(1), 1–9.

SUGGESTED READINGS

Beagle, K. G., & Dowhower, S. L. (1998). The print environment in kindergartens: A study of conventional and holistic teachers and their classrooms in three settings. *Reading Research and Instruction, 37*(3), 161–190.

Bruneau, B. J., Genisio, M. H., Casbergue, R., & Reiner, K. (1998). Developing a kindergarten phonemic awareness program: An action research project. *Reading Teacher, 52*(1), 70–73.

Buriss, K. G. (2001). Whole language vs. isolated instruction: A longitudinal study in kindergarten with reading and writing tasks. *Childhood Education, 77*(3), 187.

Button, K., & Johnson, M. (1997). The role of shared reading in developing effective early reading strategies. *Reading Horizons, 37*(4), 262–273.

Cho, B. K., & Kim, J. (1999). The improvement of children's creativity through Korean picture books. *Childhood Education, 75*(6), 337–341.

Fayden, T. (1997). What is the effect of shared reading on rural Native American and Hispanic kindergarten children? *Reading Improvement, 34*(1), 22–30.

Goswami, U. (1999). Causal connections in beginning reading: The importance of rhyme. *Journal of Research in Reading, 22*(3), 217–240.

Jordan, G. E., Snow, C. E., & Porche, M. V. (2000). Project EASE: The effect of a family literacy project on kindergarten students' early literacy skills. *Reading Research Quarterly, 35*(4), 524–546.

Kane, S. (1999). Teaching decoding strategies without destroying the story. *Reading Teacher, 52*(7), 770–772.

Karchmer, R. A. (2000). Exploring literacy on the Internet: Using the Internet and children's literature to support interdisciplinary instruction. *Reading Teacher, 54*(1), 100–104.

Kuby, P., & Aldridge, J. (1997). Direct versus indirect environmental print instruction and early reading ability in kindergarten children. *Reading Psychology, 18*(2), 91–104.

Martinez, M. G., & Teale, W. H. (1993). Teacher storybook reading style: A comparison of six teachers. *Research in the Teaching of English, 27*(2), 175–199.

McGill-Franzen, A., Allington, R.L., Yokoi, L., & Brooks, G. (1999). Putting books in the classroom seems necessary but not sufficient. *Journal of Educational Research, 93*(2), 67–74.

McMahon, R., Richmond, M.G., & Reeves-Kazelskis, C. (1998). Relationships between kindergarten teachers' perceptions of literacy acquisition and children's literacy involvement and classroom materials. *Journal of Educational Research, 91*(3), 173–182.

Morado, C., Koenig, R., & Wilson, A. (1999). Miniperformances, many stars! Playing with stories. *Reading Teacher, 53*(2), 116–123.

Moustafa, M., & Maldonado-Colon, E. (1999). Whole to parts phonics instruction: Building on what children know to help them more. *Reading Teacher, 52*(5), 448–458.

Opitz, M. F. (1998). Children's books to develop phonemic awareness—For you and parents, too! *Reading Teacher, 51*(6), 526–528.

Qi, S., & O'Connor, R. (2000). Comparison of phonological training procedures in kindergarten classrooms. *Journal of Educational Research, 93*(4), 226–233.

Reisner, T. (2001). Learning to teach reading in a developmentally appropriate kindergarten. *Young Children, 56*(3), 44–48.

Richgels, D. J., Poremba, K. J., & McGee, L. M. (1996). Kindergartners talk about print: Phonemic awareness in meaningful contexts. *Reading Teacher, 49*(8), 632–642.

Saint-Laurent, L., & Giasson, J. (1999). Four Canadian kindergarten teachers' reports about the implementation of an emergent reading program. *Elementary School Journal, 100*(2), 111–127.

Treiman, R., & Broderick, V. (1998). What's in a name: Children's knowledge about the letters in their own names. *Journal of Experimental and Child Psychology, 70*(2), 97–116.

Volk, D. (1999). "The teaching and the enjoyment and being together...": Sibling teaching in the family of a Puerto Rican kindergartner. *Early Childhood Research Quarterly, 14*(1), 5–34.

Wuori, D. (1999). Beyond letter of the week: Authentic literacy comes to kindergarten. *Young Children, 52*(6), 24–25.

CHILDREN'S BOOKS

Alarcon, K. B. (1997). *Louella Mae, she's run away!* New York: Holt.

Carle, E. (1984). *The very busy spider.* New York: Philomel.

Cronin, D. (2000). *Click, clack, moo cows that type.* New York: Simon & Schuster.

Isadora, R. (1991). *At the crossroads.* New York: Mulberry.

Hoberman, M. A. (2001). *It's simple, said Simon.* New York: Knopf.

Mennen, I., & Daly, N. (1992). *Somewhere In Africa.* New York: Dutton.

Plourde, L. (1997). *Pigs in the mud in the middle of the rud.* New York: Blue Sky.

Rogers, J. (1999). *Tiptoe into kindergarten.* New York: Scholastic.

Rounds, G. (1989). *Old MacDonald had a farm.* New York: Holiday House.

Sweet, M. (1992). *Fiddle-i-fee: A farmyard song for the very young.* Boston: Little, Brown.

Wescott, N. B. (1988). *The lady with the alligator purse.* Boston: Little, Brown.

Wescott, N. B. (1989). *Skip to my Lou.* Boston: Little, Brown.

The manner in which language and literacy develop in human beings is not known. There is no one definite explanation for these complex processes. Furthermore, new information is continually forthcoming. This demands that we read and study some more. So: If we are to genuinely assist children in their language and literacy learning efforts, if we are to be their "teachers," we need to become and remain learners about language ourselves.

Neuman and Roskos (1993)

CULTURAL CHARACTER PAPERBACK BOOKS FROM SCHOLASTIC

As asterisk indicates that a book pack is available; a plus sign indicates a predictable book. Take-Home Book Packs include a read-aloud book, an audiocassette, a card for home, and an activity sheet for hands-on activities. Phone Scholastic: (800) 724-6527.

At the Crossroads (African)

Abiyoyo (African) Big Book also available*

Amazing Grace (African American)

Angel Child, Dragon Child (Vietnamese)

Aunt Flossie's Hats (African American) Big Book also available*

Babushka's Doll (Russian)

Ben's Trumpet (African American)

Best Friends (Native American)

A Birthday Basket for Tia (Hispanic) Spanish book also available

Bigmama's (African American)

The Bossy Gallito (Cuban)

Bringing the Rain to Kapiti Plain (African) Big Book also available* +

Carlos and the Squash Plant (Hispanic) Bilingual

Chicken Sunday (multicultural)*

Corduroy (African American) Big Book available; Spanish book available*

Dancing with the Indians (African American; Native American)*

Daniel's Dog (African American)

Dinosaur Roar! (animals) Big Book also available+

Do Like Kyla (African American)

Everybody Cooks Rice (Anglo-American; multicultural)

Families Are Different (Korean; multicultural) Big Book also available*

Feast for 10 (African American)+

Flossie and the Fox (African American)*

Flower Garden (African American)+

Grandmother and I (African American)+

The Great Kapok Tree (Hispanic) Spanish book also available

Handa's Surprise (African)

Hello Amigos (Hispanic)

It Takes a Village (African)

Is Your Mama a Llama? (animals) Big Book available; Spanish book* +

Jamaica's Find (African American)*

Jamaica Tag-Along (African American)

Jonathan and His Mama (African American)

Just Us Women (African American)

A Kente Dress for Kenya (African American)

The Legend of the Bluebonnet (Native American) Spanish book available*

The Legend of the Indian Paintbrush (Native American)

Let's Eat (Spanish)

The Little Banjo (The Banza) (Animals; Haitian)

Mama, Do You Love Me? (Native Alaskan) Big Book & Spanish available* +

Miss Mary Mack (multicultural) Big Book available+

The Mud Pony (Native American)

Mufaro's Beautiful Daughters (African)

New Shoes for Silvia (Hispanic) Spanish book also available

Ricardo's Day (Hispanic) Spanish book also available

Rise and Shine Mariko-Chan (Japanese)

Saturday Night at the Dinosaur Stomp (animals)* +

The Snowy Day (African American) Big Book also available

Silly Sally (medieval English)* +

Strega Nona (medieval Italian)*

Tar Beach (African American) Big Book also available

Tell Me a Story, Mama (adopted)

Ten, Nine, Eight (African American)*

Tikki, Tikki, Tembo (Chinese)*

Too Many Tamales (Hispanic) Spanish book also available

Ty's One-Man Band (African American)*

What Mary-Jo Shared (African American)*

Whistle for Willie (African American)

Why Mosquitoes Buzz in People's Ears (African; animals)

Yoko (Japanese)

APPENDIX B

TOPICAL CULTURAL CHARACTER BOOK INDEX

ACCEPTANCE

And to Think That We Thought That We'd Never Be Friends

Building a Bridge

Cleversticks

Dragonfly's Tale

Halmoni and the Picnic

Mararget and Margarita

The Mud Family

The Singing Man

Yo! Yes?

Yoko

ADOPTION

Families Are Different

Pablo's Tree

AFFECTION; LOVE

How Do Dinosaurs Say Goodnight?

K Is for Kiss Good Night

Love Can Build a Bridge

Love Flute

Mama, Do You Love Me?

The Mud Family

On Mother's Lap

Pablo's Tree

Will You Come Back for Me?

AFRICA

At the Crossroads

Bringing the Rain to Kapiti Plain

Galimoto

Handa's Surprise

Jafta

Jafta's Father

Jafta's Mother

Mcheshi Goes to the Market

My Baby

The Singing Man

Somewhere in Africa

Why Mosquitoes Buzz in People's Ears

ALPHABET

Alef-bet: A Hebrew Alphabet

The Calypso Alphabet

Chicka Chicka Boom Boom

The Guinea Pig ABC

The Handmade Alphabet

Hieroglyphics from A to Z

K Is for Kiss Good Night

Native American Sign Language
Navajo ABC
Potluck
Turtle Island ABC

ANIMALS

Beach Feet

Bringing the Rain to Kapiti Plain

Brother Eagle, Sister Sky

Click Clack Moo: Cows That Type

Cock-a-Doodle-Do, What Does It Sound Like to You?

Coyote: A Trickster Tale from the American Southwest

Dinosaur Days

Dinosaur Roar!

Does a Kangaroo Have a Mother Too?

Fiddle-I-Fee: A Farmyard Song for the Very Young

The Forest Has Eyes

The Goat in the Rug

Going Home

Green Snake Ceremony

The Guinea Pig ABC

Guinea Pigs Far and Near

How Do Dinosaurs Say Good Night?

Hush! A Thai Lullaby

I Love Guinea Pigs

Iktomi and the Buzzard

Is Your Mama a Llama?

It's Simple, Said Simon

Louella Mae, She's Run Away

Mama, Do You Love Me?

Mice Squeak, We Speak

My Visit to the Aquarium

Northern Lullaby

Old MacDonald Had a Farm

Pigs in the Mud in the Middle of the Rud

Sammy and the Dinosaurs

The Seals on the Bus

The Shepherd Boy

Skip to My Lou

Somewhere in Africa

Ten Terrible Dinosaurs

There Was an Old Lady Who Swallowed a Trout

The Very Busy Spider

Warthogs in the Kitchen

Why Mosquitoes Buzz in People's Ears

Young Goat's Discovery

BABIES

Hush! A Thai Lullaby

Baby-O

The Lady with the Alligator Purse

Louella Mae, She's Run Away!

My Baby

BEADS

A String of Beads

Two Pairs of Shoes

White Bead Ceremony

BUILDINGS

Abuela

Isla

Tar Beach

Building a House

This Is My House

The House That Jack Built

This House Is Made of Mud

Dragonfly's Tale

BICYCLES; SKATEBOARDS

Where Is Gah-Ning?

BIRTHDAY

Not Yet, Yvette
Pablo's Tree

BLOCKS

Building a Bridge

BROTHERS

Dragonfly's Tale
Haircuts at Sleepy Sam's
Pigs in the Mud in the Middle of the Rud

BUS; SCHOOL BUS

Abuela's Weave
Baby-O
Building a Bridge
Rise and Shine Mariko-Chan
The Seals on the Bus
Wheels on the Bus

CARIBBEAN ISLAND

Hue Boy
An Island Christmas
The Banza
Juan Bobo Goes to Work
Isla

CEREMONIES; CELEBRATIONS

At the Crossroads
Dumpling Soup
An Island Christmas

Green Snake Ceremony
Not Yet, Yvette
Miss Mary Mack
Pablo's Tree
Powwow
Pueblo Girls: Growing Up in Two Worlds
Red Bird
Too Many Tamales
White Bead Ceremony

CHANTS

Baby-O
Bein' with You This Way
I Know an Old Lady Who Swallowed a Fly
The Lady with the Alligator Purse
Miss Mary Mack
The Seals on the Bus
There Was an Old Lady Who Swallowed a Trout
Twist with a Burger, Jitter with a Bug
Wheels on the Bus

CHILDREN SOLVING PROBLEMS

Abuela's Weave
Building a Bridge
Carlos and the Corn Field
Cleversticks
Galimoto
Dragonfly's Tale
Families Are Different
It's Simple, Said Simon
Love Can Build a Bridge
Miss Mary Mack
The Mud Family
New Shoes for Silvia
The Signmaker's Assistant

Max Found Two Sticks

Powwow

Red Bird

The Singing Man

EATING

Bunny Cakes

Carlos and the Corn Field

Carlos and the Squash Plant

Cleversticks

Dragonfly's Tale

Dumpling Soup

Everybody Eats Rice

Fiddle-I-Fee: A Farmyard Song for the Very Young

Halmoni and the Picnic

How My Parents Learned to Eat

Hue Boy

The Lady with the Alligator Purse

One of Three

Potluck

Red Bird

Rise and Shine Mariko-Chan

Tiptoe into Kindergarten

Too Many Tamales

Warthogs in the Kitchen

Yoko

EYE–HAND COORDINATION

Bunny Cakes

Cleversticks

Dumpling Soup

How My Parents Learned to Eat

Joseph Had a Little Overcoat

Max Found Two Sticks

My Crayons Talk

Tiptoe into Kindergarten

Warthogs in the Kitchen

EXERCISING

Bein' with You This Way

Hue Boy

It's Simple, Said Simon

Moon Jump

Susan Laughs

FAMILIES

At the Crossroads

The Day of Ahmed's Secret

Families Are Different

Hue Boy

An Island Christmas

Isla

Kelly in the Mirror

The Lady with the Alligator Purse

Louella Mae, She's Run Away!

The Mud Family

Red Bird

Skip to My Lou

Two Pairs of Shoes

Where Is Gah-Ning?

FATHERS

At the Crossroads

Carlos and the Corn Field

Cleversticks

Hue Boy

Jafta's Father

Not Yet, Yvette

Pigs in the Mud in the Middle of the Rud

Where Is Gah-Ning?

Abuela's Weave
Halmoni and the Picnic
Isla
One Smiling Grandma
My Grandmother's Patchwork Quilt
Pigs in the Mud in the Middle of the Rud
Two Pairs of Shoes

GREETINGS

Rise and Shine Mariko-Chan

GUATEMALA

Pascual's Magic Pictures
Abuela's Weave

HAPPINESS; HUMOR; SILLINESS

A Beasty Tale
Chicka, Chicka, Boom Boom
Click, Clack, Moo: Cows That Type
Famous Seaweed Soup
How Do Dinosaurs Say Good Night?
I Know an Old Lady Who Swallowed a Fly
Iktomi and the Buzzard
Juan Bobo Goes to Work
The Lady with the Alligator Purse
Louella Mae, She's Run Away!
Pigs in the Mud in the Middle of the Rud
The Seals on the Bus
Shoes from Grandpa
Silly Sally
Skip to My Lou
Susan Laughs
There Was an Old Lady Who Swallowed a Trout
Where Is Gah-Ning?

HAIR

Bein' with You This Way
Haircuts at Sleepy Sam's
Saturday at The New You
I Love My Hair
Hats Off to Hair!

HATS

Carlos and the Squash Plat

HELPING OTHERS

Abuela's Weave
At the Crossroads
Dragonfly's Tale
Going Home
The Lady with the Alligator Purse
Louella Mae, She's Run Away!
Love Can Build a Bridge
Louella Mae, She's Run Away!
Pigs in the Mud in the Middle of the Rud
Saturday at The New You

HIKING

Where Does the Trail Lead?

HOSPITAL

Love Can Build a Bridge
Going Home

HOUSES

At the Crossroads
A Beasty Tale
Building a House
The House That Jack Built

Pigs in the Mud in the Middle of the Rud
Will You Come Back for Me?

MUSIC; MUSICAL INSTRUMENTS

And to Think That We Thought That We'd Never Be Friends

At the Crossroads

The Banza

The Bravest Flute

Charlie Parker Played Be Bop

Fiddle-I-Fee: A Farmyard Song for the Very Young

Hush! A Thai Lullaby

An Island Christmas

Love Flute

Music, Music for Everyone

Northern Lullaby

Old Cotton Blues

Old MacDonald Had a Farm

Skip to My Lou

Willie Jerome

NAMES

The Day of Ahmed's Secret

Little Eagle Lots of Owls

White Bead Ceremony

PAINTING; DRAWING

The Little Shepherd Boy

My Baby

My Crayons Talk

My Name Is Georgia

Native American Rock Art: Messages from the Past

Sunpainters: Eclipse of the Navajo Sun

Tiptoe into Kindergarten

Young Goat's Discovery

PARADE; PROCESSION

And to Think That We Thought That We'd Never Be Friends

Silly Sally

PETROGLYPHS

Messages on Stones

The Mud Family

Native American Rock Art Messages from the Past

The Shepherd Boy

Young Goat's Discovery

Talking Walls

PHOTOGRAPHS

Pascual's Magic Pictures

PHYSICAL IMPAIRMENT

Good Morning Franny, Good Night Franny

The Handmade Alphabet

Susan Laughs

PRESCHOOL

Will You Come Back for Me?

Building a Bridge

Cleversticks

Yoko

PUPPETS

Louie

QUILTING, SEWING

Joseph Had a Little Overcoat

Luka's Quilt

My Grandmother's Patchwork Quilt

READING

Bunny Cakes

Click, Clack Moo: Cows That Type

The Day of Ahmed's Secret

Good Morning Franny, Good Night Franny

Jenny's Journey

A Letter to Amy

Like Me and You

The Signmaker's Assistant

Signs

Somewhere in Africa

Talking Walls

Tiptoe into Kindergarten

Warthogs in the Kitchen

SELF-CONCEPT

Abuela's Weave

Cleversticks

Hue Boy

I Am Me

I Love My Hair

It's Simple, Said Simon

Kelly in the Mirror

Yoko

SEEING; VISUALIZING

At the Crossroads

Brother Eagle, Sister Sky

The Forest Has Eyes

Pigs in the Mud in the Middle of the Rud

What Is Beautiful?

Where Does the Trail Lead?

SHOES

Jamaica and Brianna

My Best Shoes

New Shoes for Silvia

Shoes from Grandpa

Two Pairs of Shoes

SINGING

Bein' with You This Way

Fiddle-I-Fee: A Farmyard Song for the Very Young

My Mama Sings

Old MacDonald Had a Farm

The Old Man Who Loved to Sing

The Singing Man

Skip to My Lou

SISTERS

Going Home

One of Three

Pigs in the Mud in the Middle of the Rud

Pueblo Girls: Growing Up in Two Worlds

SPANISH LANGUAGE

Carlos and the Corn Field

Carlos and the Squash Plant

Margaret and Margarita

SPEAKING

Cock-a-Doodle-Do, What Does It Sound Like to You?

Does a Kangaroo Have a Mother Too?

I'm Calling Molly

Is Your Mama a Llama?

It's Simple, Said Simon

The Lady with the Alligator Purse

Mama, Do You Love Me?

Mice Squeak, We Speak

My Crayons Talk

The Very Busy Spider
Yo! Yes?

TELEPHONE

I'm Calling Molly

TOYS, MAKING

Dragonfly's Tale
Galimoto
The Mud Family

TRAVEL

Abuela's Weave
Baby-O
The Day of Ahmed's Secret
Jenny's Journey
One of Three
Pigs in the Mud in the Middle of the Rud
Red Bird
The Seals on the Bus
The Singing Man
Wheels on the Bus
Where Is Gah-Ning?

TREES

Brother Eagle, Sister Sky
The Forest Has Eyes
The Other Way to Listen
Pablo's Tree

VEGETABLES

Carlos and the Corn Field
Carlos and the Squash Plant
Dragonfly's Tale
How Are You Peeling? Foods with Moods
Hue Boy

WATER

Alejandro's Gift
At the Crossroads
The Mud Family

WEAVING

Abuela's Weave
The Goat in the Rug

WIND

Gilberto and the Wind

WORKING

At the Crossroads
Building a House
Bones, Bones, Dinosaur Bones
Fiddle-I-Fee: A Farmyard Song for the Very Young
Haircuts at Sleepy Sam's
Hammer, Nails, Planks, and Paint
The House That Jack Built
Juan Bobo Goes to Work
Old MacDonald Had a Farm
Road Builders
Saturday at the New You
The Very Busy Spider

WORRY

Abuela's Weave
At the Crossroads
Building a Bridge
Carlos and the Corn Field
Carlos and the Squash Plant
Cleversticks
Families Are Different
I Am Me!

Kelly in the Mirror

The Lady with the Alligator Purse

Louella Mae, She's Run Away

Pigs in the Mud in the Middle of the Rud

Skip to My Lou

Too Many Tamales

Will You Come Back for Me?

Where Is Gah-Ning?

WRITING

Alef-bet: A Hebrew Alphabet Book

At the Beach

Bunny Cakes

Click, Clack, Moo: Cows That Type

The Day of Ahmed's Secret

Good Morning Franny, Good Night Franny

Hieroglyphs from A to Z

In the Snow

Jenny's Journey

A Letter to Amy

Like Me and You

The Signmaker's Assistant

Signs

Writing Places

Why Write?

INDEX OF CHILDREN'S BOOKS

INDEX